Anonymous

A Journey Into Siberia

Made by Order of the King of France

Anonymous

A Journey Into Siberia
Made by Order of the King of France

ISBN/EAN: 9783744761765

Printed in Europe, USA, Canada, Australia, Japan

Cover: Foto ©Andreas Hilbeck / pixelio.de

More available books at **www.hansebooks.com**

A

JOURNEY

INTO

SIBERIA,

MADE BY ORDER OF THE

KING OF FRANCE.

BY

M. L'ABBÉ CHAPPE D'AUTEROCHE,
Of the Royal Academy of Sciences at Paris, in 1761.

CONTAINING AN ACCOUNT

Of the MANNERS and CUSTOMS of the RUSSIANS, the Present State of their EMPIRE; with the Natural History, and Geographical Description of their Country, and Level of the Road from PARIS to TOBOLSKY.

ILLUSTRATED WITH CUTS.

Translated from the French, with a Preface by the Translator.

LONDON:
Printed for T. JEFFERYS, Geographer to the KING.
MDCCLXX.

PREFACE

OF THE

TRANSLATOR.

THE difposition of this work being confiderably changed in the tranflation; the tranflator thinks it incumbent upon him to give an account of this alteration, and to offer fome reafons for having taken fuch liberty with the original.

His firft intention having been to abridge the work as much as poffible, without paffing over any material circumftance, he has reduced two volumes into one. In doing this, he has brought together all fuch parts as are more particularly connected with each other by the matter they treat of, and which are frequently feparated in the original. Thus, immediately after the journey from France to Tobolfky, is introduced the return from thence, which is at the end of the firft volume of the original. The geographical account of Ruffia is then given, together with the level of the road from Paris to Tobolfky, as it is found in the beginning of the fecond volume of the original. But, it is proper to obferve, that in the laft mentioned part, the proceffes, from which the conclufions have been obtained, are omitted; and the conclufions only produced, fo far as they were neceffary to communicate a

complete

complete idea of the height of the foil of Ruſſia, as determined by the author's calculations. The calculations have been left out, becauſe they can be of no uſe to any one, who will not analyze them, and that any reader who ſhall chuſe to take this trouble, will not ſcruple to refer to the original.

After the account of the level, the mineralogical obſervations are inſerted, but thoſe only are tranſlated, which the author has made on the foil of Ruſſia. All the extracts from the ſecond volume are cloſed with the mineralogy; the aſtronomical obſervations, electrical experiments, &c. being omitted, becauſe they are foreign to the civil or natural hiſtory of the Ruſſian Empire, and therefore not immediately connected with the chief object of this work.

The account of tame and wild animals, birds, fiſh and inſects, is then taken from the middle of the firſt volume, and introduced next to the mineralogy. By this arrangement, the whole of the natural hiſtory of Ruſſia, is brought together according to the original plan. The obſervations on the climate of Siberia, follow the natural hiſtory, and the reſt of the tranſlation is continued in the ſame order as the original.

The French meaſures have been preſerved, to avoid the fractions which muſt have interfered by reducing them into Engliſh feet, and which would have made the reading diſagreeable: and to avoid inaccuracy, which muſt have prevailed, if the fractions had been omitted in the reduction [*].

All the Ruſſian meaſures are reduced into French meaſures in the courſe of the work; but, for the convenience of the

---

[*] The French toiſe contains ſix Paris feet: the proportion of the Paris to the Engliſh foot is commonly reckoned that of 114 to 107; but from ſome late compariſons there is reaſon to ſuſpect, that this eſtimation is not perfectly accurate. This has been a further inducement to the tranſlator to uſe the Paris foot, as being the moſt fixt and determined meaſure. Vid. Phil. Tranſact. vol. lviii. p. 324.—326.

reader,

reader, the proportions of thefe refpective meafures will be given at the end of the preface, as they are collected from different parts of the original.

After the table of meafures, the reader will find the Ruffian coin reduced to Englifh, by calculating from the French coin, into which it is reduced by Mr. Chappe. In thefe calculations, the French livre has been valued at ten pence half penny sterling.

The two thermometers mentioned by the author are Mr. Reaumur's, and Mr. Delifle's. The reafons fpecified above, with regard to the toifes, have induced the tranflator to ufe the fame thermometers; but, as it is the cuftom of this country to compute by Fahrenheit's thermometer, he has fubjoined Mr. Reaumur's and Fahrenheit's fcale, with an explanation of the differences between them. It has not been thought neceffary to give Mr. Delifle's fcale, becaufe Mr. Chappe has reduced it to the ftandard of Mr. Reaumur's, whenever he has had occafion to mention it.

If the reader fhould think of comparing the tranflation with the original, he will find fome few omiffions, befides thofe above mentioned; thefe may eafily be accounted for from the principles already laid down: but, as they are of little importance, it has been judged unneceffary to take any particular notice of them. Many of the notes alfo, have been thrown into the body of the work, wherever this could be done, without interrupting the narration.

In tranflating the fcientific parts of this book, which are well worthy the attention of the learned, the tranflator's chief aim has been to be faithful and accurate: In the entertaining parts, he could wifh to have preferved the life and fpirit of the original.

Before this preface is concluded, it is thought proper to give the account of a revolution which happened a few years fince, among the Kalmuck Zongors. This is introduced towards the end of the first volume of the original; but it has been omitted in the translation, because it is much lengthened by a particular detail of the mythology of this people, which it has been judged might as well be left out; especially as their religion is in general the same as that of the inhabitants of the Thibet. But, the revolution itself, being of a curious and interesting nature, not before made public, except in the Russian language, a short extract of the account of it shall be inserted here.

"It is a matter of astonishment, that we should know so
"little of the Tartars inhabiting the southern parts of Siberia;
"and that the maps of these regions should be so imperfect as
"they are, while the Russians who live near them, are able to
"assist us so much in any inquiries we might wish to make
"concerning the nature of these people, and of their country.
"The revolution which has lately taken place among the
"Kalmuck Zongors, is a remarkable proof, that there are
"very important events which happen in this part of the
"world, entirely without our knowledge. This nation, which
"occupied an extent of country, larger than the kingdom of
"France, was totally destroyed by the Chinese in 1757, after
"a ten years war. During all this time, and till the year
"1761, this event was known to the Russian Empire only.
"All the rest of Europe was ignorant of this revolution; and
"I was informed of it only as I was travelling through Siberia,
"by some of the Kalmucks themselves, who had escaped the
"fury of the Chinese, and by some Russians living in Siberia.

"On my return from Tobolsky to St. Petersburg, in the
"month of November 1761, I communicated the information
"I had received to some foreigners I had the honor to be
"acquainted with; and some time after the Russians pub-
"lished an account of the fact in their own language.

"The

" The Kalmucks, or Eluths, are divided into three principal branches: the Kalmucks Zongors, the Kalmucks Kofkotes, and the Kalmucks Torgautes: the Kalmucks Zongors are the objects of our prefent confideration. This nation was fituated in the fouthern parts of Siberia, extending from 90 to 120 degrees of longitude; and from the 35th degree of latitude, to the 48th, or thereabouts; including in this extent of country feveral neighbouring provinces, and the leffer Bucharia, which the Kalmucks had conquered in 1683.

" The Kalmuck Zongors were governed by a Kam invefled with abfolute power, diftinguifhed by the name of Contaifch. He was confidered as the chief Kam of all the Kalmucks, and though the other branches of the Kalmucks had their particular Kams, yet they were all in fome meafure fubordinate to the chief Kam, and ufed to fupply him with troops in time of war.

" All thefe people encamp under tents; and are divided into hords or tribes, under one chief called Taifka.

" The Kam of the Kalmucks Zongors refided upon the river Ili, which empties itfelf into a lake named in the Kalmuck language *Balkach-nour*, or as fome authors call it *Palkai-nor*; it is fituated in 97 degrees of longitude and 46 of latitude.

" Thefe people became fo powerful under the reigns of Tfagan-Araptan-chon-taidji, and of his fon Galden-Tcheren, that the Ruffians and the Chinefe were equally afraid of them. The armies which thefe Kams maintained confifted of about a hundred and fifty thoufand men, during the feveral wars they carried on with great fuccefs, for the fpace of forty years, againft the Chinefe, the Tangoutes, the Ruffians, and other neighbouring powers.

" They

"They subdued the leſſer Bucharia, the capital of which is Erken.

"The Contaiſch Tſagan-Araptan made his way acroſs ſome vaſt deſerts, and ſurprized the nation of the Tangoutes, ſituated between China and India. He alſo attacked ſome Kalmucks called Chocout, ſubject to the Tangoutes, who dwell near the lake *Kokou-nour*, or the blue lake. After having plundered the Tibet, and pillaged the reſidence of the Dalai-Lama, he returned into his own dominions with an immenſe ſpoil.

"Galden-Tcheren ſucceeded him, and died in 1746; he appointed his ſon Tſebek Dorjou, aged ſeventeen years, his ſucceſſor; but the chief nobles diſliking this young prince, depoſed him, had his eyes put out, and ſent him away into the leſſer Bucharia, where he was aſſaſſinated. Some time after, the Kalmucks Zongors proclaimed Lama-Darja, aged thirty years. This prince, alſo a ſon of Galden Tcheren, was illegitimate; and therefore, by the cuſtom of the country, his election was void. Beſides, there was a legitimate heir then living, known by the name of the Noyon Debatchi, who ſhould have ſucceeded to the throne as the neareſt relation of Galden Tcheren; but Lama-Darja was ſo powerful, that the Noyon Debatchi not only concealed his pretenſions to the throne, but was even obliged to make his eſcape among the Kirſi-Koſſacks, with the Noyon Amour-Saman, and ſeveral Kalmucks.

"The Noyon Debatchi, however, had ſtill a party among the Kalmucks, which he took care to keep up while he ſtayed among the Kirſi-Koſſacks, by whoſe aſſiſtance and that of the Noyon Amour-Saman, a brave and enterprizing prince, he undertook to aſcend the throne. The Noyon Debatchi, attended by Amour-Saman, by the Kalmucks who had followed them, and by a corps of Kirſi-Koſſacks,

re-entered

" re-entered his dominions, furprized the Contaifch in the
" night-time, defeated his army, and made himfelf be elected
" Kam in the room of Lama-Darja, who had been flain in
" the engagement. Some Noyons (or princes) refufed how-
" ever to acknowledge the new Kam, and formed themfelves
" into a powerful faction. Amour-Saman being diffatisfied
" with the Noyon Debatchi fince his election, in which he had
" given him fo much affiftance, joined the rebels. Under
" fuch a chief they became formidable, but their fuccefs was
" not equal to their courage. The Noyon Debatchi gave
" battle to Amour-Saman, in which the latter was totally de-
" feated, and obliged to make his efcape into China.

" The Chinefe, who were alarmed at the great increafe of
" power among the Kalmucks Zongors, took this opportunity
" of keeping up the civil war, which had broke out among
" them. The Emperor received Amour-Saman, with the
" greateft marks of diftinction, and he was acknowledged
" Tfin-wan, or prince of the higheft rank, by the Bodko-
" Chan, a Chinefe, fent into the country of the Kalmucks at
" the head of a Chinefe army. The Kam Debatchi advanced
" towards Amour-Saman, and gave him battle; but Debatchi
" having been defeated and put to flight, was purfued and
" taken prifoner in the town of Tourfan*, from whence the
" Chinefe conducted him to Pekin.

" When the Chinefe affifted Amour-Saman, they had en-
" gaged to fix him on the throne of the Kalmucks; but it was
" by no means their intention to fulfil this engagement; for the
" Kam Debatchi was received at Pekin with the greateft
" refpect, and rather as an ally than an enemy. Amour-
" Saman then perceived that the policy of the Chinefe
" tended to the entire deftruction of his nation. Prompted

---

* The town of Tourfan or Turfan is fituated towards the northern borders of the leffer Bucharia. This battle was fought in 1754.

" by

"by these ideas, he secretly persuaded the Kalmucks and
"Mongals, who made part of the Chinese army, to revolt; he
"then put himself at their head, and attacking a body of the
"Chinese who thought themselves very secure, entirely defeat-
"ed them, and retreated into the country of the Kalmucks
"pursued by the rest of the army. He engaged in his party
"some troops of the Zongors; by the help of which he at-
"tacked the Chinese army, and obliged them to retire in the
"greatest confusion. Amour-Saman then assumed the title of
"Contaisch, with a resolution of supporting the dignity.
"Part of the nation acknowledged him, the rest preserved
"their allegiance to the Kam Debatchi, who was still a pri-
"soner at Pekin. Several hords of Mongals openly shook
"off the Chinese yoke; so that to all appearance an obstinate
"war was likely to ensue. The Emperor of China sent a
"large army into the country of the Kalmucks. He set all
"the Kalmucks free who had been taken prisoners when the
"Kam Debatchi was defeated, and treated them with great
"kindness; so that they joined themselves to the Chinese troops,
"under a supposition of their going to fight for their sovereign
"Debatchi, whom the Emperor of China still kept in safe
"custody, in order to insure the fidelity of the Kalmucks.

"At the approach of the Chinese army, most of the hords
"of the Mongals which had revolted, submitted themselves
"again, and their chiefs being taken up, and sent to Pekin,
"were there punished with death. The Zongor princes who
"were in the Chinese army, influenced the greater part of the
"troops of Amour-Saman: he was defeated, and escaped
"among the Kirsi-Kossacs, where he had before attended De-
"batchi.

"These people who live only on rapine and plunder, observ-
"ing that the Kalmucks Zongors were exhausted by civil wars,
"and unable to make any resistance, entered their country by
"force,

" force, sword in hand, spreading desolation and destruction
" wherever they passed. On the other hand, the Chinese did
" the same, under pretence of assisting the Kalmucks. These
" unfortunate people, attacked on all sides, at length aban-
" doned their native country to their enemies; and to the
" number of twenty thousand families, escaped towards Siberia;
" from whence they removed on the borders of the Volga,
" putting themselves under the protection of Russia, to which
" most of them became subject.

" Amour-Saman finding himself not in safety among the
" Kirsi-Kossacs, retired towards Siberia, in deserts and moun-
" tains almost inaccessible; but being pursued every where by
" the Chinese, he at last took refuge in Siberia, in 1757, and
" died at Tobolsky.

" The Chinese were no sooner informed that Amour-Saman
" had retreated into Siberia, than they demanded, that this
" prince should be given up to them; or, as the Russians say,
" that he should be shut up for ever. After his death, it was
" agreed that his body should be conveyed on the frontiers of
" Siberia. The Chinese sent several times commissaries to
" inspect it. At my departure from Tobolsky, I left two
" ambassadors of the Kalmucks in that city; who had been
" sent to St. Petersburg, before the reign of Amour-Saman,
" to request, that the Russians should destroy the forts they
" had constructed on the borders of the river Irtysz. These
" ambassadors, on their return to Tobolsky, were informed
" that their nation existed no more.

" According to the account the Russians give, Amour-Sa-
" man did not enter into Siberia; but retreated on the fron-
" tiers of that province, where he was soon after seized with
" the small-pox, of which he died. He had been joined by his
" wife *Bitei*, who has been seen at St. Petersburg in 1761:
" she was a daughter of Galdan-Tcheren, her first husband
" was

"was named *Ichidangin*, an elder brother of Amour-Saman,
"by whom she had a son, named *Pontsouk*.

"The unfortunate Amour-Saman made a confiderable ftay
"at Tobolfky, where he was confined a long time in the arch-
"bifhop's country houfe; but the reafons which have induced
"the Ruffians to conceal this circumftance in their account of
"the affair, have never been revealed."

Ruffian long meafures reduced to French toifes, feet, &c.

The Arcin is equal to 26 inches 6 lines $\frac{2}{10}$ths of the Paris foot.

The Sagen is equal to 6 feet 7 inches 6 lines $\frac{2}{10}$ths.

The Werft is equal to 552 toifes 3 feet 7 inches 6 lines.

The only Ruffian weight mentioned in the work is the *poede*, which contains, according to Mr. Chappe's account, forty Ruffian and thirty-three French pounds.

The French pound is reckoned equal to one pound one ounce three drachms of an avoirdupois pound; and the French quintal equal to 109 avoirdupois pounds.

Ruffian coin reduced to Englifh. The copec, equal to one penny fterling. The rouble, equal to four fhillings and four pence halfpenny fterling.

From the Scales in the Plate it appears, that M. de Reaumur's o, or freezing point, coincides with gr. 32 of Fahrenheit's thermometer. This is the general opinion, and therefore it has been thought more proper to follow it, than to adopt Mr. Martine's, who fuppofes in his *Medical Effays*, pag. 235, that *Mr. de Reaumur's freezing point anfwers to fomething above gr.* 34 *of Fahrenheit's Scale*. It may alfo be obferved, that one divifion of Mr. Reaumur's Scale, is nearly equal to two of Fahrenheit's.

It

SCALES of FAHRENHEIT's and D. REAUMUR's Thermometers.

Fahrenheit.   D. Reaumur.

PREFACE.

It is necessary to acquaint the reader, that Mr. Chappe's third volume which is a French translation of the history of Kamtschatka, printed at St. Petersburg in the Russian language, is not given here, because the same history was before translated into English by Dr. Grieve, and published by Mr. Jefferys, in 1764, in one volume quarto.

TABLE

OF

CONTENTS.

Account of the journey to Tobolſky: Page 1
    Return from Tobolſky to St. Peterſburg.   84
Of geography.   118
Of France and its frontiers.   119
Table of the longitudes and latitudes of ſome parts of France and its frontiers.   120
Table containing a journal of the road from Paris to Breſt, and to Tobolſky in Siberia.   121
Of Germany and its frontiers.   122
Table of longitude and latitude of ſome parts of Germany and its frontiers.   ibid.
Table, containing a journal of the road from Paris to Tobolſky in Siberia, Straſburg, Vienna, and Bilitz.   123
Of Poland and its frontiers.   125
Table, containing a journal of the road from Paris to Tobolſky in Siberia, Bilitz, Warſaw and Riga.   126
Of Livonia and Eſtonia.   127
Table, containing a journal of the road from Paris to Tobolſky in Siberia, Riga and St. Peterſburg.   ib.
Of Ingria, Ruſſia and Siberia, as far as Tobolſky.   128

CONTENTS.

Table of the longitudes and latitudes of some places in Russia P. 128.
Table, containing a journal of the road from Paris to Tobolsky in Siberia, St. Petersburg, Mosco and Tobolsky. 129.
Table, containing a journal of the road from Paris to Tobolsky in Siberia, through Kusmodemiansk and Solikamsky. 130
Of the level of the road from Paris to Brest, and to Tobolsky in Siberia; and of the use of the barometer in obtaining a level of the globe. 137
Of the laws by which air is condensed. 140
Table of the places on the road from Brest to Tobolsky in Siberia, the heights of which have been determined, with respect to the level of the sea at Brest, and of the Royal Observatory at Paris. 144 to 151
Remarks on the height of the soil of Russia, from St. Petersburg to Tobolsky in Siberia. 152
Mineralogical observations. 164
Of the Gypses. ib.
  I. *Solid, striated, half transparent gypse.* ib.
  II. *Crystallized, transparent gypse, resembling a pen.* 165
  III. *Transparent gypse, crystallized in form of a parallelepiped.* 166
  IV. *Transparent gypse, crystallized in form of parallelepipeds.* 167
  V. *Gypse transparent in the strata.* 168
  VI. *Mica, Muscovy glass.* ib.
Of the several mines in Siberia, between Solikamsky and Echaterinenburg. 169.
  I. *Loadstone.* 170
  II. *Loadstone.* 172
  III. *Loadstone.* ib.
  IV. *Loadstone.* ib.
  V. *Loadstone.* 173
  VI. *Loadstone.* ib.
  VII. *Cubic and greenish loadstone.* ib.
  VIII. *Iron ore in strata.* 174.
  IX. *Solid.*

CONTENTS.

IX. *Solid, blackish iron ore.*
X. *Solid iron ore, of a brown colour, inclining to red.* 176
XI. *Spongy iron ore.* — — ib.
XII. *Black spongy iron ore.* — 177
XIII. *Solid iron ore.* — — 178
XIV. *Solid, blackish iron ore.* — ib.
XV. *Reddish iron ore in strata.* — 179
XVI. *Blackish iron ore.* — 180
XVII. *Brown iron ore.* — ib.
XVIII. *Iron ore in strata.* — 181
XIX. *Solid iron ore.* — — 182
XX. *Brown iron ore.* — ib.
XXI. *Whitish iron ore.* — — 183
XXII. *Solid iron ore.* — ib.
XXIII. *Solid iron ore.* — 184
XXIV. *Solid iron ore.* — ib.
XXV. *Solid iron ore.* — — ib.
XXVI. *Solid iron ore.* — — 185
XXVII. *Solid iron ore.* — — ib.
XXVIII. *Blackish iron ore.* — ib.
XXIX. *Blackish iron ore.* — — 186
XXX. *Brown iron ore.* — 187
XXXI. *Brown iron ore.* — — ib.
XXXII. *Brown iron ore.* — — 188
XXXIII. *Solid iron ore.* — 190
XXXIV. *Brown iron ore.* — ib.
XXXV. *Solid iron ore.* — — 191
XXXVI. *Brown iron ore.* — ib.
XXXVII. *Brown iron ore.* — — 192
XXXVIII. *Brown iron ore.* — ib.
XXXIX. *Black botryoid hæmatites.* — 193
XL. *Solid iron ore.* — — ib.
XLI. *Solid iron ore.* — — 194

XLII. *Brown*

CONTENTS.

XLII. *Brown iron ore.*	Page 194
XLIII. *Blackish iron ore.*	195
XLIV. *Brown iron ore.*	ib.
XLV. *Rocky iron ore.*	196
XLVI. *Brown iron ore.*	197
XLVII. *Brown iron ore.*	ib.
XLVIII. *Solid iron ore.*	198
XLIX. *Blackish iron ore, cubic and cellular.*	ib.
L. *Blackish iron ore.*	199
LI. *Blackish iron ore.*	200
LII. *Reddish brown iron ore.*	ib.
LIII. *Brown iron ore.*	201
LIV. *Brown iron ore.*	ib.
LV. *Blackish crystallized ore.*	202
LVI. *Blackish iron ore.*	ib.
LVII. *Blackish iron ore with shining points.*	203
LVIII. *Iron ore of a yellow saffron color.*	ib.
Remarks on the iron mines of the Poias or Ryphæan mountains in Siberia.	204
Of the copper mines of the Ryphæan mountains in Siberia, and in the neighbourhood of Cazan.	208
I. *Grey coppery marle.*	ib.
II. *Copperous chist of a dirty grey color.*	ib.
III. *Greenish calcareous stone.*	ib.
IV. *Malachites.*	209
1. *Tuberous malachites.*	ib.
2. *Malachites.*	210
3. *Malachites.*	ib.
4. *Tuberous Malachites.*	211
5. *Tuberous Malachites.*	ib.
6. *Tuberous Malachites.*	ib.
7. *Arboreous Malachites.*	ib.
8. *Striated Malachites.*	212

9. *Ma-*

CONTENTS.

9. Malachites disposed in horizontal layers.	Page 212
V. Calcareous, copperous, greenish stone.	213
VI. Calcareous, copperous, reddish stone.	ib.
VII. Calcareous, copperous, and blackish stone.	ib.
VIII. Copperous and blackish marle.	ib.
IX. Marle of a greyish brown color, coppery and ferruginous.	214
X. Coppery marle of a dirty grey color.	ib.
XI. Calcareous coppery stone.	ib.
XII. Azure copper ore.	215
XIII. Copper mineralized in sand and in wood.	ib.
XIV. Copper mineralized in a calcareous earth.	216
XV. Azure copper ore mineralized in sand.	ib.
XVI. Copper mineralized in sand and in wood.	ib.
XVII. Copper mineralized in wood.	ib.
XVIII. Red copper joined to silken copper.	218
XIX. Virgin copper by flakes.	ib.
Remarks on the copper mines of the Ryphæan mountains in Siberia.	219
Of the gold mines in the neighbourhood of Echaterinenburg in Siberia.	221
Gold mines of Pifzminskaia.	ib.
I. Gold mine of Beresoufkoi.	223
II. Gold mine of Beresoufkoi.	224
Gold mine of Ouktous.	225
Gold mine of Chilovcitoetse.	ib.
Of the tame and wild animals, birds, fish and insects.	228
Of the climate of Siberia, and the other provinces of Russia.	239
Table containing the heights with respect to the sea, of places in Siberia, where the greatest cold has been observed.	259
Of the government of Russia, from the year 861 to 1767.	264
Of the Greek religion.	279
Description of the city of Tobolsky, of its inhabitants, and of the manners, and customs of the Russians.	297

Of

CONTENTS.

Of the progress of the arts and sciences in Russia. Of the genius of the nation and of education. Page 319
Of the laws, of punishments, and of exile. ——— 336
Of the population, trade, navy, revenues, and land forces of Russia. ——— ——— ——— 349
Mercantile articles exported from Russia, (v. note.) 359
Goods exported from France into Russia, (v. note.) 360
Revenues of the Russian empire, (v. note.) — 361
State of the ships of war which composed the naval powers of Russia in 1756, (v. note.) ——— — 365
Military state of the troops in Russia, (v. note.) ——— 368
Account of the annual charges of a Russian regiment, (v. note.) 378
Expence of the field troops, and the total of land and sea forces with their cost, (v. note.) ——— ——— 381

LIST of PLATES.

Map of Russia to front the Title Page.
Scales of Thermometers. (Preface) Page xii
Russian sledges. - - - - - 27
Habit of a Tartar. - - - - - 104
————Tartarian woman. - - - 105
————Russian boor. - - - - ib.
————Wife of a Russian boor. - - - 106
————A woman of Wotiac. - - - 109
————Ditto. - - - - - 110
————Samoyede woman and child. - - 111

Just published, in QUARTO,

Being proper Supplements to this Work.

I.

The History of KAMTSCHATKA and the KURILSKI ISLANDS, with the Countries adjacent.

Illustrated with Maps and Cuts. Published at *Petersburgh* in the *Russian* Language, by Order of her Imperial Majesty; and translated into *English* by JAMES GRIEVE, M. D.

II.

VOYAGES from ASIA to AMERICA.

Made by the *Russians* for completing the Discoveries of the North-west Coast of *America*. Translated from the *High Dutch* of M. MULLER, of the Royal Academy of *Petersburgh*. Illustrated with Maps. The Second Edition.

III.

The GRAND INSTRUCTIONS to the Commissioners appointed to frame a new Code of LAWS for the *Russian* Empire.

Composed by her Imperial Majesty *Catherine* II. Empress of all the *Russias*. To which is prefixed, A Description of the Manner of opening the Commission, with the Order and Rules for electing the Commissioners. Translated from the Original, in the Russian Language, by MICHAEL TATISCHEFF, a Russian Gentleman; and published by Permission.

AN ACCOUNT

OF A

JOURNEY

TO

SIBERIA.

BEING ordered by the King, and appointed by the academy, to go to Tobolſky, in order to obſerve the Tranſit of Venus over the Sun, it was my intention to embark in Holland, that I might avoid the inconvenience of conveying a large apparatus of inſtruments as far as St. Peterſburg by land; but the laſt of the veſſels deſtined for this paſſage had already put to ſea. I was therefore neceſſitated to undertake the journey by land, and this obliged me to make ſeveral new diſpoſitions very different from my original plan. M. Durieul, colonel in the King of Poland's ſervice, was then going to Warſaw; I deſired leave to accompany him, and we ſet out at the end of November 1760. I had very little reaſon to be concerned at my having miſſed the Dutch veſſel, as I learned a few days before I left Paris, that ſhe had been wrecked on the coaſt of Sweden.

The rains had made the roads so bad, that we did not reach Strasburg till after eight days travelling: we staid there two days in hopes of getting our carriages repaired, but they had suffered so much from a variety of accidents, that we were obliged to take others. All my barometers and thermometers had been broken in the night between the first and second of December, by one of the carriages falling into a ditch, five or six feet deep. I made new ones at Strasburg, while we stopped there.

Having experienced such difficulties in our journey through France, we were apprehensive we should meet with much greater in Germany; and indeed, these difficulties increased so fast, and such a number of accidents befel us, that we were forced to go to Ulm, and embark on the Danube, although I was apprized before I left Paris, that the navigation of this river was very uncertain at this time of the year on account of the fogs.

Knowing we had no particular map of the Danube in this part of its course, I took this opportunity of tracing one with the utmost precision. I wave this subject at present, as I shall have occasion to resume it hereafter.

Embarked on the Danube, we could not proceed but in the day time, and sometimes only for a few hours, because of the fogs, and of some dangerous places to be met with in this river. The fogs were the more troublesome, as the banks of the river were overflowed: there was but a small passage left between the bridges and the water; so that it was necessary to see the arches from a great distance, in order to chuse out those where the current was least rapid.

The Danube, having crossed that extensive plain in the country about Ulm, flows on between two ridges of mountains; which are at first but low and far distant from each other: they rise and come nearer together by imperceptible degrees,

degrees, till at laſt they form only a narrow paſſage at a few days ſailing from Ulm. Nothing is here to be ſeen in general, on the banks of the river, but ſteep and barren mountains: in the more fruitful parts of the country, the meadows, the ſlope of the hills, and the woods ſcattered here and there, with intervening towns and villages, afford every inſtant a new proſpect, and gratify the eyes of the contemplative traveller with a variety of objects, each more delightful than the other.

The channel of the Danube is ſo ſtraitened in ſome parts of theſe mountains, by ſeveral projecting rocks, that veſſels are never ventured to go up the river through theſe narrow places, while others are coming down. The ſailors are obliged to be very careful in going through theſe ſhort paſſages, for the rocks being perpendicular, there can be no hopes of preſervation, if a ſhipwreck ſhould happen.

From the natural diſpoſition of this place, we were unable to get on much in the courſe of the day; but as ſoon as the veſſel was at anchor, I uſed to go upon theſe mountains to aſcertain their height with the barometer. I never found any one of them more than 300 or 350 French toiſes high, but theſe were topped by others whoſe height ſeemed to increaſe as they were farther diſtant from the Danube. Theſe mountains were all covered with ſnow, although there was not the leaſt ſign of it in any part of the country about the banks of the river.

When we came near Ratiſbon, we left the veſſel, to viſit the environs of this city, with intent to make ſome inquiries into natural hiſtory. This was conſtantly our employment every time we diſembarked. M. Durieul's uncommon good nature, joined to the moſt extenſive knowledge, prompted him to be peculiarly earneſt in aſſiſting me in theſe purſuits. We had but juſt got out of the boat when that gentleman diſcovered a ſtone, on the borders of the river, with a ſingular inſcription upon it. Some ſpades were brought from the boat to clear away

away the earth from the stone; we attempted to copy the characters, with which we were unacquainted: but the length of the inscription, the intense cold, and the night coming on made us resolve to quit the talk. We determined therefore, to dig up the stone, and take it with us into the boat. Its size put us to the necessity of going for assistance to the neighbouring village. The peasants informed us, that there were many similar inscriptions all around that place. This circumstance convinced us at once that there was nothing very wonderful in our discovery. We then applied ourselves, though rather too late, to find out what this really was. It turned out that these stones were nothing more than several Jewish tomb-stones, and that the inscriptions were epitaphs in Hebrew.

Although this adventure rather disconcerted us at first, yet we resolved to entertain ourselves with it; and the exercise we had taken in the pursuit of it, had sharpened our appetites for supper. In coming away we had the good fortune to save a young man's life, who was going to throw himself into the Danube, on account of a quarrel with his mistress; being apprized of his intentions, by some persons who were running after him, we stopped him, and put him safe into their hands.

We set out the next day, and passed the bridge at Ratisbon, which was said to be a very dangerous spot, and, in support of this opinion, we were told that an ambassador had lost his life in passing it. We were convinced that the death of the ambassador had been the only foundation for this extraordinary report.

We stopped at noon the same day, to take in provisions at a small town on the banks of the Danube, and were much surprized on returning to the boat, to find a young lady on board, of fifteen or sixteen years of age: she had an air of consequence united to a most pleasing form: her down-cast eyes, her behaviour, her timidity, her dress, all bespoke her to be of good family;

family; we invited her therefore into our apartment; and she accepted of the invitation: the melancholy looks she now and then directed to us, were expressive of confusion and deep distress. We encouraged her, by paying her all possible regard; and found, after a few questions, that she lived with an uncle, a curate, at a few leagues distance from the town where we last stopped: she had ran away from him, because he wanted to compel her to take the veil. We conducted her to Passaw, where her family was.

On the 24th of December, we came to a large village. This being Christmas-eve, we went to church to hear the service, which was very long. Next day, I found that my devotion had been the occasion of my losing a portmanteau, containing great part of my linen. This was the first loss I sustained in my wardrobe, of which I brought very little back to Paris; the rest being stolen from me in the course of my journey.

After several days sailing, we arrived on the 27th at Lintz: we found about this town a large quantity of the granite stone, wrought for stair-cases, chimnies, and other ornaments. The sailors informed us, that these granites were brought from quarries in the neighbourhood of the town, where they were commonly to be met with.

The Danube divides Lintz into two parts, communicating with each other by a wooden bridge; the exact length of which, I found to be three hundred and fifty paces. I computed this distance at five hundred toises, and the depth of the river at this place, according to the mariner's accounts, is one hundred feet, or about seventeen toises. The fog, which had been thick all the morning of the 28th, began to disperse towards noon, and we immediately put to sail. The weather having been tolerably favourable for some days past, we met with very

few

few delays: and reached Vienna on the 31ft of December 1760.

I had the moft favourable reception from their Imperial Majefties at this Capital; they were pleafed to fhew their gracious attention to the Sciences and the Academy, by defiring that I might be prefented to them. While I ftayed in this city, I vifited the Emperor's cabinet of natural hiftory. From the complete feries of the articles it contains, it may be reckoned among the fineft in Europe. I have never met with any collection fo elegant in the clafs of corals.

The arfenal under the direction of Prince Lichtenftein, is remarkably curious, and deferving attention, as well from the quantity of artillery this Prince has enriched it with, as from the great ftock of arms of all kinds to be found there. They are difpofed and arranged, in a manner moft pleafing to the eye. The Prince has built a hall in the midft of the arfenal, where he has placed two beautiful marble ftatues of the Emperor and Emprefs. Their Imperial Majefties having been to fee the arfenal, were agreeably furprized with this frefh inftance of Prince Lichtenftein's attachment and zeal; but the Prince was ftill more fo fome time after, on feeing his own buft in the fame hall facing their Majefties ftatues; a condefcenfion which was the moft flattering mark of diftinction a fubject could receive, and at the fame time reflected honor upon their Imperial Majefties, whofe goodnefs and generofity captivates all who come near them. Prince Lichtenftein procured me a feries of petrified wood from the Carpathian mountains, of marbles, and of different pebbles not lefs curious.

I knew it was the cuftom at Vienna, to be very ftrict in examining every thing which came into the city. Fearing left my inftruments packed up with the greateft care, fhould receive any damage from this infpection, I had begged the favour of Count Staremberg, ambaffador from their Imperial Majefties

at

at Paris, to get leave for me to pass, without having them unpacked. He was so obliging to write, on this account, to the Baron de Cotec, comptroller of the customs. I was infinitely pleased with this gentleman's politeness, and satisfied with the orders he had given.

In the course of my voyage upon the Danube, I had observed the height of the barometer: but the use I intended to make of my observations, required that I should compare them with those made at Vienna. Here I met with Father Hell, a Jesuit, professor of astronomy, well known by his great proficiency in that science, and by his ephemerides with which he obliges the learned world every year. Father Liesganig, of the same society, and who applies himself successfully to the same studies, took the trouble upon himself of making observations corresponding with such as I should make hereafter, and of communicating those he had already made while I was on the Danube. In his observatory, we determined the magnetic variation to be thirteen degrees westward, and at the same time we compared our barometers.

Baron Van Swieten, first physician to the Empress, and member of our academy, informed me, that he used electricity with great success in the rheumatism, and other disorders of the like nature, although very little benefit is experienced from it in France. Can this difference arise from the diversity of climates, or is it owing to any injudicious method of applying the remedy?

I left this capital the 8th of January, after having experienced much kindness from the Duke de Pralin, then ambassador at Vienna. We were joined by M. Favier, who was going to St. Petersburg, as secretary of embassy: and we arrived on the 9th of January 1761 at Nikolsburg, a small town pretty well built, where there is a tolerably fine seat, and a beautiful fountain. Brünn, where we stopped the same day, is by no means an ugly town; it is fortified, although but indifferently. The citadel is placed on an eminence.

Our journey from Vienna had hitherto been over a plain where the roads were very fine; but they began to grow bad about the town of Brünn, which we did not leave 'till ten o'clock at night, having been detained there by the breaking of one of our carriage wheels. I loſt one of my barometers by this accident, and next day the other, by the carriage falling into a ditch: part of the night was ſpent in drawing it out; as we were obliged to unload it, which we did on all theſe occaſions. Theſe accidents were ſo frequent, that I was in continual apprehenſions for my inſtruments. The lights, we had provided ourſelves with at Vienna, began to fail; and without theſe it would have been impracticable for us to travel in the night, ſo that I began to fear we ſhould not reach Tobolſky in due time. The ſame day we came to the river Bianavoda; which appeared to me about thirty toiſes broad: its borders only being frozen, we waded through it. Although it was not more than two feet deep in this place, yet the horſes could not croſs it without great difficulty, the looſe flakes of ice being very troubleſome to them, as well as the frozen borders, which it was neceſſary to break. At length we arrived on the 11th at Neutiſchein, where we paſſed the night, and ſet off from thence the 12th inſtant, at ſeven in the morning. The Carpathian mountains were ſtill on our right, at the diſtance of a league, or a league and a half, ſometimes leſs. We dined at Friedeck, a ſmall town of Sileſia, pretty well peopled; where a great fair was then kept. The dreſs of the people of this town, and of the country round about, appeared to me the ſame as that of the inhabitants of Moravia: the women wear ſmall white petticoats very ſhort; they have generally a kind of coloured waiſtcoat on, and a white linen veil faſtened to the head. They wrap themſelves in this veil, which comes

down

down as low as the waift: fome of them have nothing but a piece of white crape flowing on their fhoulders; their ftockings are all plaited, as if they were made of coarfe packthread, twifted round their legs; and the whole of their drefs is as ridiculous as their figure. The men are tolerably well made, and their drefs is very fimilar to that of the country people in France.

The cold was not very intenfe, although it was now the 12th of January: the thermometer was only at three degrees below 0; a great deal of fnow fell: on the 13th, the thermometer fell to five degrees, and continued at the fame point on the 14th: but in the following night, when we were ftill at Bilitz, it fell all at once to fourteen and an half. We left this town at eight in the morning, in the midft of this intenfe cold; which I was the more affected with, as I had not before experienced any great degree of it. We reached Zator the fame day, at two in the afternoon: our baggage did not come in 'till eleven at night; for we had been obliged to have it conveyed on the country people's carts, on account of the damages our carriages had received.

Zator is a large borough town, fituated on the frontiers of Poland, of which Count Dunin is the *Staroft*, (or Lord): he was not only kind enough to infift upon our lodging with him, but feeing our carriages in very bad condition, he alfo made his people chufe out the beft fort of wood from his ftorehoufe, and gave the ftricteft orders to have them completely repaired. Notwithftanding the Count's endeavours to make our ftay as agreeable as poffible, we were preparing to fet out as foon as our carriages were ready; when we were informed, that the Viftula was not yet quite frozen over. The cold which had been fo intenfe on the 15th gave way all at once, and the thermometer was only at 0 on the 17th. It being very uncertain whether the river would foon be frozen over, we resolved

resolved to have the ice broken; and, on the 18th, we croffed the river near its head in a ferry; we arrived the 19th at Cracow, and the 22d at Warfaw.

Warfaw is the capital of Poland: it is a very fine city, and contains feveral elegant buildings; but it is remarkable, that it has not one fingle inn. A ftranger who fhould happen to come there without acquaintance, might run the rifque of lying in the ftreet. The Polanders are indeed fo very hofpitable, that fuch an incident is not likely to happen very frequently. The Marquis de Paulmy, our ambaffador, was exceedingly kind to me. He prefented me to the late King on the 23d, and to the Prince of Courland.

The women of Poland are in general handfome and amiable; they improve their underftanding by reading, and the knowledge of various languages: their full drefs is commonly after the French manner; but in undrefs, they wear a Polifh habit, which is a fort of very elegant riding-drefs. Inftead of caps, they wear a kind of dragoon's cap; this drefs is prodigioufly becoming to fuch as are well made. They love company and pleafure, but are ftrictly virtuous; which feems to be rather the effect of fuperftition, than of polifhed manners, of the climate, or of true principles of religion. It was then the carnival, a feafon devoted to pleafure: the ambaffadors, and fome of the Polifh noblemen, gave the moft expenfive entertainments; where every body was tired as ufual with form and ceremony, while the Ridotto was the only place for real amufement.

The Ridotto, is a public diverfion, in fome refpects like the mafked ball at Paris: it confifts of feveral rooms; dancing is going forward in fome, gaming in another, befides which there is one room for refrefhments. The Polanders come there in a mafquerade habit; this, according to the cuftom of the country, is often a long robe; underneath which they wear a
kind

kind of waistcoat, and their heads are shaved and covered with a cap. The Poles are generally tall and well made: the spirit of liberty shews itself in all their actions; and the haughtiness of their behaviour, seems to imply that particular respect is due to the young women they chuse to dance with. The mild and pleasing aspect of the women, the liveliness of their eyes, the slenderness of their waists, and their activity, make a remarkable contrast with the men.

The Polish dances are most in fashion at these balls; the dancers form a circle as large as the room will allow, with the persons of the first rank at the top; they turn round the room each man with his partner: the man has little to do, only twisting himself about; while the woman, whose hand he takes hold of, has more action. The music is as melancholy and tiresome as the dance; it is thought to express great dignity. After the Polish, English dances are most in use; their liveliness and spirit make up for the slowness of the former.

The kingdom of Poland is tolerably well peopled: the nobles are perfectly independent, and the nation is subjected to the neighbouring powers; from the anarchy of the government, the sovereign is without authority, the state without defence, and exposed to every invader: the lands belong to the nobles; they distribute a certain portion of land and cattle among the country people, who are their slaves. The country man enjoys the produce of the land given to him; but is obliged to work with his own oxen and horses four days in the week, to cultivate the lands of his lord, or to submit to any thing which may be required of him, even to servile employments.

Each Lord has a sort of farmer, named *Podstarofte*; to whom he allows a certain stipend, either in money or land; and under whose direction there is a *wout* or under-farmer, who gives an account every evening to the farmer of the state of the village, and the work of the day. If any one of the slaves has been remiss in coming to his business, or has behaved himself so as to displease the under-farmer, he is immediately punished: this is done by laying him along the ground with his back quite bare, one of the slaves then holds his head, another his feet, while a third is employed in flogging him severely with a whip, which they call *kantzouk*. The under-farmer drives the slaves to work with his whip, like horses, and treats them in the same manner.

While the men are employed in cultivating the lands of their Lord, the women are busied in dressing his flax, washing, or other offices peculiar to them: if neglectful, they are punished with the *kantzouk*, as well as the men. If any of the slaves attempt to evade this tyranny, by eloping from the village, they are soon sent back by the neighbouring lords, according to a settled agreement between them: in this case, they are so severely punished, that such incidents rarely happen.

The Poles have always a great number of servants, taken from among their slaves: they are allowed a certain quantity of bread every week, and a mess made of a kind of barley, cabbage, and salt, every day: they have also a livery, stockings and boots, given them, and one guinea a year for wages.

The manner of travelling in Poland requires a considerable train of attendants; it is customary on these occasions to carry every thing that is useful or convenient; all sorts of provisions, all the common utensils of life, tables, chairs, and even beds, when a visit is intended to a friend's house, where there are never more of these than are of use in the family, so that every traveller is supposed to bring his bed along with him.

The countryman alone pays the taxes in Poland, which are very moderate: the chief revenues of the lords arise from corn, butter, and honey, which the bees deposit in the trunks of of trees in the middle of the woods. Persons who are convicted of taking honey not belonging to them, are condemned to die: after their trial, they are fastened naked to the tree where the bee-hive is; their belly is then opened near the navel, sufficiently to let out all the bowels, which are twisted round the tree, and they are thus left in the most inhuman manner to expire. This sort of punishment, however, is at present almost out of use.

The fortunes of all the Polish nobility are by no means equal: the greater number have estates of their own, others live entirely on the King's bounty, who must be benevolent from necessity. The King only has the right of giving *starosties*, or considerable land estates. They belong to the family no longer than while the father lives, unless the King pleases to renew the grant to his heirs. It sometimes happens, therefore, that very opulent men in this country are reduced at once to extreme poverty: all the family is then obliged to be in the service of some of the rich people, and often of the strangers residing at Warsaw.

This state of servility is not degrading in Poland: when the Diet meets, the gentleman servant quits his master to go and give his vote. He sometimes obtains a *starosty*, and becomes a man of consequence in his turn.

All the great people of Poland call their seats palaces, although, in any other place, they would only be looked upon as the houses of private people in a very middling station. There are however some fine seats, especially the palace of the Grand-marshal of Poland.

I left Warsaw on the 27th, with Mr. Favier; we crossed the Vistula, which at this place is about sixty toises over, on the ice. The 28th, we passed through the village of Pirdeleiova. Five French people of one family had been murdered a few days before near this village, by some Russians. The mother,

mother, whose name was Lebel, carried on a considerable trade in jewels at St. Petersburg; she was then on her return from France, where she had been to make some new purchases, and had settled her daughter at the same time, whom she was taking with her into Russia with her son-in-law; an accomptant, and a maid servant. These travellers were informed on their arrival at Warsaw, that some Russian carriers were then going to set out for St. Petersburg: from a principle of oeconomy, they made a bargain with these men to conduct them into Russia. At Wegrow, the mother imprudently exposed some of her jewels. The Russians immediately laid a scheme for murdering them, and in order to accomplish this design privately, they desired the travellers to set out at two in the morning, pretending that if they made it later, they would be obliged to cross a very dangerous river the night following. The travellers consented; the two men were in one carriage, the three women in another. The Russians had contrived to separate the carriages, at some miles distance from Pirdeleiova, while the travellers slept. They began by dispatching the two men with a kind of dagger they have always at their girdle. They then went to the carriage where the women were; the young married woman was immediately slain without making any resistance; the mother defended herself as well as she could with a knife, and even wounded one of these villains. The servant, in the mean time, had escaped into a neighbouring wood, where she thought herself safe, but they followed and killed her also. They afterwards confessed all these circumstances. After having murdered this whole family, they broke open the trunks, seized the most valuable things, and then pursued their journey to Russia. An officer in the service of the Empress Queen passed by this place a few hours after the assassination: he went back to Wegrow, and acquainted the people with this horrible transaction. The curate,

curate, from whom we had the ſtory, gave ſuch a deſcription of the murderers as might enable the officer to find them out. He ſet out immediately, inquiring at every village what road they had taken. They had gone on in the great Poliſh road, intending certainly to reach the Ruſſian territories as ſoon as poſſible, where they imagined they ſhould be out of danger; but the officer made ſo much haſte, that he came up with them before they could get out of the Poliſh dominions. They were at a Jew's houſe, where they had depoſited their plunder. He had them taken up in ſpite of their reſiſtance and that of the Jew, acquainted the republic of the affair, and then continued his journey to Peterſburg.

This murder made the more noiſe in the country, as the Poles are in general very hoſpitable, and that ſuch crimes are but little known amongſt them. They never ſpoke of this affair without tears, and ſeemed to find a kind of comfort in recollecting the moſt trifling actions of theſe unfortunate travellers, in ſpeaking of their integrity, their goodneſs, and eſpecially of the mutual affection of the young married couple, which was apparent on every occaſion.

No ſooner was this incident made public in Ruſſia, than it was required that the murderers ſhould be given up. This ſtep appeared very extraordinary to the Poles, and to the ſtrangers who were then at St. Peterſburg, for the crime having been committed in the territories of Poland, the puniſhment of it certainly belonged to the republic. But the Ruſſians thought their greatneſs was concerned in the fate of theſe villains, and the Poles, by complying with their requeſt, gave a freſh inſtance of their own weakneſs.

On the 29th, at ten in the morning we arrived at Bialiſtok in very cold weather; the thermometer was eleven degrees below o in the carriage. Our journey hitherto from Warſaw had been over a fine plain, covered with granite ſtone, all the way

way from Wegrow to within seven or eight leagues of Bialiftok. Thefe granites are of different fpecies and various colours; they are to be found every where from the fize of four feet in diameter to that of two inches, and commonly of four or five inches; their form is for the moft part fpherical, which is a proof of their having been conveyed in ftreams of water.

Warfaw is entirely paved with thefe granites; but there are none to be found about Bialiftok, nor indeed any other kind of ftone. As foon as we were arrived at this borough, which may be confidered as a fmall town, we went to fee the feat of M. Branifky, Grand Marfhal of Poland.

A large avenue, with a portal of ftone at each end, leads up to the houfe: the firft portal is infulated and rather ufelefs; the fecond rifes in a cupola, and forms the gateway of the houfe. Over this portal is placed a fun-dial, and a griffin gilt underneath it, fupporting the arms of the Grand Marfhal. On coming into the court-yard, which is very large, two pteromata, built after the Roman manner, are feen on each fide; in the middle of thefe is a large pavilion. The body of the building faces the portal. The veftibule or entrance into the houfe is fmall; four columns of black marble fupport the flight of fteps, which is narrow, and has not a grand appearance: The apartments of the Marfhal and his Lady are behind the columns; the firft to the right hand, the laft to the left. The Grand Marfhal's apartments are elegant, and ornamented with a variety of fine figures in bronze; thofe of his lady are magnificent, every where fplendid with gold, and decorated with painting and fculpture, difpofed with infinite tafte. From thefe apartments I went down to fome baths, large enough to hold more than twenty perfons, but they are not properly taken care of. On the firft floor there is a fine faloon, in which however the painting is but indifferent; to the right and left are different rooms, pretty elegant, but difpofed with

lefs

less taste, and in every respect inferior to those of the Marshal's lady. The King's apartment is very beautiful; and the Queen's very rich, but antique; the bed is embroidered all over with gold.

The gardens, the groves, and the green-house, are well laid out; the park is very large, well filled with trees, and there is a fine aviary in it. This seat looks rather like the palace of a King than the house of a private man. We were treated with great civility by the Marshal's people, although their lord was absent.

The want of water is a very great inconvenience to which the town of Bialistok is exposed; the inhabitants are obliged to have it conveyed from a great distance, and this must of course be very expensive to them. The town is situated in the midst of an extensive plain, very well cultivated. We left this place the same day we arrived there, and after passing through a great many woods, in our way from Bialistok, we reached Sokolka at eleven at night.

On the 30th, at eight in the morning, the thermometer was still at 11 degrees below 0. Notwithstanding this severe cold, there was no snow to be seen any where but in the woods. At nine we came to the borders of the river Memel, the real name of which is Niemen. The river being only frozen at its borders we ferried over it, and afterwards went up a street leading to Grodno: this street, as well as the whole town, is paved with granites of various colours. The town is divided into two parts, upper and lower: the upper contains the citadel, which is insulated, and communicates with the town by means of a draw-bridge, placed over a deep gorge. The road is very good from Warsaw to this town, but farther northward the ground becomes more uneven, and interrupted with hillocks. As we were crossing a small river at the distance of a mile from Rotnica, the ice gave way, and one of our carriages stuck. We fastened all our horses, which were ten in number, to this carriage, but still found it impossible to draw it out, so that we were obliged to send for four more at eleven o'clock at night. The cold grew excessively severe; we kindled some fire in the midst of the ice and snow: at last, while we were at supper, the horses came, and with much difficulty we got out of this unlucky spot. The hills became more frequent as we advanced, and although not very steep, were still exceeding troublesome, being most of them covered with ice from top to bottom, and the horses in Poland not being shod. On the 31st, at four in the morning, we came to a river, which we crossed in a ferry, after working for two hours to break the ice on its borders. We took fresh horses at the village of Mereck, on the opposite shore, and set out from thence immediately. Having reached Olitta, we were preparing to pass the Niemen a second time, when we were told that the ferry had been carried away by the current, and that we must take the cross road to go to Kowno. The roads, however, began to be very bad, and we had scarcely got a mile on our way, before we met with other frozen hills; the ascents were very difficult, and it was impossible to get to the top without putting all the horses to one carriage: in coming down the hills, some of the horses were fastened to the back part of the carriage. We passed the whole night of the 31st of January to the 1st of February in travelling after this manner, and arrived the same day at Gniezno, a village of which Count Pascy is lord, who was then at Warsaw. Not finding any horses at this place, we sent to beg the favour of Count Pascy's farmer to get us some; he procured us some very good horses, which brought us to Darszonifki before noon, notwithstanding the extreme badness of the roads. Here we found the postilions had gone above six miles out of the road to Kowno, so that we were obliged to go back again. We

were

were in hopes, from the accounts the inhabitants of this village gave us, that the river Niemen, which was not more than three quarters of a mile diftant, would be completely frozen over, but when we came to its borders, we found the ice not ftrong enough to bear us; fo that we were obliged to go another way. Near the hamlet of Podftrava, we came to a hill, which we were labouring in vain to get up, from three in the afternoon to fix in the evening; for although it was but a low hill, yet the afcent was fteep, and covered with ice from top to bottom. We went back to the hamlet we had juft left, which was within gun-fhot of this fpot; here we refted our horfes for feveral hours, and then attempted again to pafs the hill. We took all the country people of the hamlet along with us, and burned links to fave our flambeaus. With the help of the ten horfes to one of the carriages, we got half way up the hill, but could not poffibly get any farther, although fome of us were employed in whipping the horfes, and others in pufhing up the carriage. All our attempts came to nothing, and we returned to the hamlet of Podftrava, where we paffed the night. As we were obliged to pafs all thefe frozen mountains on foot, M. Favier had got feveral falls; the laft accidents of this fort were of a dangerous nature, as he had received a number of bruifes which were very painful to him. The houfe we put up at was a kind of inn, which exhibited an appearance of the moft extreme poverty; it belonged to a Jew; there was but one bed in it for the father and mother, the reft of the family flept on pieces of very dirty rags ftrewed upon the ground. The people in this part of the country have no other light than what they get from laths of wood fet on fire, and ftuck horizontally in the wall. Here the countryman eats bread in fummer time, as well as in Lithuania, but is obliged to go without it in winter, becaufe he fells moft of his corn: the cachra is then ufed inftead of it, which is

D 2 nothing

nothing more than peeled barley, boiled in water as rice is. The better kind of people in Poland eat a great deal of pork, and four *krout*, which is nothing more than cabbage cut in pieces, and thrown into water for several months till it turns four. They have also a soup they call *barsez*; made of the juice of beet-root, turned four by being put into a cask for several months; this liquor is mixed with water, cream, and meat, when they can get it; and they reckon it a very nice dish.

The inhabitants of this hamlet are so poor, that they could scarce supply us with a little straw to lie down upon. Although we were much fatigued, yet we slept little, as the continual delays we were exposed to made us uneasy. M. Favier was intrusted with very important dispatches to the Marquis de l' Hopital, ambassador at St. Petersburg, which required so much haste, that he was frequently obliged to give the Duke de Choiseul an account of the number of obstacles we met with on our way to that capital. The countryman we had sent for fresh horses came back at four in the morning, and told us that the people would not send their horses more than half way to meet us; as they would then have been of little service to us, we resolved to attempt getting round the hill, and therefore waited till day-break. We collected all the people of the hamlet, and on the second of February, with their assistance, we at length got out of this place, where we had been detained since three o'clock in the afternoon of the 1st instant. At eleven in the morning we reached Kamstilki, and came to Kowno the same day about four in the afternoon.

On the 3d of February the thermometer rose as high as 0, which made us apprehensive of a thaw; but came down again in the evening as fast, the wind being changed to the north: our journey all this day was over a plain. On the

4th,

4th, in the morning, the cold flackened a little, and the thermometer was not more than five degrees below 0: the wind was very high, and blew up clouds of fnow, which were very troublefome to us; one of our poftilions could not ftand it, but left us in the middle of the woods, and made his efcape fo effectually, that we could not poffibly find him out, but were obliged to fend for another from the neareft village. We came to Krafki at eleven at night, and to Mittaw on the 5th inftant, about ten in the morning.

Mittaw is the capital of Courland, and the place of the Duke's refidence. It is a fine town, but in general not well built: on coming out of it we met with the palace the Duke de Biren built, while he was favourite of the Czarina Ann; which would be incomparably elegant if it was finifhed.

The roads from Kowno had been very good. We reached Olin the fame day, after paffing the boundaries of Livonia and Ruffia, at about a mile from this place. All the country was covered with fnow, and fledges began to be ufed. We came to Riga at ten at night, and put up at an inn called Krieg, where we found a number of people who had juft done fupper; the company was feated round a table, from which every thing was removed, except bottles and glaffes. Each perfon had a pipe near three feet long; they drank and fmoked alternately: fome were leaning on the table; others were ftretched at their eafe in an arm-chair, with their waiftcoats unbuttoned: nothing was to be heard but the jingling of glaffes, the clafhing of bottles, and the noife made by the fmacking of the fmokers lips. Clouds of fmoke arofe on every fide, as inconvenient to the fight as difagreeable to the fmell. They were fo thick, that perfons at the other end of the room were fcarcely difcernable. Some very pretty and well-fhaped fervant maids made their appearance now and then; they were neatly dreffed, and did

not

not seem as if they meant to pique themselves upon a profession of chastity.

We had but an indifferent supper; rest indeed seemed more necessary to us than food. We took a view of the city the next day, while sledges were preparing, on which we had our carriages placed.

Riga is a large commercial town, situated on the Dwina. Before we came into the town, we crossed this river on the ice; it is about twice as broad as the Seyne. The sea not being more than two leagues distant from Riga, the merchandize is easily brought up to the city. This town formerly belonged to the Swedes, who lost it in the time of the Czar Peter I.: it has preserved all the privileges stipulated for, when it capitulated with Russia. There are few nobles in the town, except among the strangers; the inhabitants being chiefly traders.

After dinner we went to pay our respects to the governor, who is of the Dolgorouski family; but, as he was very far advanced in years, and not well, we could not possibly see him.

We received great civilities from M. de Wittinhof, in the council of the regency of Livonia, and Knight of the Order of St. Alexander Newski. He had married the daughter of the famous General Munick, although that gentleman was banished into Siberia.

Our sledges were finished on the 7th instant, and we left Riga the same day at six in the evening. We had scarce got half a mile from the town, when we found that there was no more snow; we were then in an extensive plain, which it was impossible to pass with our sledges. The night was yet very dark, and we were far from any assistance. We attempted to fix the carriages on the wheels again; but although we had flambeaus, yet the darkness of the night and the weight of our

baggage

baggage made it impossible for us to succeed in our attempts. We ordered an interpreter, whom I brought with me from Warsaw, to desire the postilions to go into the nearest village for help: a sharp dispute immediately arose between the Russians and the interpreter. As we were ignorant of the language, we could not possibly discover what they were quarrelling about; and my interpreter being in liquor, we could neither make him listen to reason, nor hold his tongue. We were still exposed to the open air in the most severe weather, with little hope of being soon released from this situation: at last, with much difficulty we understood, that the postilions refused to go in search of assistance, on account of the darkness of the night. I came near and shewed them a rouble, a Russian coin amounting to about four shillings and six-pence English; they immediately ran off, not leaving even one man with us, and returned very quickly with the country people. It was thought sufficient to take off the sledges, which served for the fore-wheels, and to fasten them behind the carriages. We got on our way again about eleven at night, but when we had gone a few steps farther, the ropes belonging to the other sledges gave way: the country people, who had not left us, made us understand it would be absolutely necessary to take off the other sledges, and that they would do this for us, in consideration of another rouble; we had already given them two, and one to the postilions; this made altogether about eighteen shillings English. Although we were not well-pleased at being thus imposed upon, we were so anxious to get out soon from this place, that we gave whatever they asked. We went on quietly the rest of the night, and part of the next day; but as the snow grew more and more thick, and we met with nothing but sledges on the road, we were determined from what had happened to us, not to have recourse to them, till it was quite impossible to do without them. On the 8th instant there was a most violent storm; whirlwinds of snow arose on all sides; the largest objects were scarcely discernable at the distance of a few yards; the wind drove the snow with such force, that the horses stopped every minute, and it was impossible to get them on. To complete our misfortunes, one of the postilions overturned the horses, and the carriage where the baggage was, into a hole: we then gave up every thing for lost; however we got out of the carriage immediately, and after working for two hours, we proceeded again on our journey, and came at last to Lenzenhof. The wind soon grew calm, and we passed the next post to Wolmar without any accident, which was very extraordinary. The country was covered with snow, and the road was very wide; it grew narrow on coming out of Wolmar; the way was tracked over a heap of snow, gathered up by the winds between a hedge-row of trees; it was hardened only in the beaten paths; the postilions conducted us with the greatest care through this dangerous road. We were just getting out of this pass, when the carriage we were in, disappeared all at once, so that the horses heads could but just be seen, and we were buried in the carriage; there remained only a small opening at the top of the coach, by which we got out, without waiting for help. We tried in vain to disengage the carriage, by fastening all the horses of the other carriage to it: we were obliged to send for shovels from the nearest village, and after having spent the greater part of the day in this business, we at length got the carriage and horses out of the hole. We had our carriages fixed on the sledges at the next village, and arrived on the 10th at two in the afternoon at Derpt. Here we learned by some Russians, just come from St. Petersburg, that there was such a quantity of snow on the road, and the roads were so narrow, that we could not possibly travel with our carriages. The truth of this report was confirmed by the post-master, who assured us we should not be able to reach St. Petersburg in a fortnight with our carriages; we therefore left them, and took four sledges in this town, two for ourselves, and two for the servant and the baggage. I experienced, for the first time, the ease of travelling with sledges; we went on with the greatest velocity, without meeting with any accident. The cold increased however every day as we came nearer to St. Petersburg; on the 11th, the thermometer kept up at twelve degrees and a half till noon, and fell four or five degrees in the night-time. As we were almost in the open air on our sledges, we suffered much from the severe cold, which we were not used to. At length we came to St. Petersburg on the 13th of February, after a journey of about ten weeks. We had met with such a variety of accidents every day, that I despaired of reaching Siberia in time for the observation.

I went immediately to the Marquis de l'Hopital, our ambassador, who was extremely kind to me. He was just going away; the Baron de Breteuil remained minister plenipotentiary.

I had left France, in consequence of the academy of St. Petersburg having requested that of Paris to send one of its members into Siberia, where some astronomers of Russia were also to meet. These astronomers had been already gone a month, before I arrived at St. Petersburg: their departure, and various difficulties started before I came, had given rise to some doubts with regard to my journey to Tobolsky. Some of the academy of St. Petersburg proposed divers other parts of Russia, less distant, and more easily to be got at, than Tobolsky; but as the Transit of Venus over the Sun would be performed in less time in this capital of Siberia, than in any other part of the globe; it could not have been viewed to so much ad-

vantage

vantage any where else. These reasons were easily comprehended by a minister of so much knowledge as the Baron de Breteuil. Count Woronzof, High Chancellor of Russia, a lover and protector of the Sciences, readily came into his measures; the obstacles which had been raised were removed, and my departure was at last fixed for the 10th of March.

The Empress Elizabeth gave the most circumstantial orders on this occasion. All the assistances I met with in travelling through Siberia, were owing to the protection of this Princess.

When I had reached St. Petersburg, I was still at the distance of eight hundred leagues from Tobolsky. This new journey required other preparations, very different from those I had been employed in at setting out from France. I was obliged to take all sorts of provisions with me, even those which are most in common use, such as bread; and to supply myself with beds, and all the necessary utensils of life. I could not do without an interpreter, nor without a clock-maker, to mend my clocks in case of accident. I scarce had occasion to ask for any thing, but was anticipated in all my wants by the Baron de Breteuil; who was as earnest as myself about this observation, the success of which is chiefly owing to his attention; and indeed the nation is much indebted in many other respects to the conduct of this minister.

The season was so far advanced, that I began to be apprehensive, lest a thaw coming on before I could reach Tobolsky, should frustrate the design of my journey, by obliging me to remain in the midst of the woods of Siberia. I trusted, however, to the very expeditious manner of travelling on sledges, and set out from St. Petersburg on the 10th of March in the evening, with four of them. There are several kinds of these

sledges,

sledges, although in many respects they are built nearly upon the same plan *.

The sledge in which I travelled, at setting out from St. Petersburg, was close on all sides, but very heavy on account of the quantity of things I had put into it. It was

* The lower part of the sledges is made of two pieces of wood, each of which is about six inches wide, and three inches thick at the end of the back part of the sledge. The same dimensions are continued for the length of two or three feet; they afterwards gradually diminish as they come nearer to the other extremity, which is turned up in a circular form at the fore-part of the sledge, to the height of about two feet, as in the sledge at Plate I. in which there are four children drawn by two others. (The wood is bent in this manner while it is still green, and by fixing it thus, against the houses, where it is sometimes left for a year.) In the middle of, and underneath these two pieces, which are the chief parts of the sledge, there are two plates of iron, almost as thin as the iron of skates, and of the same use. These two pieces are fixed at the distance of two feet and a half from each other, by strong pieces of wood placed transversely: over this first frame a second is placed, fastened to the former by pegs, as may be seen in the forementioned sledge; but the pieces of this second frame are not so strong as those of the first. The common sledges in use, for carrying provisions and baggage, are constructed in this simple manner; they are sometimes drawn by men, but it is common to fasten several horses to them, yet more frequently one single horse, by means of two shafts fixed to the sides of the sledge; the driver then sits down on the provisions, and if the sledge is empty, he sometimes stands upright in it, while the sledge is going on with the utmost rapidity. Other sledges for travelling are of two kinds, some are quite covered, others only half over. The last are most frequent, they differ little in construction from those I have just described; upon the second frame eight wooden bars are placed, of the same height as the two bent pieces of wood; these are fastened at bottom by pegs, and at top by two beams. At the back of the sledge, a kind of top, like the head of a chaise, is formed with hoops; or rather the sledge, in this state, makes the skeleton of a carriage, known by the name of dormeuse: it is closed on all sides with leather, and most commonly with a kind of matting made from the barks of trees. The sledge thus constructed is exceedingly light; the figure of it may be seen at Plate I. Two beams fastened together behind the seat, are placed obliquely on the sides of the sledge to strengthen it; a mat fixed to the anterior border of the head of the sledge, keeps out the weather; and this may be let down, or taken up at pleasure, while another mat is put upon the feet, to prevent the snow from falling into the carriage. The most convenient sledge is that which may be seen in the middle of the Plate: it is a very light box, six feet long, three feet wide, and four or five feet high, with a door and a window on each side; there are the same conveniences in it as in a common carriage.

drawn

drawn by five horses abreast; the watchmaker and my servant were in another half covered over; a serjeant, the Chancellor was so kind to give me for a guide, chose the third sledge, where my provisions were; and my instruments were in a fourth.

As I was desirous that my attendants should be supplied with every convenience I could possibly procure them, I allowed them to lay in all sorts of provisions they liked best, except wine, because we could not carry a sufficient quantity of that for every body. I contented myself with accepting from M. Bretcuil only four flasks for my own use, in hopes indeed of finding some at Tobolsky.

I set out in the week of *Maslinitsa*, which is the week before Lent, when the Russians seldom travel, on account of the licentiousness of the common people; who are incessantly drunk during this season, and give themselves up to all kind of excess. The fear of missing my observation, hindered me from following the advice they gave me, to defer my journey, and indeed I met with nothing disagreeable from the Russians.

I travelled all night without getting out of my sledge, slept only a little in the morning of the 11th, and arrived about noon the same day at Tschoudowai. Shut up as I was in my sledge, and covered with furs, I still found it extremely cold. On coming out I went into a stove, and was much astonished to see some little children naked, and playing about in the snow, in this severe weather, while others more grown up were diverting themselves with drawing four or five of their playfellows in a sledge. These children are thus inured from their birth to the cold, which does not in the least affect them, although they are every minute exposed to the change from cold to heat, by going in and out of their stoves.

I had every thing necessary for dinner brought into the stove, and found some of my flasks emptied, and good part of my provisions gone. On making some inquiries into this matter, one of my guides told me, it was to be laid to their charge; that as for wine they liked it better than brandy, and would drink it. I was the more surprized at this declaration, and the positive manner in which it was delivered, as I had spared no pains to win all these people over, and make them attached to me. The idea of travelling alone with persons I had known only for two days, and who behaved in such a manner, did not allow me to hesitate one moment on the nature of my own behaviour; I therefore gave the fellow who said this to me, such an answer, that he was glad to get down stairs as fast as he could. After reflecting a few moments, I was well pleased with the end of this affair, and not sorry that I had shewn such spirit, as too much discretion might have been attended with disagreeable consequences upon this occasion. The Russians of this class have no other idea of subordination, than that of the most abject slavery, and acknowledge no master who does not treat them with harshness.

On the 13th I came to Gorodnia, a hamlet between Tweer and Klin: as soon as I got out of my sledge, the watchmaker asked me for one to himself; and complained of being too much crouded in the sledge where he was with my interpreter: besides that this would have brought on an additional expence, which was quite unnecessary, the difficulty of getting horses was a sufficient reason for refusing to comply with this request, which was the more extraordinary, as the method of travelling in sledges, however agreeable at the beginning of winter, grows very inconvenient towards the end of this season, especially if one person is alone in the sledge. The roads are then all divided by parallel ditches, at the distance of about thirteen or fourteen feet from each other, and holes are often met with several feet deep, in which the sledges fail; this gives the traveller such violent shocks, that he is in the greatest danger

ger of having his head broken against the sides of the sledge, unless he continues lying along. Notwithstanding this precaution, the shaking is so considerable, that it is thought much better to have several persons together in one sledge, by which means the shocks are less dangerous.

I reached Mosco on the 14th at night; my sledges were broken to pieces with the continual shocks they had received, and were in such bad condition that they could not be mended. The Chancellor Woronzof had given me a letter for his brother at Mosco, from whom I received the greatest kindness, as well as from his lady. They are held in the highest esteem in this town; and the respect their virtues insure them, is more pleasing, than that which is due to their rank. This family is the protector of strangers: sincerity and good-nature, less frequent in Russia than any where else, are conspicuous qualities in them, from the first moment they become acquainted.

M. de Woronzof assured me, that the thaw would be complete before my arrival at Tobolsky, as I had been already told at St. Petersburg; in this case it would have been impossible for me to reach this town time enough to fulfil the design I had been sent out for. I had been four days travelling from St. Petersburg to Mosco, a journey often performed in two. This delay had been occasioned by a number of unforeseen accidents; the first cause of which was the badness of the roads.

The cold, which made my attendants stay too long in the stoves while the horses were changing, also kept me back. I was then convinced of the reality of the obstacles which had been foretold to me, and of the impossibility of reaching Tobolsky in due time, without altering my plan.

I left the new sledges I had ordered, and for the sake of expedition, bought up some which belonged to the country people. I recruited my provisions, which had been much wasted; or rather indeed M. de Woronzof took care to provide

vide me with most of the things I wanted. I set out on the 17th in the morning, determined not to stop any more; the next day I told the watchmaker and the interpreter, that I would drop them on the road, if ever they went into a stove. This declaration, which they knew I should keep to, and the brandy I gave the postilions, had the desired effect; so that I met with no other delays, but travelled on in my sledge with amazing swiftness. The rivers in the north are very quickly frozen over; their frozen surface does not become uneven, as that of the Seine at Paris, but is perfectly smooth: the velocity of the sledges is then so great, that as we were upon the river Occa, one of the postilions was unable to avoid a hole where the water was not frozen, although he had discovered it from the distance of more than thirty paces; one horse fell at once into this hole, and the others, in spight of their resistance, and the postilion's efforts, would have been dragged in after him, if we had not helped them very speedily, by cutting the cords which fastened them to the sledge. There are many such holes to be met with, where the water never freezes, although the ice around is three feet thick, and the cold so very severe that it will freeze brandy and spirit of wine. I have seen upon this same river an extent of more than 200 feet where the water was not frozen. The readiest way of accounting for this appearance, is to suppose that it may be produced by some hot springs at the bottom of the river: but, on reflection, it will hardly seem possible that these springs can be considerable enough to cause such large openings. Besides, this river being exceedingly deep, however specifically light these waters arising from springs may be supposed to be, they would have time to contract a certain degree of coldness, in passing along a diameter of such length, as that, which reaches from the bottom of the river to its surface. The manner in which the congelation of the waters of this river is brought about, seems rather to difcover to us the natural caufe of this phenomenon; for, in reality, all the great rivers in the northern countries, as well as in our climates, would never freeze, becaufe of the rapidity of their current, unlefs the ice was firft formed towards the borders of the river where the waters are more at reft; thefe flakes of ice, being loofe and floating, grow bigger, and increafe daily, foon covering the furface of the waters. In this fituation the feverity of the northern froft fixes at once all thefe loofe flakes, fo that they neceffarily form a furface perfectly even; whereas the furface of frozen rivers in our temperate climates is always rough, becaufe the cold is not fufficiently fevere to bring about this confolidation fo fpeedily.

Admitting that thefe floating pieces of ice are fo quickly joined together in the northern countries, it may eafily be conceived that intervals muft be left between fome of them, on account of the different figures of thefe flakes. The large opening I have taken notice of, was probably produced in this manner; it was formed in the middle, and in the direction of the current: fuppofing therefore the river to be frozen at its borders, while the ice was floating in it, and confequently its channel much contracted at the furface of the water, the large flakes will have formed an obftacle at this place, will have been fixed there, and have left this large fpace unfrozen. It will certainly be objected, and with reafon, that although the furface of the water is frozen, the river may have ice floating beneath the frozen furface: thefe flakes will then come up to the fuperficies of the water in the places which are not frozen, fix themfelves there and fill up the empty fpaces. I imagine it to be really owing to thefe new formed flakes of ice, that fo few vacant fpaces are to be found on large rivers; but it certainly does not follow from hence, that every opening left, after the firft formation of ice, fhould neceffarily be filled up; befides, as foon as rivers are frozen over, there are

few

few loose flakes in them, and these, float but for a short time. In our moderate climates, the frost is very mild compared to what it is in the northern countries, where the thermometer falls as low as twenty or five-and-twenty degrees, and sometimes even to seventy: the temperature of the air varies likewise so considerably in our climates, that several thaws frequently take place in one winter; so that it is not to be wondered at, that there should be ice floating in the rivers most part of the time; whereas, the excessive hard frosts in northern countries; fixes at once all the loose flakes of ice; and no new pieces are formed, because the frost continues without interruption for seven or eight months in the year.

I made an observation in Siberia, which proves that there is no ice floating in rivers after the first moment of their being frozen up, and that the empty spaces left towards the current, can never be filled up with ice, during the whole course of the winter. In travelling on the Occa, and afterwards on the Volga, I met with several openings about eighteen inches in diameter: these had been made by the country people through the ice, which was more than three feet thick, for the convenience of placing nets to catch fish. This custom would not have been established, or would not certainly have been continued to this time, if there were any floating pieces of ice in these rivers; for in that case, the nets would soon have been carried away. It is evident for the same reason, that the water cannot freeze in these parts; and indeed I have always found it fluid in all the openings where I have stopped to examine the fact.

This observation, at the same time that it shews that the motion of current waters is a great impediment to their being congealed, furnishes also an argument in favor of the opinion advanced, by some natural philosophers, that the waters of the seas situated near the Pole can never be frozen, notwithstanding

standing the prodigious mountains of ice which float near the borders of these seas at the end of the winter. These mountains of ice have only been formed near the coasts, particularly at the mouths of rivers, by the flakes of ice brought down by them at the beginning of the winter: but out at sea, the water cannot be more frozen than it is at the torrid zone, and the dangers travellers have been exposed to on these seas, have arisen entirely from their not keeping sufficiently clear of the coasts.

The accident which gave occasion to this short digression happened at the distance of a few leagues from Nizan-Novogorod, where I arrived on the 20th, at one in the afternoon.

Before I reached this place, I observed from my sledge, that the small chain of mountains on the borders of the river Occa to the south, was composed of matter of various colors, disposed in layers. This mountain being perpendicular, the layers became very conspicuous, and were objects worthy of attention: I stopped the sledge to go and examine them, and was then at the distance of twenty werfts from Nizan-Novogorod. The mountain was more than one hundred feet high above the level of the stream, and the layers I have mentioned, were not more than thirteen or fourteen feet from the same point: I was for a considerable time in doubt, whether I should satisfy the great desire I had of examining these layers more particularly; for I could not get at them without passing over a heap of snow forty feet high, gathered up in this spot by the winds: this heap, towards the bottom, appeared firm enough to support me; but I was apprehensive, lest the snow should fall in with me when once I got upon it; I ventured, however, with a hatchet and hammer in my hand, followed by my servant, who soon left me to myself. The heap of snow being even with the layers, I took a sketch of it; I then examined and brought away specimens of the different substances: I

came

came down however as soon as I could; being obliged frequently to change my position, because I found myself sinking by imperceptible degrees, so that in the space of a few minutes, I was up to the knees in snow. These different layers, resembling at a distance a brick-wall, were composed of a particular species of gypse, which I shall speak of under the article of the natural history of Russia.

Although the winter season was nearly at an end, yet I did not find much snow in the flat part of the country, because it had certainly been driven from thence by the high winds into places where the current of air was more frequently intercepted. It is for this reason, we found such a quantity of it along this mountain; which I followed as far as Nizan-Novogorod, and observed in several parts the same sort of layers already mentioned. As soon as I got into this town, I waited upon M. Ismaelof, the Governor; for whom I had letters from M. de Woronzof, the High Chancellor. This minister was not only so kind to give me letters of recommendation for every place I was to pass through; but had also given orders before I left St. Petersburg, that I should be supplied with all possible accommodations on the road. I should also mention, that several other noblemen had been so attentive as to give me letters, containing orders to their stewards; from whom I received very great assistances. If I have sometimes been in disagreeable situations, this can only be ascribed to the nature of the climate, and the dispositions of the common people. It is impossible to be exempt from such incidents, in countries where the police is best regulated; much less in Siberia, so far distant from the inspection of the sovereign.

M. Ismaelof informed me, that there was a Frenchman in this town, whose name was Boudet, intrusted with educating the children of one of the principal families: he was well qualified for this employment; and was much esteemed and respected

respected in this place. He paid me a visit the same day, and conducted me to all the places I was desirous of seeing.

As I stopped at Nizan-Novogorod to have my sledges repaired, I passed the whole of the 20th instant, in seeing the town, which is most pleasantly situated, in form of a circle, upon the slope of a mountain, at the foot of which runs the river Volga: there is a large plain on the top of this mountain: the ground which is even with the river, is also disposed in a plain beyond the Volga, bounded only by the sight.

This stream is the more beautiful at Nizan-Novogorod, as it receives there the river Occa: the Volga is about two and thirty feet deep, and about three hundred and eighteen feet wide, before the Occa runs into it: this river is at least one hundred and thirty-seven feet wide. The large sheet of water formed by the confluence of these two rivers, makes a delightful view in summer time. The Governor's house is surrounded with stone walls, forming a kind of fortification, which however is not strong; the town is about eight hundred and fifty feet long, including the suburbs: it is among the second class of Russian towns, with respect to its size, and very deservedly reckoned among the first, on account of its trade, because it is the mart town of all the corn round about, which makes it very commercial. Seven or eight hundred strangers are to be seen there every day in the summer time, for the space of four months in the year: notwithstanding this, the people of the town are not rich, because the greatest part of the trade is carried on for the sovereign Prince, whose agents are so many tyrants; the rest of this trade belongs to the different noblemen, who send their corn to this market, so that the town's people have no share in it. There are indeed some few woollen-drapers and haberdashers in the town, but their shops are ill stocked, and their goods very bad; the shops are in the market, on the borders of the Volga. I met with a great concourse

of

of people in the market: the provisions sold there were chiefly frozen fish of different sorts; they are caught at the beginning of winter, and preserved 'till the end of this season by means of the cold, as well as butcher's meat and game: the people often lay in a stock of these provisions for four or five months to come.

The town is as ill-built as it is agreeably situated: most of the houses are of wood, very few of brick. There are thirty parishes in this town, and five or six convents: but there are no more than two or three priests to each parish, a number indeed more than adequate to the number of parishioners. It is customary among the Russians, to have several parishes in their towns, although they contain but few inhabitants: the number of church men is considerably increased by this multiplicity of parishes.

The young lads in this town, as well as in the neighbouring places, are married at fourteen or fifteen years of age, and the girls at thirteen: the women often breed 'till they are fifty. It will certainly be imagined from this account, that the country must be well peopled: but we shall find it otherwise, and that it is necessary to marry the girls early, in order to prevent debauchery.

My sledges being mended on the 21st in the evening, I left this place the same day at eight o'clock: the accident I had met with near Nizan-Novogorod, where one of my sledges had nearly been destroyed, although in the day-time, had made me determine not to travel on the rivers in the night. It is then impossible to see the holes; and we might all have been swallowed up, without either of us being able even to warn the others of the approaching danger; the postilions, however, assured me, that they were acquainted with the dangerous places, and that we should shorten our journey much by going along the river. I trusted to their experience, and arrived on the 22d at Kuznædemiansk, at seven in the evening, after

travelling

travelling forty-three leagues: the surface of the Volga was as smooth as glass, and not the smallest rising to be seen on it; the snow which had fallen on it had been immediately carried off by the wind, and the sledges went on with inconceivable swiftness. I sometimes got out of my sledge and placed myself behind it, in order to enjoy the pleasure of travelling so quick; the borders of the Volga are well peopled in the course of this route, so that the pleasure was heightened by seeing the river covered with a number of sledges crossing each other, running foul of, and frequently overturning each other, from the extreme rapidity of their motion. Although this was a very amusing sight to me, I could not enjoy it long: the severity of the cold, which made the thermometer fall down to eighteen degrees, obliged me to get quickly into my sledge again; neither could I bear the excessive quickness of the motion, while I stood upright on my sledge. The horses in common use are very small, and appear weak; but they are inured to labour, and get on extremely fast, although the postilions seldom lash them; they content themselves with whistling to them, and waving their hands, or speaking to them; they call these animals, mother, sister, and dearly beloved: one would imagine they are conversing with reasonable beings. I went sometimes at the rate of four leagues an hour; but was frequently delayed by the difficulty of getting horses.

Although I had met with several inconveniencies in travelling on a sledge in bad weather, I was convinced by my journey from Nizan-Novogorod to Kuzmodemiansk, that this kind of carriage is extremely pleasant at the beginning of winter: for I sat as easy in my sledge on the Volga, as I should have done in a boat in the summer time.

Kuzmodemiansk is a pretty large village; the Russians call it a town. I found about fifteen country people assembled at the gate, who took my barometer for a clock. One of the
country

country people had a chain round his neck, to which was faſtened a log of wood, about two feet and a half long, and eight inches thick: it was intended as a puniſhment, but I could not learn for what fault it was inflicted. At this place, I found all the horſes I wanted; I ſet out immediately, and quitted the courſe of the Volga with regret.

From St. Peterſburg, I had hitherto met with no eminences large enough to be called mountains: this vaſt plain is barren in many places, and cultivated in others: on the reſt, pines and birch trees are only to be found. Having croſſed the Volga at Kuzmodemianſk, I entered into a large foreſt, more than three hundred leagues long: indeed, all the reſt of the road may be looked upon as one continued foreſt, as far as the confines of Toboliky, from whence I was ſtill near five hundred leagues diſtant.

The woods in this foreſt were of the ſame kinds as thoſe I have before mentioned; but there was a greater quantity of ſnow here: it was more than four feet deep in the woods, while in the open country it was not above two feet deep at moſt. The thermometer ſtill kept up at eighteen or nineteen degrees below 0. I was obliged to run the poſts of Bolchaia and Koumia with the ſame horſes: the firſt, is not more than two leagues from Kuzmodemianſk, the ſecond, is two and a half from Bolchaia. As theſe two places were nothing more than hamlets of four or five houſes, I found neither horſes nor poſtilions there; ſo that I was obliged to go on with the ſame as far as Choumetri, where I arrived on the 23d, at ten in the morning. The people of this hamlet had run off into the woods as ſoon as I came; ſo that I was left only with the poſt-maſter; in vain we ſearched over the whole hamlet for horſes: I met with nothing but children in cradles; the mothers and daughters had hid themſelves, for fear they ſhould be made to ſerve as poſtilions. The poſt-maſter had no more than ſix horſes,

horses, according to the regulation, for the use of the court messengers, and the other horses were not able to go any farther. Some country people passed by in their sledges: they were stopped, and told that their horses were wanted; instead of making any difficulty, they immediately left their sledges, with every thing that was in them, and escaped into the woods: some of them however less swift footed than the rest were laid hold of. I asked what was the reason of their running away, and of this unusual confusion; and was told that most travellers made free with the horses, and with every thing else belonging to the inhabitants of these hamlets; who are often ill used upon asking for what was their due. The uniform of the serjeant who was with me, and the appearance of the rest of my company, had made them apprehensive of the same kind of treatment; the former postilions removed the fears of these unfortunate people; and by the help of some brandy I gave them, the quiet of the hamlet was again restored. Those we had stopped, even desired to go along with me, with such of the former postilions as were least fatigued. My journey after this was always towards the north. The cold and the snow increased daily; and houses were less frequently to be met with; so that we were obliged to travel five-and-twenty or thirty leagues with the same horses: the roads were so narrow, that there was but just room enough for a sledge, and moreover, so serpentine, that we were much incommoded by striking perpetually against the trees. The holes we likewise fell into every instant gave us such violent shocks, that I was in continual fear lest the sledges should be broken to pieces. If I met any other sledges coming from Siberia, they were laid on one side, that mine might pass by: this is the privilege of those who travel with the royal post; a bell fastened to the first horse, is the distinguishing mark, and gives notice from afar to clear the way.

The

The firſt place I came to, after leaving Choumetri, was the borough of Carewokokſzaiſk: it is dependant on the Empreſs alone; all inhabitants who are ſubject only to the ſovereign, are much happier than thoſe who are under the dominion of particular noblemen. Theſe individuals have the power of levying taxes, which they almoſt always abuſe. Beſides the claims of the nobleman, the inhabitants pay alſo one rouble (about four ſhillings and ſix pence Engliſh) to the Empreſs. The poſt-maſter's wife, a woman of forty, had had twenty children, two of them only were alive; one of five, the other of four years old; all the reſt had died before they came to that age. Here I ſtopped to get my ſledges mended, and left the place as ſoon as they were ready; the thermometer was ſtill at the ſame height of eighteen or nineteen degrees. At the diſtance of a few werſts from this borough, my ſledge was ſo violently overturned that my laſt barometer was broken. I had not left the foreſt ſince Kuzmodemianſk, and had met with no places free from trees except when I came near the houſes: the wood was either of the pine tree, deal, or birch; theſe trees had been burnt in ſome places by accident, at the diſtance of twenty or thirty leagues. It was then Lent ſeaſon, which the Ruſſians keep very ſtrictly; their food conſiſts of bad black bread, ill made and ill baked, and of oatmeal boiled in water, to which the better ſort of people add ſome oil of hemp-ſeed. Their drink is what they call *quouas*, which is nothing more than water made to ferment with bran and a little flower. This liquor is very fine, and of a yellow colour; but more four than vinegar, and has a taſte which perſons who are not uſed to it cannot bear. At other times of the year, their food is chiefly fiſh and ſome *piroquis*: the piroquis are a ſort of ſmall pies, about three inches wide, the inſide of which is filled with a fiſh they call *Siantki*. They eat their meals at a table where they place themſelves round a bowl full of water-gruel; some are seated, others stand up: some old women go about to the houses at meal-times to sell the piroquis.

The cottages appear so much the more gloomy, as the severity of the winters does not allow of any communication with the external air: the windows are generally no more than one foot high, and six inches wide; besides which, the inhabitants are almost deprived of the light of the sun, all the while that he remains in the western constellations: they are then in almost continual darkness, receiving light only from splinters of birch, which they call *louchines*; they first dry them on the stove, then fix them between the beams, to give light, or place them on a trevet; this is the business the old people are employed in, as well as in taking care to put fresh splinters as the others burn out. This custom prevails all over Russia.

Their houses are of wood, and not constructed with much skill; they content themselves with making notches at the end of each beam, that they may be firmly fastened one upon another. They take so little pains to fit them to each other, that there are large intervals between them, which they fill up with moss, to keep out the external air.. When the building is raised from twelve to twenty feet high, they cover it with boards. In houses where there are two floors, the lower floor is for the cattle, and the upper is divided into two parts, one for the milk and other provisions, the other for the family. In the last is a stove, which takes up one fourth of the room: it is generally made of brick, and is like our common ovens, with this difference only, that it is flat, and has no chimney: to supply the place of which they usually make a hole of about six inches in the ceiling, which may be opened or shut at pleasure by means of a valve. Notwithstanding the severity of the winters, they make fires in their stoves but once a day, at seven

seven or eight in the morning. As soon as the fire is kindled, the room is full of smoke; the valve being closed since the last evening, such a quantity of smoke is immediately collected that it forms a cloud, which supports itself at the height of two feet or two and a half above the floor. The people of the house must then sit on the floor, or, if they walk, must bend themselves quite forwards, the smoke being so thick, that any person standing upright in it would soon be suffocated. Strange as this custom may appear, yet there is a reason for it. When the smoke is diffused all around, and suffered to remain for any length of time in these cottages, the heat is considerably increased; so that as soon as the wood is consumed, and nothing but the embers remain: about three hours after the first lighting of the fire, the valve is opened, the smoke soon disperses, and the valve is immediately shut again till next day, to prevent any communication with the external air. The heat is then so great, that M. de Reaumur's thermometer rises to thirty-six and forty degrees; a heat which is almost as unbearable for a stranger as the severe cold of the external air. A considerable degree of heat is preserved in the cottage even till next day, when the thermometer still keeps up at sixteen or eighteen degrees above temperate.

 The furniture consists chiefly in benches placed round their cottages, sometimes a small table, and some earthen and wooden ware for their victuals, which they dress before the stove, with the embers remaining after the wood is burnt out. The women are always employed in this business, while the men build the sledges, make nets for fishing, and other instruments for hunting those animals which supply the Russians with their beautiful furs.

 All these inhabitants appear to be superstitiously attached to the Greek church; they are so strict with regard to the Lent fasts, that they make children of three or four years old keep them,

them, and never omit this duty, although they should at the same time be engaged in the most criminal pursuits.

Each family has a small chapel in the house, where the saint of the family is placed; they look upon him as the guardian deity of the cottage, and never go in or out of doors, without making signs of the cross for several minutes, bowing themselves down at the same time, and offering up some prayers to the saint. I once saw one of these country people strike his head so violently against a post in the eagerness of bending forwards, that he turned quite pale immediately: notwithstanding which he went on with his prayers. Observing that every body was looking at him without offering him any assistance, I went up to him, and made him sit down; he found himself sick, but luckily received no other injury from this excess of devotion.

The Russians take great care to ornament this chapel with small wax-lights, six or seven inches high, and about one third of an inch thick. They put other small images into it, especially such as they have received in marriage. The richer people hang up a lamp before the chapel, and on particular days they light up all these wax-candles, and leave them burning all night. Several fires happen from their carelessness in neglecting to change the lights before they are quite burnt out; by which the chapel, the saint, the cottage, and the whole village, are sometimes destroyed in a few hours. Such accidents are frequent, as this custom prevails all over Russia, even at the palace of the Empress.

The Russians have so much faith in the saints of their chapels, that they always address a short prayer to them before they undertake any thing. I was told by a Russian, who was in love with his neighbour's wife, and encouraged by her, that after having suffered a long time from the watchfulness of a jealous and troublesome husband, he contrived at length to get

get into her chamber: juft as he thought himfelf upon the point of being completely happy, the lady thinking of her faint, ran into the chapel immediately, and made her prayer to him, after which fhe returned and threw herfelf again into his arms.

On the 25th, at three in the afternoon, I came to Chlinow or Wiatka, a fmall town on a river of the fame name, where I ftopped only while my fledges were mending. The High Chancellor, M. de Woronzof, had given me a letter to M. Perminof, who was then abfent, but I received many civilities from his lady. I accepted of the invitation fhe politely gave me to dinner, and went away at eight in the evening. It was fo dark that M. Perminof fent fome of her people with me on horfeback, who rode poft with lanterns fixed to the end of large fticks. I fent them back when I had got a little better than a mile beyond the town, having a flambeau to each fledge.

All the way from Kuzmodemianfk to Chlinow it was a covered country, being only cleared and cultivated round about the villages. Thefe glades were feldom three miles in extent, and generally much lefs. Whenever I got upon any eminence, I ftopped to take a view of the circumjacent country, but could never fee any thing but woods; the fmall, clear, and open places being loft in the quantity of thefe immenfe forefts.

At the diftance of a few werfts, I got into the wood again, where I travelled all night without receiving any hurt, notwithftanding my fledges were frequently overturned. On the 26th, at two in the afternoon, I reached the hamlet Troitfkoie, where I was obliged to ftop till fix in the evening, for the repairing of one of the fledges which had received moft damage in the courfe of the laft night. I took frefh horfes at this place.

Since

Since my setting out from Mosco, which was on the 12th, I had not stopped any where except at Nizan-novogorod, where I passed one night. I had been in my sledge most part of the rest of the time, where I had very little rest, on account of the frequent shocks and overthrows I met with. My attendants did not relish this kind of life: and as they had no particular point in view to encourage them, they took some opportunity every day of shewing their dissatisfaction. I had no sooner got on a few werfts into the wood, than I fell fast asleep: some time after I waked, it was still dark night, so that I could distinguish objects only from the clearness of the snow, much shaded by a cloudy sky. I knew not at first whether I was awake or in a dream, where I was, or where I was going; but no sooner was I roused from this state of uncertainty, than I was seized with the dreadful idea of being forsaken by my attendants. Getting immediately out of my sledge, I found myself alone: I called out to each person by his name, but all was silent around me; and as I had seen their discontent increase daily, and overheard some of their discourse, I began to fear that this idea was but too strongly confirmed. The horror of my situation will easily be conceived, when I found myself alone in one of the darkest nights, at the distance of fourteen hundred leagues from my native country, in the midst of the frosts and snows of Siberia, with the images of hunger and thirst before me, to which I was likely to be exposed; I was even ignorant whether I was in the beaten track or not, which however did not seem probable.

Agitated with these thoughts, I replaced myself in the sledge, and got out of it again directly; the minute after I got into it again, seized my two pistols, and followed a track which appeared to present itself. I soon forsook this path, and immediately sank into the snow up to my shoulders; I got out again, however, with much difficulty, but so exceedingly
fatigued,

fatigued, that I continued lying in the same posture prostrate on the snow. After some little time I sat myself down, felt for my pistols, and found they were still buried in the snow. I was convinced, on looking round me, that I was still in the same track, and got back to my sledge. I was still in such agitations that I could not stay there long, but threw myself again into the same path; warned by the last accident, I proceeded with great caution, went on more slowly, and was the more uneasy at being forced to walk such a pace. I went backwards and forwards in this manner great part of the night, my thoughts always employed on my situation, and coming back now and then to my sledge. Although I was exposed to the most severe cold, I was still in a profuse sweat; notwithstanding I did not walk much; at last, pursuing the same track again, I perceived a glimmering light at some distance; on drawing near I discovered it to be a house. I went in immediately, and found my people there fast asleep; they were lying on the ground by the side of some young girls; they seemed all to be in great want of rest; I rouzed my servant, however, and left the house as quick as I could, for I was unwilling they should discover how rejoiced I was at finding them again. A light was soon brought, and I found they had left the other sledges at the bottom of the village, and brought up mine a little above it. They told me afterwards, that being much oppressed with fatigue, and seeing me asleep, they had been willing to rest themselves a little, but that being drawn in by the beauty of these young girls, the eldest of whom was not above seventeen years of age, they had stopped longer than they intended. It was evident that I was obliged to put up with this affair. Having found my pistols again, I set out at seven in the morning with the same horses. I passed by Volva, and arrived on the 28th at Berezowka, a hamlet situated in the thickest part of the forest. As it consisted only of three

houses,

houses, inhabited by poor people, I could get no horses there; and was therefore obliged to take the same on to Jouſſinewſkoe, which made five and twenty leagues, in exceeding bad roads. I found however that I had gone on at the rate of two leagues in the hour. I met with very few dwelling places in the course of these five and twenty leagues; and these hardly deserved to be called so from the scarcity of inhabitants, and their extreme poverty. I continued travelling in the same foreſt, which grew more thick as I advanced. The roads were so narrow, that the sledges we met going the other way were more inconvenient here than any where else. There was such a prodigious quantity of snow, that great caution was required in laying the sledges down on one side: nothing but the heads of the horses, turned out of the road to give room for my sledges to pass, were then to be seen. In one of these occasions, as we were passing too swiftly by one of these sledges thus laid on the side, the top of mine struck against the shaft of the other, and was carried away with so much force, that I should certainly have been killed, if the stroke had lighted upon me. This laſt shock completed the destruction of my sledge: I now remained without any covering, exposed to the severity of the cold air. Being at no great distance from Solikamſky, where I foresaw that I should be obliged to take new sledges, I did not chuse to stop at Jouſſinewſkoe to get my own mended: the rest of the sledges were also much broken. I continued my journey, but was now thrown out at a considerable distance in the middle of the snow, whenever the sledge was overturned. At length I came to Solikamſky on the 29th, at eight o'clock in the evening, after having travelled one hundred and eighty werſts in this wretched condition. Not having been into a ſtove since the 18th of the month, and therefore not having eat of any thing but what was frozen, except at Chlinow, I was the more affected

with

with the fatigue. When I came to Solikamſky I went to Mr. Dimidof's office; he had given me a letter for his ſecretaries, and had ſent them previous notice of my arrival. I was informed that they lived at the diſtance of a mile from the place, and the people offered to conduct me; but I was ſo exceedingly tired that I could not poſſibly go any farther. I had my matraſs brought immediately and laid myſelf down, but reſted very little; I felt the moſt acute pains in all my limbs, and had a cold beſides, which prevented me from ſpeaking. As ſoon as it was day-light, I was told that Mr. Dimidof's ſteward had ſent ſeveral ſledges for myſelf and my attendants, and ſome horſes to convey my baggage.

I roſe and went immediately to the houſe, where I was received by Mrs. ***, (whoſe name is not to be found in my journal) who told me, by my interpreter, that ſhe had orders from her maſter to receive me as if he was there himſelf; that ſhe deſired I would look upon the houſe as my own, and that I could give her no greater ſatisfaction than in diſpoſing of every thing in it as I pleaſed. I thanked her for her attention, then had my ſledges unladen, and ſent for ſomebody to mend them. I was obliged to give them all up, except the one which carried the baggage, and which was ſtill capable of being repaired. I was then told that my ſledges could not be ready in leſs than three days. The thermometer being at ten or eleven degrees below 0, and the country ſtill covered with ſnow, there was not the leaſt appearance of a thaw. I was not therefore uneaſy at being detained here, eſpecially as I was no more than about one hundred and fifty leagues diſtant from Tobolſky.

Mr. Dimidof's houſe is ſituated on a ſmall mountain bordering the eaſtern ſhore of the river Kama: the natural beauty of the ſituation is heightened as much as poſſible by all the embelliſhments of art, liberally beſtowed on the building, which is of wood, as well as on the garden, which is very extenſive. As the garden cannot well be kept up in winter, on account of the feverity of the feaſon, Mr. Dimidof has provided twelve very beautiful green-houſes; theſe were full of orange and lemon trees, and contained likewiſe all the other fruits of France and Italy, with a variety of plants and ſhrubs of different countries. Theſe were the only green-houſes I had met with ſince I left Moſco; but they are common in this laſt town, in St. Peterſburg, and in the neighbouring places. Without the help of green-houſes theſe towns could not be ſupplied with any kinds of vegetables during the greateſt part of the year, on account of the long continuance of the winter.

Mr. Dimidof had alſo taken care to have an apothecary's ſhop in his houſe very well ſtocked, and kept in excellent order; the direction of it was given to a man of ſkill, who diſtributed the medicines to all the ſick in the place.

The gardener was a Ruſſian, who had ſome notions of natural philoſophy, beyond what his buſineſs required; theſe notions did not indeed beſpeak a man of ſcience ſo much, as one, of an excellent capacity for acquiring knowledge. Mr. Dimidof was himſelf too intelligent not to take notice of his gardener's talents: and accordingly he had ſupplied him with ſome books of mathematics, natural philoſophy, botany, and with all ſorts of inſtruments.

The ſtay I made at Solikamſky enabled me to replace the barometer I had loſt on the road at a little diſtance from Cazan; I made two of them, and gave one to the gardener who had not any: he received it with much joy and thankfulneſs.

Solikamſky is a ſmall town on the borders of the river Kama. Iſbrants Ides, a Muſcovite ambaſſador, gives ſo high a deſcription of this place, in his journey from Moſco to China,

China*, that I determined to take a particular view of it. I rose very early in the morning on the 31st instant, in order to go into the bath, which I had been desired to do the evening before. As soon as I was up, they came and told me the baths were ready, as well as the sledge on which I was to go. I wrapped myself up in my fur night-gown, took my servant with me, and was conducted to the baths; the cold was so sharp, that I hastened across a small antichamber to a door, which I opened, thinking it led to the baths. There came out immediately such a suffocating volley of smoke, that I ran back again to the door as fast as possible, imagining the bath was on fire. Observing the Russians were as much disconcerted at my going back as I was at the circumstance, and at their astonishment, I asked my servant the reason of it: he told me, those were the baths, and that I was to undress and go into them. A Russian then opened the door again, and went in with his clothes on. I found this smoke was nothing more than the vapour rising from the baths, which formed an exceeding thick mist, and presently became snow from the extreme cold. The great heat however I found in these baths, did not agree with the notion I had that they were only to be used for cleanliness. I knew not they were intended for sweating, till I had asked several other questions, and being satisfied with the state of my health, was going away immediately, if my servant had not stopped me, and acquainted me that the baths had been all night preparing, and that the people of the house would be very much disappointed, if I should decline going into them. Prompted by these reasons, and by my own curiosity, I resolved to bathe; I therefore had the door opened, and bore at once all the heat. I undressed quickly, and found myself in a small square room, so much heated by a stove that I was instantly in

---

* Recueil des Voyages au Nord, tom. viii. pag. 9. in 12mo, edition d'Amsterdam.

a profuſe ſweat. On one ſide of the ſtove there was a kind of wooden bedſtead, raiſed about four feet; there were ſome ſteps to get up to it: the atmoſphere is exceedingly heated towards the upper part of the apartment, on account of the lightneſs of the particles of heat, while the floor keeps much cooler, ſo that theſe ſteps are contrived to prepare gradually for the degree of heat one is to experience on the bed. Being unacquainted with theſe circumſtances, and in a great hurry to get out of the bath, I went immediately and placed myſelf in the higheſt part of the room.

Here the floor had got ſuch a degree of heat, that I could ſcarcely bear the pain I felt in the ſoles of my feet, and could not have ſtaid here, if they had not thrown ſome cold water upon the ſpot, which evaporated almoſt inſtantaneouſly. I took my thermometer in with me, which in a few minutes roſe to ſixty degrees. This prodigious heat preſently ſeized my head, and made me very ſick. My ſervant, who pretended to be much uſed to theſe baths, adviſed me to ſit down, aſſuring me this giddineſs would ſoon go off; but having taken his advice, I felt ſuch acute pain that I thought I was ſitting on a plate of red hot iron. I had not time to conſider what gave me this pain, nor to find the ſteps, but fell in an inſtant at the foot of the bed, my thermometer breaking to pieces with the fall. The heat being much leſs on this flooring, I lay there at firſt without daring to ſtir, and ordered the door and the little windows to be opened directly. There was a tub of water and ſome baſons near me; I had one of them filled, and ſat down in it, while with the other I made them throw water all over me. Being a little recovered, I thought of nothing but getting out as faſt as I could, yet did not dare ſtand upright, becauſe I ſhould then have been in the hotteſt part of the atmoſphere. Attempting therefore to put on my clothes with my body bent, while I was wet, and in too great a hurry,

hurry, I found them too little for me, and the more eager I was, the lefs able was I to get them on. Overpowered with all thefe difficulties, I threw myfelf into the antichamber almoft naked, where again the extreme cold prevented me from ftaying to drefs, fo that I wrapped myfelf up in my fur nightgown, ran to my carriage, dragging fome of my clothes after me, and ordered them to drive home as faft as poffible, where I went to bed immediately. The miftrefs of the houfe was afraid, from the condition I came back in, and from my returning fo foon, that fome accident had happened to me: fhe came directly to fee me, I removed her fears, and defired I might be permitted to take fome reft, as that was the only medicine I wanted: fhe left me, and returned foon after with a bafon of tea, which fhe offered me. Obferving that I did not care to accept of it, fhe gave me to underftand by the Ruffian ferjeant, who began to know a little of French, that I had not ftayed long enough at the baths to have been fufficiently fweated; and that it was neceffary I fhould drink the tea to promote perfpiration.

Although it was by no means my intention to be fweated, yet fhe perfifted in offering me the tea with fo much kindnefs, that I took it; but as fhe promifed to bring me another bafon in a few minutes, I rofe as foon as fhe left me. My fervant had ftayed at the baths, but not finding him returned in half an hour, I was going to inquire after him, taking it for granted fome accident had befallen him. He came in juft as I was fending a man away for him; he threw himfelf directly on his bed without faying a word, at laft he told me, after I had made him feveral queftions, that he had been taken ill at the baths, and would have perfuaded me that he was fo ill, it was impoffible he fhould get over it. As he was ufed to thefe baths, I judged that his indifpofition might arife from fome unwholefome vapours, and as a change of air is the quickeft

and

and most efficacious remedy in such cases; I therefore had all the windows opened, giving orders that he should be kept quiet; and in two hours after he was perfectly recovered.

This first trial put me so much out of conceit with the Russian baths, that I would not venture into them again during my five months stay at Tobolsky, although I was frequently importuned on this point. However my curiosity was so much raised by what I learned in this town, and through the rest of my journey, of the advantages of these baths, and the method of using them, that I tried again at Echaterinenburg, on my return from Tobolsky; but the heat was too much for me to bear. Yet as I was unwilling to leave the country without being convinced by my own experience of what had been reported to me concerning these baths, I went into them again at a private house in St. Petersburg, two months before I set out for France.

These baths are in use all over Russia; every inhabitant of this vast tract of land, from the sovereign to the meanest subject, bathes twice a week, and in the same manner. Every individual, even of the smallest fortune, has a private bath in his own house, in which the father, mother, and children sometimes bathe all together. The lower sort of people go to the public baths, of which there is generally one for the men, and another for the women; they are separated from each other by wooden partitions; but as they come out of the baths quite naked, the two sexes are seen by each other in this condition, and often converse together in this posture upon indifferent subjects; they afterwards throw themselves promiscuously into the water, or among the snow. In poor and lonely hamlets, the two sexes are oftentimes all together in the same bath. At the salt-houses in Solikamsky I saw some men bathing, who came to the door now and then to cool themselves, and stood there quite naked, talking with women, who were most of them employed

employed in bringing falt provifions, brandy, or *quouas*, to the workmen. The baths of the rich differ only from thofe of the poor people in being more clean; the bathing room is generally all wood; it contains a ftove, fome tubs full of water, and a kind of amphitheatre, with feveral fteps leading up to it. There are two openings to the ftove like thofe that are in common ovens; by the lower opening the wood is put into the ftove, the other contains a heap of ftones fupported by iron bars; thefe ftones are always red hot, from the heat of the fire kept up in the ftove; the ufe of them will appear hereafter. On going into the bath a perfon provides himfelf with a bundle of twigs, a fmall pail of feven or eight inches in diameter, filled with water, and places himfelf on the firft or fecond ftep. Although the heat is lefs here than in any other part, yet it foon throws him into a fweat, the pail of water is then emptied over his head, fome little time after a fecond, and then a third. He then mounts a little higher, where the fame procefs is repeated, and at laft he gets up to the amphitheatre, where the greateft heat is felt. He ftays here one quarter, or about half an hour, and in this fpace of time warm water is frequently poured on his body. A man, who ftands before the ftove, throws now and then fome water on the red hot ftones: volleys of fteam immediately rufh out of the ftove with a noife; thefe afcend to the cieling, and fall down again on the amphitheatre, in a kind of cloud, carrying a burning heat along with it. At this time the twigs are ufed, after they have been made very foft, by holding them in the fteam as it comes out of the ftove; the man who is bathing then lies down on the amphitheatre, and the perfon next to him whips him with the twigs, expecting he will return the good office: but in many baths women are employed for this purpofe. While the leaves remain on the twigs, a confiderable quantity of the fteam is collected by a turn of the hand; this steam acts the more powerfully, as the pores are very open; and that these burning vapours are briskly driven in by the twigs, which are continually applied to all the parts of the body.

In the private baths I used, I felt such a suffocating heat on my face, when the clouds of steam were collected by the twigs, that I could not have supported it, had it lasted any time. Being willing to ascertain the degree of heat brought on by this process, I had it repeated on the thermometer, which however did not rise more than three degrees higher than it was before.

After having been flogged, water was thrown on me, and I was rubbed with soap; a person then taking hold of the twigs at both ends, rubbed me down so violently, that he was soon in as profuse a sweat as myself. Water was again poured on my body, and on the stones, and they were preparing to flog me again; but the twigs having lost their leaves, I sprang up so suddenly at the first stroke, that I pushed the operator down the stairs on the floor; and determined not to be flogged or rubbed any longer. In a few minutes my skin was all as red as scarlet. I could not bear to stay on the amphitheatre, but had my thermometer carried there, which rose to fifty degrees, while it stood at five and forty in the place where I was: I got out of these baths as soon as I could.

The Russians stay in them sometimes above two hours, and go through all the aforementioned operations several times: most of them rub their body besides with onions, in order to sweat more profusely; they get out of these baths all in a sweat, and immediately throw themselves and roll in the snow in the most severe seasons, passing thus almost in the same instant from a heat of fifty or sixty degrees, to a cold of more than twenty degrees, without feeling any inconvenience.

People

People of the first rank in Russia go to bed on coming out of the baths, and rest for some time. It is a received opinion that the baths are more beneficial to the common people, who pass immediately from this intense heat to the extreme cold, than to those, who go to bed after them.

All the Russians, in general, are much addicted to the scurvy; the languid and inactive life they lead, being shut up in their stoves all the winter, makes them very full of humors, and they perspire very little. These baths seem therefore to be absolutely necessary for them, as they might be liable to a great number of diseases if they did not use them. They produce a great fermentation in the blood and humors, and bring on plentiful discharges by perspiration. The extreme cold drives the humors back from the skin, and restores the equilibrium again. Whether these conclusions are just or not, it is an undoubted fact, that these baths are very salutary in Russia: they would certainly be very useful in Europe also for a variety of disorders, especially for rheumatic complaints. Distempers of this kind are hardly known in Russia, and many foreigners have been radically cured of them by the use of these baths.

I went to see the brass foundery and the salt-pits the day before I quitted Solikamsky; the foundery is situated on the small brook Talitza, at the distance of two wersts from the town; it consists of three furnaces, one of which only is in good order. It was my design to pay a visit to Mr. Tourchemin, who has the direction of the foundery, but he was absent. I asked for his deputy, who was not to be found, although we went all about the buildings in quest of him. I therefore returned to the foundery, desirous of gaining some information on different points; and for that purpose addressed myself to some of the workmen who appeared the most sensible, but could not, even with the assistance of my interpreter, either understand

understand them, or make them comprehend me. At length the deputy came, but was much out of humor; he took a shovel and went to work; I went up and bowed to him, signifying by my interpreter, how sorry I was to have missed of him, and begging the favor of him at the same time to shew me the mines: "They are in the middle of the yard," says he, turning his back upon me. This abrupt speech did not give me any great inclination to converse any longer with the deputy. I saw however all the mines, and brought away specimens from each, of which I shall give an account when I come to speak of the ores. The deputy, in other respects, appeared to know very well what he was about, if one could judge from the good order and regularity in which the foundery was kept. He had a sensible and sprightly look; and seemed to want nothing, but to have lived less among bears, to have been more conversant with men, and to have been born in a free country. I observed throughout the whole course of my journey, that whenever I had no letters of recommendation to the persons presiding over any of the manufactures, I always met with such kind of behaviour as I had experienced on this occasion; but on the contrary, with numberless civilities whenever I had such letters. These sort of people are slaves to a despotic superior; they are generally ignorant and excessively mistrustful, so that their behaviour is by no means a matter of astonishment.

At a little distance from the foundery is a manufacture, where most of the brass, coming from thence, is used in making houshold utensils, snuff-boxes, and other works of the like kind, which are of the coarsest workmanship. I stayed but a little while at this manufacture, and met with as bad a reception there as at the foundery.

There are salt-springs in abundance about this town; they say upwards of sixty. Notwithstanding this great number of springs, there

there are not more than two boilers in ufe; the firft forms a fquare of about thirty feet wide and two feet deep; the other is fomewhat larger *.

Thefe two boilers are placed in different falterns or boiling-houfes, at the diftance of fifty toifes from the origin of the fprings; the falt water is raifed into a refervoir by pumps, which are fet a going by horfes; the waters are afterwards conveyed to the falterns where the boilers are, through leaden pipes, fupported by props of wood. All thefe buildings were in a moft ruinous condition; at which I was the more furprized, as they are made of wood, which is common enough in this country. The produce of thefe falterns feems to be more attended to, than keeping them in repair.

One boiling is finifhed in eight and forty hours; it commonly produces fifty facks of falt, and the fack contains four *poedes* †; fo that each boiling yields two hundred *poedes*, or fixty-fix French quintals. Suppofing then one hundred and eighty-two boilings in the year, and that the *poede* of falt fells for fifty *copecs* ‡, this boiler will bring an annual revenue of

---

* According to Mr. Ifbrants-Ides's account, tom. viii. *du Recueil des Voyages du Nord*, pag. 9. Solikamfky is a large commercial town, particularly famous for its falterns, in which there are fifty boilers ufed every year, the leaft of which is ten toifes deep. A great quantity of falt is made there, which is carried away on large fhips kept only for this purpofe. Thefe falterns are fixteen or eighteen toifes in length, there are feven or eight hundred men employed in them, and they produce one hundred, or one hundred and twenty thoufand *poedes*; that is, eight hundred, or one thoufand tuns of falt.

Perhaps the number of boilers was formerly more confiderable: but it is abfurd to fuppofe them ten toifes deep. There is no river at Solikamfky capable of fupplying a building which would contain one thoufand tuns, and it is impoffible that eight hundred men fhould have been employed there in making the falt. The Kama at this place is a little wider than the Seine at high water. The fame kind of boats are ufed here as at Paris, excepting only that they are rather longer.

† One *poede* is equal to forty pounds weight of Ruffia, and to three and thirty French pounds.

‡ One *copec* is equal to about one halfpenny Englifh, or one penny French.

eighteen thousand two hundred roubles, or ninety-one thousand livres of France, the product of twelve thousand and twelve French quintals of salt.

There are now but six men employed to each boiler, formerly there were ten: the first workman is allowed thirteen copecs per day; of the other five some have ten, others eight: reckoning them one with another at nine, the expence for the workmen will amount to fifty-eight copecs *per* day, and to two hundred and eleven roubles *per annum*.

Ten square or superficial toises of wood are consumed at each boiling (the toise is equal to three *arcins* and a half); each square toise of wood costs thirty copecs, and the ten toises three roubles; so that the annual expence for wood amounts to five hundred and forty-six roubles.

Each saltern employs five or six horses: let us suppose five upon an average, each of which costs twenty copecs a day; the yearly expence for keeping the horses will then amount to three hundred and sixty-five roubles: let us then allow six other men to take care of the horses, and the pumps, at six copecs a day. Although, from the bad condition the salterns are in, it is evident hardly any thing is laid out for repairs, yet I will reckon two hundred roubles for this purpose. The buying of the horses at first costs about seven or eight roubles, and as deaths do not happen among them every year, this expence can never amount to ten roubles *per annum*. Let us even allow one hundred roubles, including the charges of harness, and in this case, the whole annual expence for the working of these salterns cannot exceed sixteen hundred roubles, or eight thousand French livres. The produce is eighteen thousand two hundred roubles, or ninety-one thousand French livres. The clear produce therefore of the first boiler will be sixteen thousand six hundred roubles, or fourscore thousand French livres; and the profits arising from the two boilers will be more than thirty-

thirty-three thousand roubles, or one hundred and sixty-six thousand French livres. The direction of these salterns is undertaken by Mr. Tourchemin; the late Mr. Showalow had it in 1762. The remainder of the profits, after these two gentlemen are paid, belongs to the Empress. On asking why two boilers only were in use, I was told, that there began to be a scarcity of wood, which is brought by the river Kama from the distance of fifty *wersts* or twelve leagues.

I found some of the people bathing at these salterns, in the same manner as I have described in speaking of common baths. After being in the baths some time, they came out quite naked, and although they were in a sweat, went immediately and rolled themselves in the snow.

As there was nothing of any consequence in this small town of Solikamsky, besides these salterns and the founderies, I left it on the second of April, at three in the afternoon, much pleased with the civilities I had met with from Mr. Dimidof's people. I soon came to the mountains called *Poias*, or *Poias Zemnoi*: they form a chain which must be considered as a branch of the large chain from Mount Caucasus. The ridge of the *Poias* mountains begins in the south, and divides Asia from Europe, reaching as far as the frozen sea. The mountains of this chain are very small, not being in general more than fifty or fourscore toises high; but the ascents are very steep: they are all covered with pines, birch, and fir trees. The roads were dreadful, and so much the more dangerous, as the nights were so exceedingly dark, that I was every instant liable to be swallowed up in the snow, which readily gave way. If, by chance, I happened to deviate in the least from the beaten track, I was exposed to very great danger. My attendants and the postilions advised me not to travel by night; but the wind being changed to the south, the frost had slackened suddenly: the thermometer was not more than two

degrees

degrees below the freezing point, and rose in the afternoon to more than three degrees above it, which made me apprehend a thaw, although such a change was not indicated by any other circumstance. Fir-trees of the greatest height seemed to yield under the weight of the snow, which was every where more than seven feet thick on the surface of the ground. No bird appeared to give notice of any change of the season: even magpyes and rooks, which are met with in great numbers on the roads all over Russia, had now quitted these deserts, where nature seemed to have become quite torpid. The marks of the sledges were the only signs of these parts being inhabited. A melancholy gloom prevailed all around, and the stillness was interrupted only by the cries of some one of our company calling out for help, when his sledge was overturned.

The inhabitants are shut up in their cottages nine months in the year, hardly ever going out as long as the winter lasts. In the beginning of September the snow is to be seen on these mountains, and soon after falls in such abundance, that every sign of an inhabited place soon disappears.

The people are then obliged to make themselves a passage through heaps of snow, collected by the winds among these mountains, where the thaw does not begin so soon as on the plains: for among the mountains it does not take place till towards the end of April, and the snow does not entirely disappear before the latter end of May; so that the delights of the summer season are not experienced here longer than about three months. In this short space of time, however, the inhabitants sow their rye, oats, and barley, and some pease, which are gathered towards the latter end of August; but these seeds seldom come to their real perfection. The soil in these mountains is dunged.

I came to Rostess on the 3d instant at midnight, exceedingly fatigued with the shocks my sledge had received, and the continual overthrows I had met with. Not finding fresh horses at this place, I was obliged to go on with the same. I travelled very slowly, on account of the declivity of the mountains we had to pass. On the 4th instant, at half an hour past nine in the morning, I was on the top of the highest of all these mountains; which, however, was not more than fourscore toises above its base. But although the height of these mountains is not very considerable with respect to the ground they stand upon, they are much higher with respect to the level of the sea, because the ground is considerably raised. When I measured this mountain, I was very near Paiadinska, where I arrived on the 4th at noon, and set out from thence immediately. I crossed the rivulet of Padira, where there is an iron foundery called Spaskoe. The ore is brought from the neighbourhood of Verkaturia. I was told in this hamlet that a woman had been devoured there by a bear at the beginning of the winter. Such accidents seldom happen, although among these mountains there are many bears, which are all black. These animals hide themselves in caverns as the winter comes on, or under old and very thick firs, where they remain during all this season without food.

At the end of the winter the inhabitants go a bear-hunting: they use rackets to walk upon the snow with; they arm themselves with pikes, and take little dogs along with them, to provoke the animal. They then wait till he comes out of his enclosure, for they would attack him to great disadvantage while he remained there, because the snow being very firm in that place, the bear would be able to avail himself of all his strength; but the instant he comes out, he sinks into the snow, and while he is endeavouring to disengage himself, the hunters easily destroy him with their pikes. The skin and fat of this animal are the only parts they reap any profit from. This account was given me at Spaskoe, and the truth of it confirmed

at

at Tobolſky, where I was alſo informed of the manner of hunting white bears, which I ſhall ſpeak of preſently. In the foreſts of theſe mountains there are a great number of wolves, foxes, hares, ſquirrels, and different kinds of fallow deer; but there are no white bears, which are only to be found more to the northward, on the borders of the frozen ocean, but their ſkins are brought all over Siberia. I have ſeen three of theſe animals alive at St. Peterſburg; they are exceedingly fierce. Thoſe I ſaw in this city were chained to a ſtake in the middle of a yard; their litter conſiſted of nothing more than a layer of ice five or ſix inches thick, formed by their excrements and the melted ſnow. This animal is much leſs bulky and more active than the black bear; his ſhape is longer and better proportioned, and his ſnout more elongated: any one may be convinced, by looking at him, of his being capable of running with great ſpeed; and the hunters have availed themſelves of this very circumſtance, in finding out how to kill him with more facility, which, however, requires a great ſhare of intrepidity. I was informed at Tobolſky, and I have no other authority for the fact, that the inhabitants go out a hunting theſe animals armed only with a ſingle pike. They are to be found near the frozen ocean, where the ſnow is as hard as the ground. They run upon the men with ſo much ſwiftneſs, that the huntſman has but juſt time to turn himſelf half round to avoid him, while at the ſame inſtant he pierces the bear with his pike.

I reached Melechina the ſame day, ſo fatigued that I reſolved to ſtay there a part of the night. I knocked at the firſt door I came to, where I waited ſome time, as every body was gone to bed; a Ruſſian came at laſt to open the door, with his lighted piece of wood in one hand, and his cap in the other. His face was ſcarce to be diſtinguiſhed on account of his looſe hair, and a long beard, which came down to his breaſt. The

firſt

first object my eyes were directed to on coming in, was an old woman, who had fallen asleep as she was rocking a child slung in a basket; her skin was wrinkled and her complexion darkened by the smoke, so that she was a very disagreeable figure. Her garb contributed to make her still more hideous. Upon a bench near her, there was a young woman, who seemed more intent upon satisfying her curiosity, than anxious to cover herself with her shift, which was the only thing she had on. The looseness of this covering, and the attitude she was in, left her much exposed; and her skin, most delicately white, appeared still more beautiful, from the contrast of the old woman, who was close to her. Near the bench were two little children lying on the ground, and some young calves in a stable: the rest of the family were laid indiscriminately in the stove, and in a kind of loft; some were asleep, and the rest were as much astonished at seeing me in their hut, as I was surprized at their situation and appearance.

The child in the basket was not a month old; he slept among a heap of straw, covered with linen, because he was newly born. Except just at this time, children are generally naked in Siberia, as well as all over Russia: they move their hands and feet about freely in the basket, without being wrapped up. This basket is fastened to a long elastic pole, which is easily moved with the foot, in order to rock them. The women, who have this care, employ themselves at the same time in spinning hemp. The children are fed with the milk of animals, by means of a horn, the end of which is fitted to receive the cow's udder: they are however sometimes suckled by the mothers. These children, although still very weak, are allowed to roll on the ground; on which they tumble over head and ears, and attempt to walk. They are left to struggle by themselves, although they are most commonly naked, or have no more covering than a shirt. In a few months they

K begin

begin to walk, at a time when they would not be able to stand up in France. Soon after they run about every where and play in the snow. These people are happily unacquainted with the use of stays, and that quantity of cloaths and confining bandages, we are here so anxious to wrap up our children in; these not only impede the growth of the muscles, but at the same time bring on deformities, which, on this account, are frequent in all other European nations, while they are seldom seen in Russia. By this kind of management the Russians are not subject to so many infirmities, and would live longer than any other set of men, if they were not so much addicted to debauchery and excesses of all kinds. They are so much inured to hard living, that although I desired the soldiers who attended me at Tobolsky to lie down in my observatory, while I was taking my observations, they chose rather to pass the night on the grass, and rose in the morning with their cloaths almost as wet by the dew, as if they had been dipped in water. They slept however extremely sound, and never felt any inconvenience from this circumstance. Their whole life, and all their exercises, bring on such a strength of constitution, as enables them to bear the greatest fatigues in war time, without injury to their health.

The moral conduct of the inhabitants is considerably influenced by this kind of life: violent passions often contribute to form great men, and are generally attendant on strong constitutions. What advantages might we not then expect, if the Russian method of educating was adopted by a nation where the nature of the government, and the moral principles instilled into young minds, direct them equally to what is honourable, glorious, and resolute? These advantages would be the more conspicuous, as luxury and effeminacy concur with the ordinary method of bringing up children, in destroying all the principles of this moral education.

It must be owned, however, that prejudices with regard to these circumstances, are not so prevalent at Paris, as they were some little time ago. Some people begin to leave off the use of swaddling cloaths; others accustom their children to go almost naked.

Among the variety of bad customs followed in bringing up children, there is none which appears more absurd than that of obliging them to make use of the right hand only. No sooner do the tender limbs of the infant begin to acquire a degree of solidity, than he is forced to feed himself with his right hand alone, which is said to be a necessary qualification in a polite education. He soon gets the habit of using the right hand preferably to the left, and becomes imperceptibly aukward in all bodily exercises or motions he is obliged to perform on the left side. It is evident, from the trouble there is in bringing children to this, that it is by no means natural to them; and the aukwardness of left-handed people is at the same time a proof of the advantage of permitting children to use both hands indiscriminately, and of the necessity of obliging them, as they grow up, to perform all the common exercises both with the right and left hand.

This method of educating, which I have taken notice of in Siberia, prevails all over Russia, except among the great, where some changes have been introduced, as they began to be civilized. However preferable this method may be to that which is used among nations addicted to luxury and ease, it must yet be confessed, that an infinite number of children die, especially among the common people, of whose families one third part is scarce ever preserved; parents who have had sixteen or eighteen children born, having often times no more than three or four alive: but there are various causes perpetually assisting in the depopulation of the several hamlets scattered abroad in these immense deserts.

The small-pox destroys almost one half of the children, and some times a greater proportion: the scurvy, and irregularities of the parents, bring on a variety of diseases unknown to other children, which are the more hurtful, perhaps, in this country, as the only remedy they have, consists in their stoves; which are very efficacious in disorders proceeding from the nature of the climate, but in venereal complaints are only palliative *. These disorders are more dangerous here than in any other place, on account of their being usually joined with the scurvy, and that the medicine proper for one of these diseases always increases the other. Venereal disorders are so general in Siberia, and in Northern Tartary, that there is reason to fear, left in process of time they should put an end to the human species in these parts. This may happen the sooner from the manner in which these people live together in their cottages, and the excess of debauchery occasioned by it. They are unacquainted with beds, and lie together promiscuously upon benches, and on the stoves, so that the children are witnesses even of the marriage rights; and the youth, being therefore sooner informed than in other places, are more disposed to give way to dissoluteness.

Although I had at first resolved to pass the night in the hamlet of Melechina, yet the unbearable smell of the room I

---

* Some authors pretend however that the Russians use the corrosive sublimate in this disorder, and particularly M. Macquer in his Chymical Dictionary (tom. ii. p. 65.) "Besides," say this author, "it is well known that the corrosive sublimate has been given internally with success for a long time past among the Tartars and the Russians, whose method of living incontinently with all sorts of women, exposes them continually to repeated attacks of venereal disorders one upon another."

I have not been able to find, in all the course of my journey, from St. Petersburg to Tobolsky, that the sublimate was in use, and I have known some rich people affected with this disease go into Europe to be cured of it. Perhaps this medicine has been laid aside, on account of the fatal consequences which sometimes attend the improper use of it.

was

was in, made me leave the place a few hours after my coming there. These inhabitants, shut up in their rooms the greatest part of the year, have no communication with the external air, except by windows of a foot square, always shut, and by a small valve, which they open for some time in the morning, to let out the smoke; so that they live constantly in infected vapors, which have been collecting and fermenting together, near nine months in the year.

On coming from Melechina I quitted the mountains, and travelled in a very extensive plain: the snow melted away so fast and so suddenly, that in some places it scarce covered the surface of the ground. At Lialinskoi, however, the thermometer remained still at seven degrees below 0. On the 5th instant, I came to this hamlet, at five in the morning, and reached Verkaturia at one in the afternoon. This is a small town in Siberia, not far from the river Tura: it is situated on rocks, and surrounded with some trifling fortifications, which have been built by the Russians since they were in possession of Siberia. The only way of passing from Russia into Siberia was through this town, ever since Gagarin's time, who was governor of this province, and who, having laid a plan for making himself master of Siberia in the reign of Peter the First, had shut up the road by Echaterinenburg, which was the most in use as being the shortest. From hence that road became neglected, and was not opened again till the year 1761, by express orders from the Empress Elizabeth. The custom-house is very strict at Verkaturia: but as I was apprized of this at St. Petersburg, I had applied for an order from the chancellor, to prevent the cases containing my instruments from being opened. They had hitherto remained just as they were packed up at Paris. I obtained this permission, notwithstanding the strictness of the regulations. Peter the First had given a general order, that all instruments relating to arts and sciences should be suffered to pass pafs unnoticed: this indulgence I could not avoid taking notice of here, as it does so much honor to that monarch; but his succeffors found themselves obliged to repeal the order, on account of the abuses that were soon made of it. The master of the custom-house, whose name was Michitas Ivan Soubatof, only asked a few general questions about my baggage, and treated me with the greatest politeness. He made me a prefent of two fable skins, a few pounds of tea, and different sorts of provisions. As I was going away, he did me the honor of a visit, with some of the principal people of the town. I had still some Luneville *liqueurs*, and some bottles of Burgundy remaining, from what the Baron de Breteuil had given me at setting out from St. Petersburg. I persuaded them to drink some with me; they were very much pleased with our Burgundy; for there is no wine in Siberia but what is brought by travellers; but our *liqueurs* were infipid to them, and too weak. As they are used to the strongest spirits, the French *liqueurs* scarce made any impression on their palates. They pressed me so much to stay at Verkaturia, that I put off going from thence till night. Mr. Soubatof persuaded me to take some refreshment at his house, where I found all his family. I could not see his wife otherwise than by her chamber door being half open: she was extremely pretty and very well dressed, but it was impossible to prevail upon her to appear any farther. I went away at eight in the evening; it was very dark, and the road exceedingly bad; so that I had all the flambeaus lighted. I travelled all night without any accident, although I had been told before I came away from Verkaturia, that I should meet with many. The weather, which was very mild when I left this town, became, to my great satisfaction, suddenly colder, at three o'clock in the morning. The thermometer fell to nine degrees below the freezing point; but as soon as the sun appeared on the horizon, it rose again with the utmost

utmoſt velocity. My courſe was now to the ſouth, and the ſnow diſappearing continually, I was determined not to loſe a moment, leſt I ſhould be overtaken by a thaw. The ſame day, the watchmaker's ſledge broke in the middle of the road. As we had no aſſiſtance at hand, it was faſtened up with cords, and with much difficulty brought on to Makhneva, where I intended to get it mended; but finding no body who would undertake to do it, I immediately bought another. While they they were getting this new ſledge ready, I dined at a houſe in the hamlet, and ſaw the Poſtilions dine: they had clubbed with ſome other Ruſſians, who were carrying proviſions to Verkaturia; they all placed themſelves round a ſmall table, the only one in the houſe, ſome on benches, others ſtanding up. A ſoup made of ſour *krout* and oatmeal, without bread, was firſt ſerved up in a ſmall wooden bowl; this they eat with wooden ſpoons: I had a fancy to taſte ſome of their bread, although it was as black as ink, but could not poſſibly eat it. This firſt bowl was taken away, and another brought up, full of ſour *krout*, dreſt with oil of fiſh. Sometimes the ſour *krout* is dreſſed with oil of hemp-ſeed, or bear's greaſe. Their drink was the *quouas* or kwas, the ſame as is uſed by the other Ruſſians, and which I have already ſpoken of. Each man paid one *ſol*, or one halfpenny Engliſh, for his dinner, which ſometimes conſiſts of peas, turnips, and radiſhes, boiled in water, with a little ſalt. It was then Lent, during which ſeaſon they neither eat meat, milk, butter, or fiſh: they take great care not to leave the leaſt remains of their victuals on the table; but gather them up very ſcrupulouſly and eat them. The table, after dinner, is the only clean piece of furniture in the houſe. Having been almoſt ſtifled with the heat, I put my thermometer upon the loft, where the people ſleep all night and part of the day. It immediately roſe to forty degrees, or near ten degrees higher than it is in the greateſt ſummer-heats at Paris. There were four or five women in this houſe, who hid themſelves behind a kind of curtain when we came in; they ſoon grew more familiar, and were much ſurprized at ſeeing us eat meat, and all our other proviſions, from which they are debarred during this Lent ſeaſon. They are ſo extremely ſtrict in this particular, that when I gave a piece of cake to one of their children, about three years old, the mother took it away immediately; and the youngeſt child, of ſeven or eight months, was the only one allowed to eat it. The exceſſive heat obliged me to throw off my fur, and I put on a French great coat. The women admired it very much, and ſurveyed, with the greateſt curioſity, every part of my dreſs, which appeared quite new to them, although this was the only road in uſe. Theſe women ſeemed more lively than any I had ſeen ſince I came from Moſco, eſpecially ſince I had travelled on that ſide of the Volga. They were alſo better made, taller, and had better complexions than I had met with in this latter part of my journey. Two girls of the houſe particularly were very pretty: they had ſomething like ruffles to their ſhifts, which I had not obſerved in any other part of Ruſſia among this claſs of people.

My route from the river Volga lay always through the ſame foreſt, where I commonly met with nothing but hamlets, in which the moſt extreme wretchedneſs prevailed. The country became more open as I got away from the mountains, and the villages more populous. The Siberian women are dreſſed generally in the ſame manner as the Ruſſians; the girls wearing their hair in treſſes, and never putting on a cap till they are married. Married women never go without caps. I left this place as ſoon as the ſledges were ready, and came to the hamlet called Babikhina, on the 7th inſtant at noon. The thaw was ſo complete, that the ſnow was melted every where except on the beaten track. A little water lying upon the rivers, yet frozen, made me ſenſible of the danger of croſſing them. Every body

was

was spurred on by this fear, and the desire of coming soon to Tobolsky, from whence I was now only seventy leagues distant; and all endeavoured to vie with each other in getting things ready at every post. I came to Tumen at midnight, and was intending to set out from thence immediately; but could find nobody who would run the risk of crossing the river, as the people at the post-house expected every moment that the ice would break up. I tried every possible expedient to persuade them to go on, but they wanted to wait till day-light before they took their resolution. I was still at the distance of sixty leagues from Tobolsky, and if I lost this night, it might prevent me from reaching the city before the breaking up of the ice; in which case I must have remained where I was, as it would then have been impossible to travel even in a boat, because the whole country is overwhelmed with torrents pouring down from all sides. I spoke to the old postilions, and represented to them, that as they had crossed different rivers with me in the course of the day without any apparent danger, these sort of passages could not possibly have become more hazardous in a few hours time. I promised to pay them double postage, and gave them so much brandy to drink, that they at last resolved to go with me. I then persuaded the people of the post-house to supply me with horses, and we crossed the river without accident.

On the 9th instant, about five in the morning, I arrived at Sozonowa, and was detained a long while at this hamlet for want of horses. I was desirous of making up the lost time, by giving brandy on the road to the postilions, in hopes of prevailing upon them to get on with the utmost expedition; but the snow being entirely melted in most places on the road, I could not, notwithstanding this precaution, reach Berozovia before four in the afternoon, and did not come to the post of Vakfarina, where I was to cross the river Tobol, till nine in the evening.

evening. I immediately afked for horfes, which were refufed, and which I was not likely to obtain, after difputing for an hour. I could not but be perfuaded of the danger there was in croffing this river; and at the perfuafion of the inhabitants, I had at firft determined to make my obfervations on this fpot; but befides the inconvenience of the fituation, I ftill wanted the authority of the fovereign to enable me to build an obfervatory, and to prevent me from being interrupted in my operations, fo that I found this impracticable. I began to be fufficiently acquainted with the people, to know that the civilities I had experienced on the road, were owing to my meeting with a few good people, and chiefly to the letters of recommendation I had from M. de Woronzof. On all occafions, where the inhabitants had been left to themfelves, I had met with the greateft difficulties, and in this inftance I had alfo much to fear from the fuperftition of ignorant people.

Befides, I was not more than twenty-five leagues diftant from Tobolfky, fo that I could have got there in twelve hours, and juft as I thought all my fatigues at an end, I began to be afraid of miffing my obfervation. I could not bear up againft this idea; a cold fweat came all over me, attended with an univerfal dejection. I was prefently rouzed from this fituation by the agitation of my mind, and propofed that a kind of way fhould be made over the ice with boards or branches of trees; but the people were fo obftinate, that they found all my propofals impracticable, and peremptorily refufed undertaking them. This made fuch an impreffion on me, that I was inclined to force them to go along with me; but the project which then came into my head, of buying up the horfes and conducting ourfelves, made me a little more calm. I went out for a moment to confider what I fhould do, and imagined this laft fcheme was the moft eligible; as my attendants feemed refolved never to leave me. I came into the houfe again pretty calm,

calm, called for something for supper, and gave brandy to every body; as the first thing necessary, after what had passed, was to bring people into good humour again.

In the mean time my thermometer was brought me, and I fixed it against the wall, to determine the heat of this place, which was suffocating. The people were as much surprized at this instrument, as the inhabitants of Kuzmodemiansk had been at the barometer, which they took for a clock. The thermometer had the greater effect on the people of Vaksarina, as it rose with great velocity when brought out of the cold air into a very hot stove. Observing they were very attentive to this phenomenon, I told them, without any particular intention, that the thermometer pointed out heat and cold; that the mercury rose in the first, and fell in the last instance. This simple explanation was not understood; they thought there was something wonderful in the instrument, which I soon perceived, and determined to take my advantage of it. The thermometer presently rose to twenty-five degrees, I then took hold of it, and very confidently told them, that by carrying it out of doors it would shew us whether there was any danger in crossing the river; and that if there was not, it would fall down to a certain point which I shewed them. This point was one degree below 0: the thermometer, at this time, was generally two or three degrees below that point in the open air; and the place I marked was more than four inches below the twenty-five degrees. They directly fixed the thermometer out of doors: I came in immediately, and spoke no more about going away. I soon perceived that ignorance and superstition were at work in their minds, already agitated by some expressions I had dropped about the design of my journey, and which they understood no more than the use of some of my instruments they had seen.

I was employed in making them drink, when the moſt ſtubborn fellow among them, who had ſlipped out without my ſeeing him, came in again, and told me with enthuſiaſm, that the animal had got down below the mark. They all ran immediately to be convinced of this fact, and I had now no difficulty to ſtruggle with, except that of hindering my interpreter from explaining that the mercury was not an animal. I preſently got a ſufficient number of horſes, and the poſtilions went away immediately: the one who had been moſt ſullen all the day, was now the warmeſt in the cauſe. I gave him the care of the ſledge where my inſtruments were; he went foremoſt, and the others followed. As ſoon as we got out of the hamlet we diſcovered the river, and this was the only object we could diſcern, in the midſt of the darkneſs which covered this hemiſphere: the faint glimmering of the ſtars, reflected in the water, which flowed on the uneven ſurface of the ice*, made us ſee the river at a diſtance, by the different ſhades of their dim light, and made an appearance of waves gently agitated. We ſoon came to the borders of the river, where all was profoundly ſilent. The firſt poſtilion was preparing to croſs it, and ſtopped ſhort. I ſtood upright on my ſledge; and called out to him *ſtoupai* (go on); puſhing, at the ſame time, my own poſtilion ſo violently, that he went on immediately. The firſt poſtilion, not willing to be overtaken, gets on at a ſtill greater rate; the others follow, and we were on the other ſide of the river in an inſtant.

I did not however enjoy the happineſs of this moment as I ſhould have done. I had but juſt croſſed the river when I was ſeized with an univerſal tremor, accompanied with convulſive ſtarts: my ſtrength, which ſeemed to have increaſed the nearer

---

* Theſe inequalities being occaſioned by part of the ice which was already melted, do not contradict my former obſervation, aſſerting that the ſurface of the frozen rivers was perfectly ſmooth.

I came to this inftant, now forfook me all at once; fo that I drank fome *liqueur* I ftill had in the fledge. I foon found myfelf relieved, and fell afleep, in which fituation I ftill remained when we ftopped at the poft of Cheftakova. I left this place immediately, and in a few hours came to Dektereva, where I was to change horfes for the laft time. As the river Irtifz was ftill between me and the city of Tobolfky, I expected to meet with frefh difficulties from the people of this hamlet; but was glad to find myfelf deceived. The inhabitants ftill continued to crofs the river at Tobolfky on the ice, becaufe this paffage being more frequented, the fnow was fo much beaten by the feet of men and beafts, that it was become united to, and confolidated with the ice, fo as to make it thicker.

At length I arrived at Tobolfky on the 10th of April, fix days before the ice broke up, after having travelled on a fledge from St. Peterfburg, about eight hundred leagues, or three hundred thoufand and eighteen werfts, in a month, although I had been delayed by feveral accidents, and by the difficulty of getting horfes.

Immediately on my arrival, I went to fee M. de Soimanof, governor of the city. He fent for his daughters; the eldeft was a widow, who came up to falute me, and took my hand to kifs it. As I was unacquainted with the Ruffian cuftoms, it put me at firft a little out of countenance, but I foon recovered myfelf. As the two other ladies, the youngeft of whom was nineteen or twenty, were coming forwards with the fame intention, I went towards them, and after having faluted them in their manner, I kiffed their hands, and immediately withdrew mine. According to the true *etiquette*, I ought indeed to have kiffed their hands, while they were doing me the fame honor, but I fhould have ftaid in my place till they came up to falute me.

The governor received me with great politeness: he convinced me of the esteem he had for the sciences, which he cultivates and is fond of. He ordered me a guard, consisting of a serjeant and three grenadiers; and at the same time supplied me with every thing I wanted.

I directly set about building my observatory, and preparing every thing which belonged to it, but could not get it finished before the 11th of May. I immediately fixed my instruments, and on the 18th instant, although the weather was cloudy, I yet found an opportunity of observing several phases of a lunar eclipse. I had prepared on the 3d of June, to observe an eclipse of the sun, invisible in France. This observation was of the more consequence, as it enabled me to determine the precise longitude of Tobolsky, which I could not expect to find from observing the eclipses of Jupiter's Satellites, because this hemisphere, in the summer time, is almost constantly lighted by the sun; and besides, this eclipse being visible also at Sweden, Denmark, and at St. Petersburg, I was sure of meeting with observations to answer mine. The sky was cloudy at the immersion of the eclipse, and although it was in June, a great quantity of snow fell; but I observed the emersion with great accuracy. The longitude of Tobolsky, resulting from this observation, being compared to that of Stockholm, communicated to me by M. Delisle, turns out to be four hours, twenty-three minutes, thirty-four seconds, with respect to the meridian of Paris.

The inhabitants of the town, not much used to see strangers, had been surprized at my arrival: they had seen my observatory construed immediately, and as its form was very different from their buildings, they thought there was something mysterious in it. They were much astonished at its being placed on a mountain, from whence I was able to take in the whole horizon; besides, that it was about three quarters of a mile distant from the town. At first, they knew not what to think; but when they saw a quadrant, clocks, a parallactic machine, and a telescope nineteen feet long, instruments they had never seen before, they concluded that I was a magician. I was busied all day in observing the sun, in order to regulate my clocks, and to try my telescopes. At night I viewed the moon and stars; and made use particularly of a small lamp, fixed to my quadrant, that I might discern the threads of the micrometer; sometimes I did not return to the city till morning, exceedingly fatigued, and the little care I took of my dress, confirmed the people in the opinion they had entertained of me.

The governor, and a few more, were the only persons who knew that I had undertaken this journey to observe the Transit of Venus over the Sun; all the rest of the inhabitants were misled by their superstition. The least ignorant among them reported a number of absurdities about this observation, and others expected at that instant the end of the world. They looked upon me as having occasioned the overflowing of the river Irtisz, which was so considerable this year, that part of the lower town was laid under water, as high as the roofs of the houses, and several persons lost their lives, in carrying their goods through the torrents of water, which overthrew and swept away the dwelling-places. Several pieces of the mountain were separated in different places, and fell into the river with a dreadful noise. Some of the inhabitants, whose houses were on the sides of this mountain, were obliged to quit them, lest they should be carried away into the river. The saltern was entirely overwhelmed, and although they were as quick as possible in endeavouring to save the salt, yet the greater part of it was lost. The plain at the foot of the mountain of Tobolsky, exhibited an appearance, to those who were on the top of the mountain, of a number of islands scattered on this watery surface, and extending as far as the sight.

This

This river overflows every year, when the snows are melted; but it had never been known to do so much damage; so that this circumstance encouraged the people in their extravagant opinions, who imagined they should see no end to their misfortunes till I was gone from Tobolsky. As my thoughts were quite taken up about the observation, I was unacquainted with all that passed on this occasion; and was so far from suspecting, that I generally left the guard at home, and went to the observatory, attended only by my interpreter, and sometimes by the watch-maker; but the guard was then ordered always to follow me. Some of the Russians advised me not to go alone to my observatory, and to take some precautions against the fury of the mob, which might lead them to any lengths. The advice was too prudent not to be followed, and from that time I determined to pass most nights in the observatory, lest they should attempt to pull it down. On the 4th instant, the wind was so high and so continual, that I was in the greatest danger of having it blown down, and was not freed from my apprehensions till the next day at noon, when the wind abated.

The event which occasioned my journey was now at hand, and the next day, being the sixth of June, was to satisfy all my inquisitiveness. M. de Soimanof, Count Pouskin, and the archbishop of Tobolsky, who all deserve more than I can say of them, having expressed a great desire of seeing this phenomenon, I had a tent pitched, in which I put a telescope for them and their families, that I might not be disturbed in my observation.

On the 5th, I was employed all day in arranging my instruments, and resolved to pass the night in my observatory. Every circumstance seemed to answer my wishes, and to flatter me that my observation would be successful. The sky was clear, the sun sunk below the horizon, free from all vapors; the mild glimmering of the twilight, and the perfect stillness of

the

the universe, completed my satisfaction, and added to the serenity of my mind. I made every body go to supper, but my contemplative situation prevented me from partaking of any food. This pleasure however did not last long, for as I went out about ten o'clock, to enjoy it in silence, I was distressed at the sight of some fogs, which partly deprived the stars of their light. I cast my eye all over the horizon, and was much dispirited on seeing already a number of clouds forming on all sides, which became thicker every instant; the darkness of the night still increased, the bright sky disappeared; and the whole hemisphere was soon overspread with one single black cloud, which damped all my expectations, and threw me into a state of despondency.

The observation of this Transit, gave the world an opportunity, for the first time, of determining precisely the parallax of the sun. This phenomenon, expected for more than a century past, had fixed the attention of astronomers, who were all desirous of sharing the honor of it. The famous Halley, who foretold it, was the first who manifested its importance, and even on his death-bed lamented the impossibility of his being witness of it. The whole learned world had taken all possible measures to assist the observation. Sovereign princes, although engaged in an expensive war, had neglected nothing that could insure the success of this important matter, which might enhance the glory of their annals, and at the same time be productive of the most substantial advantages to their subjects, and to mankind in general.

The idea of returning to France, after a fruitless voyage; of having exposed myself in vain to a variety of dangers, and to fatigues, under which I was supported only by the earnestness and expectation of success, which I was now deprived of by a cloud, at a time when I had the greatest reason to be assured of it, threw me into such a situation as can only be felt.

I had

I had not the trifling satisfaction of seeing any person who might share my anxiety. All my attendants had taken notice of it, but had gone into the observatory, where I found them fast asleep. I roused them all, they then left me alone, and I found myself relieved by their absence.

In these dreadful agitations I passed the whole night; I went out and came in again every instant, and could not continue a moment in the same position.

Such trials must have been experienced, to be sensible of the exceeding pleasure I felt, when my hopes were revived by the rising of the sun. The clouds however were still so thick, that this region was yet involved in darkness, notwithstanding the light of the sun; which was only distinguished by a reddish cast on the clouds: but an easterly wind drove this gloomy veil towards the west; and soon exposed part of the sky at the horizon. This appearance increased by imperceptible degrees; the clouds began to exhibit a whitish colour, which grew brighter every instant; a pleasing satisfaction diffused itself through all my frame, and inspired me with a new kind of life. The clouds still continued to be dispersed, the face of nature became pleasant, every thing, in short, seemed to rejoice at the return of a fine day; and as my hopes became more sanguine, the joy of my mind was still more complete.

The governor, M. Pouskin, and their families, then came up, and shared my happiness. They were soon followed by the archbishop and some of the *archimandrites*. I had strengthened my guard, apprehending that I should be interrupted by a number of curious people, but this precaution proved unnecessary, as all the inhabitants had shut themselves up in the churches, or in their houses. Although the sun was not yet visible, it was evident however that he would soon make his appearance. I prepared for the observation, and the company went into the tent I had pitched for them. My watch-maker's business was to write, and keep his eye on the clock, while my interpreter was employed in counting the time; the calmness and serenity of the air had made me resolve to bring my instruments out of the observatory, that I might move them more readily. I soon perceived one of the borders of the sun, at the time that Venus was to enter upon his disk; but on the opposite border, which was still concealed by the clouds. I stood fixed with my eye to the telescope, wandering over the immense space between us and the sun a thousand times in a minute. I was troubled by the continuance of the cloud, which at length however disappeared, and perceiving that the planet was already immersed, I prepared to observe the most material appearance, the total entry. Altho' the sky was perfectly serene, yet my apprehensions were not yet at an end. The moment of the observation was now at hand; I was seized with an universal shivering, and was obliged to collect all my thoughts, in order not to miss it. At length I observed this phasis, and felt an inward persuasion of the accuracy of my process. Pleasures of the like nature may sometimes be experienced; but at this instant, I truly enjoyed that of my observation, and was delighted with the hopes of its being still useful to posterity, when I had quitted this life.

The sky remaining clear the whole day, I went on easily with my other observations, which I dispatched a few days after, by an express, which the governor sent to the Russian court: I sent one copy to the academy at St. Petersburg, and another to that at Paris. I stayed, however, at Tobolsky till the 28th of August, to make some farther astronomical observations. During this time I was employed in acquiring some knowledge of the country of Siberia; and have joined my inquiries on this subject, with those I made in going to Tobolsky, and with other particulars, occasionally discovered in the course of my journey returning to St. Petersburg.

RETURN
FROM
TOBOLSKY
TO
St. Petersburg, 28th August, 1761.

THE instructions I had received at Paris, permitted me to stay but a short time at Tobolsky, after my observation of the Transit of Venus. When I began to think of leaving this place at the end of August, I was seized with an almost continual vomiting of blood, attended with such a loss of strength, that I could scarce support myself, and was unable to reach my observatory without assistance. My indisposition hurried me still quicker from a country where a hot bath was the only remedy for every disorder, and I was the more unwilling to submit to this, as I had already been nearly suffocated in one of them at Solikamsky. I had a very compleat medicine chest with me, and a circumstantial account of the virtues of every thing it contained; but having had the misfortune to poison a Russian, in attempting to cure him of some slight complaint, I had determined to lay aside the practice of physic: it happened very fortunately, that the dose was not strong enough to destroy the patient.

My departure, however, was still attended with many difficulties: my servant, who suffered for his gallantry at Tobolsky, was so very ill, that he could be of no use to me; besides, both

both he and the watch-maker were seized with a dread of being assassinated on our way by robbers, who were then said to commit murders every day on the road to Echaterinenburg.

I had determined to take this new route, as it would give me an opportunity of examining the mines of Echaterinenburg, and the different people inhabiting the southern borders of Siberia. These objects appeared of so interesting a nature, that I could by no means think of altering my plan.

The governor, with great politeness, offered me a guard of four soldiers to attend me to St. Petersburg. I refused it at first, thinking that the difficulties of my journey would increase in proportion to the number of my followers; but all my attendants were so dispirited, that I resolved to accept of M. de Soimanof's offer. The guard consisted of a serjeant and three grenadiers well armed. I provided ammunition and arms for all my fellow travellers; besides which, a blunderbuss was given me. I had a large carriage made for my instruments, the rest of my baggage, my provisions, and utensils. I had also two carriages commonly called *dormeuses*: the soldiers were distributed on the different carriages; and one of them was on mine with the blunderbuss. This disposition, and the military appearance it had, quieted every body. I set out on the 28th of August, to the great satisfaction of the people of Tobolsky, who imagined that the Irtisz would not return into its channel, till I was gone. I could not take my leave of the archbishop, and of M. de Soimanof and Poutkin, without being extremely affected.

Although the month of August was almost at an end, the harvest appeared still distant; the hot days were over, the insects, so troublesome in this part of the world, were gone; and the season in every respect seemed fit for travelling. My indisposition left me in a few days; but yet I did not find my journey so agreeable as I thought it would have proved: the

continual

continual rains, subsequent to the melting of the snows, hindered me greatly in crossing that extent of land between Tobolsky and the mountains. The soil being marshy for the space of near one hundred leagues, the roads were so bad, that I was obliged to send a soldier forwards, to fill up some places with fascines which would otherwise have been unpassable. I soon found it inconvenient to travel through these roads in the summer, especially with large carriages. Those which the natives use, are very small and light; they call them *Kuibics*. My large carriage, laden with baggage and provisions, was so heavy, that it sank readily into the mire, from whence it could not be withdrawn without difficulty, even with the assistance of twelve horses.

From the 28th to the 30th of August, I crossed part of the plain between Tobolsky and the mountains (called Poyas Zemnoi). We met with such quantities of ducks, that without going out of my way, I could shoot enough for myself and all my company; which was a great help to us, because I had little else but salt meat along with me. It is customary in these journeys, to lay in a stock of chickens, geese and tame ducks, which are shut up in coops. The archbishop, M. de Soimanof, and M. de Pouskin, had furnished me with a quantity of these, which I placed on the carriages, but being out of patience with the trouble they gave, I had some of them killed a few hours after setting out, and set the rest at liberty.

Notwithstanding the badness of the roads, I travelled agreeably enough for the few first days; the weather was fine, and I met with villages where I was able to take my meals; I sometimes halted on the banks of rivers; and the greatest inconvenience I felt, was from not having any bread but that of the country, which I never could relish.

On the 31st instant, I came to Tumen, a small town, part of which stands on a mountain bordering the river southward.

Its

Its fituation is as pleafant as that of Tobolfky, but it has few inhabitants. I received great civilities from M. Ivan Afananf-coifk, the Waywode; he made me a prefent of fome tea and fugar; feveral others of the inhabitants were kind enough to come and fee me, and brought me alfo fome prefents; but they frightened my little caravan, by telling us that four ruffians had been taken up the night before, at the diftance of three leagues from this town; they affured us likewife, that they went in gangs along this road; that they not only attacked and pillaged travellers, but even fmall villages: moft of thefe robbers had deferted from the recruits, or had efcaped from the mines of Echaterinenburg. This account made me more cautious; I infpected all the arms, and laid in a frefh ftock of brandy, to keep up the courage of my company; fometimes diftributing it myfelf to the poftilions, and the reft of my attendants. I had perfectly recovered my health, and every thing was done with fo much alacrity and mirth, that my people feemed to have got rid of their fears. I had eight men along with me well armed, and the blunderbufs charged with cafe-fhot, was placed on the fore-part of my carriage; fo that as I feared nothing but a furprize, I diftributed to each carriage fome flambeaux made for me at Tobolfky, and had them lighted at night.

On the 1ft of September, at three in the morning, I came to the borders of the river Pifzma, oppofite to the hamlet Kila. This river is forty toifes wide; I was going to crofs it, over a float of timber fixed to the banks at each end, and ferving for a bridge; in which manner moft of the bridges in Siberia are conftructed. But this bridge was fo bad, that as foon as the fore-horfes of the large carriage had fet their feet upon it, they fell in breaft high; feveral half rotten cords then giving way, I inftantly ordered the traces to be cut, and immediately perceived, that the current was carrying away the decayed

bridge.

bridge with the horses upon it, which were got out with much difficulty. One of the soldiers swam across the river, and went to the hamlet Kila, on the opposite shore, for assistance. This hamlet consisting of five or six houses, had been attacked on the 29th of August, by the gang of the robbers before-mentioned; three of the country people lost their lives on this occasion, but they drove off the ruffians, after having killed two of them. The soldier could not bring away more than two of the country-men; we immediately went all to work, and about seven in the morning got the carriages over, taking care not to have more than one at a time on the bridge.

At eleven at night, I came to Kuiarowskaia. My carriages were so much injured, that I stopped here to get them repaired, but could find nobody who was able to mend them; so that I was obliged to send a soldier to the neighbouring village for a cartwright; for not one of the peasants could be prevailed upon to go; such terror had the robbers spread round about. Report and fear had greatly increased their numbers and rendered them formidable. I employed the rest of the night in getting the carriages repaired, and set out at six in the morning.

As I came nearer to the chain of mountains, the soil was more cultivated, and there were scarce any marshes to be seen at Wolkava. The earth was black, as it was all the way from Tobolsky; but here it was firmer. The land round about this hamlet seemed to promise a plentiful harvest of corn, barley, and oats; but the people were apprehensive, that the cold would prevent them from ripening. I was then in fifty-six degrees fifty minutes latitude, and about one hundred and twenty-five leagues distant from Tobolsky. All this plain appeared to be but one universal marsh, which made excellent ground for pasture; it was scarce cultivated in any part, except in the neighbourhood of Pokrowskaïa and Tumen, where

I saw

I saw some very fine corn, some oats, and a small quantity of barley. The grass grows very thick in this immense plain. I found only some few small forests, scattered in the middle of the marshes; and these were chiefly of light woods, such as birch, poplar, &c. I seldom met with fir-trees before I came to Wolkava, where I was obliged to stop for the repairing of my carriages. The night was so fine that I halted in the middle of a grass plat; but it was very cold, notwithstanding a large fire was kindled; for a hoar-frost covered the ground on the third of September. I set out at eleven in the morning; and in the neighbourhood of Kosulina met with some stones for the first time, since I quitted Tobolsky; from which it was evident, that the mountains were near; and indeed I entered upon them almost as soon as I got clear of the hamlet. Here the road was dreadful, and became so dangerous in the night, that notwithstanding the light of the flambeaux, we were obliged to cross most of these mountains on foot. At length I reached Echaterinenburg, on the 4th of September, at one in the morning. My people were so much fatigued, that they chose to pass the rest of the night in the carriages, without unloading either of them. As to myself, I had my matrass laid on the ground in the small room where I was. At the same time I was told, that was the lodging appointed for me by the commandant of the town, and I must not expect any other; yet it was so small, that I could not possibly live in it. I sent a soldier forwards to the commandant, with the orders of the Empress, and to acquaint him of the intention I had of staying a few days in this town. The orders expressed that I should be furnished with all the helps and accommodations I could possibly desire; and indeed they had been hitherto punctually executed. I rose early in the morning, to learn something about the customs of the place, before I made any visit. I sent a soldier to the commandant, to inquire what time of the day I might pay my respects to him: he sent me word, that he should not be at home. This answer, which I little expected, disconcerted me exceedingly. I had letters to the principal inhabitants of the town, whom I could not go to with propriety, before I had seen the commandant, and I could not well wait till he was in a better humour. I therefore determined to call at his house, that I might not be in any particular neglectful of what I thought my duty, and then went about the town to pay my visits, fully resolved to quit the place immediately, if the inhabitants had been all as strange as the commandant; but, on the contrary, they received me with all possible kindness and civility. I went home again very well satisfied. It was then two o'clock in the afternoon; I had taken no food, any more than the persons who attended me, since eleven o'clock in the morning of the preceding day, and had no more than two roasted ducks left for eight people. I was preparing to send out for provisions, when I received some from all the persons I had visited, and in an instant my little room, of ten feet square, was filled with two sheep continually bleating, with geese, ducks and fowls. These animals made so much noise, that I was obliged to go out into the street, to learn the names of the persons I was indebted to for this kindness.

One of the soldiers immediately seized a sheep, and carried it to a good old woman in the neighbourhood; and in little better than an hour's time, he was killed, roasted, and almost eaten up.

I went in the afternoon, to return thanks to the persons who had been so obliging to me; and the fresh civilities I received from them, removed all the prejudices I had entertained on my first arrival against the inhabitants of the town. M. Artibacher, first counsellor of the chancery, and his lady, were exceedingly polite to me. I found him a chearful, intelligent,

and

and most agreeable man, although confined to his bed by an indisposition. His lady, about fifty years of age, still retained the marks of former beauty. Her countenance and behaviour were tokens of her good qualities, and of the respect paid to her by the whole town. She was fond of foreigners, and sought every opportunity of doing them service. She told me by my interpreter, in presence of her husband and all the company, that she would be my mother, and direct my house-keeping for me, while I staid at Echaterinenburg. I felt the kindness of this offer so sensibly, that I was unable to answer a word; but she was pleased to consider my silence as the sincerest mark of my gratitude. Her husband, who spoke French a little, soon rouzed my attention, by asking me divers questions relative to the intent of my journey. His lady having understood part of our conversation, which turned upon the mountains observable in the moon, on Jupiter, &c. desired her husband to ask me, if I could not shew them to her through my telescopes. It is hardly necessary to say, that my answer was such as to satisfy her. I took my leave almost immediately after, quite full of the project I at that instant conceived.

My lodging was so small, and in so much confusion, that I could not possibly receive any person in it; I therefore endeavoured to get another. The baron de Strogonof had given me a letter to his people, ordering them to assist me in every thing I wanted. After much inquiry, I learned that one of his people was in the town: and sent to desire he would call upon me. He came, and found that the letter was not from his own master, but from a relation of the same name: he offered me, however, his services, assuring me, that if he could be happy enough to be of any use to me, he knew he should oblige his master. I ought not certainly to omit mentioning, to the credit of the family of the Strogonofs, that wherever I have

have passed through any of their estates, I have been very civilly treated by their stewards. This illustrious family seems to entertain an hereditary regard for foreigners. M. Strahlemberg, and all who have travelled after him in this country, have also experienced the strongest marks of favour from them *.

I begged the favour of M. de Strogonof's steward to get me a more convenient and larger apartment: he procured me one the very next day, and I did not find out, till after I was gone, that he had given me up his own. I settled myself in it the same day, and prepared a small observatory there, intending to make some astronomical observations on this town, in order to determine its position.

The inhabitants of the town did me the honor to come to see me next day in a body, and to offer me a guard. I thanked them much for this fresh mark of their kindness, but begged earnestly of them not to send it, as the one I had was sufficient, and I had experienced that this appearance of state was often very inconvenient.

As soon as I was settled in my new lodging, I thought of entertaining Mad. Artibacher there, with some others of the town, whom I wished to be of the party. The young Count Woronzof, to whom I have many obligations, recommended me to his steward on this occasion, who lived about a mile from Echaterinenburg. He was a very civil intelligent man, and could speak French tolerably well. I begged him to prepare, for the 16th instant, the best supper he could get together, for forty people, but desired that his wife might be the only person in the secret. Provisions were collected from different places: all the preparations were carried on out of my house, so that even two hours before supper, nobody had the least suspicion of this entertainment.

* The baron de Strogonof, the senator, has a very fine cabinet of natural history.

The sky had been perfectly clear for some days past, and was favourable to my project. I went the evening before to see M. Artibacher and his lady, and invited them for the next day, to come and see the Moon and Jupiter, at seven in the evening; and at the same time desired the favor of Mad. Artibacher, to bring all her friends and acquaintance in the town with her. By this behaviour, I intended to make it appear to her that this little treat was purposely designed for her; I was desirous, however, that the principal persons of the town should be present, but would not invite one of them.

There are many foreigners, chiefly Germans, in the town of Echaterinenburg: the manners and customs therefore, of this place, differ much from those of the Russians in the other parts of Siberia, otherwise such an entertainment as this would have been impracticable, on account of the women being too closely confined.

Madame Artibacher came at the appointed time, with a large company, consisting entirely of women: I led her to the place where the telescope was fixed, which was at some distance from the house, that the preparations for supper might be unnoticed. The men joined us immediately. Being informed that it was necessary to have music at such entertainments, I had taken care to provide myself with a band.

My servant came to tell me when all was ready; I then begged the favor of Mad. Artibacher and her company, to rest themselves a little at my house. As they came in, the music struck up. All the company went into the room where the supper was, and, from the general surprize, I was convinced that the affair had been kept very secret. As Mad. Artibacher was the only person invited, I withdrew to ask the rest of the company in, left they should have gone away. There were a greater number of people than I expected, so that it was impossible for every one to sit at table. I therefore proposed, that

the

the ladies only should be seated, and that the gentlemen should be employed in waiting upon them. However extraordinary this proposal might seem at first in Siberia, where, on the contrary, it is the custom for the women to wait upon the men, yet the company came into it: M. Cléopet, a Russian, a sensible and agreeable man, assisted me in carrying this scheme into execution, which had no inconsiderable share in the pleasure I expected from this treat. I distributed napkins among the gentlemen; and then addressing myself to Mad. Artibacher, told her, that as she had been so kind to say, she would consider me as her son, the honors of my house belonged certainly to her. She answered, by a few words in the Russian language, which I understood not; but was much surprized to see part of the company go away immediately, particularly the young people, who seemed much inclined to mirth. I was going to stop them, when my interpreter prevented me, by telling me those persons had gone away in consequence of what Mad. Artibacher had said, which was: *Let those who are entitled to stay, sit down to the table.*

The company, however, was so much diminished, that there were several places vacant, even after the gentlemen were seated. All ceremony being set aside, the supper passed off very agreeably: Mad. Artibacher, as well as M. Cléopet and his lady, were as merry as possible. The last of these ladies was young, lively, fond of mirth and pleasure. I proposed a dance after supper, and although some Russians, certainly old-fashioned people, sent for their wives, who were obliged to go, yet we were not baulked of this diversion: notwithstanding this unseasonable interruption we continued dancing till four in the morning; when the company took their leave, to all appearances, very well satisfied.

This trifling entertainment had a greater effect than I could have expected; for my guests were so well pleased, that in return,

turn, the town sent me the next day the state coach, with six horses, to attend me all the time I should stay at Echaterinenburg. The governor came to pay me a visit, and by his great civilities made me forget what had passed before. I went to the principal inhabitants of the town, to return them thanks, and begged the favor of those officers, who superintended the mines, to procure me a sight of them. It was for this reason I had determined to take the route of Echaterinenburg, and to make some little stay in this town. M. Cléopet was one of the chief directors of these mines; he gave me a very high idea of the gold mines, by shewing me some specimens which were exceedingly rich. The mines are at a few leagues distance from the town: we visited them the next day; setting out early in the morning, attended by several carriages, and many persons on horseback. All the morning was taken up in seeing the mines. At two o'clock M. Cléopet took me to a small house, where he had ordered a most elegant dinner. When the dinner was almost over, all the young girls of the village were sent for: they came in their holiday dresses, and sang to us all the time we sat at the table. After dinner a little ball was given; when observing that the company flagged, I took out one of the country girls to dance with me. I was told directly, that it was reckoned the highest impropriety in Russia, to dance with a slave; so that I had no other way of repairing this offence, than by making it become general; and, after a few explanations, the whole company, men, women, farmers, and country girls, danced all together, as usual in all other countries upon such occasions. Every body was so well pleased, that the dancing continued till suppertime.

Their musical instruments are the Balalaïca and the violin. The balalaïca is a kind of guittar, which a Russian played upon: The violin is nothing more than a piece of wood, hollowed

hollowed in a very rude manner, and having but three strings made of horse hair, which, instead of rosin, are rubbed with a piece of the bark of the fir-tree, tied to the violin with a packthread. There was, however, a Tartar, who had a more perfect violin. The Russian dances did not seem to resemble any other European dances, except the Allemandes. Sometimes there are a dozen of them dancing together, sometimes two persons only, a man and a woman: most of their dances are dances of character: these appeared to me of a more ancient date, and not to agree in the least with the state of slavery in which the women are now kept by the men.

In their dances of character, a lover expresses his passion for his mistress, by the most lascivious attitudes and motions. His mistress answers him with the additional graces peculiar to her sex; which are the more alluring in these women, as the inactive lives they lead, throws a kind of languor over all their motions which gives them more expression and tenderness. Sometimes, the woman puts her two hands upon her hips, and looks stedfastly at her lover sideways, with a pair of large black eyes; while her head and body are bent to the opposite side, appearing to refuse him by this disdainful attitude. The lover then comes forward in a suppliant posture, his head reclined, his arms folded, and his two hands fixed upon his breast: and by these signs expresses submission and sorrow.

However similar the Russian dances and the Allemandes may be in point of expression and sprightliness, they still differ considerably in other respects. The Allemandes in general are full of nothing but mirth and pleasure, and there is commonly much springing up in them: the Russian dances, on the contrary, are carried on upon the level of the ground, and are rather characteristic of desire, than happiness; they are softer and have more expression.

The

The Ruffian dance is fometimes a kind of pantomime, which requires a great deal of fupplenefs and agility. This can only be danced by young people, who go through it with remarkable dexterity: they turn round on one foot, while they are almoft in a fitting pofture; they then rife up in an inftant, and throw themfelves into fome fanciful or grotefque attitude, which they vary every moment, in advancing, retiring, or turning round the room. They often dance alone in this manner, or with one woman, who has very little to do.

At fetting out from Echaterinenburg, nobody had conceived that this entertainment would keep us all day in this place: befides, I had begged the favor of M. Cléopet to fhew me the other mines; fo that it was refolved, we fhould pafs the night in this hamlet, that we might go there the next day. It was with great difficulty that matraffes were procured, and thefe were fpread in the room where we had fupped. Some laid themfelves down on them, others flept in their carriages. This buftle and confufion was far from being difagreeable to the company, but appeared, on the contrary, to renew their chearfulnefs. We went back to Echaterinenburg next day, where I was invited to different entertainments by the principal inhabitants. I ftayed here fome time, in order to make fome aftronomical obfervations, and to make myfelf better acquainted with the mines, of which I fhall give an account hereafter.

Echaterinenburg is a fmall town, founded by Peter the Firft, in 1723; it is under the jurifdiction of Tobolfky, and is the center of all the mines and founderies in Siberia; fo that the inhabitants are chiefly perfons employed in thefe mines, and are moft of them Germans. Society is upon a more agreeable footing here than in any other town of Siberia, becaufe the manners of the people are more fimilar to thofe which prevail throughout the reft of Europe.

There is one governor in the town, whose authority is only over the military. All other affairs, as well as all things relative to the mines, are adjudged by the chancery; which has the general direction of all the mines in the neighbourhood, as of those at Solikamsky, Casan, and Orenburg, whether they belong to the crown or to individuals. The chancery has the same powers and appointments as a governor, and is only subordinate to the Imperial College of the mines at St. Petersburg. The chancery has nothing to do with the mines of Colivan and Nerczinsk; these have their particular jurisdictions.

There are five jurisdictions under the court of chancery at Echaterinenburg; these are called factories. The business of these jurisdictions is to regulate matters of right, taxes, working of the mines, their revenue, and the account of the value of the crown lands. The sovereign keeps a manufactory for the working of marble and porphyry. Cornelians and sardonyxes are likewise polished here, as also a brown crystal, found in the neighbouring mines. This work is carried on by means of different machines, put in motion by water.

The garrison consists of three or four hundred men. There is an hospital here, an apothecary's shop, and different houses for the customs, and for the sale of brandy. The officers who have the direction of these last establishments, form a department, which is called the Commissariat; but this is still subordinate to the chancery.

Peter I. had ordered the establishment of a school in this place, where young people were to be instructed in the Latin, German, and Italian languages, in mathematics and drawing; but I found neither masters nor scholars here, even the clergy being unacquainted with the Latin tongue. This establishment is now reduced to one schoolmaster, whose salary is fixed at one hundred rubles, or five hundred French livres.

This

This schoolmaster was one of the persons who did me the honor of a visit just after my arrival. Altho' he was sixty years of age, yet he was so lively that I was surprized. He often addressed himself to me, but as I did not understand the Russian language, and that I was also much taken up in receiving the company, I could not possibly hold a conversation with him.

This schoolmaster came again to see me at my return from the mines, and told me, he was the grandson of a French refugee. His grandfather, whose name was Mouisset, had been a captain in the French guards, who had retreated into Russia upon the revocation of the edict of Nants. I went the next day to see him in his little cottage. He was married, and had four or five children. The good man expressed the highest joy at having a Frenchman in his house: he was no otherwise acquainted with our nation and manners, than by the tradition of his ancestors, who never spoke to him on this subject, he said, without tears, which also flowed involuntarily from him upon this occasion. I was much affected with his sensibility. He related to me all he had been obliged to undergo, before he could obtain that moderate sufficiency he now enjoyed. We then entered into some discourse on the recalling of the edict of Nants, when he told me, in a rage, that Father la Chaise had managed that affair, and that France would be ruined by the Jesuits. I could not certainly have given him a greater pleasure, than to have told him of the expulsion of the Jesuits from that kingdom, which happened about that time; but having left my country in 1759, I had not yet been informed of that event. At the same time that this schoolmaster's ancestors had transmitted to him their aversion to the Jesuits, they had also taken care to give him some knowledge of geometry and drawing: he was employed in taking the plan of the mines, and in bringing up the young people. I was so well pleased with this Frenchman, and so much affected with his situation, that I regretted much that it was not in my power to take him away with me. Besides, he was contented with his little income, and was much respected by the Russians. He had a small garden, which he cultivated himself, and which supplied him with all kinds of vegetables. He offered me some of them, assuring me, I should find them no where else. I accepted them with the more pleasure, as I had never met with any during my stay in Siberia.

I continued a few days longer at Echaterinenburg, which I quitted on the 20th instant, after having satisfied my curiosity upon the several things I had intended to notice. I was now going to cross a long chain of mountains, which obliged me to alter my plan of travelling, and to leave my large carriage, with which it would have been impossible to ascend these mountains. Instead of this, I got seven small carts, called quibiks, which are the only carriages used in Russia for baggage. They are very small, and therefore but slightly laden; as it would otherwise be impossible to travel in this country, on account of the badness of the roads. These fresh dispositions, the necessity of which I had not foreseen, would have detained me considerably at Echaterinenburg, if Count Woronzof had not been so kind to give me the letter I mentioned before; but with the assistance of his steward, and of M. Clépet, superintendant of the mines, my wants were readily supplied. I travelled pretty conveniently the first day; but as I advanced upon the chain of mountains, the roads became worse; besides, I was in want of four or five and twenty horses, and could not always get such a number.

We met with several fortified places in the course of our journey over these mountains. The fort of Grobowa is in the midst of the chain; and that of Astchitzkaia, which is the last, is in the plain. These forts are nothing more than wooden towers furrounded with palifades. They have been conftructed to keep the Bafkirs in awe, whom the Ruffians have had fo much trouble to fubdue; for, till then, they had imagined themfelves to be merely under the protection of Ruffia, and not fubject to its power.

After the chain of mountains is paffed over, the country becomes very open, infomuch that I met with none but fmall hills, fuch as are found upon every plain. The trees are fcattered here and there in clufters: I faw no other than the lighter woods here, chiefly birch.

I arrived on the 23d at the forge of Souxon, where I ftopped, in order to learn fomething about the mines of copper in the neighbourhood, which I knew to be very curious. As I had no recommendation to the director, I did not expect to be very gracioufly received, nor to be allowed the liberty of fatisfying my curiofity; fo that I made the carriages halt upon a grafs-plat, without unharneffing the horfes. The director, although a polite man, was rather fhy of permitting me to go over the forges, and examine the different works going on there. At laft, one of M. Dimidof's workmen in this manufactory, who had feen me at Solikamfky, recollected my face, and told his mafter of it. This new manufactory belonged alfo to M. Dimidof, by whofe orders I had been perfectly well received at Solikamfky. The director being informed of thefe circumftances, came up to me, while I was employed in examining the ores, which had been heaped up together in a yard; he made me a number of excufes for his referved behavior, and I went over all the moft interefting places with him again. I then thought I was going away, inftead of which I found myfelf at his houfe, where he had got my carriages conveyed, and where he had ordered a handfome dinner to be got ready. As he was a man well verfed in his own department, and well acquainted with the country, he furnifhed

me

me with many useful observations in geography, as well as on the mines, and led me, after dinner, into a room, where he had reposited the most curious pieces of ore. These consisted in a heap of wood mineralized by a dissolution of copper. They appeared exceedingly beautiful to the eye, from the variety of colors these woods exhibited; and were still more curious upon a nearer inspection, on account of the several crystallizations formed in them. I could not contain the exceeding pleasure this sight afforded me; which the Russian perceiving, began to think himself in possession of a treasure. I picked out several pieces of these woods, and my choice did not certainly light upon the least beautiful amongst them. But the director, who at first appeared to take a pleasure in offering them to me, seemed now to be rather dissatisfied with my freedom: I perceived this, and took away only a few small pieces. I desired him, however, not to build his own or his master's fortune upon this collection, which was indeed very curious to a naturalist, but of little intrinsic value. I went away extremely pleased with all the civility I had received from the director of this foundery, and arrived at Tikonofka on the 24th, at four in the morning. I found it so difficult to get horses at this place, that I could not get away before nine o'clock. Almost as soon as I came out of this village, I discovered another chain of mountains, rising almost imperceptibly. The space between the first chain and this, is merely an extensive plain, on which some few hillocks are to be found. The soil was cultivated in some places only, where, however, nothing but barley was sown; at least I did not see any other kind of grain.

The road grew worse as we advanced in this ridge of mountains, which appeared to me, in all respects, different from the former chain, where the mountains were sometimes elongated and of an easy ascent: these, on the contrary, although

rather

rather low, were so steep that it was difficult to get up them; the soil was also changed here. From Tobolsky to this second chain, the earth had appeared black and greasy; but in these last mountains, it was yellowish and more hard.

I was very near being killed, at the distance of a few leagues from Birna, by the carelessness of a postilion. The drivers in Russia, so far from taking care gently to descend the little mountains they meet with, as is customary in all other parts of the world, come down from them, on the contrary, at full speed. They cross the interval between two little hills at the same rate, and soon reach the top of the opposite mountain; but if they should happen not to clear the interval completely, it is impossible to prevent the carriage from being broken to pieces, as the horses cannot be stopped at this instant. Having crossed the river Tourka, I went up a small mountain, which I soon after descended on the opposite side. The road was winding, and upon the brink of a precipice: my coachman galloped down this mountain so fast, that not having taken care to turn short enough in an angle of the road, the horses lost the track, and I expected to see both the carriage and horses tumble down the precipice. It happened luckily, that one of the horses fell, I immediately sprang out of the carriage, and seized the others by the reins. As we were instantly assisted, this event turned out to be of no other consequence to any body but the coachman, whom his companions seized without my perceiving them, and took him to the wood, where they layed him flat on the ground, and were beating him so unmercifully with sticks, that they would certainly have killed him, if I had not intervened, on hearing him cry out. I ordered him a glass of brandy, and the moment after, he was as merry as before his punishment. He got up again on the coach box, singing, and thinking no more of what had happened; so that notwithstanding this discipline, and the strict charge

charge I gave him, to go gently down the hills, he was still inclined to gallop down them: I was therefore obliged to take a stick into my carriage, to prevent him; and, whenever we were going down a hill, I rested the stick upon his shoulders, to caution him against going fast.

At length I came to Birna, a village inhabited by Tartars; many of whom came out to meet me, at the distance of a werst from the village, expressing, by signs, their great desire to serve me. It was evident, from the candor and tranquillity observable in their countenances, that these professions were sincere; so that I followed them without any apprehensions. They placed themselves before my carriage, and conducted me to the house of the chief person in the village, who was held in great estimation among them: his merit and his virtues had entitled him to rule over them, without the form of an election. They had prepared a kind of dinner for me, consisting of honey, butter, and a few vegetables. Their houses are as neat, as those of the Siberians are dirty. In other respects they live nearly after the same manner, except that they are Mahometans.

Their dress has some resemblance to that of the Russians. The Tartars wear a woollen jacket, which they bind with their girdle; over this they have a full long robe hanging loose and flowing. They always have boots on. Their heads are shaved, except on one spot at the back part, which they cover with a small piece of leather. They wear a cap edged with fur. They are tall, strong, and well made; and their dress is perfectly becoming. Notwithstanding the mildness of their countenances, they have still the appearance of a warlike and independent people; and have indeed preserved their former privileges. In war-time, they furnish the Russians with a certain number of troops, which are kept in pay by the latter.

The

The dress of the Tartar women differs but little from that of the men; it is shorter, and they wear the girdle above the robe. Their head-dress is a cap, sometimes made in form of a sugar loaf, and covered with copecs and glass beads; a large piece of cloth fastened to the back part of the cap, and hanging down below the waist, is ornamented in the same manner. They wear boots, and might be taken for men at first sight, if not distinguished by their head-dress. They share most of their husbands labours, by whom they are very mildly treated, and there is not the least superiority on either side. The married women seemed to enjoy a perfect freedom: the girls on the contrary are much confined; but notwithstanding the watchfulness of fathers and mothers, they contrive to slip away upon some occasions, which they make the most of. In Siberia, the married women are confined, and the girls left more at liberty, which they also do not fail to take advantage of, as we have before observed, so that in all these countries the girls seem to be very troublesome.

The dress of the Russians differs from that of the Tartars, inasmuch as the first wear a kind of waistcoat instead of a tunic, and that they often leave their shirts hanging out of their breeches. Over the waistcoat, they wear a kind of jacket with a girdle. They have no boots, but wrap up their legs in cloth, which they fasten from the bottom with a cord. Their shoes are commonly made of the bark of trees. All the common people of Russia have kept their beards, and they all wear caps. The dress of the Tartars is in every respect preferable to that of the Russian men: the first is elegant, but the latter scanty. The same cannot be said of the dress of the women. That of the Tartar women is generally more rich, but not always so pleasing. The Russian women, when at home, wear above their shifts a tunic, which reaches down to their heels, and is buttoned at the fore-part. When they go out of doors, they put on a gown over this, and sometimes a mantle. Their head-dress is more like a hat than any thing else, and is usually ornamented with copecs and glass beads. The girls dress in the same manner, excepting only that they have never any caps on, and that they only bind their heads with a kind of ribband.

When I left Birna, the Tartars doubled my number of horses, on account of the mountains we were to cross, without making any difference in the price; neither would they accept of any consideration for the entertainment they had given me.

The roads became terrible at a small distance from this village; for although the mountains were but small, yet they were so steep, and the rain had made them so slippery, that notwithstanding the utmost efforts of the postilions, and the draught of the greater number of our horses fixed to one carriage, yet we were still scarce able to gain the top of the mountain, although every one of us was on foot. On our coming to other mountains, the same difficulties occurred, which were the more fatiguing both to men and horses, as each carriage required the same management. Mine being the lightest, I took the lead, in order to send assistance to the rest from the next hamlet; but I could not get farther than a mile beyond the place where I left them.

I was then on the borders of the river Tourka, in a bottom, surrounded by mountains; where the watchmaker and my interpreter soon came up with me. Having waited here two hours in vain for the other carriages, I sent back some Tartars to them, with some of the horses I had taken with me.

The other carriages appeared at one in the morning: I had left the postilions some flambeaus, which they had lighted, and which made me discern them from afar. The Tartars, who had stayed along with me, then went to meet them, and in order to give them light, they set fire at certain distances to the fir-trees they met with on the road. These trees, which were very lofty, catching the flame in an instant, were of great service to them, and at the same time exhibited a remarkable and curious sight, appearing like so many fire-works lighted upon the slopes and upon the tops of these mountains. I had all the carriages placed round a fire, and the horses were fastened to pickets in the rear. I distributed some brandy among the people, and we all eat a very hearty supper. After having rested themselves for an hour, my people set about mending the carriages, while I laid myself down by the fire upon a bear's skin: I slept very little, and rising a few hours after, I went to take a view of these mountains, while they were getting ready to march. From the beginning of this chain, I had as yet seen no other than birch-trees on the road, but at the distance of six wersts from the place where I had passed the night, I had met with fir-trees all around, as in the former chain of mountains; but with this difference, that these trees were much thicker, very lofty, and appeared to thrive well; so that these two chains seemed to differ entirely with respect to the soil and the produce; the earth is rather of a yellowish than black colour.

I set out at seven in the morning, and immediately got upon a very high and very steep mountain. We had a great deal of trouble in getting up to the top of it, because of the rain that fell, which made the way so bad, that the men, although on foot, could hardly climb up. At length we arrived about noon at the post of Pisse; a hamlet on the borders of the river which bears the same name, and situated near the end of the chain. Here again I met with fir-trees all about, and the soil was still yellowish. The firs were from three to five feet in diameter, and near fourscore feet high. The wood was very thick, on account of the number of plants and shrubs with which it abounded; when, on the contrary, in the first chain, especially in the neighbourhood of Echaterinenburg, the earth was bare, and the fir-trees we faw were very low, ftunted, and did not thrive well.

From the beginning of this fecond chain I had not feen any of the ground cultivated, as it is in the confines of Piffe, where the country begins to be more open. The corn, which had been lately fown, was already more than two inches high, and was therefore farther advanced than at Tobolfky, at the beginning of July. I only ftopped at this hamlet to change horfes, and reached Offa about three in the afternoon. This is a fmall town on the borders of the river Kama; part of it is fituated on an eminence, with a flight fortification. Offa is in the midft of a very open plain, which is almoft entirely cultivated. When I left this place, I travelled along the borders of the Kama, and at two leagues from hence, got again into the woods, which I had quitted nearly at the fame diftance on the other fide of the town. The rain had made the roads extremely bad. I did not reach Cracova till one in the morning, although I had travelled all night by the light of flambeaus. Finding no horfes in this hamlet, I refolved to pafs the night there. A large fire was kindled in the middle of the ftreet, and all my people laid themfelves down on ftraw round about it. I had my matrafs carried into the neareft houfe, where I flept. I rofe very early, and going down into the ftreet, found all my attendants faft afleep: they feemed to be fo happy, that I let them fleep on till day-break. I mended their fire, which was almoft out, looked at the carriages, and went away at eight o'clock. At noon, I came to the borders of the Kama. This river, which we croffed in a fmall boat pufhed on by oars, appeared to be more than one hundred toifes over: we were eighteen minutes in croffing it with four oars. I was affured, it was thirty or forty feet deep. The croffing of this river is very dangerous, on account of the fmallnefs of

the

the ferry ufed for this purpofe. The large carriages muft be placed acrofs the boat, fo that if there was not the greateft care taken to prevent their flipping, the boat would tip over upon the leaft motion. When I had paffed the Kama, I was in hopes of travelling in better roads, and a more populous country: it had already froze twice, fo that the mornings were very cold. The ground was covered every morning with hoar-froft; the leaves fell from the trees; and the fruits dropped from their ftalks, fo that the roads were covered with them. Every circumftance foretold the approach of winter, and nothing was to be feen, but the melancholy green of the firs. I was ftill at the diftance of four or five hundred leagues from St. Peterfburg, and as I feared being overtaken by the winter, I made very few ftops. I arrived on the 28th at Sowialova, after having experienced feveral accidents; and upon one of thefe occafions, two of my foldiers had been hurt.

Sowialova is a hamlet inhabited by the Wotiaks. I refolved to fpend part of a day with thefe people, on account of their fingular appearance and drefs. Some authors have reckoned them among the Tartars, but I could not obferve the leaft analogy between the two nations. The Wotiak men and women, in general, are no more than four feet, a few inches high, and are of a very weak and delicate conftitution. The drefs of the men is the fame as that of the Ruffians; but the drefs of the women has not the leaft refemblance to thefe I have feen in Siberia. They wear a fhift of coarfe linen, flit at the bofom like a man's fhirt; and hemmed at this opening with thread or worfted of different colors. There is alfo a little ornament of a triangular figure wrought on the right fide of the fhift. Their gown is woollen, and bears a great refemblance to the habit of the Jefuits in college; the fleeves of the upper gown are flit in the middle, to give paffage to the arms; and the lower part of the fleeve generally hangs down.

down. This gown, which reaches down to the legs, is faſtened at the fore-part merely by a girdle, curiouſly wrought. They wear alſo coarſe cloth ſtockings and ſandals, the ſame as the Ruſſians. Their head-dreſs is very remarkable: they firſt wrap up their heads with a towel, over which they faſten, with two ſtrings, a kind of helmet, made of the bark of a tree, and ornamented at the fore part with a piece of cloth and with copecs. This helmet is afterwards covered with a handkerchief, wrought with thread or worſted of various colors, and edged with a fringe. This head-dreſs is above one foot high. Their hair is divided into two treſſes, which fall down upon the breaſt with a necklace, ſuch as the Tartars wear. One of my attendants, being deſirous of examining this necklace, opened one of theſe women's ſhifts in ſuch a manner as to uncover all her breaſt, at which ſhe was ſo far from being diſpleaſed, although it was done in public, that ſhe laughed at his curioſity.

M. Strahlemberg thinks theſe people ſome of the moſt ancient in Siberia *. They have profeſſed Chriſtianity for ſeveral years paſt, but are ſo ignorant, that they have not the leaſt idea of this religion. The Ruſſians ſent them prieſts, and ſome troops, to convert them. I found a Ruſſian miſſionary at Sowialova, who was deputed to inſtruct and baptize them. Although he was unacquainted with their language, he nevertheleſs made Chriſtians of them; ſo that they ſtill adhere to all the ſuperſtitious parts of their religion.

As I was deſirous of purchaſing one of the women's dreſſes, one was brought me, which they ſold me for about a guinea. As ſoon as the people of the village were acquainted with this circumſtance, they got together, and claimed the dreſs back again; for they looked upon this as a ſacrilegious bargain,

* Tom. ii. page 153.

the punishment of which would fall on the village, becaufe they are obliged, by the articles of their religion, to bury the women with their cloaths on. The woman from whom I had bought the drefs, was called upon to anfwer the charge brought againft her: fhe owned, fhe had fold it; but alledged in her defence, that it belonged to her late mother, who lived at the time they were made Chriftians, when the Emprefs had forbidden them to bury the dead with their cloaths on. The woman was acquitted; but the Wotiaks were ftill inclined to make me return the drefs; which I fhould not have been able to keep, without the affiftance of the foldiers, who were put in a pofture of defence.

The Wotiak women are generally very ugly, and more flovenly than any other people of the north, accept the Samoyedes; according to the account I received of them from Ruffians who have travelled in that province. The Samoyedes never wear any fhift: their drefs is made of the fkin of the reindeer, in form of a bag. Their ftockings are of the fame fkin, and they fometimes wear fandals, according to the Ruffian fafhion. A Ruffian, who has travelled among the Samoyedes, made me a prefent of one of thefe dreffes, from which the plate was taken.

I did not get away from Sowialova till it was very late; I then went through feveral hamlets, inhabited by Wotiaks and Tartars, and on the 29th, at eight in the evening, reached the borders of the river Wiatka. The method of croffing this river is upon a bridge, made of two boats, pufhed on by oars. This river is not fo wide as the Kama, but the ftream is more rapid, and the paffage fo dangerous, on account of the rocks, that the watermen would not go over with us becaufe the wind was too high. I determined therefore to pafs the night on the banks of the river. A large fire was lighted; I had a kind of tent built up with branches of trees; and, after fupper, I laid

myfelf

myself down on a bear's skin. About midnight I awaked, quite frozen and covered with snow: at first, I knew not whether I was in a dream; but the snow fell all night, so that in the morning, it lay above half a foot deep on the ground. I crossed the river on this moving bridge in twelve minutes. The quantity of snow which had fallen, had made the roads so bad, that I could not reach the hamlet Scynd, without the utmost difficulty, although every body travelled this short post on foot, in order to ease the horses. I was very undetermined about the manner of pursuing my journey, and spent the greater part of the morning, considering whether I should quit my carriages and take to sledges, or whether I should still run the risque of going on with my wheel carriages. This last scheme appeared to be attended with some danger; but on the other hand I was assured, that I should find no snow when I came near Cazan, and should therefore be obliged to quit my sledges.

I set out at last with my wheel-carriages, although it snowed very hard: the number of my horses was doubled; so that I had now two and forty of them. I fed them with plenty of oats; and distributed brandy among the postilions, and by these helps arrived at Sicchi the same day, at ten in the evening, notwithstanding the extreme badness of the roads. In the course of this day's journey, I passed through several villages inhabited by Tartars, whose dress differs in some particulars from that of the Tartars of Siberia: these people were more polished, but they still preserved the simplicity and purity of their manners.

As I came nearer to Cazan, the snow diminished; and disappeared entirely at Wiscogora. Here are extensive meadows, in which the grass, pushed up a second time, displayed the verdure of the spring: the face of the country became every instant more pleasing, and the sky more serene; the hoar-frost had not yet deprived the trees of their leaves; and I saw, for the firſt time ſince my arrival in Ruſſia, ſome oaks in the neighbourhood of Cazan, and ſome fruit trees in places ſomething like orchards, inſtead of the frozen lands of Siberia, and the deſerts full of firs, and ſcarcely inhabited by any thing but animals, moſt of which are unknown in Europe. I now travelled upon little hillocks cut acroſs pleaſant groves, whoſe ſhade I ſought for, as much as I wiſhed to avoid it a few days before. The fruitfulneſs of the country was apparent from the richneſs of the villages; in which we met with gardens ſkilfully laid out, and ſtill adorned with flowers. Every object then reminded me of my coming nearer to my own country; an agreeable recollection, of which none can be ſenſible, except thoſe who have experienced it.

I arrived at Cazan the firſt of October; where a Tartar Prince was the governor, who received me very graciouſly: he had ordered an apartment to be got ready for me; but M. Weroffchin, a Ruſſian, whom I had the honor of ſeeing at St. Peterſburg, had been ſo kind as to give me a lodging at his houſe, to which I was conducted.

The next day I waited upon the governor; after a few compliments had paſſed, which I did not underſtand, we ſeated ourſelves round a table covered with a beautiful carpet; on which were placed four large pipes and a china bowl, full of Chineſe tobacco: I ſmoked for a few minutes. After this ſome *liqueurs* of the country were ſerved up, with ſweetmeats, fruits and a water melon; which laſt fruit is ſo exceedingly delicious here, that I eat nothing elſe. Melons are in great plenty at Cazan; and never do any hurt, how much ſoever one may eat of them. I found this fruit ſo much better than any I had ever met with of the kind any where elſe, that I brought away ſome of the ſeeds, but they did not anſwer in France.

The archbiſhop ſent to deſire me to come down to his country houſe, ſituated in the neighbourhood of the town; and was so obliging as to send several carriages to convey me and my attendants. I there got acquainted with a prelate, well versed in the sciences, in history and literature; and deserving the high veneration he is held in all over Russia: he was the only clergyman I met with in these extensive dominions, who did not appear to be astonished at my coming from Paris to Tobolsky, in order to observe the Transit of Venus.

I stopped several days at Cazan, and made some astronomical observations there; contributing to determine, with precision, the position of this city, which still retains some marks of its former affluence, although its trade is almost come to nothing. The houses are very well built, notwithstanding they are most of them made of wood. There is a great deal of nobility here, who live upon a very agreeable footing among themselves. All the necessary and useful things of life are in great plenty, even game, fish and fruits. White bread is also here in use, which is as little known in Siberia, as pine apples are. Wine alone is very scarce at Cazan, but the people have a method of making it with various kinds of fruits: this wine does not differ much from the natural juice of the grape either in color or in taste; but is very unwholsome, on account of the brandy, which is the basis of it.

The manners are as different from those of Siberia, as the climate. The women do the honors of their table, and add to the agreeableness of the company, of which they are a part, as at Mosco and St. Petersburg.

A great many of the inhabitants of Cazan are Tartars; who are so far from being persecuted there, that, on the contrary, they are treated with the utmost consideration; so that they are firmly attached to their sovereign. They have preserved the innocence of their manners, their probity, and their truth; and are most of them possessed of small fortunes. Their dress is much richer than that of the other Tartars I have
already

already spoken of: the dress of the women is even different in some respects, chiefly with regard to their head; for I never saw any caps there in form of a sugar loaf. Their head-dress is very similar to that of the Russians, except that they have jewels and pearls intermixed with their hair. They also make ornaments of the same kind, some of which they put upon the sleeves of their gowns; others are fastened round the neck, and hang down upon the breast.

The city of Cazan is very large and well peopled. M. de Schouvalof, one of the greatest patrons of literature in Russia, had persuaded the Empress Elizabeth to establish a Gymnasium, or school there for the education of youth. M. Werofkin, a Russian, had the direction of it: he had eight Professors under him; two for the French, two for the German, two for the Latin, and one for the Russian language; and one fencing-master, who at the same time taught dancing. The salaries of these Professors, were one hundred and fifty roubles, or seven hundred and fifty French livres. Notwithstanding the smallness of these salaries, all these different languages and exercises are taught with great success, by the attention and management of M. Werofkin. He was a man of science, and joined to all his learning the art of knowing how to manage men who were placed in a state of subordination to him; and of training up properly the youth entrusted to his care: he was a man of uncommon talents, and very fit for the situation he was placed in; in which, however, for the misfortune of this rising school, he did not long continue. His distinguished merit had raised him enemies among those who were engaged in the same pursuits. Envy and jealousy haunted him every where. Although he was at the distance of four hundred leagues from the capital, yet they were continually persecuting him: and the plots laid against him were so much the more successful, as while he was employed at Cazan in being useful to his country, he knew not from what quarter they came, or was not at hand to guard against them. In the most enlightened parts of the world, envy and jealousy are enemies from whom men of letters have most to fear, but they are less dangerous than among nations of ignorance. In a learned society, the poison of envy and jealousy stings at last those persons from whom it came, and the man of superior talents always gets the better; but in ignorant countries, the men of some little knowledge are more interested in pulling down the man of superior talents; and as the unknowing country must be guided by the first class of men, it generally coincides with their iniquitous designs. M. de Schouvalof, who was M. Werofkin's patron, and the Empress Elizabeth's favourite, had always protected him. When that Empress died he lost his influence; and M. Werofkin immediately became the victim of envy: he would have been very happy, if at the same time that he lost his place, he did not add to the number of the unfortunate people of Siberia.

I looked every where about the neighbourhood of Cazan, for the famous plant called borametz, which M. l'Abbe Lambert speaks of, in his civil and natural history. According to that gentleman's account, this plant resembles a lamb, having all the parts of that animal, with a very delicate fleece, which the women use as a covering to their heads. The plant is furnished with a small portion of blood and flesh: has no horns, but a tuft of wool in imitation of them: it lives and feeds as long as there is green grass about it; but this zoophyte, or animal plant, decays as soon as the neighbouring grass is dried up.

It cannot be imagined that M. Lambert took all these absurdities for granted, his intention in mentioning them, was certainly merely to engage travellers, to examine from whence this ridiculous fable could possibly have arisen. Notwithstanding my endeavours, I could not procure any of this

plant,

plant, which is unknown at Cazan. It is to be seen in the King's gardens, and some writers have classed it among the mosses, but it does not agree in any particular with the story given by M. Lambert.

I left Cazan at four in the afternoon, and reached the banks of the Wolga by eighteen minutes after seven. The river appeared to be about two hundred toises over in this place; and I was told it was ten toises, or sixty feet deep. The weather was calm; and the waters of this river, which is one of the finest in Europe, were not in the least agitated. I crossed the stream in a boat, pulled by six watermen, and was seventeen minutes going over. I was told at Tobolsky and at Cazan, that a great number of pirates were to be met with hereabouts, and even that the people used to amuse themselves with shooting them as they did ducks; but I never saw any of these pirates, although I travelled the space of a hundred leagues along the borders of this river. On the 8th instant, I arrived at Kusmodemiansk, after having passed through a country inhabited by another set of people called Schuwachi. Their dress is nearly the same as that of the Russians; they profess Christianity, but are as ignorant as the Wotiakes; and have, in the same manner, adhered to all their superstitions.

At Kusmodemiansk, I came into the same road I had taken to go to Tobolsky: the nearer I came to St. Petersburg, which lies more northward, the more sensible was I of the cold from one day to another, and the greater difficulties did I meet with in travelling with wheel-carriages: some rivers were already frozen over: at length, however, I arrived at St. Petersburg on the 1st of November, 1761. I spent the winter in this city with the Baron de Breteuil, who treated me with infinite kindness. I embarked in the spring, as soon as the sea would admit of it, in order to return to France, where I arrived in the month of August, 1762, near two years after my first setting out from thence.

Of GEOGRAPHY.

OUR knowledge in geography is still very much circumscribed. In the year 1761, we had determined the exact situation of a few places only, in the whole course of the distance from Strasburg to Tobolsky, which is between fourteen and fifteen hundred leagues. M. Cassini de Thury, in his journey to Vienna, has rectified several positions, between the borders of France and this capital of Austria, by geometrical observations. Russia has been the chief object of my inquiries, because it is less known than any of the other countries I have passed through.

My determinations of the geography of this country are founded on astronomical observations, made only on the places I was obliged to pass through on the road; because it is impossible to trace a map of Russia, merely from such information as may be gathered from the inhabitants, especially with regard to places from which they are at any distance. I was the more careful in making my observations on the places through which I passed, as the Russian maps of the Atlas, published in 1745, give but a very imperfect sketch of the geography of this country, where one may travel sometimes near a hundred leagues together, without finding the position of one of these places, throughout such an extent, mentioned in these maps. The road from Cazan to Ossa is an instance of this; although it lies partly through a very populous country, where there are posts erected from mile to mile, on which the distances are marked.

This Russian atlas, imperfect as it is, does credit to those who published it, and would of itself alone be a monument sufficient

sufficient to immortalize the memory of Peter the First. Before this great man came to the throne, an attempt to acquire the least knowledge of this empire, was punished with death. Since the reign of that monarch, the academy of St. Petersburg has collected several important materials towards compleating the geography of Russia: some able persons have been employed for several years past in arranging them; and the public will certainly soon reap the benefit of their labours.

Of France, and its Frontiers.

I might perhaps have omitted giving any account of the geography of this kingdom, as most of the maps are in print; but these are not in every one's possession: besides, that it will be of use for the reader to have before his eyes the disposition of my route, together with the level I have reduced it to.

Each chapter is divided into three parts. The first contains a table of the longitudes and latitudes, mostly ascertained from astronomical observations; the second, a journal of my route; and the third, the geographical accounts I have thought it necessary to give. The longitudes and latitudes distinguished by asterisks *, have been determined with the greatest nicety by astronomers of repute.

Those marked with a cross †, are less certain; and those which are not marked, are taken upon the credit of travellers.

The second column of the following table, marks the difference of the meridians between that of the royal observatory at Paris, and the meridians of the place of which the position is given. The longitudes are determined with respect to the islands of Ferro, and I have set down the longitude of Paris at 19 degrees, 53 minutes, 45 seconds, according to the last observations of the academy.

TABLE

TABLE of the longitudes and latitudes of some parts of France and its Frontiers.

Names of the Places.	Difference of the Meridians.			Longitudes.			Latitudes.		
	H.	M.	S.	D.	M.	S.	D.	M.	S.
Abbeville	0°	2	1 West	19	24	0	50°	7	1
Altorf	0°	35	25 East	23	45	0	49	17	38
Angiers	0°	11	35 W.	17	0	0	47°	28	8
Avranches	0°	14	51 W.	16	11	0	48°	41	18
Auxerre	0°	4	57 E.	21	8	0	47°	47	54
Basil	0	21	0 E.	25	9	0	47	35	0
Besan‚on	0°	14	50 E.	23	39	0	47°	13	45
Bitche	0°	20	25 E.	25	0	0	49°	2	28
Bourdeaux	0°	11	39 W.	16	59	0	44°	50	18
Brest	0°	27	23 W.	13	3	0	48°	23	0
Caen	0°	10	47 W.	17	12	0	49°	11	10
Chalons on the Marne	0°	8	9 E.	21	56	0	48°	57	12
Chartres	0°	3	24 W.	19	3	0	48°	26	49
Cherbourg	0°	15	53 W.	15	56	0	49°	38	26
Coutances	0°	15	10 W.	16	7	0	49°	2	50
Dijon	0°	10	50 E.	22	36	0	47°	19	22
Dole in Bretany	0°	16	25 W.	15	48	0	48°	33	9
Evreux	0°	4	45 W.	18	43	0	49°	1	24
Francfort on the Maine *	0.	25	0 E.	26	9	0	50°	6	0
Granville	0°	15	48 W.	15	57	0	48°	50	11
Ingolstadt †	0°	36	10 E.	28	57	0	48°	47	0
Landau	0°	23	10 E.	25	42	0	49°	11	40
Lisle	0°	2	57 E.	20	38	0	50°	37	50
Mayence	0°	24	0 E.	25	54	0	49°	54	0
Meaux	0°	2	10 E.	20	27	0	48°	57	37
Metz	0°	15	24 E.	23	45	0	49°	7	5
Munich ‡	0°	37	13 E.	29	12	0	48°	9	55
Nancy	0°	15	26 E.	23	46	0	48°	41	28
Nantes	0°	15	35 W.	16	0	0	47°	13	17
Noyon	0°	2	43 E.	20	35	0	49°	34	37
Orleans	0°	1	43 W.	19	28	0	47°	54	4
Paris	0°	0	0	19	53	45	48°	50	10
Reims	0°	6	52 E.	21	37	0	49°	14	36
Rennes	0°	16	8 W.	15	52	0	48°	6	45
Rouen	0°	4	59 W.	18	39	0	49°	26	43
Saint Malo	0°	17	29 W.	15	32	0	48°	38	59
Saint Omer	0°	0	20 W.	19	49	0	50°	44	46
Saint Paul de Leon	0°	25	21 W.	13	34	0	48°	40	55
Seez	0°	8	41 W.	17	44	0	48°	36	21
Senlis	0°	1	0 E.	20	9	9	49°	12	23
Sens	0°	3	48 E.	20	51	0	43°	11	56
Soissons	0°	3	58 E.	20	53	0	49°	22	32
Strasburg	0°	21	45 E.	25	20	0	48°	34	35
Toul	0°	14	15 E.	23	28	0	48°	40	27
Tours	0°	6	35 W.	18	15	0	47°	23	44
Troys	0°	7	0 E.	21	39	0	48°	18	2
Verdun	0°	12	11 E.	22	57	0	49°	9	18
Versailles	0°	0	51 W.	19	41	0	48°	48	18

* M. Cassini de Thuri has determined the latitude of this town, in 1762, at 50 degrees 6 minutes, instead of 49 degrees 55 minutes, as it had been always reckoned. Voyage de M. Cassini, en Allemagne, page 22. † Ingolstadt. Voyage de M. Cassini, page 139. ‡ Munich. Ibidem.

TABLE, containing a journal of the road from Paris to Brest, and to Tobolsky in Siberia.

Names of the places.	Leagues of 2000 toises.	Names of the places.	Leagues of 2000 toises.	Names of the places.	Leagues of 2000 toises.
From Paris to Brest.		Saint Brieux	2	Jaalons	2¼
		Chatelaudrin	5¼	Matougues	1
Paris from the Observatory		Guingamp	3¼	Chalons	2¼
Nanterre	3¼	Goismormant	2½	Chepy	2½
Saint Germain	1¾	Bellisle	2½	La Chaussée	2½
Triel	3¼	Pontir	2¼	Saint Amand	1¼
Meulan	2	Pontou	2¼	Vitry le François	3
Mantes	3¾	Morlaix	4	Faremont	2¾
Bonnieres	3¼	Saint Egone	2	Perthé	2¼
Pacy	4	Landivisiaw	2¼	Saint Dizier	2½
Evreux	4½	Landernau	3	Saudrup	3¼
La Commanderie	4½	Quipava	3	Bar-le-Duc	3
La Riviere	4½	Brest	2	Ligny	4
Marché-neuf	2½			Saint Aubin	2¼
L'Hottêllerie	3¾	From Paris to Strasburg.		Void	3¾
Lisieux	3½			Laye	3
Saint Aubin	2½	Paris Observatory		Toul	2½
River Diva	2	Bondy	3¾	Velaine	3
Moult	3¼	Vergalant	2	Nancy	3
Caen	4¼	Claye	2¼	Vic	7¼
Mouen	2¾	Meaux	3¾	Chateau Salins	1½
Villers-le-Bocage	3¾	Saint-Jean	2¾	Hellimer	9
Saint Martin	4½	La Ferté	2¼	Sarreguemine	6¾
Pont-Farcy	4½	Montreuil	2½	Bitche	7½
Ville-Dieu	4½	Vivret	2½	Goetzbruck	2¼
Avranches	5¼	Chateau Thierry	1¾	Grebentenberg, mt.	1
Pont-Orson	5	Pavoy	2¼	Kesleberg, mt.	0½
Dole, reckoned to Brest	5	Dormans	2½	Vimmenau	0¾
Dinant	6	Port à Binson	2¼	Bouxveiller	3½
'ego	5	La Cave	1	Brumptein	5¼
ambale	4	Epernay	2¾	Strasburg	4¼
rangles	2	Plivot	2¼		

From this journal it appears, that the distance from Paris to Brest is 145 leagues of 2000 toises each, or 127 leagues of 2282 toises, which make the 25th part of the mean degree of the meridian, which I suppose to be 1,570,060 toises; and the distance from Paris to Strasburg is 137 leagues of 2000 toises each, or one hundred and twenty leagues, reckoning 25 to a degree.

Of Germany and its Frontiers.

At Ulm I embarked on the Danube for Vienna; and in this passage traced the course of this river with great exactness, determined its windings with a compass, and computed the distances with a watch that marked the seconds.

TABLE of the longitudes and latitudes of some parts of Germany and its frontiers.

Names of the places.	Difference of the meridians.			Longitudes.			Latitudes.		
	H.	M.	S.	D.	M.	S.	D.	M.	S.
Alba regalis	1	5	10	36	12	0	47	13	0
Agria	1	11	30	37	47	0	47	42	0
Breslau	0	59	15	34	42	0	51	3	0
Bude	1†	9	52	37	22	0	47†	28	0
Caschau	1	4	30	38	32	0	48	27	0
Dillingen	0*	31	38	27	49	0	48	30	0
Grats	0	52	44	33	5	0	47	17	0
Lints	0	46	30	31	31	0	48*	16	0
Neustat	0	56	58	34	9	0	47	58	0
Nurenberg	0*	34	56	28	38	0	49†	26	0
Olmuts	1	0	49	35	6	0	49	43	0
Passau	0	42	50	30	37	0	48	30	0
Pest	1†	9	55	27	25	0	47†	29	0
Polling (¹)	0*	35	0	28	39	0	47*	48	8
Presburg	1	0	33	35	2	0	48	8	0
Ratisbon	0	38	25	29	30	0	49	2	0
Salisburg	0	41	30	30	17	0	47	34	0
Tyrnau	1*	0	55	35	8	0	48*	23	30
Vienna	0*	56	10	33	57	0	48*	12	32
Vilna	1	35	25	43	15	0	54	24	0
Ulm	0	30	25	27	30	0	48	23	0

(1) Voyage de M. de Cassini en Allemagne, page 140.

TABLE, containing a journal of the road from Paris to Tobolſky in Siberia, Straſburg, Vienna, and Bilitz.

Names of the places.	German miles of 3804 toiſes.	French leagues of 2000 toiſes.	Names of the places.	German miles of 3804 toiſes.	French leagues of 2000 toiſes.	Names of the places.	German miles of 3804 toiſes.	French leagues of 2000 toiſes.
Straſburg								
Kehl	1	2	Greyn	2	3¾	Elchingen	2	3¾
Biſchofſheim	2	3¾	Wirpel	1	2	Guntzburg	2	3¾
Stollhofen	2	3¾	Ips	2	3¾	Sommerhauſen	3	5¾
Raſtadt	2	3¾	Marbach	1	2	Auſburg	3	5¾
Etlingue	2	3¾	Molch	2	3¾	Degenbach	3	5¾
Pforzheim	3	5¾	Wiendorf	2½	4¾	Oberbruck	3	5¾
Enzweig	3	5¾	Crems	1½	3	Munich	4	7½
Calſtadt	3	5¾	Stokerau	7	13½	Anzing	3	5¾
Blochingue	2	3¾	Koreiburg	1½	3	Hag	3	5¾
Goeppingue	2	3¾	Klauſter-Neuburg	0¾	1½	Ampfing	3	5¾
Geiſling	2	3¾	Vienna	2½	4¾	Oetting	3	5¾
Weſterſtoedten	2	3¾	Wolkerſdorf	3	5¾	Markel	2	3¾
Ulm on the Danube	3	5¾	Gaunerſdorf	2	3¾	Braunau	2	3¾
Gienzburg	3	5¾	Boyſdorf	3	5¾	Altheim	2	3¾
Diling	3	5¾	Nickolſburg	2	3¾	Reit	3	5¾
Donaweſt	4	7½	Porlitz	3	5¾	Haag	2	3¾
Neuburg	3½	6¾	Brunn	3	5¾	Lambach	3	5¾
Ingolſtat	3	5¾	Wiſchau	4	7½	Vels	2	3¾
Neuſtat	3½	6¾	Kremſier	4	7½	Lints	4	7½
Ratiſbon	5	10	Biſtritz	3	5¾	Ens	3	5¾
Straubin	4½	9	Meſeritſch	2	3¾	Strenberg	2	3¾
Dekendorf	4	7½	Neutiſchein	2	3¾	Amſtoetten	3	5¾
Vilſhoven	4	7½	Friedeck	4	7½	Kemmelbach	2	3¾
Paſſau	4	7½	Teſchen	3	5¾	Molck	3	5¾
Effertingen	9	17¼	Skotſchau	2	3¾	Poelten	3	5¾
Lints	3	5¾	Bilitz	2	3¾	Perſling	2	3¾
Spilberg	3	5¾	From Weſterſtoedten to Vienna by land.			Siegharts-Kirche	2	3¾
Iten	3	5¾				Bourkerſdorf	2	3¾
Waltſe	0½	1	Weſterſtoedten			Vienna	2	3¾

The diſtance from Weſterſtoedten to Vienna, paſſing by Ulm, and following the courſe of the Danube, is 169 leagues of 2000 toiſes each; by land it is 144: and the diſtance from Straſburg to Vienna is 215 leagues of 2000 toiſes.

In this journal I have ſet down the German mile at 3804 toiſes, ſuppoſing that there are fifteen of theſe miles in a

 degree,

degree, and computing the mean degree of the meridian at 57,060 toifes of the ftandard meafure of Paris.

According to this journal, the diftance from Strafburg to Bilitz, following the courfe of the Danube, is 294 leagues of 2000 toifes, and 258 leagues computed at 25 to a degree, which league I reckon at 2282 toifes.

After having croffed the black mountains, which are parallel to thofe called Vofgi, we pafs by Wirtemberg. This country, although generally flat, is divided by a number of fmall hills. The mountains of the Danube begin about the neighbourhood of Ulm, at the diftance of a few leagues: thefe mountains are nothing more than hills at firft; they become imperceptibly clofer to each other, and are gradually elevated, as one proceeds to Vienna. The bed of the Danube is fometimes confiderably ftraitened between thefe two ridges of mountains, which at other times are feparated at feveral leagues diftance, and form large bafons.

From the fummit of thefe mountains may be feen thofe of Bohemia to the north, and thofe of Tirol to the fouth: thefe laft are a branch of that large chain, which rifes from the fea-fide in Galicia, croffes part of the globe from weft to eaft, in going from Spain through France and Switzerland, and afterwards extends as far as China.

I have been told by people of the country, that the mountains of the Danube were not fo high as thofe of Bohemia, and that the mountains of Tyrol were higher than all the chains known in Germany. I paffed within a few leagues of the Carpathian mountains which begin eaftward of Vienna. Thefe appeared to me higher than thofe of the Danube: in fome maps they have been confounded with mountains fituated weftward of the river Oder. But thefe are entirely different from the others: as they only form hillocks on the Polifh road, or fmall eminences very little raifed above the ground:

ground: they rife as they come nearer the mountains of Bohemia, of which I imagine they are a branch. I have placed a ridge of mountains on the borders of the Danube about Buda; but having not been able to fatisfy myfelf thoroughly upon this point, this ridge requires farther confirmation. I learned at Vienna, that the mountains which pafs to the north of Alba-regalis and to the eaft of Gratz, and which unite themfelves to the chain of the Danube, were as high as thofe which are on the borders of this river.

Of Poland, and its Frontiers.

The maps of Poland are exceedingly imperfect. There is not, throughout the whole extent of this kingdom, one place, the fituation of which is determined by aftronomical or geometrical obfervations.

Staniflaus Poniatowfki, King of Poland, as well verfed in the knowledge of the fciences, as in the art of government, undertook to have maps of all his dominions traced, foon after he came to the throne. The Marquis de Montalembert, of the academy of fciences, took upon him the direction of this work, which will be the more ufeful, as the compilers of it have been employed, for feveral years paft, in fettling the ground-work of thefe maps by aftronomical obfervations.

I have made out the journal of my route, by confulting people of the country. The names of the places have been looked over by fome Poles of great knowledge; but I have been obliged to take the pofitions from thofe in the antient maps, and have not had time enough to make all the obfervations neceffary to determine them with the accuracy I could have wifhed. I have taken, as I went along, fketches of the mountains or rather hillocks, I met with on the road, and the reft have been

drawn

drawn from the informations I endeavoured to acquire in travelling through this kingdom.

It is evident from the journal in the following table, that the diſtance from Bilitz to Riga, is 293 leagues of 2000 toiſes, and 257, reckoning 25 leagues to a degree.

About the confines of Brünn, ſome little hills are ſeen; theſe become higher at Friedeck, which is but a few leagues diſtant from the Carpathian mountains. Theſe hills are carried on as far as Cracow, but leſſen as they are more diſtant from the Carpathian mountains. The road from Cracow is one large plain to Grodno, at which place the little hills make their appearance again; they become higher and more numerous as far as Kowno. As I went out of the road to Lithuania, on coming from Ollita, I paſſed through Guezno, Ponorei and Podſtrava; and met with great difficulties in going through this part of Lithuania, on account of the number of mountains; although they are of ſo little height that they may be conſidered merely as riſing grounds: all the reſt of Poland is no more than one plain as far as Riga.

TABLE, containing a journal of the road from Paris to Tobolſky in Siberia, Bilitz, Warſaw and Riga.

Names of the places.	German miles of 3804 toiſes.	French leagues of 2000 toiſes.	Names of the places.	German miles of 3804 toiſes.	French leagues of 2000 toiſes.	Names of the places.	German miles of 3804 toiſes.	French leagues of 2000 toiſes.
Bilitz			Nadarzyn	2	3¾	Ollitta	4	7½
Zator	5	9½	Warſaw	4	7½	Pren	4	7½
Cracow	5	9½	Okonaw	3	5¾	Gog	3	5¾
Iwanowa	3	5¾	Staniſlawoie	3	5¾	Kowno	3	5¾
Zarnowice	4	7½	Wegrow	6	11½	Bopt	3	5¾
Naglowice	4	7½	Granne	5½	10½	Kieydan	3	5¾
Malagoſzoz	3	5¾	Pirdelciova	1	2	Montwyde	3	5¾
Radoſzyce	5	9½	Branſk	4½	8½	Peyſagola	3	5¾
Konſkie	3	5¾	Bielſk	3	5¾	Roginian	3	5¾
Inowlodz	5	9½	Bialiſtok	5	9½	Mozeyki	3	5¾
Rawa	4	7½	Sokolka	6	11½	Kraki	4	7½
Chrzconorwice	2½	4¾	Grodno	6	11½	Mitau	5	9½
Mſzczanowa	2½	4¾	Rotnica	6	11½	Riga	6	11½
Zabiawola	2	3¾	Merecz	4	7½			

Of

A JOURNEY TO SIBERIA. 127

Of Livonia and Estonia.

The geographical measures of Russia are werst, which are each divided into 500 sagens, or fathoms, and each fathom into three arcins.

The arcin is 26 inches, 6 lines, and three tenths, according to the Paris royal foot *: the sagen is six feet, 7 inches, 6 lines, and 9 tenths: the werst is 552 toises, 7 inches, and 6 lines; 103 wersts and one third are equal to one degree of the meridian, which I compute at 57,060 toises.

TABLE, containing a journal of the road from Paris to Tobolsky in Siberia, Riga, and St. Petersburg.

Names of the places.	Wersts of 552 toises.	French leagues of 2000 toises.	Names of the places.	Wersts of 552 toises.	French leagues of 2000 toises.	Names of the places.	Wersts of 552 toises.	French leagues of 2000 toises.
Riga			Knitas	21	5¼	Waivota	17	4¼
Nevermuhlen	11	3	Uddern	23	6¼	Narva	20	5¼
Hilchensfer	14	3¾	Derpt	24	6¼	Jamburg	21	5¼
Engerharsdof	18	4¾	Igafor	22	6	Opole	15	4
Roop	21	5¼	Torma	22	6	Cyrkowicie	24	6¼
Lenzenhof	20	5½	Nenal	24	6½	Koskowa	21	5¼
Wolmar	18	4¼	Kansk	16	4½	Kipina	19	5
Stackel	19	5	Kleinpungern	22	6	Gorieloi	20	5¼
Gulber	20	5¼	Pourroi	15	4	St. Petersburg	21	5½
Teiglis	17	4¼	Fockenhof	16	4¼			

According to this journal, the distance from Riga to St. Petersburg is 146 leagues of 2000 toises each, or 128, allowing 25 leagues to a degree; there are no mountains to be met with in all this extent.

* This result is taken from what was settled between M. Delisle and M. Winsheim, in the month of March 1738, in consequence of a commission for regulating the weights and measures. The arcin of Russia was compared with the French foot, sent from Paris, by M. de Mairan of the academy of sciences.

Of Ingria, Ruſſia, and Siberia, as far as Tobolſky.

TABLE of the longitudes and latitudes of ſome places in Ruſſia.

Names of the places.	Difference of the meridians.			Longitudes.			Latitudes.		
	H.	M.	S.	D.	M.	S.	D.	M.	S.
Cazan	3*	7	38	66	48	15	55°	47	22
Echaterinenburg	3	55	0	78	40	45	56°	51	42
Iſland of Ago	1†	18	20	39	28	45	58°	56	0
Moſco	2*	20	53	55	7	0	55°	45	46
Narva	0	0	0	0	0	0	59°	23	27
Nova-Uſolia	3†	36	52	74	6	45	59°	23	54
Revel	1	27	50	41	51	15	59°	26	22
Riga	1†	25	15	41	12	30	56°	56	24
Saigatka	3†	24	38	71	3	15	56°	43	15
St. Peterſburg	1*	52	0	47	53	45	59°	55	0
Sarapul	3†	22	38	70	33	15	56°	26	45
Tobolſky	4°	24	18	85	58	15	58°	12	22
Veretia	3†	37	1	74	9	8	59°	22	41
Uſt-Ykſkoi	3	18	38	69	33	15	55°	51	50

If theſe longitudes and latitudes are compared with thoſe of the beſt maps extant of Ruſſia, it will be found, that there are ſometimes errors in theſe of one degree and a half in the longitudes, and of half a degree in the latitudes. The ſame errors are alſo obſerved in the Ruſſian maps themſelves ‖. I have been attentive to theſe differences in the maps of my journey; but I cannot flatter myſelf ſo far, as to ſuppoſe, that I have not committed any other errors, in attempting to rectify the antient geography by theſe new obſervations.

‖ According to the Ruſſian Atlas, the longitude of Saigatka is 72 degrees 31 minutes; and its latitude 57 degrees 12 minutes.

TABLE,

TABLE, containing a journal of the road from Paris to Tobolſky in Siberia; St. Peterſburg, Moſco, and Tobolſky.

Names of the places.	Werſts of 552 toiſes.	French leagues of 2000 toiſes.	Names of the places.	Werſts of 552 toiſes.	French leagues of 2000 toiſes.	Names of the places.	Werſts of 552 toiſes.	French leagues of 2000 toiſes.
St. Peterſburg			Murom	30	8¼	Oſſa	35	9¾
Iſchora	35	9¾	Monakhova	25	7	Piſſe	20	5½
Toſna	23	6¼	Pogoſt	29	8	Birma	54	15
Loubana	26	7¼	Bogorodzkoe	39	10¾	Tikonoſka	32	8¾
Tſchoudoiwa	32	8¾	Niſan-Novogorod	30	8¼	Orda	16	4¼
Spakoi	25	7	Zimenki	25	7	Sabarca	20	5½
Podbereſchie	23	6¼	Tatinets	31	8½	Souxon	10	2¾
Novogorod	22	6	Belozericha	35	9¾	Solotoukouſka	13	3½
Bronitſkoi-ïam	35	9¾	Fokino	29	8	Baikoiva	17	4¾
Zaitſowo	30	8¼	Soumka	34	9½	Aſtchitzkaia	20	5½
Kreſteſkoi	31	8½	Kuzmodemianſk	20	5½	Biſertzkaia	20	5½
Jachelbiza	39	10¾	Eſkeren	30	8¼	Klenouſkaia	25	7
Zimnegorſkoi-ïam	23	6¼	Czebakſcar	26	7¼	Kirgiſchanſkaia	29	8
Jedrowa	22	6	Coſki	30	8¼	Grobowa	23	6¼
Chotillowſkoi-ïam	35	9¾	Ilineva	31	8½	Bilimbaeuſkoi	23	6¼
Wyſzneiwoloczok	36	10	Weſovaïa	23	6¼	Echaterinenburg	52	14¼
Vidropuſk	33	9	Cazan	27	7½	Koſulina	21	5¾
Torjok	36	10	Wiſocogora	20	5½	Belojarſkaia	24	6½
Mednoie	33	9	Schurillena	29	8	Volkava	25	6¾
Twer	28	7¾	Sumacourſa	23	6¼	Kamyſchlowſka	22	6
Gorodnia	37	10½	Sicchi	22	6	Kroſnoiarka	22	6
Zawidowo	21	5¾	Louga	27	7½	Pyſchmintkaia	14	3¾
Klin	27	7½	Scynd	20	5½	Kuiarowkaia	14	3¾
Pieſzki	30	8¼	Soromacou	25	7	Belecoſkſou	44	12
Tchernaïa	24	6½	Neſnimacan	25	7	Demenova	12	3¼
Moſco	28	7¾	Caccy	25	7	Malſchova	39	10¾
Dereunia-Novaïa	35	9¾	Derichova	22	6	Tumen	36	10
Bounkova	26	7¼	Jouſki	40	11	Sozonowa	46	12¾
Kirjana	29	8	Sowialova	25	7	Pokrowſkaia	31	8½
Lipni	28	7¾	Zaſerin	35	9¾	Iſtinſka	[illegible]	9[illegible]
Undola	17	4¾	Caſachewa	30	8¼	Wakſarina	34	[illegible]½
Wolodimer	22	6	Bapka	20	5½	Cheſlakova	2[illegible]	[illegible]
Soudogda	35	9¾	Reſeſtoinka	15	4¼	Dekhetereva	36	1[illegible]
Mochók	30	8¼	Cracow	20	5½	Tobolſky	43	1[illegible]¾
Dratſchewo	26	7¼						

TABLE, containing a journal of the road from Paris to Tobolsky in Siberia, through Kusmodemiansk and Solikamsky.

Names of the places.	Wersts of 552 toises.	French leagues of 2000 toises.	Names of the places.	Wersts of 552 toises.	French leagues of 2000 toises.	Names of the places.	Wersts of 552 toises.	French leagues of 2000 toises.
Kusmodemiansk			Solovetskoie	33	9	Martinskaja	25	6 3/4
Bolcaja	10	2 3/4	Troiskoie	22	6	Jaiwa	35	9 1/4
Koumia	50	13 3/4	Krontegowskoi	25	6 3/4	Moltchana	35	9 1/2
Choumetri	30	8 1/4	Jekaterinskoi	25	6 3/4	Rostess	37	10 1/4
Carewokoksaisk	30	8 1/4	Tikowskaja	35	9 3/4	Paiudinska	40	11
Polovinoi-vrag	50	13 3/4	Loenskoie	25	6 3/4	Melechina	40	11
Jaransk	40	11	Kaigorodock	35	9 3/4	Lialinskoi	22	6
Voskresenskoie	34	9 1/2	Volva	34	9 1/2	Verchaturia	12	11 1/2
Tchernaia	47	13	Berezowka	25	7	Saldinskoi	27	7 1/2
Kotelnich	46	12 3/4	Joussinewskoe	30	8 1/4	Makhneva	37	10 1/4
Jouriewskoie	20	5 1/2	Zezewskaia	15	4 1/4	Fomina	28	7 3/4
Orlow	26	7 1/4	Kosineskoie	36	10	Babikhina	53	14 1/2
Pouitriskoe	21	5 3/4	Loginova	32	9	Tourinsk	53	14 1/2
Chlinow	30	8 1/4	Sirinskoe	28	7 3/4	Sladkaia	50	13 3/4
Slobodskoi	28	7 3/4	Nikonowa	25	7	Rogestuenkoie	50	13 3/4
Prokosiewskoi	30	8 1/4	Solikamsky	30	8 1/4	Tumen	51	14

By this journal it appears, that the distance from Kusmodemiansk to Tumen is 433 leagues of 2000 toises each, and from St. Petersburg to Tobolsky 859 leagues; whereas, from St. Petersburg to Tobolsky, by Cazan, is no more than 782 leagues of 2000 toises, or 685 leagues at 25 to a degree.

From these different journals, the following distances are ascertained in leagues of 2282 toises, or 25 to a degree.

From Paris	to Brest - - - - - - - - - -	127
	to Strasburg - - - - - - - - -	120
	to Vienna, following the course of the Danube	308

This

This laſt diſtance, and the following, are fifteen leagues leſs going by land.

From Paris { to Warſaw - - 467
to St. Peterſburg - - - 762
to Tobolſky, by Cazan - 1447

From Breſt to Tobolſky - - 1574

All the road from St. Peterſburg to Moſco, an extent of 200 leagues, is one continued plain, except at Waldai, where there are mountains in the middle of the road, which however are nothing more than hillocks, or riſing grounds. The road, as far as Moſco, is almoſt entirely made with pieces of deal wood, three, four and five inches thick; ſometimes they are made with faggots placed along ſide each other, and covered with earth four or five inches thick, but there is no earth laid upon the deal. When the road is ſpoiled, a new one is made by the ſide of the other.

A great quantity of wood is uſed in this method of making the roads; and indeed nothing but cluſters of fir-trees are to be met with throughout this ſpace, which in other reſpects is fine, and cultivated, eſpecially in the neighbourhood of Moſco, and the bridges are alſo kept in good repair; but after this town, the roads are very bad. From St. Peterſburg to Waldai the ground is raiſed only about 45 toiſes above the level of the ſea: it riſes all at once to about 200 toiſes. Moſco is in a large plain, elevated 259 toiſes above the level of the ſea.

Wolodomer is ſituated on a hill bordering the river Kliazma. There is an archbiſhop belonging to it. The river is nearly as broad as the Seine, and the hill not more than 30 toiſes above the level of the river, the borders of which are marſhy, as is likewiſe the whole plain as far as Murom. Almoſt all the ground lying between theſe two towns is uncultivated: nothing but sand is be seen there, and fir-trees, which are most of them stunted and do not thrive well.

Murom is a small town, partly situated on a mountain, about 20 toises above the river Occa, which is 100 toises over, and 4 deep.

The Wolga is one of the finest rivers in the known world. The southern side of it is bordered by a hill from Nisan-Novogorod to Kusmodemiansk. All the ground to the south of this river is raised about 50 toises above the level of the stream; and is extremely well cultivated throughout this plain as far as Cazan: there is very little wood to be met with in this part, and the people are sometimes obliged to fetch it from ten leagues distance; while there are nothing but immense forests to be met with northward of the river.

Cazan is the lowest of all the places upon the road from Mosco: the ground rises immediately as one goes to the north. At some distance from Cazan the beauty of the country disappears, and gives place to forests of fir-trees. The soil is not much cultivated; it forms a plain as far as the river Kama, which one must cross over to get to Cracow, where the mountains begin.

Before one comes to Cazan, there is another road at Kusmodemiansk leading equally into Siberia: this was the way I went in going to Tobolsky: the road is very little cultivated except in the neighbourhood of Chlinow. There are nothing but thick forests to be seen as far as Solikamsky, situated on the borders of the Kama, where the chain of mountains, known by the name of Poias Zemnoi, begins.

I crossed these mountains at this place as I was going to Tobolsky, and passed over them again at my return by Echaterinenburg, Ossa and Cracova, six leagues more to the south. I took drawings of the several mountains on these two roads;

I determined

A JOURNEY TO SIBERIA. 133

I determined their heights with the barometer, and their distances with my watch, which marked the seconds.

This chain of mountains is forty leagues broad at Solikamsky. In going from this town, the mountains continue rising to the middle of the chain: from whence they diminish immediately, so that they are made shelving on both sides with a ridge in the middle. The highest part is at Jaiwa and near Kiria. At the first of these places the ground is 376 toises above the level of the sea, and at the last, the mountain of Kiria is 440 toises; but, as the river Kama is 187 toises above the level of the sea, it follows, that these mountains are not raised to any considerable height above the ground they stand upon; but their ascents are very steep. There are sometimes plains of several leagues upon the summits of these mountains.

I passed by the way of Echaterinenburg on my return from Tobolsky to St. Petersburg. Here the chain begins to the east of Echaterinenburg: it rises as it comes nearer the middle, and terminates at the Fort Bisertzkaia. It is about 40 leagues long; but these mountains did not appear so high as the others: they were not more than about 250 toises high about the middle. The mountain of Klemouskaia was 309 toises. After this chain, a plain of more than 20 leagues follows, and then a fresh chain appears, the mountains of which, rise by imperceptible degrees towards the middle; they afterwards lessen and terminate on the borders of the Kama. This second chain is not more than about 30 toises wide. The highest mountains are 212 and 287 toises; and the level of the river at Ossa being 153 toises above the level of the sea, it follows, that these mountains are not raised more than about 150 toises above the ground they stand upon.

The chain of the Poias mountains, or rather the middle of this chain, is pointed out in all the maps; but the second chain, which must be traversed in going to Ossa, and which is continued

along

along the eastern border of the Kama, is no where to be found. Having stopped some days at Solikamsky and at Echaterinenburg, I had an opportunity of acquiring all the information I wished for, with respect to this country, which is pretty well known between these two towns, on account of the Mines, and the number of persons frequently passing from one to the other. I had besides some particular plans, on which I marked all the observations that occurred to me, or that were communicated by others, concerning the places where it was not possible for me to go. I have mentioned nothing from my own observations, but what I met with in the course of the route; and there is not one single mountain, the design of which has not been taken upon the spot: those which are out of the road, have only been represented from the informations I was able to gather in the country. All these mountains are covered with fir-trees. The woods have been omitted in the maps, to make them less confused. I saw the second chain only at the place where I crossed from Orda to Ossa: it is totally different from the chain of Echaterinenburg: I have carried it on, along the eastern border of the Kama, without being able positively to ascertain, whether it is really continued so far. The Poias mountains are a continuation of the Rymnic mountains, and the new chain appears to me to be a branch of the same, which joins the Poias mountains in the neighbourhood of Kongour. This opinion is founded upon the following reasons.

The chain which I crossed in going from Orda to Ossa, is continued towards the south; I saw it myself from the road, after I had passed the Kama, and was told by all persons I conversed with on the subject, that it went on in the same direction; but I have not been able to get much information about that part which extends towards Menzelinsk. All the mountains expressed in my maps near this place, have only
been

been drawn from analogy to what I had seen: there is no other authority for them, and I cannot even venture to affirm, that this chain of mountains is continued towards the south, in the manner I have expressed it, but it appears probable to me that it is; besides, that this circumstance seems to be indicated by the course of the river Kama. For, if we follow the course of this river on the map, we shall see that it is directed from west to east towards its source, and that the chain of the Poias mountains makes it form suddenly a right angle at Solikamiky, and turns its course towards the south, in an opposite direction to the chain. The same chain throws it again out of its natural course at Offa; and it is probably by the same means that it returns to the west, where it opens into the Wolga.

After having passed this chain, the rest of the way to Tobolsky is nothing but one plain full of marshes.

Before I finish this article, I shall make some observations on the limits of Asia and Europe. Some modern geographers had fixed them, with M. Gmelin, on the river Oby; but this opinion has not been adopted by the majority: besides, that it was founded upon a supposition of imaginary lines being drawn across some large deserts. The limits marked out by the Poias mountains, which in that case divide Asia from Europe, have been judged more proper; although it has been necessary, in adopting these limits, to trace some imaginary lines in several places, either for want of being sufficiently acquainted with these chains of mountains, or from their not being continued from the frozen sea to Mount Caucasus, of which they appear to be a branch. Whatever is the reason, these limits are still very doubtful in some places. They may, however, be naturally traced by the streams and rivers bordering these chains of mountains, in the way M. de Strahlenberg has determined them. For, setting out from the mouth of the river Don, in the black sea, and following its course as far as the

the 49th degree of latitude, there is only one line of ten leagues, drawn over the Wolga at Tſarichin, where this ſtream makes almoſt a right angle. The eaſtern border of the Wolga may afterwards ſerve as a boundary, as far as the mouth of the Kama, which muſt then be followed to the mouth of the Koiwa. This laſt river would fix the boundary as far as the place where its ſource begins; the river Peczora would then be found at the diſtance of five leagues directly northward, and this might determine the limits as far as the frozen ſea, into which it opens. This boundary, fixed by nature, leaves no uncertainty behind it, and will limit, almoſt every where, the chain of mountains which divides Aſia from Europe.

Of the level of the road from Paris to Brest, and to Tobolsky in Siberia: and of the use of the barometer in obtaining a level of the globe.

THE internal parts of the earth, so far as we are acquainted with them, are composed of different layers of earth, sand, marl, clay, calcareous and vitrificable stones. In all these layers sea-shells are found, sometimes collected into heaps, which are extended throughout whole provinces. All these layers, produced by the sediments which have been deposited by the waters, in the various changes the globe has undergone, exhibit appearances corresponding to these changes, in the several mountains, plains and valleys; which appearances, determine the order of these revolutions and their respective periods: but the solution of these problems requires a previous knowledge of the height of these different layers, with respect to one common level, the angle of inclination they fall into in the mountains, the direction of their slope, the situation of metals, minerals, and of all the materials produced by animal and vegetable substances, as also the height of the mountains, and the rivers, with their slopes.

The additional knowledge we acquire by the levelling of the globe, comprehends the history of nature, and furnishes us with the most interesting discoveries in all branches of science.

The use hitherto made of the barometer in levelling, has been chiefly confined to the determination of the different heights of mountains, undoubtedly, because of the difficulties arising from the variation of the atmosphere: the height of a mountain indeed is measured in a few hours, and it is an easy matter either to know what changes the atmosphere has undergone

gone in such a space of time, or to make proper allowances for them. But when the barometer is used for the levelling of the ground, every circumstance seems to concur in assisting to produce false conclusions. The variations of this instrument in Europe, are about two inches, and therefore, the results in these countries are liable to similar errors, when observations made at the same time, in places far distant from each other, are compared: but, in small distances, the variations of the atmosphere being generally uniform in a given extent of country, very accurate results may be obtained, if care is taken to compare the barometers, and to allow for the trifling difference almost always to be observed in these instruments. And indeed, from observations made at the same time at Perpignan and at Paris, it has been found, that the variations of the atmosphere have been nearly the same in these two places *: This hypothesis is confirmed by the observations made at Paris, and in the province of Auvergne, upon Mount Dor †, by those made at Genoa ‡, in Spain, Italy, and England §. I have also established the validity of this opinion by a series of observations I have made at Bitche, and by others at Brest and at Paris at the same time. I think therefore, I may venture to affirm, that the variations of the atmosphere are generally uniform in a distance of about 150 leagues, and consequently that the respective height of two places, at such a distance, may be obtained with precision, by observations made at the same time with the barometer, provided that a number of these observations are collated; for this method of levelling is liable to error from several circumstances. Storms, hurricanes, and other phœnomena of this kind, may happen in one pro-

* Volume académie 1740, Mem. de M. Cassini.
† Volume académie 1705, Mem. de M. de Maraldi, page 219.
‡ Volume académie 1708.
§ Volume académie 1703.

vince,

vince, without producing any perceptible alteration in others, although they fhould not be at any great diftance.

The variations of the atmofphere are fo uncertain at confiderable diftances, that if we content ourfelves merely with comparing obfervations, made by the barometer, in places widely diftant from each other, we fhall be liable, in fome inftances, to fall into miftakes of more than 260 toifes; but we fhall have nothing of this kind to fear, if, in the courfe of our journey, we frequently repeat thefe obfervations on the rivers, and on the mountains, and keep an exact journal of all other local circumftances; efpecially if, at the fame time, we are fupplied with plans of the country we are travelling through. The obfervations made on the rivers ferve to determine their flope; the times when the variations of the atmofphere have taken place are then known, and may be properly attended to.

Of the laws by which air is condensed.

MESSIEURS Mariotte, Caffini, Maraldi, Bouguer, and several other natural philofophers, have fettled the laws by which air is condenfed and rarefied. Thefe laws, although very different among themfelves, will anfwer the obfervations pretty well in fmall heights of about 200 toifes; but will be found not to agree in more confiderable heights.

If the height of a mountain of 2000 toifes is determined according to M. Mariotte's rules, this height will turn out to be about 300 toifes too little*; and nearly as much too great according to M. Maraldi's †. The refults from M. de Caffini's rules are in a medium between the two preceding, and he fuppofes that the air is rarefied in a reciprocal ratio to the fquare of the weight it carries.

M. Bouguer's ‡ opinion is, that the weight of the upper air diminifhes in geometrical progreffion, in proportion as one rifes above the level of the fea, while the heights increafe in arithmetical progreffion; and the logarithmal tables, being a feries of numbers in arithmetical progreffion, anfwering to other numbers in geometrical progreffion, he fuppofes, that the heights of the barometer are indicated by numbers, and the heights of the air by logarithms. This rule is confirmed by all the obfervations he has made on the Cordelleiras mountains, by diminifhing the heights one thirtieth part §; but he thinks it takes place, only in the interval, between the height of 600 and that of 2500 toifes ‖.

---

* Volume académie, 1705, Mem. de M. de Caffini, page 61.
† Volume académie, 1733. Mem. de M. de Caffini, page 40.
‡ Figure de la terre, et Mem. académie, 1753.
§ Figure de la terre, page xxxix.
‖ Volume académie 1753, page 529.

In the level I took, of the road from Paris to Tobolſky, I have never had an opportunity of meaſuring any confiderable heights, and I have found, in every inſtance, that the laws of condenſation, ſettled from experiment by M. Maraldi, have anſwered exactly to my obſervations, provided I took care to determine for each barometer I made uſe of, the quantity of air ſuſtained by a line of mercury on a level with the ſea. Thoſe who have made experiments of this kind, have almoſt always differed in the reſults, as may be ſeen by the following account.

According to M. Mariotte one line of mercury anſwers, on a level with the ſea, to - - - 10 toiſes 3 feet.

According to
{ M. Maraldi to   10   -   -
  M. de Caſſini to   10   -   - 5
  M. de la Hire to   12   -   -
  M. Picard, to   14   -   - 1 }

This account is ſufficient to indicate, the miſtakes one may fall into, by making uſe of tables calculated from theſe obſervations. Theſe differences are attributed to collections of vapours, which may exiſt in ſome parts of the atmoſphere, and make it more heavy for a time; to the ſituation of the places where the experiments are made; and to the immediate elaſticity of the air, more or leſs powerful at different times. It is probable, that theſe phyſical cauſes contribute greatly in producing the different reſults, mentioned by divers natural philoſophers, with regard to the quantity of air one line of mercury, at a level with the ſea, can ſuſtain. I imagine, however, that theſe diſagreements have chiefly been owing to the barometers, with which the obſervations have been made. Barometers made with the ſame accuracy, of equal diameters, and filled with the ſame mercury, will agree perfectly in their height and progreſſion; but this equality will no longer ſubſiſt, if they are differently conſtructed. In order to aſcertain this

by

by experiment, I made five barometers at Bitche, in 1753; the diameter of the tubes was from one line and a half to three: besides this, they were all different, either in the manner of boiling the mercury, or with regard to the glass, or the mercury itself, which was more or less depurated. I found by a series of observations, that these barometers hardly ever agreed either in their height or in their progression; so that the prodigious difference there appears between Mr. Picard's results, and those of the other philosophers, can only be owing to the construction of his barometer.

M. Duhamel, of the academy of sciences, has one large barometer, which does not rise more than half a line, while the others rise a whole line; but the mercury in this barometer has not been boiled, and it is suspected that this difference arises from some particles of air still resting against the sides of the tube.

All these inconveniences are prevented, by determining, for each barometer, what quantity of air, one line of mercury, at a level with the sea, can sustain. This quantity will be different, if it is supposed, that barometers, however well constructed, may vary a little in their progression. The mistakes committed, will be in proportion as this difference is more or less considerable. Let us suppose, for instance, that the mercury rises two lines in one barometer, while it rises but one in M. Duhamel's; it is evident that if the level of the same ground is taken with these two barometers, the same object will be about twice higher by the second, than by the first barometer, supposing, that one line of each, sustains an equal quantity of air; but notwithstanding these different progressions, the same results will be obtained, if the quantity of air, answering to one line of mercury, has been determined in each barometer by experiment: and for this purpose I have settled a table for each barometer I have made use of. This table points

A JOURNEY TO SIBERIA.

out the quantity of air, fuftained by each line of mercury, in proportion as one is raifed above the earth, from the level of the fea. The method I take for this purpofe is very fimple, I go up with my barometer to the top of a mountain, leaving marks at all the places where the mercury finks one line: after I have well fatisfied myfelf by repeated trials, that the atmofphere has not varied, and that each mark anfwers to one line of mercury, I then determine the height of each mark by a level; and knowing already the height of one of thefe marks, with refpect to the level of the fea, I alfo know the quantity of air anfwering to one line upon this fame level. It will even be fufficient, to obferve the barometer, at the bottom and at the top of the mountain, admitting, that the laws of the condenfation have been fettled by M. de Caffini, or M. de Maraldi. I have always found M. de Maraldi's agree perfectly with my obfervations; which it muft be faid have only been made on places not much elevated above the level of the fea.

I have given, in the following table, the heights of all the places on the road from Breft to Tobolfky. The firft column contains the names of the places; the fecond, the height of each place with refpect to the level of the fea, reckoned by toifes; the third, the height of the mercury above that fame level. In the fourth column, the height of the mercury is determined, with refpect to the level of the river Neva; and in the fifth, the mean heights of the barometer are indicated.

The heights of each place are given in this table with the fractions, which has not been done fo much to fhew with what precifion they may be determined, as to give the real refults of the calculations.

TABLE,

TABLE of the places on the road from Brest to Tobolsky in Siberia, the heights of which have been determined, with respect to the level of the sea at Brest, and of the Royal Observatory at Paris.

Names of the places on the road.	HEIGHTS in toises with respect to the level of the sea at Brest.			HEIGHTS of the mercury, with respect to the level of the sea at Brest.		relative of the mercury between the observatory and each place.		mean of the barometer.		
I.	II.			III.		IV.		V.		
FRANCE.	toif.	ft.	in.	lin.	12ths	lines.	12ths	inch.	lin.	12ths
Brest, level of the sea	0	0	0	0	0	— 4	1	28	1	1
Brest, the town	18	0	0							
Morlaix, level of the sea	0	0	0	0	0	— 4	1	28	1	1
Pontou	32	2	0	2	11	— 1	2	27	10	2
Bellisle	41	4	0	3	9	— 0	4	27	9	4
Guingamp	32	2	8	2	11	— 1	2	27	10	2
Chatelaudrin	37	5	9	3	5	— 0	8	27	9	8
Lambale	16	2	8	1	6	— 2	7	27	11	7
Iego	1	4	11	0	2	— 3	11	28	0	11
Mountain, ¼ of a league from Dinant	55	2	0	4	11	+ 0	10	27	8	2
Dinant	27	3	4	2	6	— 1	7	27	10	7
Dole	0	5	5	0	1	— 4	0	28	1	0
Avranches	37	5	0	3	5	— 0	8	27	9	8
Mountain, 1 league from Pontfarci	134	0	0	11	5	+ 7	4	27	1	8
Pontfarci, river Vire	15	3	0	1	6	— 2	7	27	11	7
Villers-le-Bocage	60	0	7	5	4	+ 1	3	27	7	9
Caen, river Orne	1	4	5	0	2	— 3	11	28	0	11
River, Dive	2	4	4	0	3	— 3	10	28	0	10
St. Aubin	74	5	5	6	7	+ 2	6	27	6	7
Lisieux, on the mountain	30	2	5	2	9	— 1	4	27	10	4
Marché Neuf	75	1	0	6	8	+ 2	7	27	6	5
Evreux, river Iton	8	4	8	0	9	— 3	4	28	0	4
Pacy, river Eure	9	0	4	0	9	— 3	1	28	0	4
Bonnieres, river Seine	10	2	8	1	0	— 3	1	28	0	0
Mantes, river Seine	12	2	7	1	2	— 2	11	28	11	11
Meulan, river Seine	13	2	4	1	3	— 2	10	27	11	10
Triel	31	2	0	2	10	— 1	3	27	10	3
Poissy, river Seine	14	4	7	1	4	— 2	9	27	11	9
St. Germain on the mountain	60	0	5	5	4	+ 1	3	27	7	9
St. Germain, river Seine	16	5	7	1	7	— 2	6	27	11	6
Paris, Pont-royal	21	1	7	1	11	— 2	2	27	11	2
Paris, observatory	45	3	5	4	1	— 0	0	27	9	0

TABLE

TABLE of the places on the road from Brest to Tobolsky in Siberia, the heights of which have been determined, with respect to the level of the sea at Brest, and of the Royal Observatory at Paris.

Names of the places on the road.	HEIGHTS in toises, with respect to the level of the sea at Brest.			HEIGHTS of the mercury, with respect to the level of the sea at Brest.		relative of the mercury between the observatory and each place.		mean of the barometer.		
I.	II.			III.		IV.		V.		
FRANCE.	toif.	ft.	in.	lin.	12ths	lines.	12ths	inch.	lin.	12ths
Denainvilliers	85	5	7	7	5	† 3	4	27	5	8
Meaux, river Seine	32	5	7	2	9	— 1	4	27	10	4
Castle-Thierry, river Seine	44	3	0	3	8	— 0	5	27	9	5
Dormans, river Marne	48	0	0	4	0	— 0	1	27	9	1
Epernay, river Marne	51	5	0	4	2	† 0	1	27	8	11
Chalons, river Marne	56	2	3	4	7	† 0	6	27	8	6
Vitry-le-François, river Marne	62	5	7	5	2	† 1	1	27	7	11
Bar-le-duc, river Orne	70	1	0	5	9	† 1	8	27	7	4
Toul, river Moselle	105	0	0	8	5	† 4	4	27	4	8
Castle Salins, river Seilles	119	0	0	9	6	† 5	5	27	3	7
Hellimer	140	0	0	11	1	† 7	0	27	2	0
Sarreguemine, river Sarre	115	0	0	9	2	† 5	1	27	3	11
Bitche, river	155	5	0	12	5	† 8	4	27	0	8
Castle of Bitche	202	5	0	0	0	† 0	0	0	0	0
Strasburg, river, Rhine	80	0	0	6	6	† 2	5	27	6	7
Pavement of the cathedral	86	2	0	0	0	0	0	0	0	0
Top of the steeple	159	4	0	0	0	0	0	0	0	0
Mountain of Donon	524	2	0	36	0	† 31	11	25	1	1
Raon, on the plain	258	2	0	19	4	† 15	3	26	5	10
Bouxveiller	129	1	0	10	3	† 8	2	27	2	10
Bromptein	88	3	0	7	2	† 3	1	27	5	11
Benfeld	95	3	0	7	8	† 3	7	27	5	5
Chatenai	112	3	0	9	0	† 4	11	27	4	1
St. Mary, at the mines	202	1	0	15	6	† 11	5	26	9	7
Mountain of St. Mary, at the cross	447	0	0	31	2	† 27	1	25	5	11
Entrance of the mine of St. Nicholas	286	0	0	0	0	0	0	0	0	0
Depth of the mine, 101 toises 2 feet	0	0	0	0	0	0	0	0	0	0
Bottom of the mine, 184 toises 0 feet	0	0	0	0	0	0	0	0	0	0
Epfig	112	3	0	9	0	† 4	11	27	4	1
Vangenmille	95	0	0	7	8	† 3	7	27	5	5
Foot of the mount. of the castle of Rose	113	4	0	9	1	† 5	0	27	4	0
Top of the mountain	211	4	0	16	2	† 8	1	26	8	11

TABLE of the places on the road from Brest to Tobolsky in Siberia, the heights of which have been determined with respect to the level of the sea at Brest, and of the Royal Observatory at Paris.

Names of the places on the road.	HEIGHTS in toises, with respect to the level of the sea at Brest.			HEIGHTS of the mercury, with respect to the level of the sea at Brest.		relative of the mercury between the observatory and each place.		mean of the barometer.	
I.	II.			III.		IV.		V.	
	toif.	ft.	in.	lin.	12ths	lines.	12ths	inch.	lin. 12ths
FRANCE.									
Vimmenau	103	4	0	8	4	† 4	3	27	4 9
Mountain Kesselberg	219	0	0	16	8	† 12	7	26	8 5
Mountain Grebentenberg	230	0	0	17	5	† 13	4	26	7 8
Goetchebrick	190	0	0	14	8	† 10	7	26	10 5
Determined Heights.									
Gundershoffen, river Zinsel	92	0	0	0	0	0	0	0	0 0
Aldorf	86	0	0	0	0	0	0	0	0 0
Mulhausen	95	0	0	0	0	0	0	0	0 0
Robach	97	0	0	0	0	0	0	0	0 0
Utweiller	100	0	0	0	0	0	0	0	0 0
Neuveiller	113	0	0	0	0	0	0	0	0 0
Meltzenheim	96	0	0	0	0	0	0	0	0 0
GERMANY.									
Ulm, Danube, river	189	4	0	14	8	† 10	7	26	10 5
Donawert, Danube, river	175	5	0	13	9	† 9	8	26	11 5
Ingolstat, Danube, river	166	4	0	13	1	† 9	0	27	0 0
Ratisbon, Danube, river	154	3	0	12	2	† 8	1	27	0 11
Passau, Danube, river	131	3	0	10	6	† 6	5	27	2 7
Lintz, Danube, river	114	5	0	9	3	† 5	2	27	3 10
Iten, Danube, river	108	0	0	8	9	† 4	8	27	4 4
Waltse, Danube, river	107	1	0	8	8	† 4	7	27	4 5
Wiendorf, Danube, river	95	3	0	7	9	† 3	8	27	5 4
Vienna, Danube, river	80	0	0	6	6	† 2	5	27	6 7
Observatory of the Jesuits	107	0	0	8	7	† 4	6	27	4 6
Wolkersdorf	87	2	6	7	1	† 3	0	27	6 0
Gaunersdorf	93	4	6	7	5	† 3	6	27	5 6
Nickolsburg	94	5	0	7	8	† 3	7	27	5 5
Brenn	108	0	8	8	8	† 4	7	27	4 5
Wischau	137	1	5	10	10	† 6	9	27	2 3

TABLE of the places on the road from Brest to Tobolsky in Siberia, the heights of which have been determined, with respect to the level of the sea at Brest, and of the Royal Observatory at Paris.

Names of the places on the road.		HEIGHTS in toises, with respect to the level of the sea at Brest.			HEIGHTS of the mercury, with respect to the level of the sea at Brest.		HEIGHTS relative of the mercury, between the observatory and each place.		mean of the barometer.		
I.		II.			III.		IV.		V.		
		toif.	ft.	in.	lin.	12ths	lines.	12ths	inch.	lin.	12ths
POLAND.											
Malagozcz, on the river	mean	153	0	0	12	10	† 8	9	27	0	3
Inowlodz	mean	126	0	0	10	9	† 6	8	27	2	4
Warsaw, Vistula	mean	98	0	0	8	6	† 4	5	27	4	7
Wegrow	mean	120	0	0	10	4	† 6	3	27	2	9
River Bug	mean	121	0	0	10	5	† 6	4	27	2	8
Grodno, river Niemen	mean	120	0	0	10	4	† 6	3	27	2	9
Kowno, river Niemen	mean	35	0	0	3	2	— 0	11	27	9	11
RUSSIA.											
Roop	mean	4	0	0	0	5	— 3	8	28	0	8
Stackel	mean	12	0	0	1	2	— 2	11	27	11	11
Teiglis	mean	13	0	0	1	3	— 2	10	27	11	10
Derpt	mean	18	0	0	1	8	— 2	5	27	11	5
Nenal	mean	19	0	0	1	9	— 2	4	27	11	4
Narva	mean	15	0	0	1	5	— 2	7	27	11	8
Jamburg	mean	17	0	0	1	7	— 2	6	27	11	6
Kipina	mean	20	0	0	1	10	— 2	3	27	11	3
St. Petersburg, Neva, river		17	4	3	1	6	— 2	7	27	11	7
Tschoudoiwa		38	2	0	3	3	— 0	10	27	9	10
Spakoi		42	3	0	3	7	— 0	6	27	9	6
Bronitskoi-ïam, Lake		34	4	2	2	11	— 1	2	27	10	2
Zaitsowo		45	2	0	3	10	— 0	3	27	9	3
Krestskoi		45	2	0	3	10	— 0	3	27	9	3
Jachelbiza		44	4	0	3	9	— 0	4	27	9	4
Zimnegorskoi-ïam		135	0	0	10	9	† 6	8	27	2	4
Jedrowa		190	1	0	14	9	† 10	8	26	10	4
Chotillowskoi-ïam		183	1	0	14	3	† 10	2	26	10	10
Vidropusk		197	2	0	15	3	† 11	2	26	9	10
Torjok		189	0	0	14	8	† 10	7	26	10	5
Twer { Volga, river		178	3	1	13	11	† 9	10	26	11	2
Twer { Town		179	0	0	14	0	† 9	11	26	11	1

TABLE of the places on the road from Breſt to Tobolſky in Siberia, the heights of which have been determined with reſpect to the level of the ſea at Breſt, and of the Royal Obſervatory at Paris.

Names of the places on the road.	HEIGHTS in toiſes, with reſpect to the level of the ſea at Breſt.			HEIGHTS of the mercury, with reſpect to the level of the ſea at Breſt.		relative of the mercury, between the obſervatory and each place.		mean of the barometer.		
I.	II.			III.		IV.		V.		
	toiſ.	ft.	in.	lin.	12ths	lines.	12ths	inch.	lin.	12ths
RUSSIA.										
Gorodina	185	1	0	14	5	† 10	4	26	10	8
River Seſtra	174	1	0	13	7	† 9	6	26	11	6
Klin	178	4	0	13	11	† 9	10	26	11	2
Moſco, river Moſco	269	0	0	20	2	† 16	1	26	4	11
Koupavena	268	3	0	20	1	† 16	0	26	5	0
Bouinkova, river Kliaſma	253	3	4	19	1	† 15	0	26	6	0
Lipni	227	1	0	17	4	† 13	3	26	7	9
Undola	221	5	0	17	0	† 12	11	26	8	1
Wolodimer	230	0	0	17	7	† 13	6	26	7	6
River Kliaſma	202	2	5	15	7	† 11	6	26	9	6
Soudogda	190	1	0	14	9	† 10	8	26	10	4
Murom	158	0	0	12	5	† 8	4	27	0	8
River Occa	152	1	0	12	0	† 7	11	27	1	0
River Tioſſa	158	1	0	12	5	† 8	4	27	0	8
Monakhova	170	4	0	13	4	† 9	3	26	11	9
Pogoſt	170	1	0	13	4	† 9	3	26	11	9
Bogorodzkoe	172	0	0	13	6	† 9	5	26	11	7
Volga, river Volga	127	3	6	10	2	† 6	1	27	2	11
Niſan-Novogorod, mountain	178	0	0	13	11	† 9	10	26	11	2
Zimenki	172	4	0	13	6	† 9	5	26	11	7
Tatinets	122	2	10	9	10	† 5	9	27	3	3
River Sondevia	122	5	0	9	10	† 5	9	27	3	3
Belozericha	154	2	0	12	2	† 8	1	27	0	11
Cremianki river	127	1	0	10	2	† 6	1	27	2	11
Fokino	126	1	0	10	1	† 6	0	27	3	0
River Sura	118	2	0	9	6	† 5	5	27	3	7
Koumka	119	3	0	9	7	† 5	6	27	3	6
Kuſmodemianſk	120	3	0	9	8	† 5	7	27	3	5
Volga river	111	3	9	9	0	† 4	11	27	4	1
Lſkeren	170	0	0	13	4	† 9	3	26	11	9
Czebakſar	106	5	10	8	8	† 4	7	27	4	5
Coſki	169	10	0	13	3	† 9	2	26	11	10

A JOURNEY TO SIBERIA. 149

TABLE of the places on the road from Breſt to Tobolſky in Siberia, the heights of which have been determined with reſpect to the level of the ſea at Breſt, and of the Royal Obſervatory at Paris.

Names of the places on the road.	HEIGHTS in toiſes, with reſpect to the level of the ſea at Breſt.	HEIGHTS of the mercury, with reſpect to level of the ſea at Breſt.	relative of the mercury, between the obſervatory and each place.	mean of the barometer.
I.	II.	III.	IV.	V.
RUSSIA.	toiſ. ft. In.	lin. 12ths	lines. 12ths.	inch. lin. 12ths
Ilineva	174 0 0	13 7	† 9 6	26 11 6
Caſan, Volga, river	96 4 8	7 10	† 3 9	27 5 3
Wiſocogora	108 0 0	8 9	† 4 8	27 4 4
Schurillena	117 0 0	9 5	† 5 4	27 3 8
Sumacourſa	157 0 0	12 5	† 8 4	27 0 8
Sicchi	141 0 0	11 3	† 7 2	27 1 10
Louga	150 0 0	11 10	† 7 9	27 1 3
Scynd, river Wiatka	128 0 0	10 3	† 6 2	27 2 10
Soromacou	206 5 0	15 10	† 11 9	26 9 3
Neſnimacan, river Unjak	200 5 0	15 6	† 11 5	26 9 7
Caccy	215 0 0	16 6	† 12 5	26 8 7
Derichova	189 3 0	14 1	† 10 7	26 10 5
Jouſki	177 5 0	13 10	† 9 9	26 11 3
River Zi	167 1 0	13 1	† 9 0	27 0 0
Sowialova	174 2 0	13 7	† 9 6	27 11 6
Zaſerin	149 3 0	11 10	† 7 9	27 1 ?
Gavarilla, river Sciwa	145 0 0	11 6	† 7 5	27 1 7
Caſachewa	163 0 0	12 10	† 8 9	27 0 3
Bapka	156 0 0	12 4	† 4 3	27 0 9
Nevolna	159 1 0	12 6	† 8 5	27 0 7
Summit of a mountain	201 1 0	15 7	† 11 6	26 9 6
Same mountain	186 3 0	14 6	† 10 5	26 10 7
River near the mountain	166 2 0	13 1	† 9 0	27 0 0
Cracow	164 5 0	12 11	† 8 10	27 0 2
Oſſa, river Kama	152 5 0	12 1	† 8 0	27 1 0
Piſſe, river Piſſe	151 5 0	12 0	† 7 11	27 1 1
Mountain Grivenina	195 0 0	15 1	† 11 0	26 10 0
Summit of the mountain, at ¼ of a league from the river Jourka	287 1 0	21 5	† 17 4	26 3 8
River Tourka	210 3 0	16 2	† 12 1	26 8 11
Summit of the mountain, 3 leagues from Birma	250 5 0	18 11	† 14 10	26 6 2

TABLE

TABLE of the places on the road from Breſt to Tobolſky in Siberia, the heights of which have been determined, with reſpect to the level of the ſea at Breſt, and of the Royal Obſervatory at Paris.

Names of the places on the road.	HEIGHTS in toiſes with reſpect to the level of the ſea at Breſt.	HEIGHTS of the mercury, with reſpect to the level of the ſea at Breſt.	relative of the mercury between the obſervatory and each place.	mean of the barometer.
I.	II.	III.	IV.	V.
	toiſ. ft. in.	lin. 12ths	lines. 12ths	inch. lin. 12ths
RUSSIA.				
Pirma, river	189 0 0	14 8	† 10 7	26 10 5
River Tourka	178 3 0	13 11	† 9 10	26 11 2
Mountain, 5 leagues from Tikonoſka	211 4 0	16 3	† 12 2	25 8 10
Tikonoſka, river Irinen	168 0 0	13 2	† 9 1	26 11 11
Orda	176 1 0	13 9	† 9 8	26 11 4
Sabarca	228 2 0	17 5	† 13 4	26 7 8
Solotoukouſka	186 4 0	14 6	† 10 5	26 10 7
Baikoiva	192 2 0	14 11	† 10 10	26 10 2
Aſtchitzkaia, river	196 0 0	15 2	† 11 1	26 9 11
Biſertzkaia, river	236 4 0	18 0	† 13 11	26 7 1
Touſz, rivulet	246 5 0	18 8	† 14 7	26 6 5
Mountain	309 0 0	22 10	† 18 9	25 2 3
Klenouſkaia	219 2 0	16 9	† 12 8	26 8 4
Kirgiſchanſkaia	240 1 0	18 3	† 14 2	26 6 10
Grobova	256 3 0	19 4	† 15 3	26 5 9
Bilimbaeuſkoi, river Czauſova	252 5 11	19 1	† 15 0	25 6 0
Flat mountain	269 1 0	20 2	† 16 1	26 4 11
Foot of the mountain	235 4 0	17 11	† 13 10	26 7 2
Mountain of Chriſtal	270 2 0	20 3	† 16 2	26 4 10
Echaterinenburg, river Iſet	220 0 1	16 10	† 12 9	25 8 3
Koſulina	212 5 0	16 4	† 12 3	25 8 9
Belojarſkaia, river Pyſzma	188 4 9	14 8	† 10 7	26 10 5
Kamyſchlowſka, river Pyzma	161 3 4	12 8	† 8 7	27 0 5
Pyſchminſkaia, river Pyzma	151 5 2	12 0	† 7 11	27 1 1
Kuiarowſkaia, river Pyzma	145 0 +	11 6	† 7 5	27 1 7
Kila, river Pyzma	120 4 8	9 8	† 5 7	27 3 5
Malſchova	108 3 0	8 9	† 4 8	27 4 4
Tumen on the mountain	146 2 0	11 7	† 7 6	27 1 6
River Tura	110 3 0	8 11	† 4 10	27 4 2
Sozonowa	102 0 0	8 3	† 4 2	27 4 10
Pokrowſkaia	97 3 0	7 11	† 3 10	27 5 2
Berozoviar, river Tobolſky	89 5 4	7 7+	† 3 3	27 5 9

TABLE

A JOURNEY TO SIBERIA.

TABLE of the places on the road from Brest to Tobolsky in Siberia, the heights of which have been determined, with respect to the level of the sea at Brest, and of the Royal Observatory at Paris.

Names of the places on the road.	HEIGHTS in toises, with respect to the level of the sea at Brest.			HEIGHTS of the mercury, with respect to the level of the sea at Brest.		relative of the mercury, between the observatory and each place.		mean of the barometer.		
I.	II.			III.		IV.		V.		
RUSSIA.	toif.	ft.	in.	lin.	12ths	lines.	12ths.	inch.	lin.	12ths
River Irtysz, at Tobolsky	68	4	10	5	8	† 1	7	27	7	5
Tobolsky, on the mountain	97	1	1	7	11	i† 3	10	25	5	2
Solikamsky, river Kama	187	1	6	14	6	† 10	5	26	10	7
Jaiwa, river	375	5	0	27	0	† 22	11	25	10	1
River Sicchema	260	2	0	19	7	† 15	6	26	5	6
Top of the mountain	342	2	0	24	11	† 20	10	26	0	2
River, at the foot of the mountain	296	4	0	22	0	† 17	11	26	3	1
Top of the mountain	390	3	0	27	11	† 23	10	25	9	2
Moltchana	326	4	0	23	11	19	10	25	1	2
River Koswa	345	2	0	25	2	† 21	1	25	11	11
Rostess	404	1	0	28	9	† 24	8	25	8	4
Beginning of the mountain	440	2	0	30	11	† 26	10	25	6	2
Top of the mountain	471	2	0	32	9	† 28	8	25	4	4
River Padira	366	2	0	26	5	† 22	4	25	10	8
Paiudinska	313	4	0	23	1	† 19	0	25	2	0
Melechina	262	5	0	19	9	† 15	8	26	5	4
Top of the mountain, 13 wersts from Melechina	265	2	0	19	11	† 15	10	26	5	2
River Lialia	221	1	0	16	11	† 12	10	26	8	2
Lialinskoi	192	3	0	14	11	† 10	10	26	10	2
Verchaturia, Tura, river	160	0	0	12	7	† 8	6	27	0	6
Makhneva	211	3	0	16	3	† 12	2	26	8	10
Babikhina	153	1	0	12	1	† 8	0	27	1	0
Turinsk	143	0	0	11	4	† 7	3	27	1	9
Rogestuenskoie	117	5	7	9	6	† 5	5	27	3	7
Tumen, Tura, river	110	3	0	8	11	† 4	10	27	4	2

Remarks

Remarks on the height of the soil of Russia, from St. Petersburg to Tobolsky in Siberia.

IT was my first intention to have thrown these remarks into a note; but M. de Mairan's ingenious paper, upon the general cause of heat in summer and cold in winter, which I knew nothing of when this work was first committed to the press, has obliged me to be more explicit on this subject.

Russia may be considered as one immense plain, extending from St. Petersburg to Tobolsky, divided by a chain of mountains from south to north, at the seventy-fifth degree of longitude. In different parts of this plain, some eminences or platforms are to be met with, as at Mosco, Caccy, and near the origin of the Kama. I have crossed this vast plain from west to east, over an extent of about 700 leagues; the distance from south to north is 400 leagues. The Baltic sea lies to the west of this plain, the river Irtysz to the east, the Frozen Ocean to the north, the sea of Azow and the Caspian to the south.

If we cast our eyes on the general map, it will be observed that the countries to the north and to the south of the road I travelled through, are in general the lowest; as most of the rivers have their origin in the confines of this route. Some of them empty themselves into the southern seas, others into the Frozen Ocean; all the eastern rivers into the Irtysz, and all the western into those seas which are the boundaries of this part of Russia.

Petersburg and Tobolsky are the two extremes of this part of Russia from west to east. The first of these towns is 18 toises above the level of the sea, the second, 68. The extreme points of the north and of the south are the level of the sea.

According

According to the level I have taken of this part of Ruſſia, greateſt height of the country, between St. Peterſburg and Jachelbiza, an extent of near one hundred leagues, is only 45 toiſes; the ſmalleſt 18: and if the medium between theſe two reſults is taken, the mean height of this plain will be 31 toiſes, which differs only 14 toiſes from the two extremes. It has appeared to me from geography, and the informations I gained in the country, that this firſt plain extends itſelf more or leſs along ſide the ſea northward, and in ſome places ſouthward. There are generally no mountains to be ſeen on theſe ſhores, except in the ſouthern part of Ruſſia.

The diſtance from Jachelbiza to Oſſa is about 400 leagues; the whole of which extent may be conſidered as a ſecond plain.

In ſome places, however, there are hillocks, riſing grounds, or platforms, to be met with, as at Moſco, Caccy, and near the origin of the Kama. Theſe platforms are ſometimes 30 and 40 leagues in diameter. The height of the platform at Moſco is 269 toiſes above the ſea; that at Caccy, 215. The mean height, therefore, of theſe platforms is computed in even numbers at 240 toiſes*. The platform, where the Kama riſes, is at leaſt 240 toiſes †. The higheſt part of the reſt of the plain, is the level of the Kliaſma at Wolodimer, which I have deter-

---

* I at firſt ſuppoſed this height at 220 toiſes. This alteration has obliged me to make others; but they do not affect the inferences drawn from thence in another part of the work.

† I have not taken the level of this part of Ruſſia, but we may ſtill have a pretty exact idea of the height of this platform, by conſidering the ſlope of the Kama, which I have determined at 2 feet, 6 inches, 9 tenths *per* league. The diſtance from the origin of the Kama to Solikamſky is indeed about 130 leagues; and ſuppoſing the ſlope of the Kama at 2 feet, 6 inches, 9 tenths *per* league, the whole ſlope of the Kama, from its origin to Solikamſky, will be 55 toiſes: and the level of the Kama at Solikamſky being 187 toiſes above the level of the ſea, the height of the ſource of this river will be 242 toiſes. This height will, however, be rather more conſiderable, not only becauſe the ſlope of the river is greater towards its origin, but alſo becauſe it may reaſonably be imagined, that the higheſt point of the platform is not at the ſource of the river.

mined at 202 toifes; and the loweft is the level of the Volga at 96; confequently, the mean height of this fecond plain is 149 toifes above the level of the fea, or 150, to make even numbers; and therefore the platforms are 90 toifes higher than this fecond plain.

The chain of mountains, known by the name of the Poias or Ryphæan mountains, begins at the diftance of a few leagues from Offa: it divides into two ridges towards the fouth, feparated from each other by a vaft plain. The loweft part is Tikonofka, the height of which has been determined at 168 toifes; the higheft is Sabarca, 228 toifes. The mean of the third plain is therefore 198 toifes. I had at firft reckoned this plain among the number of platforms; but the divifion of the foil of Ruffia feemed to me more exact by admitting this third plane, which is the bafis of all the mountains.

I croffed this fame chain at Solikamfky, about 60 leagues more to the north. The level of the Kama at Solikamfky, and that of the Tura at Verchaturia, fhould be confidered as the places which point out the level of the third plane towards the north: the firft 187 toifes; the fecond, 160. The mean height, therefore, of the third plane is 173 toifes, and as I have already determined this towards the fouth at 198; the medium between thefe two refults, will bring out the real height of the third plane to be 185 toifes above the fea.

The higheft mountain of the firft chain is 287 toifes. If this is compared with the height of the third plane, determined at 185 toifes, the mean height of the firft chain will turn out to be 235 toifes, 50 toifes above the third plane, and the higheft mountain 102 toifes above it. The higheft mountain of the fecond chain is that which ftands weftward of Klenoufkaia; its height is 309 toifes. By comparing this to the height of the third plane, the mean height of the fecond chain appears to be 247 toifes, 62 toifes above the third plane, and the higheft mountain 124.

The

The higheſt mountain on the road to Solikamſky, is that which ſtands to the eaſt of Kiria; its height is 471 toiſes above the level of the ſea. If this is compared with the height of the third plane, determined at 185 toiſes, the mean height of the chain will be 328 toiſes above the level of the ſea, 143 above the third plane, and the higheſt point 246 toiſes above the ſame plane.

From theſe different combinations, the following reſults are produced.

Mean height of the firſt chain, above the level the ſea, - - - - - - - 236 toiſes.
Mean height of the ſecond chain, - - 247
Mean height of the chain at Solikamſky, - - 328

On an average, mean height of the chain, - - 270

I have determined the mean height of the third plane at 185 toiſes; conſequently, the mean height of the chain is 85 toiſes above the third plane, and the higheſt mountain is 286 toiſes.

From this chain to the Irtyſz, there are about 120 leagues. The higheſt ground, throughout this extent, is at the foot of the mountains: its height continues leſſening as far as the Irtyſz; ſo that this ground forms a ſlope, the higheſt point of which is at Verchaturia on the north, and at Belojarſkaia on the ſouth road. Verchaturia is 160 toiſes above the ſea, and Belojarſkaia 189. The mean height, therefore, of the higheſt part is 175 toiſes: the level of the Irtyſz at Tobolſky being the loweſt point, and the height of the level of this river being 68 toiſes; the ſlope of the ground from the chain to Tobolſky, an extent of about 120 leagues, will be 107 toiſes.

This part of Siberia forms a new plane, which is inclined, whereas the others are parallel to the horizon. This plane makes an angle of about two degrees and an half with the horizon at Tobolſky. It riſes more and more towards the ſouth, and ſinks towards the north.

From theſe different reſults it may be concluded, that Ruſſia, from St. Peterſburg to Tobolſky, a diſtance of 700 leagues, is compoſed of four planes, each of them parallel to the horizon *, except the laſt.

The firſt plane, from St. Peterſburg to Jachelbiza, a diſtance of 100 leagues, is raiſed above the level of the ſea at Breſt 31 toiſes. There are no mountains on this firſt plane.

The ſecond plane, extending about 400 leagues from Jachelbiza to Oſſa, is raiſed 150 toiſes above the level of the ſea, and and 119 above the firſt plane. Hillocks of inconſiderable height are found upon this plane, as well as ſome platforms: theſe are 30 or 40 leagues in diameter: their mean heights are 240 toiſes above the level of the ſea, and 90 toiſes above the ſecond plane, on which they ſtand.

There is a third plane, extending about 90 leagues, from Oſſa to Echaterinenburg; the height of which is 185 toiſes above the level of the ſea, and 35 above the ſecond plane. On this third plane, the ridge of the Poias mountains is ſituated, the height of which is 270 toiſes above the level of the ſea, 85 above the third plane, and the higheſt mountain 286.

The fourth plane forms a ſlope from the chain to the Irtyſz, ſo that its angle of inclination is two degrees and a half at Tobolſky. Its height at the foot of the mountains is 175 toiſes, and at Tobolſky, which is the loweſt point of this part of Ruſſia, 68 toiſes. The ſlope, therefore, of the ground from the chain to Tobolſky, an extent of about 120 leagues, is 107 toiſes. This plane afterwards riſes towards the ſouth, and comes near the level of the ſea towards the north.

* It is ſuppoſed that each plane has particularly one uniform curvature, compoſed of ſmall planes, parallel to the viſible horizon, which extends about two leagues.

This divifion agrees, in fome refpects, with the idea preceding travellers have had of the foil of Ruffia. They have all found that it rofe on advancing towards the Poias mountains; but they have alfo fuppofed that it rofe equally to the eaft of thefe mountains: and by giving a confiderable height to thefe different planes, they have reprefented this country as the higheft part of Europe. According to my level, thefe feveral planes not only appear of a moderate height, but the ground alfo, inftead of rifing to the eaft of the Poias mountains, finks on the contrary for the diftance of near 120 leagues; and the level of the ground at Tobolfky is no more than 68 toifes above the level of the fea; this turns out very differently from what former travellers have advanced: neverthelefs their authority, and that of the natural philofophers, who have adopted this opinion, is fo refpectable, that I have thought myfelf obliged to pay a particular attention to this point.

Although the opinion of all thefe travellers was not founded on any obfervation publifhed in their works; yet as their accounts agree perfectly with each other in this point, I was fo ftrongly prepoffeffed in favor of what they have advanced, that I took it for granted this part of Ruffia was extremely high; fo that when I found, upon calculations made from my obfervations, that the refults were directly contrary to the received opinion; I imputed the difference to fome miftake in the obfervations, and endeavoured to deceive myfelf on every circumftance which feemed to be in favor of them. I was indeed fo well pleafed with thinking myfelf miftaken, that I would not liften to the truth; but at length I was fo much difgufted with this bufinefs, which had taken up more than two months of my time, that I had once refolved to omit this part of my journey, and to give up the barometer for ever. I took up the bufinefs again, however, feveral months afterwards, and confined myfelf to the obfervations alone. A firft calculation,

haftily

hastily made, convinced me, by the agreement of the results, that I was in the right. I laid aside an opinion, contradicted by all my observations, and was afterwards guided only by facts.

Ifbrants Ides imagines that the mountains of Verchaturia are 5000 toises high; I have determined the mountain of Kyria, the highest in the country, at 471 toises above the level of the sea; and if considered with respect to the ground on which it stands, it is no more than 286 toises high. This result, founded upon exact observations, cannot be controverted; any one may be convinced of this by examining in the last table of the levelling, the process by which it has been determined.

M. Gmelin gives an account of some observations made by the barometer at Kyria, on the 4th of December 1742 *, and at Verchaturia at the same time; but he gives the observations only, without drawing conclusions from them. According to these observations, the barometer at Verchaturia was higher than at Kyria by 17 lines, which are equal to 269 toises †.

The hamlet Kyria is situated in a plain, which makes part of a mountain standing to the east of the hamlet. I have settled the height of this mountain at 471 toises above the level of the sea. I did not take notice of the barometer in the

---

* Voyage en Siberia de M. Gmelin, édition Françoise, p. 248. t. ii. "On going away from Verchaturia, we were inclined to measure, by means of the barometer, the height of the neighbouring mountains, cal'ed the Ryphæan mountains, in the village of Kyria, which stands westward of the mountain, but not on its top. M. Muller observed, on the 4th of December, 1742, that from eight in the morning till two in the afternoon, the height of the barometer was 26 Paris inches $\frac{10}{12}$. The same day, and the same hours, at Verchaturia, it was at 27 inches $\frac{6}{12}$."

† Height of the barometer at Verchaturia - - 27 inches $\frac{1}{2}$
   At Kyria - - - - - - - 26 26

Relative height between Verchaturia and Kyria - - 1 37
The mean height of the barometer at Verchaturia, being reckoned at 27 0 6, 1 inch $\frac{6}{12}$, or 17 lines, will be found equal to 269 toises.

hamlet

hamlet Kyria, but I obferved it, on the 4th of April, at fix in the morning, in the plain at a fmall diftance from Kyria, where I ftopped a little while. According to my obfervations, the place where I took them turned out higher than Verchaturia by 280 toifes, 2 feet*, whereas I had determined from the obfervations of M. Gmelin, that it was only higher by 269 toifes, which makes a difference of 11 toifes. According to my obfervations, the barometer fhould be higher at Verchaturia by 18 lines $\frac{4}{11}$, while M. Gmelin has obferved this relative height at 17 lines only: this trifling variation may arife from a difference in the barometers, from the fpot not being exactly the fame, and perhaps alfo from fome difference in the temperature of the air. I have been lefs anxious, however, about making our refults agree, than in fhewing, from M. Gmelin's own obfervations, how inconfiderable the height of this mountain is †. It will be feen hereafter, from the fame obfervations, that the earth, to the eaft of thefe mountains, is likewife very low; and if M. Gmelin was really acquainted with this country, when he afferted ‡ "That there are large plains in "Siberia *(vaftos ibi extare campos)* which are raifed as much "above the reft of the earth, and as far diftant from the

---

* Height of this place above the fea   -   -   440 toifes 2
  Height of Verchaturia   -   -   -   160   0

  Relative height   -   -   -   -   280   2

And if the exact heights of the barometer, with refpect to the level of the fea, are compared, it will be found that the barometer at Verchaturia is higher than at the fame fpot in the plain by 18 lines $\frac{4}{11}$.

† It may perhaps be objected, that I have not attended to the corrections which the temperature of the air requires. This is the only circumftance in which this correction can be of any confequence. In my obfervations made in fummer time, the difference could only be 2 or 3 toifes, and fometimes 6 or 7, but here it becomes more confiderable: but this alteration is far from adding to the height of thefe mountains, fince, on the contrary, it makes them lower. The height of Kyria would then be 102 feet or 17 toifes lefs, and that of Verchaturia, 7 toifes.

‡ Paffage quoted by M. de Mairan.

"center,

" center, as many mountains of no inconfiderable height are
" in other countries *(montium non exiguæ molis)*;" the miftake
muft have arifen from his following the opinions of former
travellers, without attending to his own obfervations.

M. de Stralemberg has alfo fpoke very clearly upon the
great height he afcribes to this country; fo that this traveller,
to whom we are indebted for many ufeful remarks on Siberia,
has given us frefh proofs of the impropriety of advancing facts
not fupported by obervations. The paffage quoted from M. de
Stralemberg, by M. de Mairan, is as follows*: "The northern
" countries of Afia, *fays Baron Stralemberg, a Swedifh officer,*
" *and a man of learning, who was a prifoner feveral years in Ruf-*
" *fia and Siberia,* are confiderably higher than the European
" countries, as much fo, *he adds,* as a table is, with refpect
" to the floor it ftands upon: for, when we travel from the
" weft, going out of Ruffia, and pafs on to the eaft, by the
" Ryphæan mountains, to get into Siberia, we find that
" we always rife, rather than defcend, as we advance."
From this authority, joined to M. de Gmelin's, M. de Mairan
concludes with reafon, that if we muft rife, rather than defcend, on going from the Ryphæan mountains, to the eaft of
that chain of mountains which feparates Europe from Afia,
it follows, that how little foever thefe mountains are raifed,
the vaft plains of Siberia muft of neceffity be upon a level with
the tops of pretty high mountains.

My obfervations are directly contrary to thefe facts and this
affertion; fince it appears from thefe, that, on travelling eaftward from the Ryphæan mountains, the ground rather falls
than rifes from this chain of the Irtyfz, throughout an extent
of about one hundred and twenty leagues; of which one may
be convinced without the teftimony of my obfervations. We

---

* Mémoire de l'Académie Royale des Sciences de 1765. This paffage is taken from the defcription of Ruffia, French tranflation, tom. i. p. 332.

need only cast an eye upon any map whatsoever of these countries, and we shall find a number of rivers, whose source is in the Ryphæan mountains, and their course eastward from thence, emptying themselves into the Irtysz, at the distance of one hundred and twenty leagues from the chain: from whence it is evident, that the soil must be on a continual descent from the Ryphæan mountains to the east. I have determined the slope of these rivers by the most accurate observations; and have found, that the slope from the mountains to Tobolsky is 107 toises; the height of the Irtysz at Tobolsky 68 toises above the level of the sea, and 47 toises above the level of the Seine at Paris.

M. de Mairan mentions also another passage in the same part of his *Memoire*, pag. 256. It is asserted as a fact, in Cellarius's geography, quoted by this learned academician, that the Ryphæan mountains are constantly covered with snow. Although this would be no proof that the mountains in these northern countries were very high, yet I shall take upon me positively to deny the fact. I crossed these mountains at Echaterinenburg in the month of August, and they were not then covered with snow: at the end of May, the snow disappears from the mountains of Solikamsky, although they are higher, and their situation is more to the north than those of Echaterinenburg; and if there was any foundation for the fact mentioned by Cellarius, it would not certainly have been unnoticed by Mess. Gmelin, Stralemberg, Muller, and several other travellers, who have passed through this country.

Although it is evident, from what has been already said, that this country is not so high as it has been thought to be, yet it may not be improper to establish the validity of this opinion by some farther proofs, which would be sufficient of themselves to determine the point.

All philosophers know, that the variations of the barometer become less in proportion as we rise in the atmosphere; so that, in considerable heights, the mere observations of the barometer, compared to the mean height of this instrument at the level of the sea, are sufficient to determine the degree of elevation. If we suppose this country to be raised one half league only above the level of the sea, instead of two leagues and a half which M. Isbrants Ides gives to these mountains, then, the barometer will be six inches lower upon these mountains than at the level of the sea; and the mean height of the barometer in these places would only be 22 inches, for the mercury would never rise to 23. Now, I have observed, in the place acknowledged by all travellers to be the highest of the chain, that the barometer was at the height of 25 inches, 11 lines, $\frac{3}{12}$, upon the top of the mountain of Kyria, on the 4th April, at eight in the morning; and M. Gmelin, in a place a little below this, observed it at 26 inches, 5 lines; the barometer in these places being about 4 inches above the mean height of 22 inches. It is therefore evident from these observations, that these mountains cannot be more than about 400 toises high, instead of 2500, as M. Isbrants Ides asserts.

If all my observations made in Russia are examined in the same manner, it will still be found, that this country is lower than it has been supposed to be, since the barometer was in all places very high. During my stay at Tobolsky, from the 23d of April to the 28th of August, I observed the barometer at 28 inches, 10 lines, $\frac{4}{12}$, on the 28th of April, nearly as at Paris; and the lowest point was 27 inches, 6 lines, on the 24th of June. These facts are so clear, that they will not even admit the supposition of the country being higher than I have computed it. It is therefore certain, that all travellers have been mistaken in giving such an excessive height to the Ryphæan mountains and to this country; it is equally certain, that the

ground

ground falls, instead of rising, from the Ryphæan mountains towards the east; and that the country lying eastward of these mountains, far from being on a level with the tops of any pretty high mountains, is, on the contrary, lower than most plains of a moderate height in Europe; since the Irtysz at Tobolsky, one hundred and twenty leagues distant from the mountains, is no more than 68 toises above the level of the sea.

My only intention, in these remarks, has been to make it appear, that the part of Russia I went over is lower than it has been imagined; and I have not had the least design of controverting M. de Mairan's ingenious system on the causes of cold in winter and of heat in summer. In speaking hereafter of the climate, I shall prove, that the part of Siberia, to the east of Tobolsky, is not of so great a height, as that the almost incredible cold which prevails there, can be ascribed to this circumstance: this is owing to some particular and local causes, and those which I have assigned are equally applicable to M. de Mairan's system.

MINERALOGICAL OBSERVATIONS.

THE sandy tract of Poland extends all over Russia, as far the mountains which separate Siberia from the rest of this empire. I could not make myself acquainted with the nature of this soil, till my return from Tobolsky to St. Petersburg; for as I had set out from this capital in winter-time, the ground was covered with snow. I shall hereafter speak of the superficial soil of this country, and shall at present confine myself to the examination of that part of the chain of the Ryphæan mountains, lying between Solikamsky and Echaterinenburg. I have examined this part with the greatest care; having also had an opportunity of examining the internal parts of the earth, by going down into the mines which are worked there.

Before I enter upon my account of the mines, I shall just speak of the gypses which are found in Russia, in the neighbourhood of Cazan, and in Siberia. I have already mentioned them in the detail of my journey, where I referred to some farther particulars on this subject, which I introduce here, to preserve the order of the route.

Of the Gypses.

I. *Solid, striated, half transparent Gyps.*

This is found on the Occa, four leagues westward of Nisan-Novogorod. It forms a bed of two inches thick, in the mountain situated to the south of this river. This gypse lies between two beds of red clay, of a moderate firmness. The layer

layer of gypſe is 6 toiſes above the level of the river, and conſequently 131 above that of the ſea*.

This gypſe is white, made up of long and ſparkling fibres: it is compact, it divides itſelf into lamellæ; and is harſh to the touch. Theſe lamellæ are not eaſily rubbed to powder between the fingers: they appear at firſt like ſo many ſmall fibres, reducible into a pretty fine powder, but hard to the touch. It does not effervesce with acids, and when calcined puts on the whiteneſs of ceruſs. The parallel fibres, of which it is compoſed, ſeparate upon the ſlighteſt preſſure; it then ſticks to the finger, is ſoft to the touch, and falls into a ſaponaceous powder, like that of the Chineſe gypſe, to which it has ſome reſemblance; but does not decrepitate in the fire as that does; beſides, its fibres, even before calcination, are coarſer, leſs compact, and have not the ſilkineſs of the Chineſe gypſe.

This gypſe conſiſts of three beds. The fibres of the two lower beds, run in the ſame plane, perpendicular to the baſe, but the upper bed is compoſed of oblique fibres.

II. *Cryſtalliſed, tranſparent Gypſe, reſembling a pen.*

This gypſe is not unlike a pen. The lamellæ, or cryſtals, of which it is made up, terminate all upon one line as the feathers upon a quill. The planes of the large lamellæ make angles of about 50 degrees, and the ſmall ones of 70 degrees, with this line.

This gypſe divides itſelf into layers in the direction of planes, perpendicular to thoſe of the large lamellæ: its ſurface is as ſmooth and ſhining as well poliſhed glaſs. Theſe layers are not pliable in the leaſt, and therefore break very eaſily. They

---

* Niſan-Novogorod is 127 toiſes, three feet, above the level of the ſea. This height, and the ſlope of the Occa, being given at 4 feet, 6 inches, &c. we find the height of this bed to be 130 toiſes, 4 feet.

may be subdivided into others so thin, as not to produce any great alteration in the color of paper. The parts which compose this gypse are so small and so smooth, that it is impossible to distinguish them through a magnifying glass. The small lamellæ are formed into a kind of parallelepiped. If we strike these solids in a direction perpendicular to their base, they all separate into parallelepipeds, composed of lamellæ similar to those we have just before been mentioning.

This gypse does not effervesce with aqua fortis. It decrepitates in the fire, loses its transparency, and divides itself into lamellæ, which are perfectly smooth, and of a grey pearl color. It has a silken feel, when powdered between the fingers, and is soft to the touch as the former, but less friable. It is found on the Volga, at some leagues southward of Cazan.

III. *Transparent gypse, crystallised in form of a parallelepiped.*

This gypse forms a kind of oblique parallelepiped. It is composed of two parallelograms and eight trapeziums. The lower base, as well as the upper, is a parallelogram whose correspondent angles are equal, and the remaining angles of which are obtuse and acute; the obtuse angles are of 129 degrees, the acute of 51. The lower base is somewhat larger in all directions than the upper. Each surface is composed of two oblique trapeziums, all the sides of which are unequal, even those of the correspondent trapeziums. These surfaces are inclined, and form obtuse angles at the points of contact. These angles are equal on the correspondent surfaces, of 160 degrees on the large sides, and 110 on the small sides. If sections were made parallel to the base of this parallelepiped, and passing through the line of contact of these trapeziums, we should then have four sections, about one tenth of an inch
distant

distant from each other, becauſe the ſides of theſe trapeziums are all unequal.

This gypſe, although it is an inch thick, is tranſparent enough, to let one diſtinguiſh a black line, when it is laid on paper. Its color is rather browniſh. When cut with a knife, parallel to its baſe, it divides itſelf into lamina as thin as the Ruſſian glaſs, or *glacies mariæ*, but different from the latter inaſmuch as they have no kind of elaſticity, and are as brittle as glaſs. The ſurfaces of theſe lamina are as ſmooth as the beſt poliſhed glaſs. They even reſemble ice of a browniſh hue.

This gypſe decrepitates in the fire, loſes its tranſparency, becomes very light, and of a fine ſilken white color: its ſurface remains ſmooth; it does not effervesce with aquafortis; its lamina are diſtinguiſhable, but are not ſo thick. It is ſo friable when calcined, that it falls into ſmall leaves on the ſlighteſt touch. It may be rubbed down between the fingers to a very fine ſoft powder. This gypſe is found on the Volga, to the ſouth of Cazan.

IV. *Tranſparent gypſe, cryſtalliſed in form of oblique parallelepipeds.*

This gypſe is compoſed of ſeveral parallelepipeds reſembling the laſt, but they are not ſo regular, although they are moſt of them furniſhed with the ſame number of ſides. They differ almoſt all in ſize, and form various groups, which make this figure altogether very irregular, although, in general, it has ſome reſemblance to an inclined parallelepiped, compoſed of ſix parallelograms. To each of theſe parallelepipeds in particular, may be applied what has been ſaid of the laſt. The principal difference is in the color, which in theſe is rather yellowiſh than brown. This gypſe is found on the Volga, ſouthward of Cazan.

V. *Gypſe*

V. *Gypſe tranſparent in the ſtrata.*

This gypſe comes from the Poias mountains, between Echaterinenburg and Solikamſky, but I know not from what particular ſpot. It is diſpoſed in layers. The piece I have, forms a plate three inches long, two inches wide, and four lines thick. It is as diaphanous as glaſs, and is of the color of white glaſs. The ſame peculiarities may be obſerved in it as that of N°. III, with this difference, that native ſulphur is ſometimes found in it.

VI. *Mica, Muſcovy glaſs.*

This kind of gypſe is found in ſeveral parts of Ruſſia, eſpecially in Siberia, where glaſs is made of it. It is ſometimes two feet and a half ſquare, and commonly five or ſix inches. It is one third of a line in thickneſs, and is ſo tranſparent that one may read through it: its color is a light brown, inclining to yellow.

It makes a certain noiſe when ſcraped with the point of a knife, or any other inſtrument; it is ſo tough, that it muſt be bent backwards and forwards ſeveral times before it will break, and is compoſed of an infinite number of lamina. At firſt it ſeparates readily into ſix or ſeven lamina in its longitudinal direction; each of which become flexible and more tranſparent. The ſurfaces are very ſhining, and as ſmooth as the beſt poliſhed glaſs. Each of theſe lamina is eaſily ſubdivided into three others: they are then ſo tranſparent, that the color of objects is not much affected by them; they are alſo ſo pliable that they may be twiſted round the finger like paper, and will immediately recover their common form. If one of theſe lamina is farther ſubdivided, it falls into ſpangles, which may be blown away.

This mica resists fire and acids: it does not decrepitate, but makes a noise something like butter beginning to melt in a pan, which seems to proceed from the separation of the lamina: it then becomes four lines in thickness, instead of one third of a line as it was before. A number of about thirty lamina more or less distant from each other may be distinguished in it; and although they should be brought together with the fingers, they immediately return to their natural state.

This mica, after being made red hot, is still pliable: it acquires a white color as bright as silver. It loses its transparency when left to its original thickness of one third of a line, and becomes half transparent again when divided into twenty lamina. It may then be subdivided into an infinite number of other lamina of different sizes, like the silver leaves used by the gilders. When it is rubbed for any time in the palm of the hand, it falls into spangles which stick to the skin.

Of the different mines in Siberia, between Solikamsky and Echaterinenburg.

Ice and snow cover the country on which I have made the following observations for most part of the year. It is commonly spoken of by the Russians, as of a new Peru, in which mines of gold and silver, and precious stones abound. Although much may be taken off from this account, it is still certain, that mines of gold and silver are to be found within the frozen soil of Siberia, as within the parched territories of the torrid zone; but these mines, at least those of the Poias mountains, are never to be found among those immense rocks, which form ridges of mountains, extending over an infinite space, and crossing the globe. The mines in Siberia are rather found in plains situated on the tops of low mountains: they are one or two feet below the surface: their extent and difposition is such as to furnish the naturalist with an unusual appearance. The copper and iron mines equally deserve our attention. Those of iron are every where distributed in heaps, and do not keep any invariable order in their situation. That I may proceed with regularity, I shall treat particularly of each ore.

To fulfil this undertaking, I brought away a large collection of all the ores of this country, with remarks serving to illustrate the history of them. These remarks I made on the spot, and collected the materials from the pits, which had been made to raise the ore. Whenever it was not possible for me to go to the spot, I consulted the persons in the country who had the direction of the mines. At my return into France, I was assisted by M. le Sage, well known for his progress in chymistry; and M. Bouchu, correspondent of the Academy of Sciences, was also kind enough to take upon himself all the experiments made on the iron ores.

I. *Loadstone.*

This iron ore is in general not easily melted; it produces a very bad iron, and that in small quantity. The loadstone of Siberia is on the contrary a very rich ore. It is found in different parts of the Poias mountains, between Echaterinenburg and Solikamsky. That which I am most acquainted with, is from the mountain Galazinski, situated about ten leagues out of the road in going by Echaterinenburg, and sixteen leagues westward of the forge of Bilimbaeufkoi [*]. In

---

[*] This forge belongs to Count Strogonow. The ore is melted and the iron prepared here, as in almost all the forges I shall have occasion to speak of. By a forge we are therefore to understand the place where the furnaces are, and where the metal is put into fusion.

this place, I found heaps of this ore above twenty feet high: I judged it at first sight to be loadstone; and indeed it is called magnetic ore: but when torrefied, it loses its attractive property. I readily got some that had not been exposed to fire, and knew it immediately to be loadstone. I brought away more than twenty pounds of each; but before I give any particular account of this ore, I shall just mention what the director of the forge told me about it.

The mountain from whence it is taken is more than 20 toises high: the ore is found at the bottom in beds separated by the earth; but the summit of the mountain is formed only by rocks of loadstone.

The crude loadstone of the mountain of Galazinsky is hard and compact; it strikes fire against a steel; it is of an iron colored brown; and course shining lamellæ are to be observed in it when broken. Having torrefied some pieces of this loadstone, it lost its power of attracting the filings of iron; but if applied to some filings thrown upon a loadstone not torrefied, the filings were attracted by the calcined loadstone, although not so powerfully as before calcination. This loadstone, calcined and pounded, falls into a powder, resembling the filings of iron, and equally subject to the powers of the common loadstone.

The torrefied loadstone I brought with me from Bilimbaeuskoi, is exactly the same, in every particular, as the crude loadstone which I calcined at Paris.

The crude loadstone loses two pounds on each hundred by calcination.

Produce *per* hundred { not torrefied, - - 58
{ torrefied, - - 60

The regulus of the first fusion does not run kindly, is irregular, and colored.

The regulus of the second fusion takes the mould well, is sharp, and colored with blue and red; and the flags are red.

The torrefied loadstone at Bilimbaeufkoi produces forty-three *per* hundred. The regulus is well fused, but irregularly shaped: it is deeply colored with blue and yellow; and the flags are reddish *.

II. *Loadstone.*

In the neighbourhood of the forge Utinfkoi, on the borders of the river Czaufowa.

This loadstone is of the same kind as that of the mountain of Galazinski, but less perfect, being mixed with a quantity of ferruginous, and sometimes copper earth.

III. *Loadstone.*

In the neighbourhood of Vifimkoi, of the same nature as that of No I. but more compact and smoother, and possessed of stronger attractive powers.

IV. *Loadstone.*

This is found to the south-east of Solikamsky: it is of the same nature as No I. of middling magnetic power, and containing many earthy particles.

---

* This ore being the same as that of No I. the produce should be similar: however M. le Bouchu's experiments cannot be doubtful, because they are made twice upon the crude ore; but as I brought several loadstone ores with me, it is probable that I may have been mistaken in the number I gave to him. Many chymists are of opinion, that a regulus of iron cannot be obtained by experiments made on small quantities. M. le Bouchu has invalidated this opinion; and it will be seen by what follows, that the result of these experiments scarcely differs from some of those I made on the spot, in the working of these mines at large.

V. *Loadstone.*

In the neighbourhood of the forge of Serebrianſkoi. It is of the ſame nature as the others, and extremely hard. It ſtrikes fire with ſteel. Its iron color is not ſo bright, and the ſhining ſpangles are leſs: it ſeems very rich in iron.

VI. *Loadstone.*

From the mountain of Galazinſki, already ſpoken of N_o II. it has been calcined at Bilimbaeuſkoi, and produced after this new trial 47 *per* hundred: in the country the produce is reckoned at 50 *per* hundred.

Loadſtone is found alſo in other parts of this chain, where it is very common. It ſeems all of the ſame kind. The variety of appearances to be obſerved in it, depend on the greater or leſs quantity of earthy particles with which it may happen to be combined. The product mentioned at Nº I. and II. ſeems to indicate the two extremes of the richneſs of the ore, one of which conſequently brings 60 *per* 100, the other 43.

The loadſtone is found only in that chain, whoſe direction is from ſouth to north.

VII. *Cubic and greeniſh Loadstone.*

This is found in the mountains ſituated to the ſouth of Solikamſky, at the diſtance of twenty leagues from this town. This ſtone is very hard, compoſed of ſmall cubes, grouped together in all kinds of forms, in a greeniſh ſubſtance. The cubes are of a bright luſtre, of the color of iron: iron filings adhere equally to the cubes or to the greeniſh ſubſtance. The ore,

when

when reduced to powder, exhibits some shining spangles of an iron colour, and a greenish dust. The loadstone attracts these two substances equally. This ore calcined becomes of a black color, inclining to blue. The green disappears, it attracts no more the iron dust, unless that is previously thrown upon another loadstone reduced to powder; it falls into small cubes of a brown iron color. The greenish particles are no more to be seen in it: the iron seems mineralised in this ore by arsenic. It loses by calcination 7 *per* 100, and produces a regulus ill shaped, of several colors, and brings 55 and a half *per* 100.

VIII. *Iron Ore in Strata.*

Iron ore of Bilimbaeufkoi, five leagues to the south-west. This ore is compact, of a yellow color, inclining to red. The martial earth is mixed with a little clay; it is disposed in strata. In some places, black metallic particles may be observed, more compact than the rest of the ore.

This ore, when crude, is not attracted by the loadstone, but becomes so in a small degree when calcined, by which operation it loses 8 *per* 100.

Produce *per* 100 { when crude, after two fusions, - 28
{ calcined, - - - - - - 32

In the first experiment on the crude ore, the fusion was imperfect, and the produce was put into the crucible again. The ore calcined was colored, as in the first trial.

IX. *Solid, blackish Iron Ore.*

This is found to the south of Bilimbaeufkoi, in the small mountain of Galazinski, from whence I took it. It is disposed in rocky masses, from two to six feet in diameter. It is found in a ferruginous earth, the produce of which is almost as rich

rich as that of the rocky ore itself. When the ore is broken, cavities are sometimes found in it, the inside of which is lined with a ferruginous earth of the deepest black color. By the help of a magnifier, small round tubercles may be distinguished in it. The inside of these cavities sometimes appears as if it was lined with the most beautiful black velvet. In other places, the cavities are very large and extremely irregular. The inside of the ore is vitrified, it is shining and browner than the rest. This vitrification has probably been brought about by a volcano. The rest of the ore, which forms the rock, is very compact, of a brown color, inclining to red in the broken parts; and covered outwardly with a yellowish oker.

The loadstone does not act upon this ore in its crude state, but attracts it powerfully when calcined; it loses by this operation 13 *per* 100.

Produce *per* 100 { when crude, - - - 51 $\frac{1}{2}$
{ calcined, - - - 53

At Bilimbaeuskoi, the produce is reckoned at 50 *per* 100.

The regulus in these two experiments is well-shaped: yellow and red colors are to be observed in it, and some tough flags.

Iron ore is to be found in other parts of this mountain, with cavities, as in the foregoing; the inside of which, does not exhibit the same appearances. This ore is decompounded, and may be said to consist chiefly of pure ferruginous earth. There are still some solid parts in its inside, which seem to indicate that it is the same ore as the foregoing: the produce, however, is very different. It is not subject to the powers of the loadstone when crude, but becomes so, to a great degree, when calcined; by which it loses 10 *per* 100.

Produce *per* 100 { when crude, - - - 34
{ calcined, - - - 52

In the firſt fuſion, this ore is colored with yellow, blue and red, and produces an ill-ſhaped regulus.

In the ſecond fuſion, it produces green flags, and a regulus well-ſhaped, ſharp, and colored with blue and yellow.

X. *Solid Iron Ore, of a brown color, inclining to red.*

This is found about ſeven leagues to the ſouth-weſt of Echaterinenburg. It is compact. Its outward ſurface is covered with a yellow oker, of a reddiſh brown in the breakings of its ſolid parts. In the other parts it is friable. Theſe ſhew a decompounded ore, and ſome blackiſh parts, which are ſtill ſolid.

This ore, when crude, is not acted upon by the loadſtone; but is ſlightly attracted by it, after calcination; by which it loſes 14 *per* 100.

Produce *per* 100 $\begin{cases} \text{when crude,} & - & - & - & 48 \\ \text{calcined,} & - & - & - & 48\frac{1}{2} \end{cases}$

In the country, the produce is reckoned at 45 *per* 100.

The fuſion was imperfect in the firſt experiment on the crude ore; it was therefore put into the crucible again, and a regulus was obtained, well-ſhaped, ſharp and colorleſs.

The calcined ore produced a regulus well-ſhaped, ſharp, and colorleſs.

XI. *Spongy Iron Ore.*

This is taken from the neighbourhood of Bilimbaeuſkoi, near the mountain of Galizinſki. It is internally full of ſmall cells like thoſe of a ſponge; with this difference, that they are ſometimes formed by thin plates. This ore is partly decompounded: it is black in ſome places, and brown in others: ſome of the plates are ſhining, and as if they were vitrified.

In general, it shews nothing but an oker of a deep yellow. Sometimes, however, solid particles may be seen in it, which resemble exactly the ore N° VII. Their color is a reddish brown.

This ore, when crude, is not acted upon by the loadstone, but becomes subject to its powers after calcination; by which it loses 10 *per* hundred.

$$\text{Produce } per\ 100 \begin{cases} \text{when crude,} & - & - & 40 \\ \text{calcined,} & - & - & 47 \end{cases}$$

In the country the produce is sometimes reckoned at 50 *per* 100.

The crude ore produces a regulus well shaped, sharp, and colored in several places with blue, red and lively yellow.

XII. *Black spongy iron ore.*

This is found to the south of Bilimbaeufkoi, at a small distance from that of N° X, to which it bears some resemblance; but it still very different in several particulars. It is full of cavities, as the pumice stone, and is nearly as light, whereas the other ore is rather heavy. The inside of this last ore is homogeneous, and of a very dark black color. It is covered externally with an oker of a bright yellow, which indicates a state of decomposition. When crude it is not attracted by the loadstone, but becomes subject to it after calcination; by which it loses 13 and a half *per* 100.

$$\text{Produce } per\ 100 \begin{cases} \text{when crude,} & - & - & 28 \\ \text{calcined,} & - & - & 32 \end{cases}$$

In the country the produce is reckoned at 35 *per* 100.

The crude ore produces a regulus well shaped, sharp, and colored with deep blue and red.

The ore calcined produces a regulus well shaped, sharp, and colored in some places.

XIII. *Solid iron ore.*

I could only get this ore in its calcined state: it is situated to the north of Bilimbaeufkoi, but I am not acquainted with its exact situation. Although calcined, it is very solid, compact, and heavy. It is black in some places, and of a deep red in others. It did not appear to be affected by the loadstone.

This ore produces green flags, a regulus well shaped, sharp, of a blue color, and 54 *per* 100. In the country it is reckoned to produce 45 *per* 100.

XIV. *Solid blackish iron ore.*

This is found in the neighbourhood of Wolofzkoie, one league and a half distant from Bilimbaeufkoi southward. It is hard and very compact. At its broken parts shining points are to be observed: its color is brown inclining to black. Its surface is irregular and rugged, without cavities. Some small stones are to be observed in it. This ore partakes a little of the hœmatites: it is covered with a ferruginous earth of a bright yellow.

This ore is not subject to the loadstone, except when calcined; it is then friable, of a blueish color on the inside, and reddish without. It loses 12 *per* 100.

Produce *per* 100 { when crude, - - 55
{ calcined, - - 61

In the country the usual produce is reckoned at 50 *per* 100.

This ore, in its crude state, produces a regulus well shaped, sharp, colored with red and blue: when calcined, the regulus is also well shaped, sharp, and some few colors are still to be seen in it.

In the same place is found another iron ore, bearing a great resemblance to the first. It is solid, compact, and brown on

the

the infide: feveral fhining points are to be obferved in it, which appear to be chryftalline. It is not fmooth on the broken furface as the firft, except in fome places, which are of a blackifh brown, and feem to have fome analogy to the hœmatites. This ore is covered externally with a ferruginous earth of a bright yellow: it is not attracted by the loadftone till after calcination; when it ftill remains very hard, and lofes 5 and a half *per* 100.

Produce *per* 100 { when crude, - - 46½
{ calcined - - 50

This ore produces, both when crude and calcined, a regulus well fhaped, fharp, and colored.

In the neighbourhood of the fame place another ore is likewife found, which I only got in its calcined ftate: it is then very hard, compact and heavy: it is blueifh on the infide, and outwardly reddifh. It is not much affected by the loadftone. It produces yellow flags, a regulus well fhaped, yellow, and 16 *per* 100.

XV. *Reddifh iron ore in ftrata.*

This is taken from the neighbourhood of Schaitanfkoi, to the eaft of Bilimbaeufkoi: it is very hard, compact and heavy, of a brown inclining to red, or rather of the color of wine lees. On its infide are alfo to be obferved fome fhades of a bright yellow; and it is covered on the outfide with a yellow ferruginous earth. In fome parts one may difcover little fhining tubercles of a very deep black, which bear a great refemblance to the hœmatites. On its broken furface longitudinal ftreaks are to be feen; but thefe feem to be formed from the ftrata of which it is compofed, and which are varioufly colored.

The loadstone does not attract this ore when crude; and but inconsiderably when calcined: it is then friable, the strata become more evident, and are disposed in thin plates. Its inside is colored with different shades of red, sometimes very dark. It loses by calcination 15 and a half *per* 100.

Produce *per* 100 { when crude, - - 35
{ calcined, - - 51

The crude ore produces green flags, a regulus well shaped, colored with yellow and red; when calcined, it produces green flags, a regulus well fused, but irregularly shaped and colored.

XVI. *Blackish iron ore.*

This is found southward of the forge of Schüralinskoi, near the origin of the river of Rez. It is very hard and compact, and breaks into small shivers: it is full of cavities, in which is observed some oker of a light yellow, and sometimes brown. The solid parts of the inside of this ore are of a brown black color, its outward surface is rugged.

The crude ore is not subject to the loadstone, but when calcined is slightly affected by it: it then becomes of a very dark red, and loses 13 *per* 100.

Produce *per* 100 { when crude, - - $51\frac{1}{2}$
{ calcined, - - $58\frac{1}{2}$

The crude ore produces a spongy regulus of a yellow color; when calcined, the regulus is well shaped, sharp, and colorless.

XVII. *Brown iron ore.*

This is taken from the neighbourhood of Caravievi, twenty leagues to the south of Echaterinenburg; it is hard and compact. Various substances are to be observed on its inside. The ore, in general, is of a dark brown color, and in some places

places black. Some shining points are discernable in it, which appear to be the ore chrystallized: in the brown parts some mica may be distinguished, and other small shining points which seem to be chrystal. In some places talc is found of a white color inclining to yellow: it is disposed in thin plates. It separates readily, and is as easily rubbed to powder between the fingers. Its external surface is irregular, of a brown color intermixed with yellow shades, arising from a ferruginous earth.

The loadstone does not attract this ore when crude, but acts powerfully upon it after calcination, when it remains still very hard. It is colored with blue and several shades of red: it loses by calcination 13 *per* 100.

The crude ore produces a regulus well shaped, not colored, and 39 *per* 100. The calcined ore is reckoned in the country to produce 40 *per* 100.

XVIII. *Iron ore in strata.*

This is found in the neighbourhood of Echaterinenburg: it is disposed in strata one third of a line thick. These strata are of a black color inclining to blue; they are divided by yellow oker, which forms one stratum of very little thickness. This ore is sometimes of a dark brown color, and of a brown inclining to yellow: it breaks into shivers. Its external surface is rugged, and covered with yellow oker. In some parts a blackish spongy surface may be distinguished, which exhibits myriads of pores through a magnifying glass.

The crude ore is not affected by the loadstone; but is slightly acted upon by it after calcination: it is then puffed up, very friable, and of a very dark red color. It loses 11 *per* 100 by calcination.

Produce *per* 100 {when crude, - - 36½
                    calcined, - - 41¾

XIX. *Solid iron ore.*

This comes from the neighbourhood of Echaterinenburg; I only got it in its calcined state; it is then friable. Its inside is in general of a dark red, and in several places of a shining black color. In some places points of a bright red may be observed. This color disappears by the application of aquafortis, and returns again instantaneously. The external surface of this ore is reddish; it is slightly affected by the loadstone, and bears some resemblance to the hæmatites.

It produces 42 *per* 100, red flags, the surface of which is covered with a kind of white enamel, and a regulus well shaped, sharp, and of a bright yellow color.

XX. *Brown iron ore.*

This is to be found in the neighbourhood of Echaterinenburg; it is very compact. Its outside is generally of a dark brown color. There are some cavities in it, the inside of which is lined with a very black ferruginous earth, with tubercles in some places. Some shades of a deep yellow oker are also to be distinguished in it; its external surface is covered with a bright yellow oker. This ore, when crude, is not subject to the loadstone, but when calcined is powerfully attracted by it; and becomes extremely friable. Blueish colors with reddish shades are to be seen in it. It loses 14 *per* 100 by calcination.

Produce *per* 100 {when crude, - - - 38
                    calcined, - - 45

In the first experiment with the crude ore, the regulus was well shaped, sharp, and colorless. Calcination produces some tenacious tough flags, a regulus well fufed, but irregularly fhaped, and of a yellow color in fome places.

XXI. *Whitifh iron ore.*

This comes from the neighbourhood of Echaterinenburg; it is very compact, foft to the touch, although of a clear whitifh brown color; various colors, fuch as black and yellow, appear on its broken furface. It feems to be compofed of a ferruginous earth, combined with clay. Its external furface is of a dirty light yellow color. It is not much affected by the loadftone till after calcination, when it ftill preferves its hardnefs, acquires fome fhades of red, and lofes $6\frac{1}{2}$ *per* 100.

This is a very poor ore; being not well feparated in a firft experiment, the produce was expofed a fecond time to fufion, and fmall pieces of metal were obtained, well fhaped, and yielding 6 *per* 100 for the produce of this crude ore.

XXII. *Solid iron ore.*

This is found in the neighbourhood of Echaterinenburg. I got it only in its calcined ftate; it is then very compact. Its infide exhibits various colors, and fhining black, which fhews its analogy to the hæmatites: in other places it is reddifh and of a different grain. Several fhining points may be obferved in it, which appear like the mica. In fome places points of a lively red may alfo be feen: it is flightly affected by the loadftone, and its external furface is of a reddifh hue.

This ore produces 54 *per* 100, fome tough flags of deep yellow and red colors.

There is another mine worked near this of N° XXII, the ore of which differs only from the preceding; in producing 61 *per* 100.

XXIII. *Solid*

XXIII. *Solid iron ore.*

This comes from the neighbourhood of Echaterinenburg: it is calcined, black and reddish. The black parts are the hæmatites ftriated longitudinally. It is fparkling and fhining in thefe places: it is but flightly fubject to the loadftone; it produces green flags, inclining to blue, a regulus well fufed, irregularly fhaped, of a lively yellow color, and 54 *per* 100.

XXIV. *Solid iron ore.*

Calcined ore from the neighbourhood of Echaterinenburg. It is a kind of hæmatites of a deep black color. It is compact, and fhining where it is broken. There are cavities in it filled with a ferruginous earth, of a deep red in fome places, and a lively red in others.

This ore is flightly affected by the loadftone. It produces beautiful green flags, a regulus well fhaped, fharp, and 63 *per* 100. The regulus is yellow underneath, and in fome places white.

XXV. *Solid iron ore.*

Calcined ore from the neighbourhood of Echaterinenburg. Its infide is of a deep black color, but not bright: it is very friable; and fhining particles are fometimes to be feen in it.

This ore is more powerfully attracted by the loadftone, than any I have yet mentioned. It produces flags of a violet color; a regulus well fufed, irregularly fhaped, of deep yellow, red, and blue colors, and 63 *per* 100. It contains a fmall portion of copper.

XXVI. *Solid*

XXVI. *Solid iron ore.*

Calcined ore from the neighbourhood of Echaterinenburg: compact and hard. Different red colors are to be discerned on its inside: some are inclined to brown, others are of a light red, and others again are only disposed in small spots much resembling dull vermilion; it stains the fingers. Although it has lost its chief properties by calcination, it still appears very analogous to the hæmatites.

This ore is not subject to the loadstone; it produces a regulus well shaped, sharp, of a yellow color, and 54 *per* 100.

XXVII. *Solid iron ore.*

Calcined ore from the neighbourhood of Echaterinenburg. It is partly of a brown color inclining to black on its inside; but when reduced to powder is of a deep red. Streaks may be observed in some parts of it, which bear a great resemblance to the hæmatites: it is of a red color inclining to brown, and sometimes lighter in the other internal parts. Its external surface is covered with a spongy ferruginous earth, of a deep red color: some black parts are distinguishable in it, smooth and shining, as in the hæmatites.

The loadstone has no effect upon this ore. It produces green flags, a regulus well fused, irregularly shaped, of deep blue and yellow colors, and 61 *per* 100.

XXVIII. *Blackish iron ore.*

This is taken from the neighbourhood of Echaterinenburg; it is very solid and compact, and breaks into small shivers. Some brown parts are apparent on the broken surface, among which

which the mica shews itself; the other parts are of a dark black: all the parts are smooth and shining, and indicate the hæmatites in this place, but without any appearance of regularity. This ore, after calcination, becomes of a red color inclining to blue.

The loadstone acts powerfully upon it when calcined; by which process it loses 15 *per* 100.

$$\text{Produce } per \text{ 100} \begin{cases} \text{when crude,} & - & - & 53 \\ \text{calcined,} & - & - & 58\tfrac{1}{4} \end{cases}$$

This ore produces green flags, and a spongy regulus, of deep blue and yellow colors.

XXIX. *Blackish iron ore.*

From the neighbourhood of Echaterinenburg. It is hard, compact, and very heavy, and breaks into small shivers; it appears to be formed of two layers, the one of a black color rather inclining to blue, and the other of the same kind of substance, combined with yellow oker, somewhat inclining to red. Its outward surface is of a yellowish oker. The black parts of this ore seem very similar to the hæmatites, without putting on any regular appearance. On the broken surface smooth and shining parts may be observed.

The loadstone does not affect this ore in its crude state, but acts upon it after calcination, by which it becomes friable, of a blueish color with different tints of red; and when pounded, is of a red color inclining to blue. It loses 11 *per* 100 by calcination.

$$\text{Produce} \begin{cases} \text{when crude,} & - & - & 52 \\ \text{calcined,} & - & - & - & 59 \end{cases}$$

This ore, both crude and calcined, produces tough flags, a regulus well fused, and ill shaped, of a deep blue and rather yellowish colors.

XXX. *Brown*

XXX. *Brown iron ore.*

From the neighbourhood of Echaterinenburg; hard, compact and very heavy. It breaks into shivers; it is of a very fine grain, and its color in general is a deep brown. In some places still browner parts may be observed, the grain of which is not quite so fine; these contain a great deal of the mica, and, in some spots, oker of a deep yellow. On the broken as well as on the external surface, some parts may also be observed of a beautiful black color, smooth and shining, and very analogous to the hæmatites.

The loadstone acts upon this ore only after it has been calcined. It this state it is very friable, of a red color consisting of three different shades, one of which is rather blueish. It loses 12 *per* 100 by calcination.

Produce *per* 100 { when crude, - - 41
{ calcined, - - 50

This ore produces, after these two experiments, green flags, a regulus well shaped, sharp, and colored.

XXXI. *Brown iron ore.*

This is found on the road from Echaterinenburg to Bilimbaeuskoi. It is hard and very compact, breaks into small shivers, and exhibits a smooth surface of so fine a grain, that it is impossible to distinguish the particles which compose it, even with a magnifying glass. This ore is of a deep brown color. Many cavities are to be observed in it, with layers of a black substance, shining and full of tubercles. This black substance appears to be the hæmatites. When this ore is pulverised it is of a deep yellow color.

In its crude ſtate it is not affected by the loadſtone, and very ſlightly when calcined; in which ſtate it becomes extremely friable; of a light blue, mixed with ſome red colors. It loſes 21 *per* 100 by calcination.

Produce *per* 100 { when crude, - - 53
{ calcined, - - 63

This ore, in its crude ſtate, produces green and tough flags, a regulus well fuſed, ill ſhaped, of yellow and lively red colors.

XXXII. *Brown iron ore.*

This is taken from the mountain of Guaſcheminskoe, near to Echaterinenburg, weſtward. It is hard and compact, and breaks into ſmall ſhivers. It is of a fine grain, eſpecially in thoſe parts which are analogous to the hæmatites; but the ſurfaces are not ſhining in theſe parts, as in the preceding ores. It is in general of a pretty deep brown color: ſurrounded in ſome places with a reddiſh oker, in others with a light yellow oker. This ore when reduced to powder is of a deep yellow.

In its crude ſtate it is not ſubject to the loadſtone, but is powerfully affected by it after calcination, by which it becomes very friable, and exhibits two different kinds of red, one of which is light. It loſs 16 *per* 100.

Produce *per* 100 { when crude, - - 43
{ calcined, - - 50

This ore, when crude, produces at firſt a regulus not well ſeparated; but on being fuſed a ſecond time, it comes out well ſhaped, ſharp, and colorleſs, as when it is calcined.

In the ſame mountain is found another ore reſembling that of Nº XXXI. It is hard, compact, breaks into ſhivers, and the grain of the broken ſurfaces is ſo ſmooth, that the parts
which

which compose it can scarce be distinguished with a magnifying glass. In some places it is of a yellowish brown, in others of a blackish brown color. In the last places there are some shining spots which indicate the hæmatites; but this is not regularly disposed, nor is it furnished with any thing like tubercles. This ore is surrounded by oker of a reddish yellow color, and sometimes whitish: it acquires a deep yellow when reduced to powder.

When crude, the loadstone does not affect it, but acts powerfully upon it when calcined: it is then very friable, of a blue color, with red and whitish tints. It loses 13 and a half *per* 100.

In its crude state, it produces a spongy regulus, partly in grains, colored, and 51 *per* 100.

The mountain in which these two ores are found, is three leagues distant from Echaterinenburg: the ore is disposed by heaps, in kinds of pits which are from 15 to 30 feet in diameter, and generally 25 feet deep. These mines extend over a space of 1700 toises from south to north, and 200 toises from east to west. When the turf is raised, a yellowish earth, two feet thick, presents itself, and immediately below this the mine appears. The ore is found in loose lumps, of irregular and oftentimes odd figures: these lumps are commonly surrounded with a yellow and reddish oker, more or less deeply colored; they are often prodigiously large, weighing as much as three thousand weight. Mattocks, however, are the only instruments used for separating them from the mass, and they are broken with a hammer. At other times they are only two or three inches in diameter. They are inclosed in a ferruginous earth combined with clay, and in a kind of very rich mine in grain, which however is never worked. There is no kind of calcareous matter in any of these mines, of which I convinced myself both on the spot,

and

and at Paris, by examining the different earths I brought with me.

The ore in lumps is not equally plentiful every where. When one pit is worked out, another is fought for by following the metallic channels, by means of which all thefe pits communicate with each other. I counted one hundred of thefe upon the fpot. It is reckoned in the country, that the ore, in lumps, produces 50 *per* 100, and that in grain, 40.

XXXIII. *Solid iron ore.*

This comes from the neighbourhood of Echaterinenburg. Although calcined, it is very folid, compact, and of a blackifh brown color: there is a little of the hæmatites to be obferved in it, and it abounds with cavities, full of a deep red colored ferruginous earth. It is attracted by the loadftone. It yields a regulus badly feparated at the firft fufion: but being fet on to the fire again, the ore is obtained in fmall grains, well fhaped, of a pale yellow; and 44 *per* 100 is produced.

XXXIV. *Brown iron ore.*

This comes from the neighbourhood of Echaterinenburg. It is hard, compact, breaks into fmall fhivers, and is of a light brown amber color. Although there are but few particles which feem to partake of the hæmatites, yet I believe it bears a great analogy to that ftone.

The loadftone does not affect this ore when crude, but acts powerfully upon it when calcined. It then becomes friable, of a blueifh color. It lofes 10 *per* 100 by calcination.

Produce *per* 100 { when crude, - - - 56
{ calcined, - - 64

In its crude state it produces green slags, a regulus well shaped, sharp, of yellow, red and blue colors. When it is calcined the slags are also green, the regulus irregularly shaped, very sharp and colored.

XXXV. *Solid iron ore.*

Calcined ore from the neighbourhood of Echaterinenburg. In this state it is hard and compact, uneven on its broken surface, of a reddish brown color, and in some places blackish. This ore is scarce affected by the loadstone. The first fusion does not separate it well, the second produces a regulus well shaped, sharp, of a yellowish color, and 56 *per* 100.

XXXVI. *Brown iron ore.*

From the neighbourhood of Echaterinenburg; hard, compact, of a clear brown color, and an equal shade on its broken surface: where one may however observe one layer covered with a black color like velvet. This matter placed between the two layers has no degree of thickness. The grain of the ore is very fine, and furnished with the mica. Several parts of its external surface are full of tubercles, where some shining particles may likewise be seen; so that, according to all appearances, this ore is very analogous to the hæmatites. It is of a red color, mixed with yellow, when reduced to powder.

The loadstone does not affect it in its crude state, but acts powerfully upon it, after calcination; by which it becomes friable, of a beautiful deep red, and loses 15 *per* 100.

Produce *per* 100 { when crude, - - 69
{ calcined, - - 79

This ore, both in a crude and calcined state, produces green, tough slags, and a spongy regulus, colored.

XXXVII. *Brown*

XXXVII. *Brown iron ore.*

From the neighbourhood of Echaterinenburg; hard, compact, uneven on its broken furface, of a blackifh brown color, and a tolerably fine grain. There are cavities in it full of a very hard cryftallization, but without any regularity. This cryftallization fhould feem to indicate native iron: it is of the moft beautiful black: and fome fhining particles are obferved on its outward furface, which partake of the hæmatites. This ore is of a dull red color when pulverifed: it is but little affected by the loadftone, and that only when calcined: it is then friable, colored with red, and produces a fine deep red color when ground.

Produce *per* 100 { when crude, - - 50
{ calcined, - - 54

The crude ore yields a regulus, irregularly fhaped, of a yellow color; and when calcined, a regulus, well fhaped, fharp, and colorlefs.

XXXVIII. *Brown iron ore.*

From the neighbourhood of Echaterinenburg; hard, compact, uneven on its broken furface, and of a grain rather coarfe. Its general color is a lightifh brown, and in fome places a fhining black, like a beautiful varnifh. It indicates the hæmatites; and fometimes even tubercles are to be obferved in it. This ore, when powdered, is of a dufky red. When crude, it is not fubject to the loadftone, but it is powerfully attracted by it when calcined: it then becomes friable, and of a red color inclining to blue.

Produce *per* 100 { when crude, - - 41
{ calcined, - - 47

The

The crude produce required a second fusion, the regulus was then well shaped, sharp, and colorless.

XXXIX. *Black botryoid hæmatites.*

Iron ore from the neighbourhood of Echaterinenburg. The tubercles of this hæmatites seemed to have been formed like the stalactites, but with striated concentric layers. It is of a black shining color on its surface, as also at its broken parts: it breaks into shivers, and the striæ divide into distinct needles like those of antimony: these are likewise brittle. This hæmatites is formed upon a common iron ore, hard, compact, and of a dark brown color with some yellow shades. The hæmatites, reduced to powder, is of a deep yellow, as well as the ore; but the color of the ore is the lightest: they are neither of them attracted by the loadstone. Having calcined a piece which contained these two ores, the hæmatites preserved its color, but lost its brightness; the iron ore became of a reddish black. I afterwards reduced these two substances to powder, the hæmatites was gritty to the feel, of a dark brown inclining to a reddish color: the iron ore pulverized was softer to the touch, resembling the hæmatites in color, but lighter. The loadstone acted powerfully on this ore; it also acted on the hæmatites but not with any considerable force. I repeated this experiment several times, and found that the loadstone acted even more readily on the small needles, which were not reduced to powder. As I did not think it necessary to give up this piece for experiments, I could not determine the produce of this ore; besides that some idea may be formed of it from what has been said.

XL. *Solid iron ore.*

This comes from the neighbourhood of Bilimbaeuskoi; it is calcined, hard, compact, of a dark red color with brown shades,

shades, uneven on its broken surface: the grain of it is coarse, and contains a great deal of the mica. When pulverized it is of a beautiful deep red, and hardly affected by the loadstone.

This ore produced, by a second fusion, a regulus well shaped, sharp, and 47 *per* 100.

XLI. *Solid iron ore.*

Calcined ore from the neighbourhood of Bilimbaeuskoi; it is very hard, extremely uneven on its broken surface, and of a blueish color: its keeps its color, after it is pulverized; with this difference, that it then becomes darker: it is as powerfully attracted by the loadstone as filings of iron are. It produces a regulus well fused, irregularly shaped, of a yellow color in some places, and 62 *per* 100.

XLII. *Brown iron ore.*

From the neighbourhood of Echaterinenburg; hard, compact, of a fine grain, and smooth on its broken surface. It is disposed in lamellæ, divided by a beautiful black layer of no thickness. This substance surrounds the ore in some places; it is shining, and resembles the hæmatites (N° XXXVIII.) The ore is of pale brown inclining to a reddish color. In some places, chiefly on its outside, oker may be observed. This ore, when pulverized, is of a yellowish color inclining to brown, not subject to the loadstone, but powerfully attracted by it when calcined; it then becomes friable, blueish, with reddish shades, and of a fine deep red color, when pounded. It loses 13 ¼ by calcination.

Produce *per* 100 { when crude, - - 37½
{ calcined, - - 43.

This

This ore, when crude, required a second fusion: after which it produced a regulus well shaped, sharp, and colorless, as when calcined.

XLIII. *Blackish iron ore.*

From the neighbourhood of Echaterinenburg; compact, hard at its broken surface; blackish, shaded in some places with a reddish color, in others with a fine shining black, indicating the hæmatites, but is of no thickness. It abounds with numbers of little tubercles. In the reddish parts the mica is found: the grain of the ore is tolerably fine; in these parts it is porous, and its broken surface uneven.

This ore, pulverized, is of a deep yellow, and not affected by the loadstone; when calcined, it is hard and solid, of a dark black color, but dull; when reduced to powder, after calcination, it acquires a reddish black color, and is powerfully attracted by the loadstone. It is reckoned, in the country, to produce 52 *per* 100.

XLIV. *Brown iron ore.*

From the neighbourhood of Echaterinenburg, partly decompounded: the solid part is hard, in general compact, and of a light brown color; but several layers are to be discerned in it. Some of them are composed of light yellow oker; and these have commonly very little thickness: the others bear a great resemblance to the black hæmatites. These last are sometimes half a line thick: the decompounded parts consists of a fine light yellow oker, sometimes mingled with blackish shades. In the solid parts of this ore, which have no analogy to the hæmatites, a small portion of the mica may be distinguished, with several crystalline particles. It contains many irregular cavities.

This ore, when pulverized, is yellowish, and not affected by the loadstone; when calcined, it is blueish, and shaded with red veins; if pulverized, after calcination, it is then powerfully attracted by the loadstone, and acquires a fine deep red color. It loses 13 *per* 100 by calcination.

Produce *per* 100 $\begin{cases} \text{when crude,} & - & - & 44\frac{1}{2} \\ \text{calcined,} & - & - & - & 50 \end{cases}$

This ore, both crude and calcined, produces a regulus well shaped, sharp, and colorless.

XLV. *Rocky iron ore.*

From the neighbourhood of Echaterinenburg. It is a kind of yellowish grit, porous and hard. The particles of sand are coarse and equal. It is shaded in some places with a blackish color; this seems to indicate the existence of the iron, which is clearly seen by the naked eye at the broken parts; where it is scattered about in different places in small blueish and shining spangles.

This ore, pulverized, is of a deep yellow, it is the only one in which I have hitherto found particles in this state affected by the loadstone without being calcined. When this dust is exposed to the loadstone, the particles of iron disengage themselves to fix upon the loadstone, like the filings of iron. This ore, when calcined, is of a blackish brown, and becomes still more subject to the powers of the loadstone. It appears to me, that there is but a very small quantity of the sulphur that mineralizes the iron in this ore; but the metallic part is not for this reason more plentiful; for the ore is so poor that it is never worked. It loses 8 *per* 100 by calcination.

XLVI. *Brown*

XLVI. *Brown iron ore.*

From the neighbourhood of Echaterinenburg; hard, compact, and heavy. It is compofed of different fubftances irregularly difpofed; one is of a pale brown, another blackifh, and a third of a yellow oker, folid in fome places. The brown fubftance is uneven at the rugged broken part; the grain of it is coarfe, and interfperfed with feveral fhining cryftalline particles. The blackifh fubftance is in general of a very fine grain; the parts which compofe it are not to be diftinguifhed by the naked eye. It feems very analogous to the hæmatites, which is found in fome parts of it. Its broken furfaces are fmooth and fhining, and the grain cannot be here difcerned even with a magnifying glafs. The oker appears to be a decompounded part of the ore.

This ore, pulverized, is of a dufky red; it is but flightly affected by the loadftone, and that only when calcined: it is then friable, blueifh, with various tints of red: when pulverized, it acquires a deep red color, and yields confiderably to the loadftone. It lofes 12 *per* 100 by calcination.

Produce *per* 100 { when crude, - - 42
{ calcined, - - 48

This ore produces, in both thefe experiments, a regulus well fhaped, fharp, and colorlefs.

XLVII. *Brown iron ore.*

From the neighbourhood of Echaterinenburg; hard and moderately heavy, of a fine grain, fpongy in fome parts, and feems to indicate the hæmatites. The yellow oker furrounds it, and fome of this may be perceived on its infide, chiefly in the cavities which are found there.

This ore, pulverized, is yellow, reddish, and not acted upon by the loadstone. Calcined, it is friable, blueish, and powerfully attracted by the loadstone. It loses $16\frac{1}{2}$ per 100 by calcination.

Produce per 100 { when crude, - - 52
{ calcined, - - - - 58

This ore, when crude, produces green, tough, colored flags. When calcined, the regulus is well shaped, sharp, and colored.

XLVIII. *Solid iron ore.*

Calcined ore from the neighbourhood of Echaterinenburg; hard, compact, and heavy; of a black color inclining to blue, and brown in some places. The hæmatites may be seen dispersed indiscriminately through it, and some reddish oker.

This ore, pulverized, is of a dusky red, and is affected by the loadstone. It produces a regulus irregularly shaped, of a yellow color, and $55\frac{1}{2}$ per 100.

XLIX. *Blackish iron ore, cubic and cellular.*

This is taken from the neighbourhood of Echaterinenburg; it is partly solid and hard, partly cellular. The solid part consists only of cubes of the size of common dice: there are, however, some of them whose surfaces are not more than four lines over. These cubes are irregularly disposed. On all their surfaces, longitudinal fibres, parallel to the sides, may be observed; but the fibres of one surface always run in a contrary direction to those of another. The outside of these cubes is shining, and of a blackish color, and the substance, when pulverized, acquires a yellowish brown color. The loadstone has scarce any power over it, only attracting, very inconsiderably, some of its parts. When it is calcined, its color is then a dark reddish

reddish brown. The ore, in which these cubes are found, is of a blackish brown, as hard and as compact as the cubes; its grain is fine at the broken part, and tolerably smooth. When pulverized, it is of a yellowish brown inclining rather to red, and the loadstone has no effect upon it. The cellular part resembles a honeycomb, with this difference, that the cells are of various forms. Their sides are not the 20th part of a line thick. These cells are sometimes found empty, sometimes filled with a black substance, and at other times with a dark brown kind of matter. The general color of the cellular part of this ore is brown inclining to black: when pulverized, it is of a brown inclining to yellow, and not attracted by the loadstone: it becomes subject to it in a slight degree when calcined, and its color then becomes black inclining to blue.

The solid part of this ore is covered externally with a layer of bright yellow oker. In some parts are observed collections of mica mixed with this oker, and between the cubes there are cavities lined with crystallizations of a crystal matter. This crystallization arises in little tubercles of a yellowish brown color, and is certainly produced by the metallic part: it sometimes covers the faces of the cubes. This ore loses $11\frac{1}{2}$ per 100 by calcination.

Produce per 100 { when crude, - - - 45
{ calcined, - - - 54

When crude, it requires a second fusion; it produces then a regulus well shaped, sharp, and of a yellow color; as it does likewise when calcined.

L. *Blackish iron ore.*

From the neighbourhood of Echaterinenburg; composed of two substances; one of a blackish color inclining a little to red; and the other of a dirty brown. The blackish substance

substance is hard and compact: its grain is fine, and smooth on the broken surface. In some parts a shining matter may be observed, indicating the hæmatites. There are some cavities in it, the inside of which is lined with crystallized tubercles of a dull black color.

The other dirty brown substance is but in small quantity; it is tolerably hard, porous, rugged, and of a moderate consistence. This ore, when pulverized, is of a yellow color inclining a little to red; it is not then affected by the loadstone, but is powerfully attracted by it when calcined: it is then friable, blueish, and, when pulverized, of a dark brown reddish color. It loses 13 *per* 100 by calcination.

Produce *per* 100 { when crude, - - 45
{ calcined, - - 52

The crude ore requires a second fusion: it then produces a regulus well shaped, sharp, and colorless, as when it is calcined.

LI. *Blackish iron ore.*

From the neighbourhood of Echaterinenburg; friable, disposed in bright scales, of a deep black color: it contains but a little iron, and a great quantity of copperous pyrites. The mine is not worked.

LII. *Reddish brown iron ore.*

This is found in the low mountains situated to the east of Melechina, and to the west of Verchaturia. It has scarce any consistence, being nothing more than a ferruginous earth, the parts of which are somewhat consolidated; it is of a reddish brown color. In some parts of it are found silky copper fibres, which in other parts are crystallized under the form of vitriol.

It is not affected by the loadstone even after calcination. It is then very friable, of a deep red, and when pulverized of a beautiful red inclining to blue. It loses by calcination 21 *per* 100: and produces green flags, a regulus well shaped, sharp, of a bright yellow, and 52 *per* 100.

LIII. *Brown iron ore.*

From the mountains situated westward of Zernoistoznskoi, northward of Echaterinenburg. It is composed of different substances confusedly mixed together; but they each of them preserve their particular characteristics. In some places the ore is of a shining black, in others dull; it is of a fine grain; these parts seem to bear some analogy to the hæmatites: the other parts indicate nothing more than a ferruginous earth, of a brown color inclining to yellow, sometimes a dark brown. There is much crystal dispersed in the inside of this ore. It becomes friable by calcination; and when pulverized is of a dark red color, and is not affected by the loadstone.

It loses by calcination 13 *per* 100, and produces a regulus well fused, some red colors, and 39 *per* 100.

LIV. *Brown iron ore.*

From the neighbourhood of Echaterinenburg; hard, compact, of a rough grain. A great deal of mica may be observed in it, and upon its outside a layer of a light red color, which appears to be cinnaber. It also contains a black shining substance, which is owing to the hæmatites. This ore when pulverized is of a beautiful red, and is not affected by the loadstone. When calcined, it preserves its hardness; the colors are deeper and of a fine red; and when pulverized, after calcination, the loadstone acts upon it. It loses 13 *per* 100, and produces

produces a regulus irregularly shaped, of red and blue colors, and 47 per 100.

LV. *Blackish crystallized ore.*

Found in the neighbourhood of Bilimbaeufkoi. It is a ferruginous earth, hard in some places; but in general of a moderate confiftence. It is full of brownish cryftals, difposed in leaves, but unequally diftributed. They sometimes form small cells, filled with a blackish ferruginous earth, which is at other times of a bright yellow. The general color of this ore is that of fnuff. The loadftone has no effect upon it, and but little when it is calcined; it then becomes friable, of a very deep red color inclining to blue. It loses $18\frac{1}{2}$ per 100, and produces a regulus well shaped, sharp, colored, and 47 per 100.

LVI. *Blackish iron ore.*

From the neighbourhood of Echaterinenburg; hard, compact, heavy, of a very fine grain in its blackish parts, and coarser in those which are of a light reddish brown. There is a small quantity of mica to be obferved in it, and some parts of a shining black, which feem to indicate the hæmatites. This ore, pulverized, is of a yellowish brown, and is not affected by the loadftone. Calcination gives it a red color inclining to blue: it is of a very deep red when pulverized, and yields to the loadftone. It loses 15 per 100 by calcination.

Produce per 100 { when crude, - - $44\frac{1}{2}$
calcined, - - 49

This ore produces green tough flags and a fpongy regulus, deeply colored. The fame appearances are obferved when it is calcined, with this difference, that the regulus is then well shaped.

LVII. *Blackish*

LVII *Blackish iron ore with shining points.*

This is found in the neighbourhood of Echaterinenburg: it is composed of a black ferruginous earth, a fine yellowish sand, white shining points, some of which are mica, others crystal. A copperous earth is also to be observed in it. This metal sometimes appears in it under the form of silky copper, and is often crystallized as rough emeralds. These several substances form a kind of granite, friable and very light, and a greyish sand when this is pulverized. This ore exhibits nearly the same appearances after calcination, with this difference, that the loadstone then attracts slightly some of its parts. It loses 13 *per* 100. It is so poor an ore, that in the experiments made on small quantities, there are scarce any particles of iron to be extracted: it seems to be richer in copper.

LVIII. *Iron ore of a yellow saffron color.*

From the neighbourhood of Echaterinenburg. It is a ferruginous earth of a saffron color, light and so friable that it may be rubbed to powder between the fingers. It then falls into a kind of sand, which tinges the fingers with a bright yellow inclining to a saffron color. In some places blackish parts may be observed, some mica, and several copperous parts of a green color, sometimes under the form of silky copper. Crystals are also found in it, and a saponaceous substance resembling the asbestus.

This ore, calcined, is easily pulverized; the loadstone then attracts some of its particles. It contains so little iron, that it is scarce possible to obtain a few particles from experiments made on small pieces; it appears richer in copper.

Remarks on the iron mines of the Poias or Ryphæan mountains in Siberia.

In all the ores I have mentioned, the iron is mineralized by fulphur, and combined with a vitrifiable earth, often with clay; but I never found any calcareous earth mixed with any of them. I convinced myfelf of this while I was in Siberia, in the mines I vifited there, and have been farther confirmed in the opinion by an accurate obfervation I made of the fact at my return to Paris.

Of all thefe mines, to the number of fixty-one, taken from different places, there is not one difpofed in veins. They are all found in heaps, fcattered here and there; and ought therefore to be reckoned among the ores, carried by fome revolutions in the earth, from one place to another.

Among all thefe ores, there is but one (N° **XLV.**) which is attracted by the loadftone; all the reft require calcination, after which they become more or lefs affected by it.

Thefe mines, although in heaps, and difperfed to all appearance without order, do ftill obferve one unvariable rule. All thofe from the neighbourhood of Echaterinenburg; bear a great analogy to the hæmatites; and they are alfo the richeft. Thofe from Bilimbaeufkoi have a greater refemblance to rocky ores, and fome of them appear to have been expofed to fire in volcanos.

Thefe mines are almoft always found in low mountains, and on the borders of rivers. They are not generally more than three feet below the furface; they are feldom more than four and twenty or thirty feet deep, and oftentimes much lefs. The bottom of them is on a level with the rivers, fo that by the pofition of thefe mines, and the levelling of the road, the height

height of each particular mine might be determined with respect to the level of the sea; but it will be sufficient to determine the mean height of the bed in general, by calculating the height of the highest and lowest points.

The highest place, where the iron ore is to be found, is on the river Czausova, southward of Bilimbaeuskoi, eighteen leagues distant from thence, and this place is 272 toises above the level of the sea *.

The mouth of the river Kofwa may be reckoned as the lowest place where the iron ore is to be found: it is 184 toises above the level of the sea †.

It is therefore certain, that the highest iron mines in the Poias or Ryphæan mountains, are raised 272 toises above the level of the sea, and the lowest 184 toises; if the medium between these two results is therefore taken, the mean height of the known mines of iron will turn out to be 128 toises above the level of the sea; whereas the highest measured mountains are 471 toises high, others are 309; the mean height, therefore, of these mountains is 290, and the soil or plane, upon which these mountains stand, is 150 toises.

From this calculation it appears, that the iron mines are found about 70 toises above the surface of the soil, or in the lowest mountains: this agrees perfectly with their general position; for they are seldom found in the higher mountains, or in the middle of the chain.

---

* The height of Bilimbaeuskoi is 252 toises, 5 feet, 11 inches; and the slope of the river Czausova is 6 feet, 7 inches, 4 tenths per leagues; so that the distance of this place, from the iron mine being known, the height of that mine appears to be 272 toises.

† The mouth of the Kofwa is in the Kama, 26 leagues distant from Solikamsky, which is 187 toises above the level of the sea; and the slope of the Kama being 1 foot, 11 inches, $\frac{7}{10}$ per league, the height of the Kofwa, at its mouth, will be 184 toises.

All thefe ores are calcined in the open air, before they are put into the furnaces. They are collected in heaps, two feet deep, upon piles of wood, arranged for that purpofe in dry places. The lumps of ore are not in general more than about three or four inches in diameter.

Thefe mines produce an iron of a peculiar quality, ductile, or harfh and brittle. Thofe which produce a harfh and brittle iron, are generally the richeft, as the mines of load-ftone, and the chief part of thofe from the neighbourhood of Echaterinenburg, moft of which may be claffed among the hæmatites; but it is ufual to mix feveral forts of iron ore together, combining fuch as are malleable and ductile, with others which are rich, harfh, and brittle.

The iron arifing from thefe combinations is perfect, and better for certain purpofes than that of Sweden or Spain; it is pliable and ductile, and preferves at the fame time a degree of folidity, not to be found in Spanifh iron. This iron is tough both when cold and hot, and its angles are fmooth. If we ftrike it with the fharp part of a hammer, a dent is made in it as in lead; and when cold, it cannot be eafily broken. Its grain is fo fine, that it can fcarce be diftinguifhed with the naked eye: its broken furface refembles fteel. It is indeed ufed in works of the greateft nicety. I once took up a bar of it fifteen feet long, three inches wide, and feven lines thick; and having fixed it between two branches of a tree, I twifted it readily about the tree, and brought it back again with as much eafe, without fplitting it, or making any cracks at the angles. I brought away fome fpecimens of it: our workmen were aftonifhed at the goodnefs of this iron, which is not fufficiently known in France; if it was more known, it might turn out to the advantage of both nations.

For

For 100 poedes *, or 3300 weight of France, a meafure of coal is confumed three arcins high †, three long, and two wide, (or 6 feet 7 inches high, 6 feet 7 inches long, and 4 feet 5 inches wide.)

Some of thefe forges bring to thofe in whofe poffeffion they are, 4000 roubles, or 20,000 French livres, after all expences are deducted; and there are 2000 roubles, or 10,000 livres, allotted for the workmen and other expences.

The contractor buys this iron at twelve French fous, *per* poede; he fells it again on the fpot for 50 fous, and at St. Peterfburg, by wholefale, at 80. It was conveyed, during the winter feafon, upon fledges, and in the fummer by water. It is fold to the Englifh, who are the principal traders. I was informed of all thefe circumftances at Echaterinenburg, from perfons who fuperintended thefe mines.

I have not feen, in any place, iron forges better fupplied and better kept than thofe which belong to Count Woronzof, near Echaterinenburg. The perfon who had the direction of them was a Ruffian, very well acquainted with this bufinefs. The mines of Bilimbacufkoi belong to Count Strogonof. The forge confifts of one furnace and three fledges: it produces 20,000 poedes *per annum*, or 660,000 quintals of France, which, in French coin, are worth 6000 livres, at 50 fous *per* poede. In 1761, this forge was in a very bad condition, moft of the workmen having deferted.

---

* The poede is equal to 40 pounds of Ruffian weight, and 33 pounds of France.

† The arcin is equal to 2 feet, 2 inches, 6 lines ½ of French meafure, royal foot.

Of the copper mines of the Ryphæan mountains in Siberia, and in the neighbourhood of Cazan.

I. *Grey coppery marle.*

This has some kind of consistence, although it is friable. It is composed of two layers; aquafortis shews that a cretaceous substance abounds in each. It contains very little clay, and a great deal of coarse sand; so that this marle is not tough, but easily rubbed to powder between the fingers. One of the layers is grey inclining to a reddish color; a small quantity of greenish copperous earth is to be observed in it. The other layer has scarce any thickness; it is of a sea-green inclining to grey, which color is owing to the copper. Every circumstance seems to indicate a dissolution of this metal, the particles of which have been conveyed and deposited in this marle. It is found in the neighbourhood of Cazan, and contains so little copper that the mine is not worked.

II. *Copperous schist of a dirty grey color.*

Some clay, sand, and a green copperous earth is found in this stone. It does not effervesce with acids. It is disposed in flakes, and breaks easily into shivers. These three substances form a light stone, the parts of which are pretty well connected; it is of a coarse grain, and of a dirty grey color inclining to green. It is found in the neighbourhood of Cazan.

III. *Greenish calcareous stone.*

This stone is hard and compact, composed of calcareous earth, of sand, and of a copperous earth. This earth resembles verdigrease;

verdigreafe; and is fometimes found in layers. The grain of this ftone is coarfe, its parts are not very clofely united; and it is eafily reduced to fand between the fingers. The copper appears to have been depofited in this ftone, as in that of N° I. It comes from the neighbourhood of Cazan. In many different places we find fome marle and calcareous ftones, fimilar to thofe of N° I. and III. Some contain more, others lefs copper. This metal is fometimes depofited in clay, but not frequently. I have brought away fpecimens of all thefe: they differ fo little from each other, that I have not fpoken of them diftinctly, in order to avoid repetitions. The copper is alfo fometimes found in pure fand, with fcarce any mixture of calcareous earth. The metal is then difpofed in ftrata, and fometimes ferves as a gluten to the fandy particles, which are eafily reduced to fand.

IV. *Malachites.*

The malachites is found in the cavities of copper mines, under the form of ftalactites and ftalagmites. That of Siberia is very beautiful, may be polifhed, and is fit for all kinds of jewels. It is fometimes full of tubercles, fibrous, and difpofed in layers: it is produced by copper which has been in a ftate of diffolution.

1. *Tuberous malachites.*

This malachites is a ftalactites, refembling an acorn, full of tubercles, crowned with a cup of the fame kind. The cavity, which receives the head of the acorn, is internally of a whitifh green color, as the external furface of the acorn is alfo. Thefe two parts confift of layers half a line thick, more or lefs. They are all of a different green, fometimes of a fine fea-green,

green, a deep and a blackish green. Each layer is of a homogeneous green; but with a magnifying glaſs it appears that theſe are compoſed of other layers: one may diſtinguiſh ten or eleven of them. The acorn is hollow, the cup concave on the inſide and convex on the out. This ſtone explains perfectly well the formation of theſe malachites. They ſeem to have been produced by ſtalactites formed by the ſide of each other, and covered by layers of the ſame kind of matter.

2. *Malachites.*

This malachites muſt have formed a layer covering ſome ſtalactites. The cavities which are in it indicate the number of the ſtalactites. The ſurface of the cavities is of a whitiſh green color, they are convex externally, and of a darker green. It is diſpoſed in layers, as the preceding.

3. *Malachites.*

This muſt have been a covering to ſome ſtalactites. It conſiſts of 11 layers, three quarters of a line thick, and each of theſe is compoſed of other layers of the thickneſs of a hair. The 11 layers are of a beautiful green color, more or leſs deep. The lighteſt is a deep ſea-green. Some blackiſh layers may now and then be diſtinguiſhed. This malachites is very hard, its parts are perfectly well combined; and it exhibits on its broken ſurface, and in ſome of the layers, only an appearance of perpendicular fibres, all tending to the center of the cavity, or the tubercle they belong to. The outward ſurface of this malachites is covered with other layers of the ſame kind of matter, whoſe cavities are in an oppoſite direction to the former.

4. *Tuberous*

4. *Tuberous malachites.*

This is the same malachites polished on one side, and rough on its external surface. Each stalactites appears to be formed of different layers: the lightest of which are of a beautiful sea-green. It is sometimes found in the center of several stalactites, which are generally black, and surrounded with various layers of the same kind of matter, of a beautiful green color more or less dark, and mixed with other black layers. The intervals between the stalactites are filled up with the same kind of matter, disposed also *per stratum*.

5. *Tuberous malachites.*

This malachites is polished on both sides. It differs only from some of the other malachites in its color, which is darker and more splendid.

6. *Tuberous malachites.*

This is formed by tubercles of different sizes, collected in an irregular manner, and is covered with several layers of the same kind of matter. At its base one may discover some iron particles mineralized by sulphur.

7. *Arboreous malachites.*

This might be ranged in the class of the tuberous malachites, but the tubercles are so disposed, as to put on exactly the appearance of leaves in the broken parts. It is in other respects similar to those I have before mentioned, with this difference only, that it is very full of cavities.

8. *Striated*

8. *Striated malachites.*

This malachites is not tuberous as the others; it is composed of several layers, almost imperceptible to the naked eye, and of threads perpendicular to these layers, and tending to the same center. It is hard and compact, and there are no cavities in it as in the others.

9. *Malachites disposed in horizontal layers.*

This differs entirely from the rest, with respect to the layers which compose it. They are horizontal, half a line in thickness, generally of a dark green color, and some of them are blackish. One may observe some fibres in it perpendicular to these, chiefly in the upper layer; which makes one third part of the thickness of the malachites.

M. le Sage thinks, that the malachites is formed by the combination of a greasy matter with the copper; and upon this principle makes an artificial malachites which produces, by analysis, the same appearances as the natural fossils [*]. By the experiments he made on the malachites of Siberia, he found that they produced 62 and 63 pounds of copper *per* 100. The malachites I brought with me from Siberia, have been taken from the copper mines situated to the south of Solikamsky, and to the north of Souxon.

---

[*] This curious dissertation has been read at the academy, and will appear in the third volume of the foreign memoirs.

M. le Sage dissolves the copper by a volatile alkali, freed from the sal ammoniac, by means of a fixed alkali. The volatile alkali acquires an azure color. This solution being exposed to the air in a vessel, the alkali is decompounded; its greasy part remains combined with the copper, and gives it a green color. If the evaporation is made imperceptibly, crystals are obtained of the most beautiful green color, but collected without order; this is what he calls artificial malachites.

V. *Calcareous.*

V. *Calcareous, copperous, greenish stone.*

This stone is hard, compact, and very heavy: it is compounded of a calcareous earth, of clay, sand, and a coppery earth: there is but little of the calcareous earth in it. It shews a coarse grain on its broken surface of a sea-green color, and in some places a beautiful azure blue. This ore is found in the neighbourhood of Solikamsky.

VI. *Calcareous, copperous, reddish stone.*

This is compounded of a calcareous earth, of clay disposed in flakes, of sand, and of a copperous earth. This last is sometimes found among the flakes of clay; where it is always combined with the calcareous earth. The copperous matter forms layers, not more than the sixth part of a line in thickness. It is of a sea-green, mixed with the sand and calcareous earth. This stone is friable, and of a very coarse grain.

VII. *Calcareous, copperous, and blackish stone.*

This is hard, compact, and of a fine grain. It appears entirely calcareous, and contains very little copper, which is, however, distinguishable in some parts of it by green and blue spots. This ore is found to the south of Solikamsky.

VIII. *Copperous and blackish marle.*

This is disposed in flakes; it contains a little sand, some copperous green earth, and upon one of its surfaces there is the mark of a striated texture, disposed in the form of a fan. It is found to the south of Solikamsky.

IX. *Marl*

IX. *Marl of a greyish brown color, coppery and ferruginous.*

This marl is moderately solid. The clay is disposed by flakes in it. The ferruginous earth is of a deep red, scattered here and there as well as the coppery earth. These two metals are always combined in it with the cretaceous part. The copper is distinguished by its green color. This is a very poor ore, and is found in the neighbourhood of Solikamsky.

X. *Coppery marl of a dirty grey color.*

This is mixed with small sand and a coppery earth, sometimes green, sometimes blue; it is very friable, and disposed in layers; it is found northward of Niz-Czusowoi, and is a very poor ore.

Besides these ores, we find several copper mines in the Ryphæan mountains, from the 58th degree of latitude, as far as to the north of Solikamsky. I have brought specimens of them from fourscore different places; but as they are of the same nature as those already spoken of, I shall not enter into a description of them. The copper in these mines is always combined with the cretaceous part of the marl. All these mines are found in the lower or newly-formed mountains: these mountains appear to be all composed of marl, in which the cretaceous part prevails, and calcareous stones, sometimes sandy.

XI. *Calcareous coppery stone.*

This stone is hard, compact, and of a fine grain. It is compounded of a calcareous earth and small sand. In some places one may discover black argillaceous particles disposed in flakes. The copper is here joined with the small sand, and especially with the earth, to which it gives a sea-green color, sometimes light, and often very dark. The coppery matter is sometimes crystallized in small cells like those of the honey-comb, the sides of which are very thin. The copper in these crystals appears to be combined with pure marl. This ore is pretty rich, and is found to the south of Souxon.

XII. *Azure copper ore.*

This is hard, compact, and heavy. It contains a calcareous earth, some sand, and copper. The metallic part gives various colors to the several layers which compose it; two of these layers are of a shining bright azure blue; those in the middle are of a pale green. According to M. le Sage's opinion, mentioned under the article of the malachites, the copper in the azure part is mineralized by a volatile alkali, and, in the green part, by the greasy matter produced from the volatile alkali decompounded. This ore is pretty rich, and is found to the south of Echaterinenburg.

XIII. *Copper mineralized in sand and in wood.*

In this ore some blend, or black jack, may be distinguished, which at first appeared to me to be iron; it contains also some sand, wood and copper. It forms a very hard and compact stone in the sandy parts, and in those which contain the black jack. The vegetable parts are so friable that they are easily separated. The copper is distinguished by large spots of a fine green grass color. The wood is black, and resembles a coal, the parts of which are combined with a greasy earth. The copper is crystallized in several parts of this vegetable, under the form of small cells such as are before mentioned. They are sometimes of a bright green,

green, deep and blackish, and moſt of them are ſhining; ſo that theſe cryſtallizations may be conſidered as vitreous. The copper is every where joined to a calcareous earth; which is not found but where the metal is. This ore is found northward of Souxon.

XIV. *Copper mineralized in a calcareous earth.*

This ore contains a little ſand, and a great deal of copper united to a calcareous earth: it is of a pale green, inclining to a ſea color. It is porous and pretty hard, and is found to the ſouth of Souxon.

XV. *Azure copper ore, mineralized in ſand.*

This is a ſandy friable ſtone, of a very coarſe grain. The copper is diſtinguiſhed in it with the naked eye, by a number of ſpots of a light azure blue. In ſome places this metal gives a greeniſh color to the ſand, which is of a dirty grey color; but by means of aqua fortis we find that the copper is always united to a calcareous matter. This ore is found to the ſouth of Echaterinenburg; and is pretty rich.

XVI. *Copper mineralized in ſand, and in wood.*

This ore differs only from that of N° XIII. in having a leſs quantity of ſand and black jack. There are many parts in it of an azure blue, ſometimes diſpoſed in layers, and frequently in ſpots. It is richer than that of N° XIII. and is found to the ſouth of Souxon.

XVII. *Copper mineralized in wood.*

It is evident from the ſpecimens I have brought of this, that it has belonged to a tree of at leaſt one foot in diameter: the

inſide

inside is reduced almost to a very friable coal, although its parts are combined with a greasy kind of matter: the copper is sometimes crystallized in small cells, such as those before mentioned; but these crystallizations are only found in general among the fibres of the wood, which has entirely changed its natural appearance. The bark of the tree is distinctly seen in it, four lines in thickness: it is divided into two layers; one of an azure blue color, the other of a pale green, nearly the color of verdigrease. This wood is taken from the mines in the neighbourhood of Souxon. I have been told upon the spot, that whole trees were sometimes found in the beds of these ores. I took the specimens I brought with me, from a collection which filled the greatest part of a room more than twenty feet long. The wood contains more or less copper, according to the different places it comes from: its colors are of various hues; but are always either green or of an azure blue.

The copper mines of Souxon extend round about this neighbourhood as far as 150 wersts, or 30 leagues. They are found in mountains which are an hundred toises high, and more especially in those whose slopes are considerable; they are disposed in beds which follow the slope of these mountains; here they form irregular channels: these commonly unite in one principal channel, which is a kind of center, from whence the branches extend sometimes the length of a mile. These mines are generally placed nearly in the middle of the height of these mountains. They approach them by soughs digged in the sides. They are about 78 feet deep. They are obliged to support the earth with timber. They only use the mattock, and sometimes the sledge hammer.

The produce of these mines is but indifferent. The richest of them do not yield more than 4 *per* 100, and the others much

much lefs. They are mixed one with another. I have had some specimens of this ore from 70 different places, but they are all of the same nature, of which I convinced myself by the same experiments. The copper is always united to a calcareous earth: I have never found it in veins of quartz, nor mineralized by sulphur, nor by arsenic.

XVIII. *Red copper joined to silken copper.*

The red copper is so very analogous to the red silver in this mine, that it is only to be distinguished from this metal by fusion. It is found scattered among the silken copper ore; which resembles much the silken copper of China; but is more solid. I know not how this red copper is mineralized; but it appears to me, that it may be ranged in the class of virgin copper. The silken part of this ore is of a beautiful green; mixed with a little calcareous earth: it is as rich as it is scarce; and found in the neighbourhood of Echaterinenburg.

XIX. *Virgin copper by flakes.*

The virgin copper is found in this ore dispersed in small flakes, in a kind of reddish-oker. The copper is of a yellowish red; one may discover, in some places, a small quantity of calcareous earth; and in others it resembles solid cinnaber. The oker is friable. This ore is found to the south of Echaterinenburg. In the neighbourhood of this town may sometimes be found some copper ore mineralized by sulphur in quartz; but this is not common.

Remarks

Remarks on the copper mines of the Ryphœan mountains in Siberia.

The copper mines we are acquainted with in the Ryphæan mountains are never difpofed in veins; they are found in the lower or newly-formed mountains: where they are commonly difpofed in beds fcattered here and there, and they often form different branches terminating at laft in one. The mines of Solikamfky obferve the firft of thefe orders, thofe of Souxon, the laft. I was informed by people of the country, well verfed in thefe matters, that all the other copper mines are arranged in the fame manner. This feems alfo to be indicated by the nature of thefe laft ores, as they are all of the fame kind. Some few of thofe brought from the neighbourhood of Echaterinenburg are an exception to the general rule.

I have brought away 160 fpecimens of copper ore from different places: they are all in marls or in calcareous ftones, partly compofed of fand; but the metallic fubftance is almoft always found in the cretaceous part, and oftentimes in wood, as in the neighbourhood of Souxon. The nature of thefe ores fhews plainly, that they have been recently formed. It fhould feem, as if the copper had been firft diffolved, and afterwards carried to, and depofited in the places where it is found; but in this cafe we might expect to find it mixed indifcriminately with the feveral kinds of matter of which thefe mountains are compofed, whereas, on the contrary, it is only found united to the calcareous fubftances, whether thefe happen to be mixed with clay or with fand.

Moft of thefe ores are of an azure blue color, and the reft are green, either dark, fea color, or color of verdigreafe. According to M. le Sage's fyftem, the azure ores are mineralized by a volatile alkali, and the green part by a greasy matter produced from the volatile alkali decompounded; so that the azure is changed into the green.

The copper mines from the 58 degree of latitude, to Soliamsky, situated in the 60 degree, are all found in marl, in which the cretaceous part commonly prevails, and sometimes the argillaceous part. The low mountains situated westward of the Ryphæan mountains, are all of the same nature, from the 58 to the 60 degree of latitude.

These mines are found at the depth of a few feet, and follow the course of the soil to the level of the rivers *. From these facts and from the levelling, the mean height of the metallic coppery bed of Offa at Solikamsky turns out to be 172 toises above the level of the sea. There are also some copper mines to the east of the Kama as far as Menzelinsk; but these are so poor, that it is not worth while to work them. I am little acquainted with this part of the soil, but from the specimens I have had, it appears to be the same as the rest. The height of the metallic bed in the confines of Menzelinsk, may be computed at 126 toises above the level of the sea †. If this is compared with the height of Offa, which is 152, the mean height of the metallic bed, from the 55 degree and a half of latitude, to about the 57 degree and a half, will be 139 toises; whereas I have computed that from Offa to Solikamsky at

---

* From this account, Offa may be confidered as the loweft point of the metallic coppery bed, in the weftern part of the Ryphæan mountains; and the mines to the north of Solikamsky, as the higheft. Offa is 152 toises, Solikamsky 187, above the level of the fea: the slope of the Kama, being then known to be one foot 11 inches, and fuppofing the flope of the small rivulet Wifzera to be the fame, the height of the metallic bed in this place will be 192 toises; and since that of the Kama at Offa is 152 toises, the mean height of the coppery bed is therefore 172 toises. The mines in the neighbourhood of Souxon may be ranged upon the same plain, Solotoukoufka being 185 toises above the level of the fea.

† The height of Menzelinsk is calculated from that of the Kama at Offa, and from the given flope of this river.

172; so that it rises in proportion as it advances northward the length of the Kama.

We have seen that the mines in the neighbourhood of Echaterinenburg were different from the others; they are also ranged in a different plane. We find by the levelling * that the copper mines situated about the 57 degree of latitude, and mineralized by sulphur in the quartz about the confines of this town, are 238 toises above the level of the sea: and if the medium is taken between the three coppery beds; the mean height of the coppery bed will be found to be 183 toises above the level of the sea.

Of the gold mines in the neighbourhood of Echaterinenburg in Siberia.

These are almost the only ones which are found in quartz and disposed in veins. I got plans of these mines, and went over them with the greatest attention, with a design of giving a complete history of them. I marked all the observations I made upon the plans, and brought away specimens of all the kinds of matter I found there.

Gold mines of Pisminskaia.

This mine is situated to the north of Echaterinenburg, in 78° 48′ of longitude, and 57° 4′ of latitude. The cham-

---

* The highest place where the copper ore is found in the quartz, is on the river Czausova, 15 leagues to the south east of Bilimbaeuskoi. The height of Bilimbaeuskoi being given at 253 toises, and the slope of the river Czausova at six feet seven inches, the height of this place will be found to be 264 toises above the level of the sea. Kosulina, which is 213 toises high, may be considered as the lowest place; and consequently, the mean height of the copper mines is 238 toises.

bers of this mine are directed from south to north, and its veins from west to east.

The gold ore is discovered by a white earth, inclining to a grey color, mixed with some layers of a ferruginous earth. The soil has been scarcely dug two feet deep, before the veins of gold make their appearance; they run 10 toises from west to east, and sometimes 30; and are four or five inches broad at the upper part, which is always the richest. The vein afterwards diminishes in breadth and quality, as it gets lower down. These veins represent pretty exactly a semicircle, of which the upper part is the diameter. They are from two or three to 10 toises distant from each other, and rather inclined to the horizon. The matter which separates them is a blueish hardened clay, which seems to contain some of the asbestus, as well as the white earth already mentioned. We also find a vitrifiable earth in it, of a moderate consistence, some yellow, black and red oker, pretty hard. The red oker is a sure sign of the vein not being rich; and as soon as it appears in any quantity, the vein is neglected. The mine is almost always terminated at the lower part, by a layer of this oker. This mine is 14 toises deep; and the water is found immediately underneath it.

The vein consists generally of quartz, separated in different places by various kinds of matter, which I shall mention hereafter. It is necessary, on account of these substances being slightly connected together, to prop up the chambers with timber. The wood is arranged in the same manner as in building the houses in Russia, so that in some places the ground cannot even be seen between the beams.

The gold is commonly seen in the quartz, and often in a very friable oker. It is found in small spangles, which are separated here, as every where else, by washing. There are workmen employed in conveying out of the chambers all the

substances

substances they find there. Such as appear to contain gold are laid in heaps near the criminals who have been condemned to labour in the mines. Their feet are chained down, and they are fastened to a seat made from a piece of a rock. They separate, with a hammer, the ore from the parts in which this metal is not apparent. Other workmen are busied in collecting the ore, and carrying it to the mills prepared for grinding and washing it.

The veins of the quartz are separated by sand, by the white earth before mentioned, by clay, sometimes solid, sometimes soft, and by a grey stone, vitrifiable and pretty hard; but the form alone of the veins, and their direction from west to east, observes such an unvariable law, that it is difficult to imagine, how they can have been combined with the other substances, most of which appear to have been successively conveyed into these places. A small quantity of lead is found in the quartz, some pyrites, native sulphur, and several brown crystals, like those of Bohemia and Saxony. They differ only from those crystals, which are called topases, in being a little harder.

The lower part of this mine is 206 toises above the level of the sea.

I. *Gold mine of Beresouskoi.*

This is situated to the north of Echaterinenburg; in 57° 1′ latitude, and 78° 54′ longitude.

The veins of this are also disposed in parallels, except in a few places. The direction of those which are situated westward is from south to north-west; consequently, they make an angle of about 45 degrees with the east. The direction of those veins whose situation is eastward is more similar to the veins of the mine of Pifzminskaia, being frequently from west to east; and such veins as are thrown the farthest out of this

this direction, make an angle of about 30 degrees from the east towards the south. The internal texture of the earth in this mine differs only from that of Pifzminfkaia, with regard to a few substances I shall now take notice of.

There is less quartz in the veins of the mine of Berefoufkoi, than in those of the former; and the gold is most commonly found in a black ferruginous earth, often cryftallized in cubes. This is the richeft of all the ores. Veins of vitrifiable stone of a grey color, fometimes reddish, are also to be found in it. This stone is full of mica, and feveral small brown cryftals. At other times cubes of quartz and ferruginous earth form a layer five or fix lines thick upon thefe ftones, and upon others of fand; to which they are fo flightly attached, and fo loofely connected, that they may eafily be feparated with the finger. This ftone is likewife found in veins where iron is cryftallized in cubes. I have already mentioned thefe in fpeaking of the iron ores. Thefe two cubic iron ores are the fame. Having defired M. le Sage to analyfe them, he found that thefe cubes produced 70 pounds *per* quintal; and, according to this learned chymift, the iron is mineralized in them by a marine acid *.
The bottom of the mine is 200 toifes above the level of the fea.

II. *Gold mine of Berefoufkoi.*

In 70° 50' of longitude, and 57°. of latitude. The veins may likewife be confidered as parallel: fome of them, however are directed from weft to eaft, while others make an angle of about 23° from the eaft towards the fouth, and

---

* M. le Sage intends to prefent to the Royal Academy of Sciences, a differtation upon this cubic ore, for which reafon I have not enlarged upon it. It differs, however, from that of N°. XLIX, as the cubes are larger, and that, when reduced to powder, it is flightly attracted by the loadftone.

from the east towards the north. The internal texture is in other respects the same as the first; and the bottom of the mine is 201 toises above the level of the sea.

Gold mine of Ouktous.

In 78° 49′ of longitude, by 56° 50′ of latitude. Most of the veins are in the same manner parallel: others make an angle of about 20° and some of 40° from the east towards the north. The internal texture of the earth is nearly the same as in the mine of Beresoufkoi, with this difference, that the veins in the mines of Ouktous are sometimes 63 toises in length, whereas in the other they do not exceed twenty toises. The bottom of the mine is 216 toises above the level of the sea.

Gold mine of Chilovoitoetse.

In 79° 17′ of longitude, by 56° 31′ of latitude. The veins are somewhat irregular, but their general direction is such as to form an angle of about 25° from the east towards the south. The veins are about 40 toises long; and the bottom of the mine 207 toises above the level of the sea.

The produce of these mines is so trifling, that it does not always clear the expences, although labour is at an exceeding low price, on account of the slaves who are employed there. The silver mines are not worth mentioning. They are less useful to the kingdom of Russia, than they are to natural philosophers, to whose consideration they present a number of interesting inquiries.

We have seen that the mine of Ouktous was the highest of all these, being 216 toises above the level of the sea, and that of Beresoulkoi, of 200 toises, the lowest. Consequently, the mean height of this metallic bed is 208 toifes. I have determined that of the coppery bed at 183 toifes, and that of the ferruginous bed at 228 toifes. The beds of iron and thofe of gold are therefore nearly of an equal height: and if we recollect what has been faid in the account of the iron ores, it is certain that they are all in vitrifiable fubftances, among which I have not found the fmalleft particle of calcareous matter. I have made the fame obfervation, on upwards of fourfcore fpecimens of gold ores, with this difference, that thefe are found in quartz. The copper is the only ore found in a calcareous matter. Thefe feveral facts feem to point out the height of the vitrifiable and of the calcareous matter in this chain. They are founded on a number of obfervations, concurring to eftablifh this truth; which has been farther confirmed to me by all the inquiries I have made on the fpot, in the courfe of my journey, either northward or fouthward. In all the lower parts of thefe mountains I have conftantly found calcareous ftones, and vitrifiable ftones in all the higher parts.

It follows, therefore, from thefe feveral obfervations, that the calcareous matter rifes in thefe mountains as high as 183 toifes; this is ftill farther confirmed by the height of the vitrifiable matter, which is found at 218 toifes. In the laft heights the gold and iron mines are placed, in the firft the copper mines.

I have determined the height of the moft elevated plane of Ruffia, from St. Peterfburg to Tobolfky, at 185 toifes above the level of the fea; and the mean height of the chain ftanding upon this plane, at 270 toifes; from whence it may be concluded, that the copper mines and the calcareous earths terminate at the height of this firft plane, and that the gold and iron mines are found at the lower part of the vitrifiable fubftances, at 52 toifes above the mean height of the chain.

As

As most of the ores appeared to me, on the spot, recently formed, and conveyed there, I imagined that the real mines should be searched for in the middle of the chain, in higher places; but I was informed by the directors of these mines, and by all the miners I consulted, that frequent attempts had been made to look for them in these places, but as these attempts had always been fruitless, the design was now quite given up.

I shall close this article, with some remarks on the teeth of the Mamout, so much talked of by travellers. Monf. d'Aubenton has demonstrated that these teeth, were the real elephant's tusks. I have brought pieces of some of them, which must have belonged to an elephant of the largest kind. We cannot discover by any astronomical knowledge, whether the temperature of this climate was ever similar to that in which these animals are produced.

M. Franklin, a celebrated English natural philosopher, informed me, as he went through Paris, that he had found several tusks in America, which were ranged in the class of elephant's tusks: and told me at the same time, that they had found several jaw bones there belonging to the same animal. I desired him to get me one of those jaw-bones, which he was so kind as to send me. It was found out here not to be the jaw of an elephant; but, at the same time, nobody knows what animal it has belonged to If there were any accurate observations which made it evident that there are in America tusks similar to those of the elephant, as M. d'Aubenton has made it appear concerning the tusks found in Siberia, and if it could likewise be proved, that the jaws I received from M. Franklin belong to the same animal, it would then be certain, that there had been an animal different from the elephant, but furnished with the same tusks, and that animal might have existed in Siberia.

Of the tame and wild animals, birds, fish, and insects.

THE Ruffians live upon very indifferent forts of food, especially in the country from Mosco to Tobolsky, as may be seen in the account already given. There is however great plenty of all the neceffaries of life throughout this extent of land, except bread and wine. The rivers abound with fish, and the country with all sorts of game. The peafants feldom eat butchers meat, and lefs frequently game; and feem to care very little about this kind of food. They live chiefly on fifh, because they can be fupplied with it eafily in large quantities. Fifh is fo plentiful, efpecially in Siberia, that, inftead of buying it from the fifhermen, it is often the cuftom to make bargains with them for the chance of a certain number of drafts. One may always get fifh enough to keep a whole family for feveral days, for the value of four or five pence Englifh. Game may alfo be had at a very low price; but the Ruffians drefs it badly, and in the moft uncleanly manner. In other places, many people are enticed by the luxuries of the table; but a ftranger in Ruffia eats only to fupport life.

The partridge is very common at Tobolfky, and all over Ruffia, as well as the moor-cock, the wood-hen, and the quail; but all thefe birds have a difagreeable fifhy tafte. There are alfo infinite numbers of aquatic birds round about Tobolfky, and in all the northern parts of Siberia; but moft of them, as well as the birds of prey, are met with in the reft of Europe.

I brought away the following birds from the country about Tobolfky.

The fea peacock.	The grey plover.
The fea pie.	The leffer godwit.
The Swifs lapwing.	The greenfhank.

The

The wigeon.
The pin-tail duck.
The tufted duck.
Gargany and teal.
The common mallard.
The large ash colored sea gull.
The black and white gull.
The great curlew.
The scoter.
The diver.

All these birds have been described in other works, I have only taken notice of the two last, because they differ in some respects from those Mr. Brisson has described in his treatise on birds.

The diver of Siberia seems to be the same as that Mr. Brisson has described, under the name of the red neck diver *;.

(tom..

* *The red neck diver.*
It is rather larger than the tame duck; from the extremity of the bill to that of the tail, it is one foot, eleven inches, six lines long; and two feet, three inches, seven lines long, to the extremity of the nails; its bill, from the tip to the corners of the mouth, is two inches, ten lines long; its tail one inch, ten lines; its foot, two inches, eight lines; the middle one of the three anterior toes, together with the nail, is three inches, one line; the external toe, three inches, three lines; the internal one, two inches, eight lines, and the posterior one, only eight lines. Its flight is three feet, eight lines; and its wings when close, hardly reach beyond the root of the tail: the top of its head is covered with small feathers brown in their middle part, and ash-colored at their edges; all the rest of the head, the throat and sides of the neck, as far as about two thirds of its length, are ash-colored: the occiput and the under part of the neck, as well as the sides of it near the body, are covered with small brown feathers, edged on both sides with white; which makes them appear variegated with longitudinal spots, some white, others brown; the feathers, however, of the neck nearest the back, instead of being bordered with white, are only marked on their edges with small spots of this color; the back, the rump, and the upper parts of the tail, are of a shining brown color; the feathers on the shoulder are of the same color, some of them being marked with small white spots. On the lower part of the neck, there is a spot of a beautiful chesnut color *, four inches long, and about eighteen lines broad at its lower part: its figure is that of an Isosceles triangle, with its apex towards the throat. The lower part of the neck, beneath this spot, is covered with feathers

of

* In the diver I brought with me, this spot is of a beautiful chesnut color; but is not more than two inches six lines in length; its breadth, at the lower part, is fifteen lines, and at the upper part eight. Above this spot, the lower part of the neck is covered with small feathers, brown in the middle, and edged all round with white: the breast, the belly, and the legs, are of a very fine silken white color, like that of the Didappers.

tom. vi. page 111. N° 111.) the description here given of it is the same as that gentleman's. The differences I have observed will be mentioned in a note.

I have ranged the second bird in the class of the sea ducks; it as some analogy to the scoter † described by Mr. Brisson, (tom.

of a brown color in the middle, and edged all round with white. The breast, the belly, and the legs, are of a beautiful white; the sides are covered with brown feathers, most of which are edged with white; those under the tail are also brown, and almost all tipped with white; the feathers underneath the wings are white; some of the largest of them, however, are rather ash-colored on their outside; the small feathers on the tops of the wings, and the large ones, at the greatest distance from the body, are of a shining brown color; the large and middling sized feathers nearest the body are of the same color, and marked on their edges with a few small white spots; the wing is composed of thirty feathers of a dark and almost blackish color, but much lighter at their origins on the inside only: the two nearest the body are moreover marked with small white spots, placed on their edges, near their extremities: the first feather is very short; the second the longest of all: the tail is composed of twenty brown feathers; the middle ones are rather longer than the side feathers; these continue decreasing gradually in length to the outermost on each side, which is the shortest; so that the end of the tail is rounded: the bill is black; the feet, the toes, together with the membranes, and the nails, are blackish; but the inside of the feet and toes is inclined to a reddish cast. This diver is found in the northern seas, builds its nest on little eminences met with in rivers, and lays but two eggs. *From Mr. de Reaumur's cabinet.*

† *The scoter.*

It is somewhat larger than the tame duck; from the extremity of its bill to that of its tail its length is one foot, eight inches, three lines; its bill, from the tip to the corner of the mouth, is two inches three lines long; its tail, three inches, three lines; its foot, two inches; the outward toe with the nail, three inches, the middle toe, two inches, eleven lines; the inward toe, two inches, two lines, and the hind toe, ten lines. Its wings, when close, extend as far as the middle of the tail; their length from the pinion is ten inches; the head, the throat, the neck, and the breast, are of a deep black polished color; the back, the rump, and the coverings of the upper part of the tail are of the same color, but neither so deep nor so shining; the sides and the belly are blackish; the small feathers underneath the wings are of the same color; the large ones are ash-colored; the small feathers on the outside of the wings, as well as the large ones, are of the same black color as the back: the feathers of the wings are of the color of the back on their outside; those which are nearer the body are blackish on their inside, and those which are at the greatest distance are ash-colored: the feathers of the wings decrease in length in proportion as they are nearer the body.

tom. vi. pag. 420, N° 28.) of which you may be convinced by comparing my description with his; which I have copied wherever there was any affinity between the two birds, in order that they may be better known.

Pelicans, swans, and some few didappers, are also found about Tobolsky. There is an infinite variety of sea peacocks; as there are scarcely two of them to be found alike.

The rivers and lakes of Siberia, as well as those of Russia, contain almost all the same kinds of fish as are found in Europe, trouts, pikes, tench, breams and carp; but eels, crawfish, the common salmon and smelts, are very scarce. All sorts of sturgeon are to be found here, and whitings, haddocks, and small cods, are the most common of all.

The rivers of Siberia abound with many other kinds of fish unknown in Europe. Among these is the sterlet, which is so very like the sturgeon that there is scarce any difference, except that it is much smaller and much more delicate. It is so fat that it may be fried without oil. The fat of it is yellow, and is collected for the use of the kitchen. The people are very careful of its eggs, as well as of those of the sturgeon; they fry them a little in oil, with salt and spices of the country.

---

body. Underneath the flag part of the wing there is a transverse white band, composed of twelve feathers arising from the bend of the wing; when the wings are close, that part of this white band, which remains exposed, is three inches long, and about eight or nine lines broad. These white feathers cover the large ones. The bill forms a small black eminence, on which the nostrils are placed; at its upper part it is one inch, six lines long, from the tip to the feathers, and eleven lines to the part where the eminence begins [*]: the breadth of the bill is one inch, and it is of a brimstone color; two black streaks are seen on both sides of the nostrils; they diverge towards a round part which is bent on the lower bill; the bill is denticulated, like that of the common duck. This scoter is found in the marshes round about Tobolsky in Siberia. *From the collection of the Marchioness of Aligni.*

[*] This eminence has no the least analogy to the tubercle in the scoter described by Mr. Brisson.

These

These eggs, dressed in this manner, are known by the name of caviar, which is put up in pots like mustard; this food is as much esteemed as the sterlet.

This fish and sturgeon are very common at Tobolsky, and consequently the caviar also; but this last kind of food, and the sterlet, are very dear throughout the rest of Russia. At Tobolsky, a sterlet, two feet long, sells sometimes for no more than sixpence English. All other fish are exceedingly cheap there, as they are in general all over Russia.

The tame animals fed at Tobolsky, and from thence to St. Petersburg, are oxen, horses, some sheep, dogs, fowls, geese, and ducks in great plenty.

The oxen * are of a very small breed, as well as the horses; these last animals run with great swiftness, and are almost indefatigable: they run through a post of twenty leagues with the greatest ease and without any inconvenience.

There are scarce any oxen or horses to be found beyond Tobolsky; the method of travelling there is with dogs harnessed to the sledges.

The wild animals are black and white bears: the first are very common, the last are found on the borders of the Frozen Sea. There are common wolves in all the forests, as well as lynxes, boars, elks, a kind of stag very like the fallow deer, and foxes, which, although of the same species, are still very different with respect to the color of their skin; some being perfectly white, others yellow inclining to red. Some are grey, with a black streak on the back; these are much valued: the most scarce and most beautiful are perfectly black. The skin of one of these sometimes sells for three or four hundred roubles or two thousand livres of France. They are commonly found towards the eastern part of Siberia; in the way from Tobolsky

---

* The oxen of the Ukraine are very large.

†

Tobolſky to Kamtſchatka. Ermines and ſables are alſo moſt common in the ſame places: the fine ſables are extremely dear, as the lining of a man's ſuit of cloaths ſells for five or ſix thouſand livres, and ſometimes twenty; although I myſelf never ſaw any furrs of this price in Ruſſia. In France, the tails of the martins are much valued: in Siberia, this part of the ſkin of the animal is the leaſt in repute; becauſe the hair of it is too harſh: the moſt beautiful martins indeed have ſeldom fine tails; they are perfectly black, or have but few grey hairs: the back is the part moſt valued, ſo that furriers, who chuſe to be ſupplied with fine furrs, cut up all theſe ſkins, and ſew the backs together, in order to match them; this makes the kind of furr that is ſo very dear. Beſides that, the ſkins of ſables are thicker of hair than thoſe of the martins of other countries; the ſhag is alſo longer, ſofter, and the furrs that are made of it are much lighter.

The gulo, or glutton, is alſo found in Siberia, in the diſtrict of Hinſk; as well as otters, beavers, the iſatis, or fox of Siberia, rein-deer, and the ſayga, a kind of wild goat, which is chiefly found, as well as the otters and beavers, in the ſouthern part of Siberia, near the origins of the rivers Irtyſz, Jeniſſea, and the Oby. The otters, beavers, and the rein-deer, are more common at Kamtſchatka, they are not to be found in the reſt of Siberia, except in the eaſtern parts.

The inhabitants collect themſelves in companies to go a hunting theſe animals; they go at the cloſe of the winter, from the month of March to the end of April, taking proviſions with them for ſeveral days. I have been aſſured that they ſometimes go in rackets, as I have mentioned before, but I never ſaw this done in Siberia, ſo that it does not appear to be commonly the cuſtom. They catch the ſmall animals with ſpringes and nets, and the large ones with traps.

They cloath themselves with the most common furrs, chiefly with sheep skins: they sell the others to pay their taxes and their lords.

The furrs of Jenisseik are more valued than those of the Oby and the Lena. I have only mentioned the names of all these animals here, as they are perfectly well described in the natural history of the king's cabinet by Messrs. Buffon and Daubenton.

Partridges and hares are white in the winter, and squirrels grey. These animals regain their natural color in summer; the partridges while they are moulting, and the quadrupeds by shedding their coats. Although the same phoenomenon be observed in some other countries, I was so struck with it in Russia, that I resolved to examine whether it was to be accounted for from the nature of the climate or the species of these animals. I found no difference between the hares of Russia and those of France to outward appearance, except that the skins of the first are thicker of hair. They have also underneath their paws a kind of down, like that of swans; but there is no hair underneath the paws of hares in our temperate climate.

If the excessive cold in Russia was really the cause of the white color in these animals, they ought not to grow white when fed in a stove during the winter time. I fed a hare in the summer time at Tobolsky, intending to make this experiment, which I could not succeed in, because my hare died before I left Tobolsky; but passing through Mosco, at my return from Siberia, I saw a lady who had a tame squirrel, which was already turned grey at the end of October, though it was always kept in a very hot stove. I do not think the point can be determined from this one fact; which is, however, sufficient to throw doubts upon the opinions of those, who imagine that the whiteness of hares and partridges is a consequence of the excessive cold.

cold these creatures are exposed to in Russia; they seem rather to be of a different species from those of our climates.

The insects of Siberia and Russia are very little known. Notwithstanding the pains I took to acquire some knowledge of them, yet I am scarce able to give any fresh information to naturalists on this subject.

The variety of objects I was engaged in throughout my journey, did not allow me, as I was alone, to collect insects myself, because I could not stay long enough in the country. I was in hopes to have met with some assistance in the places where I stopped, by promising rewards to all persons who would supply me with insects; but yet I had not one brought to me. I can, however, venture to say in general, that most of the insects of Russia are of the same species as those which are found in marshes and ponds; they commonly appear in Siberia about the month of July.

There are such numbers of large gnats, especially at Tobolsky, that they are very troublesome to the inhabitants, even in their own apartments. As I was unacquainted with this inconvenience, I took no care at first to guard myself against these flies, so that I could not be one moment at ease from the itching occasioned by their bites: my legs, my face, and hands, were so considerably swelled, that I was obliged to keep my bed for several days. I did not venture out afterwards without boots, covering my face with a veil, and putting gloves on, according to the custom of the country. Soldiers who stood centry took the same precautions; and I have seen some of them cover their faces with pitch. As I was obliged to have my face uncovered, in order to make my astronomical observations, I had a fire made with peat round my observatory, so as to raise a considerable smoke; this made the insects disappear, and when I was going to take my observation I had the fire put out again.

The large gnats are not the only insects with which the inhabitants of Tobolsky are incommoded; the air being also full of small gnats, they form clouds, which are always in motion, and are continually sticking against one's face, but are more troublesome than hurtful.

Clouds of locusts and dragon-flies appear sometimes in these regions. I have been assured, that, in the years 1749, 1750, and 1751, there were such multitudes of locusts in Ukraine, that they destroyed all the corn round about Bielgorod, as well as all the vegetables and the leaves of the trees: and there appeared at Tobolsky, on the second of July 1761, such a great number of dragon flies, that the noise they made, tempted me to go out of my room in order to find out the cause of it. From the observations I made, it appeared that these insects formed a column, extending from the river Irtysz to my observatory; it was therefore about 500 toises long: the height of the column was not above five toises. It made its first appearance about eight o'clock in the morning, and continued passing till one in the afternoon, following the banks of the river in its course from north to south. These insects flew with inexpressible swiftness. In order to have some idea of this, I fixed my eyes upon one cloud of these flies, with a watch in my hand, which marked the seconds, and began to run as fast as possible, attempting to follow it; in nine or ten seconds I perceived the cloud began to get beyond me. I then measured the ground I had gone over, and found that it covered between 19 and 20 toises. I convinced myself, by several repeated experiments, that this column of insects moved at the rate of 20 toises in nine seconds, and consequently fourscore thousand toises, or three leagues and a half in an hour; so that as the column had been five hours in passing, it must at least have occupied a space of seventeen leagues in length: I have made it appear, that the column was also five toises in breadth, and

five

five in height; it must therefore have contained an infinite number of insects. They appeared at first under the form of a cloud, which seemed to graze the earth, so that we were afraid to come near it; and when once got into it, our faces were struck every instant with the quantity of these flies, which were perfectly similar to those we have in France.

From all that has been said it appears, that game and fish are found in Siberia, and that butchers meat is common in some places; but that corn does not grow kindly in this province. It is brought hither from parts of Russia situated in Europe. Monopoly makes it dearer in Siberia, on account of the frauds which prevail there, in spite of the watchfulness of the governors; so that the people seldom eat any bread.

The Russians, indeed, in general know not how to make bread: in Siberia, they do not separate the bran from the flower; their bread is neither leavened nor baked, so that if one throws a bit of it against the wall, it sticks there like plaister; it is sour and black. There was no other kind of bread in use at Tobolsky all the while I was there, except at the archbishop's. The bread is so bad, that those who were along with me determined not to eat any of it, till all the biscuit I brought with me from St. Petersburg, which I intended to keep for my return, was consumed.

The archbishop has his flower sifted, and has small loaves made of it, two or three inches in diameter; he was so obliging as to send me now and then a dozen of them, which was a very considerable present: he sent some also to the governor on feast-days; they were cut into small slices, one of which was given to each guest.

Wine is known at Tobolsky by report only: the persons who go from St. Petersburg or Mosco into Siberia sometimes take a few bottles with them; but travellers are generally less anxious about providing themselves with wine for these journies, on account of their being obliged to supply themselves with every other necessary of life. The liquors in use at Tobolsky are the same as those I have already mentioned in several parts of this work. The common people drink quouas, and the other inhabitants drink beer, mead, and other liquors made with brandy.

A confiderable revenue arises to the sovereign from brandy, which is made only from corn, all over Russia. The people, who undertake this contract, sell a tun of brandy to the crown for thirty roubles*, or a hundred and fifty livres of France; and the crown sells it again to the public at 90 roubles, or 450 livres of France. All the Russians are forbidden to make brandy, on pain of the most severe punishments. The nobility alone are permitted to provide themselves with some for their own use.

* The tun contains 480 French quarts; and I have been assured that 24 of these distilled, produce about two quarts of spirit of wine.

Of the climate of Siberia, and the other provinces of Ruffia.

THE vaſt empire of Ruſſia extends about nineteen hundred leagues * from weſt to eaſt, that is, from the iſland Dago to Cape Tchuktſchi, which bounds it to the eaſt †. About fourteen hundred and ſeventy of theſe leagues are taken up by Siberia alone, and the remaining four hundred and thirty make up the reſt of Ruſſia. The breadth of the latter part, from Azoph to its boundaries in the Frozen Ocean ‡, is five hundred and twenty-five leagues. The greateſt breadth of Siberia, from its ſouthern boundaries towards Selinginſki §, is near ſeven hundred leagues ¶.

I was told, in paſſing through Solikamſky **, a city ſituated in the weſtern limits of Siberia, that in the year 1761, Mr. de L'Iſle's thermometer had ſunk down to two hundred and eighty degrees, which anſwers to about ſeventy of M. de Reaumur's. This extreme and almoſt incredible degree of cold appeared the more aſtoniſhing to me, as the thermometer, on which it was obſerved, was expoſed on a wall

---

* One degree contains five and twenty of theſe leagues, or 2282 toiſes, ſuppoſing the mean degree of the meridian to be fifty-ſeven thouſand and ſixty toiſes.

† The longitude of the iſland of Dago is about forty degrees, and that of Cape Tchuktſchi, two hundred and nine.

‡ Azoph is at the forty-ſeventh degree of latitude, and the limits of the north about the ſixty-eighth degree.

§ The limits of the ſouth are at about forty-nine degrees of latitude, and extend as far as ſeventy-ſeven degrees.

¶ Theſe are the greateſt dimenſions. The mean length of Ruſſia, as far as Siberia, is about three hundred and fifty leagues; its mean breadth four hundred. The mean length of Siberia may be reckoned fourteen hundred and ſeventy leagues, its mean breadth, five hundred.

** Longitude, ſeventy-four degrees four and twenty minutes; latitude, fifty-nine degrees, thirty-five minutes.

to the north, in an open yard, so that I did not conceive it was possible a man should live in the degree of cold he must necessarily be exposed to, in crossing the yard to take the observation; and I was still confirmed in this opinion, by what I had myself experienced from the cold in Russia. I had often feared not being able to support it, though M. de Reaumur's thermometer fell only to about two and twenty degrees. My breath was then used to freeze about my lips, and to make one entire icicle with my beard, which I had shaved only once since my leaving Mosco, at Nisan-Novogorod, where I had made some stay. The rest of my body, indeed, was guarded by the quantity of furrs I was covered with, besides that the very snow which fell, would sometimes defend me, as it lay five or six inches deep about my sledge; yet the air I breathed, pressed with such force upon my breast, which had never been affected before, that I was like to sink under the acuteness of the continual pain. This induced me to suspect the validity of what I had been told about the seventy degrees of cold: besides, that mercury condensed in a thermometer, to a certain degree, requires a far more intense cold to keep up its condensation; so that supposing the cold of Solikamsky four times more severe than what I had been exposed to, although such a degree of cold must have been excessive, and scarce possible to be conceived, yet it would still have been much less intense, than what the inhabitants of the place must have really felt.

Being desirous of gaining every possible light on this extraordinary fact, I went to see the thermometer the Russian had made use of; it was fixed on a plate of copper divided with the greatest nicety; and the height of it, ascertained for that day, according to the known rules, agreed exactly with my thermometer, made with the greatest accuracy on M. de Reaumur's principles; so that I could no longer be in any doubt about the goodness of the instrument. I called therefore for the diary

diary of obfervations made throughout the whole year, and from examining the progreffion of the thermometer, received the moft fatisfactory evidence of the truth of this aftonifhing fact. To fuch extreme cold, the frequent accidents, which happen to travellers in Siberia, are certainly to be attributed. I was affured at Solikamsky, that the cold fometimes increafed fo confiderably in a few hours, as to ftrike both men and horfes dead, who happened to be at too great a diftance from any houfe to fhelter themfelves fpeedily from it.

In common cold weather, it frequently happens, that fome parts only of the body are frozen; in this cafe, it is ufual to rub them with fnow, by which the circulation is immediately reftored. When fuch an accident happens to the face, which generally lofes all fenfation in thefe exceffive frofts, the perfon affected in this manner muft be told of it; for without this effential piece of fervice, which people do each other by turns, the frozen part would foon be loft.

The climate of Tobolsky is very cold. In the year 1735, M. de Reaumur's thermometer was obferved to be at 30 degrees in this city [*]; it appears, however, that the winters are lefs fevere there than at Solikamsky. Although the winter of 1761 was very rigorous in this capital of Siberia, it by no means came up to what was felt at Solikamsky.

The foil of the country about Tobolsky is very fit for agriculture; a layer of black earth from one to two feet deep, being every where to be met with. This earth is fo fat as to make clay ufelefs; and fo light as to be ploughed eafily with one horfe. Notwithftanding all thefe circumftances, fo favorable to the cultivation of land, this is ftill extremely neglected, owing as much to the lazinefs of the inhabitants, as to the feverity of the cold, the length of the winters, and the

---

[*] M. De Lifle, vol. acad. 1749, pag. 2. des mémoires.

almoſt continual rains which follow the thaw. Theſe are the ſeveral cauſes, on account of which, the little corn that is ſown ſeldom comes to perfection.

In our more temperate climates, at the beginning of May, nature ſeems to revive, and to impart new life to all that breathes or vegetates; the trees are adorned with freſh leaves, and the face of the whole country with an agreeable verdure, the different ſhades of which form a variety of pleaſing landſcapes. The birds have already choſen their mates, begin to enliven nature with ſport and ſong, and fill every hedge or green tree with ſounds of joy. The lark ſeems to give the ſignal of the riſing morn; now he ſoars above the clouds, making the air ring with his warbling notes, and now, in an inſtant lights on beds of flowers, with which the meadows and fields are enamelled. All nature is beautified, and inſpires cheerfulneſs and pleaſure in our climates, while dreadful winter ſtill reigns at Tobolſky. Inſtead of that verdure, and thoſe flowers whoſe fragrance is ſcattered far around; the continued melting of the ſnows, forms and keeps up torrents in the mountains, ſome of which ruſh into the neighbouring rivers, ſwell them, and overflow the country; others roll over the immenſe plain beneath, ploughing it up in all directions, and ſpreading confuſion and deſtruction all around. Then the plain, viewed from ſome neighbouring hill, appears like a new ſea, formed, on a ſudden, in the midſt of a continent. The ſky is then almoſt always darkened by clouds, whoſe vapours frequently fall down in rain, ſometimes in ſnow or frozen miſts, which are the more alarming, as they are always driven by impetuous winds, and therefore occaſion more acute pains than are felt from a much greater degree of cold. This ſeaſon of the year uſually paſſes in this alternation of rain, ſnow, and miſts. On the 4th of June, the whole country was three times covered with ſnow, which diſappeared as often; ſoon after, the air became

more

more temperate by the approach of the sun to the solstice; this luminary, at that time of the year, is almost always upon the horizon, so that one may read with the utmost ease at midnight. Although the heat lasts but for a short time, yet even in this interval the vegetables suddenly shoot up. The corn was already a foot high on the 22d of June; but instead of the fruit-trees, which grow in almost all other places, nothing is to be seen in these nearly desert countries, except fir-trees, appearing as old as the earth itself: their form, which is ever the same, and the gloominess of their color, saddens the most cheerful disposition. In these solitary woods, the only persons to be met with, are some of the unfortunate inhabitants of these climates, in search of birch-trees, into which they make an incision, in order to collect the sap, from whence their mead is afterwards prepared.

I have often walked along the banks of the river Irtysz, at the distance of several leagues from Tobolsky, in hopes of seeing landscapes embellished with a multitudes of houses; instead of which, I met with nothing all along this river, but a vast plain, covered by the mud the waters had deposited before they subsided; and pools of stagnated water on all sides, whose borders were strewed with dead boughs, and trunks of trees which had been rooted up. Although it was near the end of July, the ground had not yet acquired firmness enough to make the treading it entirely safe. Spurred on by the desire of getting some birds I was unacquainted with, I ventured to stop a few minutes in the same spot; but, being too intent upon my object, did not perceive the ground had given way, till after I had shot one of the birds; I then attempted to fetch it, but found myself stuck so fast, as not to be able to stir. At last I got out of this place, by supporting myself with my gun, but gave up my bird, and was not tempted to go in search of others. I got back to the boat in which I had come down the river, and did not quit it again till I came to the firſt village, ſituated on pretty high ground. Every thing in this village beſpoke the utmoſt miſery. I walked round about it, and found ſome corn had been ſown there, which was as fine as one could wiſh to ſee it, but ſo backward for the ſeaſon, that the inhabitants deſpaired of there being time enough for it to ripen.

No European fruit is to be found at Tobolſky, except the currant, which is ſometimes met with in the woods. The fruits of the country are the glouguat, and a kind of raſberry. The glouguat bears a great reſemblance to our currants. Theſe fruits have a little tartneſs and are looked upon as antiſcorbutics. The people are alſo very careful in gathering the fruit of a kind of pine, very like the cedar. There are indeed but few of them growing in the neighbourhood of Tobolſky itſelf, but they are found in plenty about Verchaturia. The fruit of this tree is in great requeſt; it is eaten raw; and beſides this, an oil is extracted from it for the common purpoſes of the table.

It has been attempted in vain to ſow vegetables at Tobolſky. Radiſhes, a few ſallads, and a kind of green curled cabbage are almoſt the only ones which have ſucceeded; but the inhabitants have rhubarb of the ſecond ſpecies in their gardens, the leaves of which they make ſallads of, as they do of dandelion and nettles, when they begin to ſprout.

A Ruſſian had brought a young apple-tree with him from Moſco, which he had raiſed in a hot-houſe; this year (1761) it bore an apple about the ſize of a crab. It was produced in a large diſh at a grand entertainment, cut into ſmall ſlices, and given to ſome of the gueſts; among the reſt, one piece was offered to me, but I found it ſo ſour and ſo bad, that I could never bring myſelf to chew it, and was therefore obliged to

ſwallow

swallow it whole like a pill, that I might not appear wanting in civility.

The pasture is excellent, the grafs grows every where equally well; confequently, the inhabitants have a great deal of cattle. I had read in fome book of travels, that, during the whole fummer, the ground at Tobolſky was never thawed more than a few feet below the furface, and an inhabitant of the city had alfo affured me of the fact; notwithſtanding which my daily obfervations made me fufpect the veracity of the Ruffian, as well as that of the author. I frequently endeavoured to get the ground digged: the difficulty of having labourers in a country where all are flaves, made me refolve to apply to the governor: he was fo kind as to give me up a dozen criminals, who were chained and condemned to labour at the public works, like the galley-flaves with us. I had the ground digged by them ten feet deep and found it not frozen. I had intended going ftill deeper, but having increafed the pay of thefe unfortunate wretches, which was only one half-penny Englifh a day, they fent for large quantities of brandy, made the guard drunk, and efcaped while they were afleep. I found their irons in the woods a few days after, but the governor not having thought proper to truft me with any more criminals, I was obliged to give up the work. They had already gone four feet deeper without finding the earth frozen. I then thruft my fword in it (for I travelled in a lay habit) up to the hilt with the utmoft eafe. It is very certain therefore, that the ground at Tobolſky thaws entirely, fince the thaw prevails as far as fixteen feet deep. This experiment altered the idea I had conceived of the climate of Tobolſky, and made me ftill more cautious of advancing facts from tradition and hearfay; for I am perfuaded the numerous miftakes found in the writings of fome travellers, proceed rather from their credulity, than from their want of truth.

Not having travelled beyond Tobolsky, I cannot speak of the remaining part of Siberia from my own remarks. But modern travellers, having gone through this country with thermometers, and with a spirit of observation, far beyond that of their predecessors, have been enabled to communicate a very accurate description of the climate of this vast country, which it is necessary to give an account of in this work.

According to Mr. Gmelin's observations*, made at Argunskoi in Siberia †, the climate is so cold in all this country, that many places are found where the ground never thaws more than three feet deep. People who work in the silver mines, in the neighbourhood, have made cellars in the parts which have been already digged up, to preserve their provisions from the severe cold felt at Argunskoi even in the summer. Nevertheless the air is so cold in these cellars, that the ice, which is formed there in winter, does not melt in the summer, although the thermometer was a little above the congealing point on the 17th of July, 1735.

The same traveller felt the greatest cold of Siberia, for the first time, in the city of Jenisseik ‡, towards the middle of December. "The air seemed frozen, and like a mist,
" though free from clouds. This extreme condensation of the
" air hindered the smoke of the chimnies from rising; the
" sparrows and magpies used to fall down and die of cold,
" if they were not instantly taken up and carried into warm
" places. When the door of a room was opened, a mist was
" immediately formed round the stove, and, within the four

---

* Gmelin, voyage en Siberie, edition Françoise, tom. i. pag. 252 and 258.
† Latitude, fifty degrees, fifty-three minutes; longitude, one hundred and thirty-six degrees, forty-two minutes.
‡ Latitude, fifty-eight degrees, twenty-seven minutes; longitude, one hundred and ten degrees, forty minutes.

"and twenty hours, the windows were entirely covered with
"ice, three-tenths of an inch thick *."

Mr. Gmelin went through the fame city again on his return to St. Peterſburg in 1739 †, and made feveral obſervations there, to afcertain whether the cold was equally fevere. "On
"the 22d of October, at midnight, Mr. de Liſle's thermo-
"meter fupported itſelf at one hundred and ninety degrees,
"which anſwer to twenty-one degrees below the freezing
"point in M. de Reaumur's. Mr. de Liſle's thermometer fell
"towards the end of January at Jeniſſeik, to two hundred
"and fifteen degrees, which anſwer to thirty-eight of M. de
"Reaumur's. From that time the froſt gave way. The
"river of Jeniſſea thawed on the 8th of April, and in three
"weeks the country reſumed its verdure. This is a plain
"proof that winters differ from each other here, as well as
"any where elſe.

"According to the fame traveller ‡, the cold began to be
"felt at Olekminskoi §, in the year 1736, towards the end
"of Auguſt; the trees loſt their leaves on the firſt days of
"September; all the grafs was withered, fome fnow fell, and
"the cold formed a frozen fleet. On the 9th of September,
"the ice began to float on the river Lena, and a few days
"after, large pieces were taken out of it, more than two feet
"thick, which the inhabitants turned to a very proper uſe.
"Their windows do not ſhut cloſe, nor can the uſual preſerva-
"tives of skins and dung defend either the rooms or cellars from
"the intenſe cold. It is cuſtomary, therefore, to take large
"clear pieces of ice, about the fize of the window, which are

* Gmelin, tom. ii. pag. 181 and 182.
† Gmelin, tom. ii. pag. 51.
‡ Id. i. pag. 352 and 355.
§ Lat. fixty degrees, twenty minutes; longitude, one hundred and thirty-feven degrees.

"placed

"placed on the outside; a little water is then poured on
"them, and the window is made.

"The cold is so sharp at Jakutsk *, that, a few years be-
"fore 1736, a waywode, who was obliged to go from his
"own house to the chancellor's office, not more than about
"eighty steps off, had his feet, hands, and nose frozen, and
"did not recover without the greatest difficulty; although
"his body was covered with a very large furr, and his head
"wrapped up in a furr-hood †. Towards the end of June,
"the ground is often found frozen for three feet deep. In
"1685, as the people were digging for a well, the ground
"was found frozen thirteen toises deep in the month of
"July ‡; yet the river thawed on the 11th of May 1737, and
"on the 14th the frost was quite gone.

"The city of Tomsk, although situated much more to the
"south §, is still exposed to very sharp frost. In the midst
"of April, the air was already warm and agreeable; but it
"changed on a sudden towards the 15th of May; we then
"had snow, rain and sleet; and felt one day of cold unknown
"before at this season ∥."

The city of Mangasea, situated on the river Jenissea, is in
a very cold climate ¶. Mr. Gmelin speaks thus of it **.
"I have mentioned the fine days we had, before we left
"Jenisseik, towards the end of May ††. When we arrived

---

* Latitude, sixty-two degrees; longitude, one hundred forty-five degrees, forty-two minutes.
† Tom. i. pag. 381, 411, and 412.
‡ I imagine this to be an error of the press, and that it should be thirteen feet.
§ Latitude, fifty-seven degrees, three minutes; longitude, one hundred and two degrees, thirty-eight minutes.
∥ Gmelin, tom. ii. pag. 164.
¶ Latitude, sixy-five degrees, thirty-six minutes; longitude, one hundred and seven degrees.
** Tom. ii. pag. 54.
†† Tom. ii. pag. 51.

" at Mangafea, we thought we had paffed from fummer to
" winter, although it was on the 10th of June: we were then
" indeed at 65 degrees, 36 minutes, north latitude. The
" ground was covered with fnow, which ftill continued falling;
" the ice was extremely thick, and did not melt even in the
" day-time. This bad weather foon ceafed, and we were not a
" little furprized at the fudden change we were witneffes of.
" As foon as the air had acquired fome degree of heat, it
" preferved it; the vapours and clouds, which had darkened
" the face of the heavens, difappeared at once, and, fo foon
" as the 12th, we were able to live without fire. The next
" day we faw fome fwallows. The heat of the fun increafed:
" on the 11th, there was no fnow to be feen, the grafs grew
" vifibly; fo much, that if ever man could be faid to fee it
" grow, it was at Mangafea."

M. Delifle, of the Royal Academy of Sciences, in the long ftay he made at St. Peterfburg, has collected all the obfervations, made in Siberia, by the different academicians fent into Ruffia: he has alfo lived among moft of them at their return, and from them has received all the informations he could defire. The account he gives of the cold in Siberia is too interefting to be omitted *. He has likewife made a table of his obfervations, from which an accurate idea may be formed of the almoft incredible frofts of Siberia, and of thofe which prevail throughout the reft of Ruffia.

It appears from this table, that, in 1735, the cold made Mr. Reaumur's thermometer fall down to feventy degrees at Jenifeik, as it has been already obferved it did at Solikamfky in the winter of 1761. In the fame year 1735, the cold was much lefs intenfe at Tomfk, fince it anfwered only to fifty-

* Vol. de l'Acad. Roy. des Sciences de Paris, an. 1749, pag. 1. des mémoires.

four degrees and a half of M. Reaumur's thermometer. At Irkutſk *, it was at thirty-two degrees, although this city is ſituated in one of the moſt ſouthern provinces of Siberia; and at Tobolsky at thirty degrees, notwithſtanding this city ſtands about ſix degrees northward of Irkutsk †.

It happens not unfrequently, even on the borders of China, that ſo great a degree of cold is felt, as to make M. Reaumur's thermometer fall to thirty degrees; and the places where this has happened, are nearly in the parallel of Paris, where the greateſt cold, in 1709, was fifteen degrees, and one quarter.

The obſervations made on the cold at Aſtracan, mention facts as extraordinary as any of thoſe I have been relating. Aſtracan, though ſituated under the parallel of the middle of France ‡, is ſtill expoſed to the moſt ſevere cold, even ſuch as is felt in moſt northern parts of Europe. According to Mr. Lerch's obſervations §, the river Volga froze on the 14th of December 1745; the cold increaſed daily, and Mr. Deliſle's thermometer fell, on the 27th of the ſame month, to one hundred and eighty-four degrees; which anſwer to ſixteen degrees of Mr. Reaumur's. In the beginning of January 1746, the cold at Aſtracan anſwered to twelve degrees of Mr. Reaumur's thermometer: it increaſed every day to the 16th. Mr. Deliſle's thermometer was at one hundred ninety five degrees and a half, which anſwer to four and twenty degrees and a half of M. Reaumur's; and while this very ſevere weather was felt at Aſtracan, the winter was exceeding mild in the northern parts of Europe.

---

* Latitude, fifty two degrees, eighteen minutes; longitude, one hundred twenty-two degrees, thirty-eight minutes.

† Latitude, fifty-eight degrees, twelve minutes, twenty-two ſeconds; longitude, eighty-five degrees, fifty-ſix minutes, forty ſeconds.

‡ Latitude, forty-ſix degrees, fifteen minutes; longitude, ſixty-eight degrees, twelve minutes.

§ Volume de l'Académie de Berlin; année 1746, pag. 257.

When we come to speak of the cold felt in the other parts of Ruſſia, after what has been ſaid of Siberia, the climate appears very different, altho' ſtill extremely cold. It grows more temperate as one comes nearer to the weſtern boundaries of Ruſſia. From Mr. Deliſle's table it appears, that the cold at St. Peterſburg * makes Mr. Reaumur's thermometer fall from ſeventeen to thirty degrees: I have not met with any obſervations made at Moſco, but it is generally enough known, that the cold is ſo ſevere there, though it ſtands much more to the ſouth than St. Peterſburg †, that in ſome winters the inhabitants can hardly bear it. If water is thrown up into the air, it often falls down again in ice. The winter in theſe two laſt mentioned cities, uſually continues for ſeven or eight months, and ſometimes longer. The climate grows more temperate as one draws nearer to the ſouth; in the Ukraine it is very mild.

Notwithſtanding the degree of cold I have mentioned, corn grows in many of theſe places. The ground in general is very fit for agriculture in ſome part of Siberia; where a black kind of earth is met with, like that of Tobolſky, and conſequently exceedingly fertile; ſo that if the ſoil does not every where produce corn, it is for want of a ſufficient heat to bring about the vegetation of plants.

The province of Nerczinſk is very fruitful, and more ſo than any other part of Siberia: here the corn comes to its full perfection, and all kinds of fruits are produced: this fact is authenticated by all the travellers.

Although the ground never thaws at Argunſkoi below a certain depth, yet a kind of wild buck-wheat grows there,

---

* Latitude, fifty-nine degrees, fifty ſix minutes; longitude, forty-ſeven degrees, fifty-three minutes.

† Latitude, fifty five degrees, forty-ſix minutes; longitude, fifty-five degrees, ſeven minutes.

which differs from the common fort in being lefs, and not angular *.

Corn thrives pretty well between the forts Olekminfkoi and Vitimfkoi, notwithftanding the extreme cold felt there †. On the 10th of Auguft 1736, the hay was got up at Vitimfkoi: moft of the corn was reaped; and in kindly years the harveft is never later, although fome cold nights had already been felt.

The frozen foil of the province of Jenifeik, and the lazinefs of the inhabitants, are equally the caufes of this province being almoft uncultivated though it is one of the moft extenfive.

The province of Irkutfk is of a great extent; it is uncultivated and barren; full of defert and dry plains, over which one may travel for feveral days without meeting with one fingle tree. There are many falt lakes in this province.

The climate of Jakutfk is by no means fit for corn, altho' barley has fometimes been feen to grow and ripen there; but as it has failed feveral times, the fowing of it has been long fince neglected. The other kinds of corn have never been known to ripen. This diftrict is not only too far north, but likewife too much to the eaft. The earth, however, is black and greafy, as in the beft foil of Siberia ‡.

All the other parts of Siberia, from the town of Ilimfk to the fea of Kamtfchatka, are barren, dry and defert §. The inhabitants of thefe laft regions live contentedly without bread: their food confifting of vegetables, fifh, and game; and the pulp of young pines, which they fcrape off, dry it, reduce it to powder, and afterwards mix it with their victuals ‖. Corn, however, is imported into thefe parts of Siberia, but in very

---

* Gmelin, tom. i. pag. 259.
† Gmelin, tom. i. pag. 338. and 349.
‡ Gmelin, tom i. pag. 411.
§ Defcription de l'Empire de Ruffia, par M. le Baron de Strahlenberg, tom. i. pag. 28. ‖ Gmelin, tom. i. p. 388.

fmall

small quantities, on account of the length of the roads, and the difficulty of feeding the horses.

According to Mr. Gmelin *, there is no pasture to be found about the town of Okotskoi; nothing grows there but small willows, the young shoots of which can be eat by the horses. It often happens, that in going from this town † to Jakousk, where the horses must be brought back, the winter sets in while the people are on the road; in which case most of the horses perish, so that it is scarce possible to save one out of a hundred.

The regions of the south part of Siberia, towards the borders, produce no corn, or very little, as far as the confines of Astracan. This, however, appears to be the only part of Siberia fit for human beings to live in: the climate is mild, and the soil seems as if it would be very fertile, if cultivated; but for want of inhabitants, nothing besides deserts are to be met with, which form a powerful barrier against the Tartars. The cold is sometimes very severe there as I have before observed: but this is to be looked upon as an extraordinary circumstance, not resulting from a general law.

The rest of the Russian empire is cultivated in several places; its mean length, from west to east, is about three hundred and fifty leagues, and four hundred from south to north. It is not equally peopled throughout, nor equally fit for agriculture. All the country between the Frozen Sea and the parallel of St. Petersburg, situated about the sixtieth degree of latitude, is hardly peopled at all: nothing but forests and marshes are to be seen there; and no corn, or at least very little. This climate produces no fruit, nor even any of the common vegetables ‡. This part, which is barren and almost

---

* Tom. i. pag. 416.

† A town situated on the borders of the sea of Pengina. It has a port; where people embark for Kamtschatka.

‡ Strahlemberg, description de l'Empire de Russie, tom. i. pag. 26, and all the travellers.

desert,

desert, extends three hundred and fifty leagues from west to east, and two hundred from north to south. The remainder of Russia extends still two hundred leagues towards the south, and this is the only part where the soil appears fit for agriculture. The Ukraine is an exceedingly fruitful province, in which there is plenty of every thing. Most of the lands are cultivated in all the other provinces, from fifty-six degrees of latitude to the parallel of St. Petersburg; yet the corn thrives there but indifferently *.

Hitherto the climate of Russia has been considered only with regard to its produce, we shall now see that it affords new objects, of a very interesting nature. By these we shall find a confirmation of that generally received opinion, that the more we advance towards the east under the same parallel, going from Europe, the more the cold increases; and this observation holds good as far as towards America, which is authenticated by Mr. Delisle's memoir, already spoken of. These are his words †.

"From what I know of the methods people take to pre-
"serve themselves from the extreme colds of Russia and Sibe-
"ria, and what happens in warm rooms during these ex-
"cessive colds, I cannot think they are ever more severe than
"those of which captain Middleton gives an account to the
"Royal Society of London, and which he experienced in the
"English colony at Hudson's Bay, under fifty-seven degrees
"three-fourths of latitude.

"Although the houses in which people are obliged to shut
"themselves up for five or six months in the year are built of
"stone, the walls of which are two feet thick; although the
"windows are very narrow, and supplied with very thick

---

* Strahlemberg, tom. i. pag. 28.
† Volume de l'Académie de Paris de 1749, page 13.

"shutters,

"shutters, which are shut up for eighteen hours every day:
"although very great fires are made four times a day in these
"rooms, in large stoves, built on purpose; although the
"chimnies are shut quite close when the wood is consumed,
"and nothing but the burning embers are left, in order the
"better to keep in the heat; yet all the inside of these rooms,
"and the beds, are covered with ice three inches thick, which
"the people are obliged to remove every day. The only light
"they have, in these long nights, is procured from balls of
"iron, of four and twenty pounds, made red hot, and hung
"up before the windows. All liquors freeze in these apart-
"ments, and even brandy in the smallest rooms, notwith-
"standing a great fire is continually kept in them.

"Those who venture out in the open air, defended even
"with double and triple coverings and furrs, not only about
"the body, but also about the head, neck, feet and hands,
"are nevertheless benumbed with the cold at first, and cannot
"return into the warm rooms, without losing the skin of
"their face and hands, and sometimes having their toes
"frozen.

"We may have still a better idea of the external cold,
"from the account captain Middleton gives of the lakes of
"standing water, which are not more than ten or twelve
"feet deep, freezing down to the bottom; this happens also
"to the sea, which freezes to the above-mentioned depth;
"although the ice is not more than nine or ten feet thick in
"rivers nearest the sea, and where the tide is strong.

"The extreme cold sometimes makes the ice crack with
"an astonishing noise, as loud as the explosion of a cannon.

"With regard to the earth, Mr. Middleton thinks it is
"never thawed at the bottom; because, having had it digged
"five or six feet deep in the course of the two months during
"which

"which the summer lasts, he had found it still frozen, and white as snow.

"These effects are greater than those commonly felt in Siberia; which would induce one to believe, that the frosts of Hudson's Bay, and the neighbourhood, are at least as severe as the most intense frosts of Siberia. The only way of being perfectly assured of this, is by observations made with thermometers, as accurate as those which have been made use of to determine the cold in Siberia."

These last observations make it more and more certain, that the cold increases as one advances eastward, so that this fact is now incontrovertable. This phenomenon has been chiefly accounted for in Siberia, from the prodigious height which has been attributed to the soil of this country, and the quantity of salt found in it. The disposition of the soil in Siberia has still been considered in another light. This country forms an inclined plane from the Frozen Sea as far as the frontiers of China, where the soil is highest, because the two empires are separated in this spot by chains of mountains. The sun, situated towards the horizon of these mountains, cannot therefore impart much heat to this inclined soil, when it enlightens that hemisphere, because its rays will only glance over that surface of the globe. The extreme cold of this country is perfectly well accounted for from the combination of these several causes. But in what manner does the general effect proceed from either of these causes? It has been already shewn, that the soil of Siberia is not so much raised as it has been hitherto supposed to be. These points deserve to be farther discussed, for which purpose I shall be obliged to repeat some of the facts already advanced, in order to avoid confusion. Laurentius Lange asserts, that the ridge of mountains which separates Russia from Siberia is more than two leagues high [*]."

---

[*] Journal du voyage de Laurent Lange à la Chine, tom v. pag. 378. du recoeuil des voyages au nord, edition d'Amsterdam, chez Jean Frederic Bernard.

A JOURNEY TO SIBERIA.

"The mountains of Verchaturia," says he, "are situated between that place and Solikamſky. We paſſed over them in ſuch extreme cold weather, that the coverings of our ſledges were not ſufficient to protect us from it; and we were in ſo much danger of loſing our noſes, that we could not poſſibly proceed more than twenty werſts without ſtopping. We had fifty werſts to go over theſe mountains, which are, I believe, at their higheſt point, nine werſts high."

The firſt travellers have determined the great height of theſe mountains of Siberia, from obſervations ſuch as theſe. Moſt of thoſe who have come after them have been led away by the ſame prejudices, and have confirmed them; ſo that they have been afterwards conſidered as known facts: yet it is evident, from the level I have taken in the courſe of my journey, not only that theſe mountains are not very high, but likewiſe that the ground of Siberia, at leaſt as far as Tobolſky, is very low. As this has been already proved under the article of the levelling, it will be ſufficient to obſerve here, that the height of the middle of the chain near the hamlet Roſtcſs, which is the moſt elevated point, is four hundred and ſeventy-one toiſes above the level of the ſea at Breſt, inſtead of five thouſand toiſes, which Laurentius Lange ſuppoſes it to be; and that the Irtyſz at Tobolſky is no more than 69 toiſes above the level of the ſea, four and twenty toiſes above the level of the great Obſervatory, and forty-eight toiſes above the level of the Seine at the Pont-Royal.

With regard to the other parts of Siberia, where theſe extreme colds have been obſerved, I cannot take upon me to determine, with preciſion, the height of thoſe lands, as I have never been upon the ſpot. M. Gmelin, however, has made obſervations there with the barometer, of which Mr. Braün has given an extract in the memoirs of the academy of St. Peterſburg *: but this extract, and mere observations of the barometer, are not always sufficient to determine exactly the height of the places, where they have been made. I have made use of other methods to fix the exactness of my observations in the level I have taken. From the slope of the rivers which cross Siberia, one may, however, obtain results, which, though not exact, will still be sufficient to let us know, whether the height of these parts is such, as to be the principal cause of the cold in Siberia.

The river Loire has a very considerable slope: so that supposing the rivers of Siberia, which run across plains of five or six hundred leagues, to have equal slopes, the heights deduced from thence must be greater than they should be; therefore, by stating the mean slope of the Loire at four feet, seven inches, eight lines, *per* league of 2000 toises †, the heights calculated from thence will be found in the following table.

If all the rivers I have calculated from, were supposed to have the slope of the Irtysz, the height of these places would be less by about one fourth part.

* Tom. vi. p. 425.

	feet.	inches.	lines.
† The slope of the Loire at Rennes, by leagues of 2000 toises, is,	6	11	4
At Orleans,	4	7	10
At Angiers,	2	3	11
Mean slope.	4	7	8

TABLE,

TABLE, containing the Heights, with respect to the Sea, of Places in Siberia where the greatest Colds have been observed.

Names of the places.	Longitudes.		Latitudes.		Distances of the rivers at their mouths.	Heights above the level of the ocean at Brest, determined by the mean slope of the Loire.	Heights above the level of the ocean at Brest, determined by the mean slope of the Irtysz.	Mean heighs above the ocean at Brest.
	d.	m.	d.	m.	leagues or 2000 toises.	toises of France.	toises of France.	toises of France.
Astracan	68	12	46	15		observed		
Solikamsky	74	24	59	35		observed	——	187
Echaterinenburg	78	40	56	44		observed	——	220
Tobolsky	85	57	58	12		observed	——	69
Tomsk	102	38	57	3	500	426	132	279
Irtysz. Lake Saisan*	103	30	47	54	760	626	201	413
Mangasea	107	0	65	36	200	154	53	103
Jenisseik	110	40	58	27	440	380	115	247
Irkutsk	122	38	52	18	900	775	236	505
Kiringa	125	54	57	30	750	18	197	407
Nerczinsk	133	48	51	48	660	549	172 in the mountains.	549 531
Argunskoi	136	42	50	53	637	531	166	
Olekminskoi	137	0	60	20	640	533	167	350
Jakutsk	145	52	62	0	400	349	105	227

* The lake Saisan, where the Irtysz rises, is about seven hundred and sixty leagues distant from the gulf Obkaia, in the direction of the course of the river: supposing, therefore, the slope of this river equal to that of the Loire, determined at 4 feet, 7 inches, 8 lines per league of 2000 toises, the level of lake Saisan will then be 626 toises above the level of the sea. I have calculated from my observations the slope of the Irtysz at Tobolsky, so that its mean slope may be reckoned at 1 foot, 7 inches, per league, and the lake Saisan would then be no more than 200 toises above the level of the sea. This height should however be more considerable, because the slope of this river must increase as one comes nearer to its origin; and I suppose we may come pretty near the truth, by taking the medium between these two results. This medium fixes the height of the lake Saisan at 413 toises above the level of the frozen sea.

In this manner I have determined the heights of all the places mentioned in the preceding table, except the four first; these have been determined by observations mentioned in the article of the levelling of Russia. The heights of Nerczinsk and Argunskoi, have been determined merely from the slope of the Loire; because I suppose the slope of the river Amour to be very steep, its course being entirely among the mountains; whereas the other rivers of Siberia, having their course in the immense plain, which extends from this chain as far as the frozen sea, must consequently have their slopes much less steep. We must not indeed expect, as I before hinted, very accurate results from these calculations; they furnish us, however, with a comparative point approaching nearly to the real situation of these places; whereas other travellers have all asserted, that Siberia was very high, without giving us any idea of the real height of the soil; and and those who have done this, as Laurentius Lange, have been led into the grossest mistakes.

L l 2

The refults mentioned in this table confirm the obfervation all travellers have made, that the foil rifes continually as one advances from Tobolfky towards the eaft. This city, fituated in a latitude of 58 degrees, appears to be the loweft of all the places in Siberia lying under the fame parallel: and indeed all the rivers, whofe origin is to the weft or to the eaft of the Irtyfz, difcharge themfelves into this river. The places fituated about the parallel of Tobolfky, and mentioned in the foregoing table, are, Solikamfky, Tomfk, Jeniffeik, Kiringa and Olekminskoi. All thefe are among the number of places, in which the fevereft cold of Siberia has been felt. In the year 1735, it was obferved, at 30 degrees at Tobolsky, while at Tomsk it was at 53 degrees and a half, and at 70 degrees at Jeniffeik. The greateft difference of this cold is 40 degrees between Tobolsky and Jeniffeik, while the difference of the refpective height of thefe two cities above the level of the fea, is no more than 178 toifes, which the town of Jeniffeik has above the other. Now, fo trifling a difference in height can have no relation to the difference of cold experienced at Jeniffeik, and at Tobolsky; befides, the cold, in the fame winter, was lefs fevere at Tomsk by 18 degrees, than it was at Jeniffeik; although the city of Tomsk is the higheft, being 279 toifes, and that of Jeniffeik only 247. It is hardly neceffary to dwell any longer upon this fubject, in order to prove that the fmall differences in the heights of the above mentioned places cannot poffibly produce thofe prodigious differences in the degrees of cold which the travellers have related.

The true caufe, therefore, of the different degrees of cold felt in Siberia, feems to be accounted for from local circumftances, and from the quantity of falt found in feveral parts of it; which may be ftill farther confirmed by the following obfervations.

According to M. Gmelin's remarks before mentioned, the ground is not thawed at Jakutsk at the end of July. He even fufpects suspects that there are no springs in this part, because the earth is always frozen. At Argunskoi, though nearly under the same parallel as Paris, several places are found, where the ground never thaws more than three feet deep, and these may be considered as perpetually frozen spots. This town, however, is not raised more than 531 toises or thereabouts, above the level of the sea. Mr. Bouguer has observed the perpetual frozen spot at Peru, to be 2434 toises above the level of the sea *. He thinks that according to the parallel of Paris, it should be 1500 or 1600 toises. This spot should therefore be the same at Argunskoi, since that town is nearly in the same latitude. It might be suspected from this observation, that the earth at Argunskoi is higher than I suppose it to be: but we must not confound the frozen spot observed in Siberia by Mr. Gmelin, with that remarked at Peru by Mr. Bouguer; since they are owing to two very different causes. I do not even imagine, that there are any mountains in Siberia of such a height, as that the constant frozen spot mentioned by Mr. Bouguer, can be found upon them; and indeed all the travellers, who have passed over the mountains situated between China and Siberia, have never taken notice of such a spot. But let us return to our subject. The constant frozen spot, of which M. Bouguer speaks, is owing to the prodigious height of the mountains called Cordeleirias des Andes; for it is well known that the cold increases in proportion as we rise in the atmosphere, which fact Mr. Bouguer accounts for. The air being less dense and more transparent as we get farther from the earth, is therefore less heated by the immediate action of the sun, on account of the readiness with which the rays pass through any very transparent body; whereas, towards the surface of the earth, the denser air must be more heated by the mere action of the sun. The heat is still increased by the contact and vicinity of bodies

* Figure de la terre, pag. 48.

more denfe than thofe it furrounds, and upon which it is diffufed; confequently, the air muft be lefs heated than the more denfe bodies contiguous to it. If we place a thermometer in the fun, and another in the fhade, the firft fhall fometimes rife in fummer-time 14 or 15 degrees above the latter. This thermometer points out the ftate of the atmofphere, and the firft fhews the effect produced by the immediate action of the fun upon the earth.

Thefe few remarks, applied to the conftant frozen fpot obferved by Mr. Gmelin, prove, with the utmoft evidence, that it cannot be owing to the height of Argunfkoi, and that the caufe of it muft be very different from that which produces the conftant frozen fpot in the Cordeleirias mountains; for, if that was the cafe, the furface of the earth at Argunskoi would be perpetually covered with fnow and ice, as at Peru; and the cold would increafe in proportion as we got higher in the atmofphere, whereas it is juft the contrary. The froft at Argunskoi is only found at the depth of three feet; the furface of the foil being completely thawed. The climate is alfo pretty temperate in fome places, fince it admits of the growth of vegetables. Nerczinsk, although fituated under the fame parallel, and only at the diftance of 15 leagues to the northweft, is in a temperate and exceedingly fertile climate; neverthelefs it is a few toifes higher than Argunskoi. Therefore the caufe of the conftant frozen fpot in Siberia, is different from what it is at Peru; it does not of courfe imply any remarkable height, and it is a miftake to attribute the exceffive cold of Siberia to the prodigious height which has been improperly given to this country. This degree of cold is certainly owing to the falt in Siberia; which indeed is found in great quantities about Solikamfky, at Jeniffeik, at Irkutfz, and in the Baraba. The extreme cold before mentioned muft therefore be attributed to local and particular circumftances. The want

want of cultivation, may likewife be reckoned among the general caufes. As we travel towards the eaft, the earth becomes lefs populous, uncultivated and defert. We meet with nothing but immenfe forefts, which prevent the fun from acting upon the furface of the earth; and marfhes and lakes, whofe waters abforb the rays of the fun, and reflect very few of them. The cultivation of land has a confiderable influence upon the nature of a climate.

Men live however in Siberia, though often expofed, for feveral minutes, to cold which finks Mr. Reaumur's thermometer to 70 degrees; while, in the baths, they experience a heat which make it rife to 60 degrees. M. Tillet has made it appear, that a woman in France bore, for the fpace of ten minutes, a degree of heat which made the fame thermometer rife to 112 *. It was imagined, from Mr. Boerhave's account, that men could not bear a heat above 54 degrees, and that both animals and vegetables muft perifh in cold below 34 degrees. It has been alfo thought, for a long time, that it was not poffible to make an artificial heat exceeding 32 degrees; till Mr. Braun, of the academy of St. Peterfburg, congealed mercury, by a degree of cold, equal to 470 of Mr. Delifle's thermometer, which anfwers to 170 degrees of Mr. Reaumur's †.

Thefe truths fhew what progrefs we make in the knowledge of facts, and feem to bring us nearer to that of primary caufes, which however may yet be for ever hidden from us.

* Volume de l'Académie de Sciences, de l'année 1764, pag. 195. des mémoires.
† Differtation de Mr. Braun fur le froid artificiel, imprimée à Saint Peterfbourg, en 1759.

Of the government of Russia, from the year 861, to 1767.

ACCORDING to the annals of Poland and Russia, the last of these kingdoms has been governed by a succession of Princes, Grand Dukes, or Czars, all of the same family, from the year 861 * to 1596. The first of these sovereigns was named Rurich; the last, Fedor Iwanowich. During this interval of more than 700 years, the eldest sons have always succeeded of course, without having any disputes with their brothers, or any of their subjects. So long a filial succession should seem to prove, that Russia was then a free state. But the same annals, and all historians, assert, that the nation was ever governed by absolute princes. According to all probability therefore, the government must have been rendered milder by some particular customs, since it does not appear that the state was exposed to any remarkable commotions till the death of Fedor Iwanowich.

Fedor Iwanowich died in 1596, leaving no children. Some historians assert he was poisoned, and his daughter also, by Boris Godonow, his minister and favourite. The princess died before her father. Boris Godonow, having acquired great authority under the reign of the Czar Fedor, caused the young Demetrius, legitimate heir to the crown, to be murdered at Uglicz in 1597 †: he afterwards dispatched the murderer he had employed. The castle of Uglicz was razed by his orders, and some of the inhabitants of the town were murdered, in order to make him appear innocent, and to give a striking

---

* According to some historians, since the year 700.
† This prince was brother to the Czar Fedor, by another mother.

proof

proof of his attachment to the royal family. This defpotic tyrant did not ftop here; he alfo deftroyed, under different pretences, all the princes who could poffibly have any pretenfions to the crown, as well as all perfons in office who were attached to them; and heaping crimes on crimes, Boris feized upon the throne in 1598, and taking advantage of the confternation of the people, caufed himfelf to be crowned by them. Seated on a throne, ftained with the blood of his kings, he was haunted with fear and miftruft. He thought himfelf furrounded by traitors, or new pretenders. He pronounced fentence of death againft every one of whom he entertained the flighteft fufpicion: the blood of the innocent was continually fpilt; the fword of tyranny flamed all around, wickednefs became virtue, and virtue, languifhing and debafed, did not dare to fhew her head. By repeated crimes Boris eftablifhed the moft fhocking flavery, by which he expected to fecure to himfelf the poffeffion of the throne; but was foon after driven from it by a new ufurper, who was himfelf affaffinated in 1606. From this time, Ruffia became a fcene of anarchy and confufion; frefh pretenders to the throne perpetually rifing up, who were fucceffively affaffinated or dethroned; the commotions increafed daily, and continued till the year 1613.

Although the realm of Ruffia had never been elective, yet, under fuch circumftances, the nation was obliged to chufe a fovereign. Michael Romanof, grandfather of the Czar Peter, was elected this year, in an affembly of the chief nobles; and the Ruffians fubmitted themfelves to a youth of fifteen, without making any conditions*. From the readinefs with which they confented to a change of the old conftitution, it may be concluded, that it had not been formed by them, that they had

---

* M. de Voltaire, tom i. page 80, édition de Paris, chez Panckoucke.

not the leaft notion of liberty, or that they were extremely degenerated.

Alexis Michaelowitz, his fon, came to the throne in 1645, without any other form of election. His reign was difturbed with feditions and civil wars; chiefly occafioned, it feems, by the defpotic fway, which Morozou, favourite of the Czar, exercifed over the empire. Mr. Voltaire obferves, "That this "part of the world being lefs reftrained by manners than any "other, it was neceffary it fhould be reftrained by corporal "punifhments, and that thofe punifhments gave birth to "flavery *.

After the death of the Czar Alexis, which happened in 1677, the nation became more and more enflaved. This prince had been twice married. From the firft marriage he had the two princes, Fedor and Iwan, with fix princeffes; the fruits of the fecond, were Peter the Firft, and one princefs. Fedor came to the throne at 15 years of age, and died in 1682, without children †. Perceiving that his brother Iwan, too ill-favored by nature, was unfit to reign, he named, on his deathbed, his fecond brother Peter, who was not more than ten years old, his fucceffor to the throne. The princefs Sophia, daughter of Fedor, from the firft bed, formed the defign of placing herfelf at the head of the empire. This princefs, whofe fchemes were the more dangerous, on account of the fuperiority of her underftanding, continued ftirring up the moft bloody rebellions for the fpace of about feven years. In thefe calamitous times, treafons and public murders conftantly prevailed. The nation was in the utmoft confufion and diforder. The Strelits fpilt blood on all fides, and practifed unheard-of cruelties; the life of the fovereign was as much expofed as that

---

* M. de Voltaire, page 83.
† M. de Voltaire, page 87, et fuivantes.

of his subjects. Sophia was at length shut up in a convent; but the nation, inured to rebellion and slaughter, was with difficulty restrained from repeating the same crimes. Peter the First, in 1689, taking the reins of government in his own hands, conceived the design of reforming and civilizing his nation: but being more absolute than any of his predecessors, he drew the bands of slavery still closer. The vast projects of this great man are well known; he died in 1725, in the midst of his labours, and the Empress Catherine his wife in 1727.

Peter Alexiowitz, grandson to Peter I. succeeded to the throne, and died in 1730. The prince of Olgorouki, and count d'Osterman, who composed the high council, suppressed the will of the Empress Catherine, and raised a report, that Peter II. on his deathbed had, named the princess, dutchess dowager of Courland, his successor. She was the daughter of John, elder brother of Peter I*, but by another wife. This princess being kept from the throne by the children of Peter I. was obliged to consent to terms, by which her power was limited. The prince of Olgorouki, and count d'Osterman, had proposed to keep the reins of government in their own hands; but she had scarcely ascended the throne, when she assumed the same authority as the sovereigns her predecessors.

This princess had brought with her, her favourite Biren, a native of Courland. In the name of the Empress Ann, he ruled the Russians with a rod of iron. He seemed already to have conceived the design of making himself one day master of the throne. He subdued the nation by inflicting punish-

---

* The will of the Empress Catherine, which had never been made public, regulated the succession of the Russian empire: the dutchess of Holstein, and the princess Elizabeth, daughter of Peter I. and of the Empress Catherine, were to succeed to Peter Alexiowitz, Strahlemberg, tom. i. pag. 225.

ments, and sending a number of exiles into Siberia. After the death of the last prince of the house of Ketler, the Empress Ann created him duke of Courland; and at her death, in 1740, she appointed him regent of the empire, till the majority of her niece's son, who was only two months old. This young prince was proclaimed Emperor by the name of Iwan, or John III. and the duke of Biren, though hated by the nation, had the title of regent.

The princess of Brunswic, the Emperor's mother, could not however bear the sway of the regent; she therefore thought of shaking it off, and pitched upon general Munic, a stranger in Russia, to assist her in the undertaking. Munic was well acquainted with Biren and with the Russians; and assured the princess, that as she had thought of this scheme, she was in the greatest danger of being arrested with her party, if Biren himself was not arrested within four and twenty hours. Munic took this task upon himself, and went away immediately. In order to remove all cause of suspicion from the regent, he set out with intention to pay him a visit; but returned when he had got half way to the house, fearing lest he might be followed by some spy from the princess, and be suspected of betraying her. He went directly home, where he remained till midnight, on the 18th of November 1740. He then took a few trusty soldiers with him, and seized upon Biren in his bed; Biren was banished a few days after into Siberia, where he was shut up in a house, built in the middle of a marsh, and the princess of Brunswic was declared regent.

The various revolutions Russia had already experienced, made way for others, and facilitated the success of them. The people, always enslaved, were not attached to their sovereign, either by laws or affection: so that the crown was exposed to every

every one who had courage enough to seize upon it, by policy or superior strength.

Lestoc, a foreign surgeon, attached to the princess Elizabeth, daughter of Peter the First, in conjunction with an ambassador of an European power, formed the design of placing her upon the throne. Just as the design was going to be carried into execution, the regent was informed of it by advices she received from Brussels. She sent for the princess Elizabeth, and mentioned the circumstance immediately; firmly persuaded that she could not be able to impose upon her in the first instant of surprize. The countenance of the princess Elizabeth, and her mildness, convinced the regent of her innocence. Elizabeth went home, told Lestoc, that the conspiracy was discovered, and that she renounced the empire. Lestoc heard her, retired, and went to dispose every thing for fixing her upon the throne in a few hours.

Lestoc, having seen the chief conspirators, went to the billiard-table towards eight in the evening; there he found a suspicious person, whom it was necessary to hinder from going about the town; the passion this spy had for play, made it easy for him to effect his purpose. He engaged him in a few games at billiards, and detained him till the arrival of one of his emissaries. Upon that, Lestoc soon finished his game. He went away almost immediately, and took a turn round the palace, to see that every thing was in its usual state. From thence he went to the parade, where he waited till eleven o'clock for another emissary, whom he had sent to general Munic's, and to count d'Osterman, the prime minister's house. Upon being informed that every thing was quiet, he returned to the princess Elizabeth, and had two sledges brought into her court-yard. With an air of satisfaction he told her, all was disposed for placing her on the throne. She rejected every proposal, and refused to hear any thing farther. He then took out of his pocket two small drawings hastily taken upon cards. One of them represented the princess Elizabeth in a convent, where they were cutting off her hair, and Lestoc was upon a scaffold. In the other, she was represented ascending the throne amidst the acclamations of the people. Lestoc, at the same time that he gave her these two drawings, desired her to chuse between the two situations; she chose the throne.

Lestoc now spoke to her only about the success of the enterprize: he persuaded her to put on the ribband of the Order of Russia, and led her to her sledge. He placed himself behind her, with the late Mr. Woronzof, then page to the princess. There were two officers in the other sledge; and Elizabeth, attended only by four persons, advanced towards the palace, to seize upon the empire. Twenty soldiers, however, who had been gained over, waited for the princess as she passed along. She went directly up to the guard. At the sight of this small troop, the drummer prepared to sound the alarm, Lestoc burst the drum at once with a knife. The princess appeared immediately, with that noble mien which captivated all hearts: she told the soldiers in a few words, that the sole right of the throne, which the regent had usurped, was vested in her, as daughter of Peter the First; then ordered them to take the oath of allegiance, and to follow her. She spoke to slaves; they prostrated themselves before her, and joined her small company. Lestoc distributed the confidential people in the most suspicious posts, and kept the rest along with him; their fidelity he was assured of, as he was always at hand to command them. All the guards of the palace yielded at the bare command of Elizabeth. She came at last to the door of the regent's chamber, who was fast asleep, and had the emperor her son, the young Iwan, by her side. Here Elizabeth first met with opposition; the officer on guard presented his bayonet, and not only put himself in a posture a posture of defence, but also threatened to kill all those who should come forward. Lestoc immediately cried out to him with a loud voice, *Wretch, what doest thou mean? ask mercy of the Empress.* The slave instantly betrayed his sovereign; and Elizabeth entered the apartment with her followers. The regent had been awakened by the noise she had heard. The princess Elizabeth addressed her first, and the regent said, *What, madam, is it you?* She was directly seized, carried out of the palace, with the young Iwan her son, and conducted to the house of the princess in the same sledges which had brought her rival; where she was carefully watched. Elizabeth seated on the throne of her forefathers, commanded as empress in the palace, and all obeyed. In the mean time Lestoc sent some trusty soldiers to arrest Munic and d'Osterman. A few hours were scarce elapsed since the princess Elizabeth came out of her house, before the regent was dethroned. All suspicious persons were seized, and five or six thousand men took the oaths of allegiance to the princess Elizabeth, determined to murder both the regent and their emperor, if Elizabeth should command them, or to assassinate her, if the regent could possibly take the command for one instant. The rumour of the princess Elizabeth's accession to the throne began, however, to spread: but the persons who propagated the news in public, were looked upon as very dangerous people, so that it was customary to run away from them without answering one word.

Lestoc had had an eye to every circumstance. While he was conducting his sovereign to the throne, the manifesto which proclaimed Elizabeth empress, was printing; and almost as soon as the sun shone upon the horizon, she was acknowledged throughout the capital, and soon after by the whole nation.

The regent, sent back at first into her own dominions with her son, had already got as far as Riga, when fresh orders came

came to ſtop her. Being brought back to St. Peterſburg, ſhe was there impriſoned for ever, as well as her ſon. Munic and d'Oſterman were baniſhed into Siberia; and in this revolution, which took place from the 5th to the 6th of October 1741, there was not one drop of blood ſpilt. The Empreſs Elizabeth reigned till the year 1762, frequently diſturbed with the apprehenſions of being dethroned in her turn. She ſent for her nephew the duke of Holſtein, and married him to a princeſs of Anhalt-Zerbſt.

Leſtoc, attached to his ſovereign from her infancy, enjoyed alſo the peculiar happineſs of being truly favored by her, although he had placed the crown upon her head. He was created count of the empire, and married one of the maids of honor belonging to the empreſs. Her majeſty beſtowed favors upon him inceſſantly: but at a time when he was in the higheſt eſteem, Beſtuchef, his avowed enemy, a ſubtle and crafty man, opened a treacherous plot he had been meditating againſt him for a long time. He gained ſo far upon the weak mind of the Empreſs Elizabeth, as to cauſe Leſtoc and his wife to be arreſted. They were exiled into Siberia, and all their poſſeſſions confiſcated. Beſtuchef in his turn was likewiſe baniſhed. The Ruſſian court appeared more quiet on the outſide for a long time; but internally, envy, jealouſy and miſtruſt, reigned throughout this immenſe palace. The Grand Duke did not live with his wife. The princeſs of Anhalt-Zerbſt, born in a free country, and brought up in the midſt of the muſes and the arts, was not dejected by this event. Her genius, and the knowledge ſhe had acquired, ſupplied her with the moſt agreeable relief; amidſt the commotions of the court ſhe contrived to live in a ſtate of tranquillity. She had married the duke of Holſtein, with no other view than that of obtaining the right of ſucceſſion to the throne, which was granted to her. While ſhe lived in this
retired.

retired manner, she employed herself entirely in acquiring an insight into men, and learning the arts of government. As her thirst after knowledge was unlimited, she passed her leisure hours in the cultivation of the sciences, of the arts, and of literature. Perceiving the talents the princess Daschkof was possessed of, she made her partner of her pleasures. But the Grand Duke, jealous even of her amusements, put her to the necessity of keeping up her correspondence in a private manner with this young princess, sister to the lady Woronzof. I have read a letter of this young princess upon friendship, which would not be disowned by our best writers.

I was still at St. Petersburg, when the death of the Empress Elizabeth, who suffered under a tedious illness, was daily apprehended. She was beloved by the whole nation, who feared the reign of Peter III. She died in the month of January 1762.

Peter III. ascended a tottering throne, of which he would perhaps have been for ever deprived, had the Empress lived seven or eight days longer. At the instant of his accession to the empire, some orders, not rightly understood, excited commotions which seemed to portend a revolution expected by every body. Some private persons had even taken care to place their fortunes in the hands of the ministers belonging to their respective nations. But Mr. Glebof, a Russian, had been bold enough to give some advice to Peter III. during the illness of the Empress. The instant of her death, Peter III. assumed the command, and was acknowledged Emperor. The Empress, his wife, came, and fell at his feet; and striking her head against the ground, paid him homage as the first of his slaves. All his subjects also took the oath of allegiance, and he enjoyed the empire in peace. He immediately recalled all exiles from the reign of the empress Ann, and I had the singular satisfaction of seeing Biren, Munic, and Lestoc, all together at St. Petersburg.

Peter III. quitted his old palace, to take poffeffion of the new one, leaving the emprefs in the former. He gave himfelf up in an indecent manner to pleafures and diverfions, at which the emprefs, whom the Ruffians had always held in the higheft refpect, was never prefent.

About a month after his acceffion to the throne, he went to the fenate, and declared that he granted the privilege of freedom to the nobility. The fatisfaction this news filled the nation with, was too great to be defcribed. In the firft fit of enthufiafm, they propofed to erect a ftatue of maffy gold to him; but fomebody obferving, that there was not gold enough in the whole empire for fuch a purpofe; the juftnefs of the reflection determined the Ruffians to confine themfelves to a ftatue one foot high, which was to be placed in the fenate-houfe. A ftatue of bronze was foon after fubftituted in the place of this, and at length the nation feemed refolved for one of marble.

It was neceffary, however, that the emperor fhould publifh an edict, in order to confirm this grant of freedom to his people; fo that, in confequence of the reprefentations of fome officers of ftate, Peter III. limited the freedom granted to the nobility, to the permiffion of not ferving in the army, and being allowed to travel with his confent. In confequence of this edict, a Ruffian officer, defirous of quitting the fervice, applied to the emperor for leave. The emperor afked, *What is your rank? Captain*, replied the officer. *Well then*, faid the emperor, *I make you a lieutenant, and you fhall ftill ferve*; and accordingly he did ferve as lieutenant.

Part of the nation, however, was pleafed with the emperor's familiarity; but his public and private conduct were both equally difguftful to the more fenfible people. Entirely abforbed in his pleafures, a fudden revolution removed him from the throne, and fixed the emprefs there in his ftead. From that moment the lives and fortunes of the subjects depended on the sole will of that princess. They prostrated themselves before her, swearing the most faithful allegiance to her, as to the sovereigns her predecessors. But the unexpected deaths of the emperor, and of the young Iwan, conspired to secure to her the possession of the empire.

As soon as the sovereign is on the throne, he is supposed to have no more relations, and no one dares to claim any connection with the royal family. A foreign courtier, having found that the countess of Woronzof was related to the empress Elizabeth, went immediately and complimented her with the news, which he thought was a discovery of political importance: the empress turned pale, and told him he was mistaken.

It was forbidden, on pain of death, to keep any coin stamped with the image of the young Iwan. The people dare not play with roubles, which bear the impression of the sovereign. One cannot pass before the palace, facing the emperor's apartments, without pulling off one's hat, or letting down the glass, if one is in a carriage; otherwise one is exposed to insults from the soldiers. Any person who should write the name of the empress in small caracters upon a letter, would be liable to be severely punished for it.

These trifling circumstances are mentioned merely to give an idea of the extent of the absolute power of Russian monarchs.

The nobility dare not come near the throne without fear and trembling. They are banished into Siberia for the slightest political intrigue, and their possessions being confiscated, one whole family thus falls a victim to the artful insinuations of the courtier. When I was at St. Petersburg, I was one day on a visit at the house of a stranger, who was in office; being desirous of information, I asked whether the prince Iwan was living or not: it was immediately whispered in my ear, that in Russia no one spoke of that prince. We were, however, no more than three Frenchmen in the room, which was upwards of thirty feet square. On the eve of the death of the empress Elizabeth, no one dared to inquire concerning her health; and when she was dead, though it was universally known, yet every body was afraid to speak of it.

The mutual distrust, in which people live in Russia, and the total silence of the nation upon every thing which may have the least relation either to the government, or to the sovereign; arises chiefly from the privilege every Russian has, without distinction, of crying out in public, *Slowo Dielo*; that is to say, I declare you guilty of high treason both in words and actions. All the bystanders are then obliged to assist in taking up the person accused. A father arrests his son, and the son his father, and nature suffers in silence. The accused, and the accuser, are both conveyed immediately to prison, and afterwards to St. Petersburg, where they are tried by the secret court of chancery.

This tribunal, composed of a few ministers chosen by the sovereign, leaves the lives and fortunes of all families at their mercy. This jurisdiction is of so odious a nature, that a subject, who shall even be indifferent to these agents of tyranny, is often found guilty, although the accuser should not be able to bring convincing proofs of the crime; and this happens chiefly when the impeacher answers for the guilt of the person accused, with his own shoulders; that is to say, submits to receive the punishment of the knout. If he bears this without recanting, the person accused is found guilty, condemned to death, and part of his estate forfeited to the accuser. If some very extraordinary circumstances indicate the innocence of the person accused, the impeacher is then punished a second time. He is also punished, but only once, when,

when, not having demanded the trial of the knout, he is found incapable of proving the guilt of the man whom he impeaches.

This jurisdiction has been established, merely that tyranny might enjoy the privilege of sacrificing all such persons as have become the object of despotic jealousy. It was therefore necessary that the crime of the false accuser should not be punished with death; and the punishment of the knout was always made milder in his favor.

The nobility, thus bowed under the yoke of the most dreadful slavery, do not fail to retaliate upon the people: the people are slaves to them, to the sovereign, or to the waywodes who represent him.

Two kinds of slaves are distinguished in Russia among the people: some belong to the sovereign, others to the nobility. The first only pay tribute to the empress, the others both to the sovereign and to their lord. The nobles estimate their riches by the number of farmers which belong to them. The slaves of the crown pay in to the royal treasury, the sum of one hundred and ten copecs, or four shillings and seven pence of English money, and the others pay two shillings and eleven pence to the crown*. The lords impose what tax they please upon their slaves, and sometimes seize upon the small fortune they may have acquired by their abilities. If these slaves, by cultivating the land and by industry, do not get enough to pay the lord, he allows them to hire themselves to merchants, strangers, or other persons who have no slaves. For this purpose, he gives them a passport only for a few years. The slave is obliged to remit his wages annually to his lord, who gives him up what he thinks proper out of them.

The lords sell their slaves, as cattle is sold in other parts of the world. They chuse out from among them the number of

* The article of the taxes shall be more fully spoken of under that of the revenues of the Russian empire.

servants they want; and treat them with great inhumanity. They are not allowed a civil power of life and death over their servants, any more than over their other slaves; but as they have the privilege of punishing them with the *padogi*, they have them chastised in such a manner, that they may be said, in fact, to have acquired the right of putting them to death.

In weighty offences, a lord, according to law, ought to bring his slave to be tried at the ordinary courts of justice. In 1761, the senate published an edict, whereby all the lords were allowed to send any slaves they were displeased with to work in the mines; but the lords prefer, and will ever do so, chastizing them at home, and keeping them to themselves.

This people, thus oppressed by slavery, is now governed by the empress of Anhalt-Zerbst; a woman of an extensive genius, who is sensible of the defect of such a kind of government, and is wholly employed in reforming it. She will not certainly confine the privilege of freedom to the nobility, but will extend this advantage to all her subjects. Humanity pleads for it, and true policy demands it. Without this circumstance the empire of Russia would be nothing more than a feudal government; and which, considered in this view alone, would multiply petty tyrants, and destroy all sovereign authority. Happy the nation, if sensible of the blessing of being governed by such a prince; all whose endeavours tend to procure happiness to this people, which under Peter III. was on the point of falling into its primitive state of barbarism. She is erecting a monument to Peter the First, in order to immortalize, and convey to the latest posterity, the memory of that great man: she encourages the arts and sciences, and every branch of political administration; and shews that very nation, that she alone was worthy to fill the throne of Peter the First.

Of the Greek Religion.

THE religion which prevails in Siberia, as well as throughout Russia, is the Christian religion of the Greek church. It was first established in Russia by Wolodimer in the year 987. In the reign of the Czar Fedor Iwanowitz, the metropolitans of Russia were ordained by the patriarchs of Constantinople. Jeremy, patriarch of Constantinople, came to Mosco in 1588, and consecrated Job patriarch of all Russia. From this time, the patriarchs of Russia were consecrated by the bishops of the country: but according to Strahlemberg, they were still confirmed by the patriarch of Constantinople, till the time of the patriarch Nicon, who first shook off this subjection. According to Voltaire, in his history of Russia (pag. 66.) the period of this independance may be traced as far back as the time when the first patriarch was appointed in Russia.

The Greek church differs from the church of Rome chiefly in the following articles: The Greeks administer baptism by dipping, the Romans by sprinkling: the last consecrate with unleavened bread, the first with leavened bread, and they also administer the Lord's Supper in both kinds. The Romans believe that the Holy Ghost proceeds from the Father and the Son; the Russians, that the Holy Ghost proceeds from the Father by the Son. The precision of scholastic divinity has made a great difference between these two assertions; from whence many disputes have arisen. Notwithstanding this, several of the fathers have often used both these modes of expression, In the Romish church, the pope is acknowledged as the first bishop by divine right, and as such is the center of the unity of the church. The Russians do not admit the pope's supremacy; and, in their catechism*, they condemn the opinion of the Romans concerning purgatory: but they believe, that those who die in actual sin are not always damned, but that they may be redeemed even from the greatest crimes, by prayers and alms offered up for the dead †.

* I translated from the Latin what is here related from the Russian catechism, which was lent me for a few days in the year 1765, by the Russian ambassador's chaplain. It was published at Breslaw in 1751, by John James Korn.

† Are there not some among the dead, who are in a middle state between salvation and damnation?

Answer. There is no such state; but it is certain that many persons have been taken out of hell, not by repentance after death, but by the pious offices of the living, and the prayers of the church; particularly by the sacrifice of the mass, which is commonly offered up for all the living and the dead. Otherwise, these souls cannot be ransomed by their own works, nor by repentance; neither can they do any thing to deliver themselves from hell.

65. What are we to think of alms and pious offices for the relief of the dead?

Ans. Theophylact gives the following commentary on the words of our saviour, in the 12th chapter of St. Luke: *Fear him who has the power to cast you into hell.* Observe, says Theophylact, that Jesus Christ does not say, *Fear him who after death casts you into hell,* but, *fear him who has the power to do so;* for all men in general who die in sin, are not cast into hell; but it is in the power of God either to punish them in this manner, or to have mercy upon them. I observe this on account of the offerings and alms offered up in favor of the dead, as they are of great use even to such as have gone out of the world defiled with the most heinous crimes. Let us therefore persist in our endeavours, by prayers and almsgiving, to appease the wrath of him, whom it doth not always please to exert the power of forgiveness, which is still ever in his hands. We must then conclude from the doctrine of scripture, and this father's exposition, that it is absolutely necessary to say prayers, to give alms liberally, and above all to offer up mass for the dead, as they are not able to do any of these works in their own behalf.

66. What are we to think of purgatory?

Ans. A temporary punishment for the purification of souls, is no where mentioned in sacred writ. On the contrary, it is on this account that Origen's opinion is censured by the church. It is evident enough, that when the soul is once separated from the body, it can no longer be a partaker of any sacrament of the church; for if the soul could itself atone for any faults committed, it might certainly receive some advantages from the sacrament of repentance. This opinion being quite contrary to the true orthodox doctrine, it is with reason that the church offers up the holy sacrifice, and prayers to God, for the pardon of those who have formerly sinned during their life; and not that they may be purified by any punishments they undergo. The saying of mass, together with the prayers and alms offered up by the living in their behalf, are of themselves sufficient to relieve and redeem them from hell.

This catechism insists much on the necessity of almsgiving at church, in order to be happy in the other world. It was by means of this doctrine, that the Russian clergy enriched themselves so much, during the warmth and zeal of the first christians. The Czar Wolodimer, while the Tartars were employed in subduing part of his dominions, went himself through another part of them with his patriarch Cyrus, teaching this doctrine to his subjects, which was by no means agreeable to the poorer sort. The priests canonized the Czar Wolodimer, but his successors forbad any farther donations to the church, and, after a tedious war, expelled the Tartars from Russia.

According to the 28th article of this catechism, "God intro-
" duces the soul into the body, as soon as the organs are
" formed. It immediately expands itself all over the frame,
" in the same way as fire insinuates itself in all the parts of a
" red hot iron; but its chief residence is in the head and the
" heart."

In other parts of the same work, however, the spirituality of the soul is admitted.

The 18th and 43d articles of the catechism declare, that,
" the intention alone of committing a mortal sin does not
" quite give death to the soul, although it gives it a deep
" wound. No sin can be truly mortal, unless actually com-
" mitted. All others are in the class of venial sins, which
" are to be atoned for by prayers and good works."

Peter I. abolished patriarchs in Russia, and in the year 1719, instituted a perpetual synod in their stead. It consists of a president, an office which the czar reserved for himself, a vice-president, who is an archbishop, six counsellors, who are bishops, and six archimandrites or abbots. The synod is obliged to refer all important matters to the Czar in the senate, where they go in a body, and take their seat below the senators*.

The Russian clergy is divided into two bodies, monks and regular priests, who are called *Popes*. All the monks of Russia are of the order of St. Basil, whose institutions they follow. They live together in common: they are not allowed to eat meat, but live entirely on fish, eggs, and a milk diet. They are even to abstain from this sort of food in Lent season, as well as on Mondays, Wednesdays and Saturdays throughout the year.

The superior clergy, consisting of archbishops, bishops, and archimandrites or abbots, are taken from the monks; so that they are all obliged to follow the rules of Saint Basil's order: but the archimandrites are the only persons among the superior clergy who live in communities; which are all subject to the archbishops and bishops. The priests cannot have any of the dignities of the higher clergy: they are all married; they must wed a virgin before they are consecrated, and are obliged to abstain from saying mass, whenever they have indulged themselves the night before. If they become widowers, and are no longer of use in maintaining their children, they generally turn monks; and in case of competition for a bishopric or an abbey, the monk who has been married has the preference. It is customary for the children of priests to continue in their church, and take orders, although they are allowed to follow any other kind of life.

All the riches of the Russian clergy are divided among the bishops and monks. The priests are very poor, because the livings and parishes are too numerous; most of their profits depend on casual circumstances.

---

* Stæhlemberg, tom. ii. pag. 103. M. de Voltaire in his history of Russia, tom. i. pag. 229. says, that the synod ranks with the senators.

The bishops are named by the synod, but the nomination must be confirmed by the sovereign. The bishops nominate to the abbeys, and all the preferments of the inferior clergy: they may be removed, as well as the abbots, and depend entirely on the bishops pleasure. This excessive subordination gives the bishops too much power over the inferior clergy: the monks and priests are no better than so many slaves; they appear in a submissive posture, and in a state of humiliation, whenever they come before the bishops. The priests are not held in much esteem in society, or among the monks, who are their superiors: their condition would still be more wretched, if their wives did not contribute to make the monks behave more mildly to them.

The clergy of Russia are ignorant, drunken and libidinous. The bishops and priests are less addicted to women than the rest: the first on account of their years, the last because of their wives: but they make up for this in drinking.

They make their wine with plants, a few drugs, and some brandy. They have beer, and a sort of mead, the basis of which is the fluid oozing from the birch-tree at the beginning of summer. Their favorite drink is brandy, and another liquor they call *crematum*; which is so strong, that the first time I drank of it, I thought I had swallowed aqua fortis: it produced so violent an irritation in my mouth, that I could neither speak nor spit out; I resolved from that time never to drink any more *crematum*.

One of these prelates, in other respects an agreeable man, asked me to go and see his library, and immediately shewed me the way to it. I followed him, very anxious of knowing what books he had, and he led me into an insulated building in the midst of a garden. We came into a very neat and well-lighted gallery; several niches, of a foot square, were made in the wall. The prelate opened the doors of them, and I perceived

they

they were filled up with casks. These casks, containing various liquors, and surrounded with ice, filled the whole building, and constituted his library. He had built a very pleasant apartment above this kind of icehouse.

I met with priests in company, and especially monks, so drunk, that they were obliged to be carried away on a litter, decent people being put to the blush by their actions and discourses. The clergy are often found in the streets unable to walk home.

We must not, however, form our opinion of all the Russian clergy from this disadvantageous representation of them. In the course of my journey, I have met with clergymen of abilities and of irreproachable manners, among which I could mention some archimandrites and priests of Tobolsky, to whom the archbishop gave an excellent example in this particular. This prelate had not indeed much knowledge besides what concerned his ministry: but a zeal, better directed, seemed only to be wanting to complete his caracter.

The Sorbonne proposed to the Czar, in 1717, a reunion of the Greek with the Roman church: and every thing that passed on this occasion is well known. If this society did not succeed in the attempt, they acquired at least so high a reputation among the clergy of Russia, that they imagine no man in France can be learned, unless he is a member of that illustrious body.

It would be very useful, if the esteem in which this society is held in France, could be extended to those who give themselves up to the education of our youth. The Russians have the greatest respect for their governors and teachers; and consider them as the fathers of their pupils. If the education in Russia does not answer as it might be expected from such behavior, it is because honor and virtue can only spring up in the soil of liberty.

The nobility of Ruffia never enter into the priefthood; fo that there is no intermediate ftate in the ecclefiaftical body, which is made up entirely of the common people, or the children of the priefts, who are often the moft diffolute; fo that the ignorance and depravity of the Ruffian clergy are the natural confequences of their not having received any principles of education. Their power was dangerous only in the times of the primitive church, as they were then a better conftituted body; and that the whole nation was inflamed with zeal, which is no where to be found at prefent, but among the lower clafs of people.

The revenues of the church being increafed, and having never been expofed before Peter I. to the changes, to which the fortunes of individuals are fubject, the clergy became more opulent than the greater part of the nobles. Religious zeal being grown much cooler among thefe, they have looked with a jealous eye on the immenfe poffeffions of the monks, oftentimes acquired by the confifcation of eftates belonging to their anceftors. Hence the clergy, inftead of being fupported by this body of the ftate, have, on the contrary, always had enemies among all the nobility. Peter I. ventured to leffen the power of the ecclefiaftic body: he abolifhed the dignity of Patriarch; he did not however deftroy religion, which he reverenced, nor its influence on the minds of men, by attacking fuperftition, and rectifying abufes. He had formed a defign of diminifhing the revenues of the monks, and bringing them back to their firft inftitution; and gave out a decree for this purpofe.

The common people are bigotted even to fanaticifm in favor of the Greek religion: this extravagance increafes the farther we get from the capital; but thefe very people are fo little acquainted with their religion, that they are perfuaded they fulfil all its duties, by complying with fome external ceremonies, and especially by keeping the Lent fasts with the greatest strictness. In other respects, they give themselves up to debauchery and to every kind of vice. Morality is less to be met with among the Russians, than among the Pagans their neighbours. The opinions of the Russians with regard to Christianity are so extraordinary, that it should seem as if that religion, so well adapted in itself for the happiness and good order of society, had only served to make this people more wicked. A murderer being taken and condemned, and being asked in the course of his trial whether he had kept the Lent fasts; appeared as much surprized, as the most upright man would have been, if his honesty had been called in question. He immediately answered with warmth, that he was incapable of neglecting the duties of his religion. Yet this very man was at the head of a set of ruffians, and whenever they seized upon any travellers, he readily gave up all the booty to his companions, if they did but deliver him these unhappy victims alive. He first undrest them, and tied them naked to a tree, without any regard to their sex: he then opened their breast near the heart, and drank their blood. He declared, that he took great pleasure in seeing the dreadful contorsions and convulsions of these wretched people. This fact, though it may seem scarce credible, was told me by some Russians.

Such examples are rarely to be met with in Russia; and I have mentioned this only to shew that, in this country, less attention has been given to form the manners of the people by religion, than to oblige them to observe certain ceremonies, which do not always improve the morals of mankind.

There have been few sects of the Greek religion in Russia, and this may perhaps be owing to the ignorance of the clergy. The sect of Razholniki is the only one which has maintained itself to this day. M. de Voltaire says, it arose in the twelfth century. These sectaries have neither priests nor churches: they

they hold their meetings in private houses. They live together peaceably in their hamlets like brothers. They avoid any intercourse with the Ruſſians, whoſe bad morals would diſturb their ſociety. They are exceſſively ignorant, and think it a great ſin to repeat *Hallelujah* three times, therefore they only ſay it twice. The biſhops of Ruſſia give the bleſſing with the fore and middle finger; but theſe ſectaries pretend that it ſhould be given only with the three other fingers. They would not allow a prieſt who has drunk brandy to adminiſter baptiſm. Theſe abſurdities, and others of like nature, caracterize the ſect of Razholniki. The cruel perſecutions they have ſuffered from the Ruſſians have made them become ſo violently fanatic, that they think they may be allowed to kill themſelves for the love of Jeſus Chriſt; and indeed, when they are perſecuted, they gather themſelves together in one houſe, to which they ſet fire, and periſh in the flames.

I was aſſured at Tobolſky of the authenticity of theſe facts, related by Mr. Voltaire and Strahlemberg, and was ſurprized that the clergy were not thereby induced to be more mild in the exerciſe of their religion. Meekneſs is every where recommended throughout the goſpel, and our holy religion is neither tyrannical nor cruel: ever conſiſtent with moral and political laws, it teaches us to love our brethren as children of the ſame God, and makes us truly Chriſtians and good members of the ſtate.

Upwards of one hundred thouſand families have been driven from Ruſſia by perſecution, and have taken refuge among the Tartars, who have always been profeſſed enemies to the Ruſſians. The remaining families are ſtill more ſtedfaſt, and reverence thoſe perſons who have periſhed in torments as martyrs. One woman eſpecially, (for fanaticiſm ſeems to be carried to a higher pitch in that ſex) holds the firſt rank among the ſaints of this ſect. Being accuſed of making the ſign of the croſs with three fingers, she was condemned to die; and while they were leading her to execution, she continued exhorting people of her persuasion, to keep stedfast in the faith of their fathers: and notwithstanding the blows they inceslantly gave her, she was every instant lifting her hands up to heaven, and making the sign of the crofs with three fingers.

The number of sectaries daily increased on account of these persecutions; several believers abjured their religion, because of the cruelty of the clergy; and such as might have been brought over by a milder treatment, were rather confirmed in their errors, so that there never was an instance of any one of the Razholniki sect being converted.

In such circumstances, the sovereign steps into the assistance of his faithful subjects, as a father to that of his children: religion prescribes it to him, and the safety of his kingdom demands it. Peter I. was thoroughly convinced of this, and gave the most express orders, that the Razholniki sect should not be persecuted; and by a few examples of severity, made the prelates become true Christians, and good citizens.

After the death of Peter I. the persecutions began again, under his successors. There were several people in prison on this account while I was at Tobolsky; from whence they were now and then taken out on great festivals, that they might behold the ceremonies of the church, under the vain expectation of their being moved by the sight.

I sometimes conversed with the archbishop and the abbots of the country on this unfortunate sect of Razholniki. One day, I asked one of them in jest, whether these sectaries, who would only repeat Hallelujah twice, would go into hell or purgatory, for as to heaven that was surely out of the question. His face was instantly crimsoned over, and his inflamed eyes bespoke the nature of his answer: we have no purgatory, said he, as in your Romish church; they will be irremissibly damned.

ned. He could say no more, and though in other respects he was a good man, and ever inclined to relieve the distressed, he would have thought perhaps he had done a very meritorious action, if he could have annihilated me that instant.

Among the number of Saints in Russia, after Saint Nicolas, Saint Andrew is one of those in whom they place the greatest confidence. His relics are at Novogorod. The priests say, that when the Greek and Roman churches separated, this Saint set out by sea from Rome, where he embarked on a mill-stone: his oar was a reed, which became petrified the instant the mill-stone was put in motion. His baggage came after him in a kind of trunk, which also floated on the waves: it contained, as the archbishop of Tobolsky thinks, some ornaments of the church. This great Russian Saint arrived at last, after a long voyage, at Novogorod, where his trunk came a few days after him. He then offered something to a fisherman for the chance of his first draught, and the bargain appearing advantageous to the latter he readily agreed to it: but when, instead of fish which he expected, he saw a trunk in the net, he claimed it as his own; and, after many disputes, the affair was referred to the court of law established in the place. The Saint, to shew that he was in the right, gave an inventory of his effects, which being found, upon opening the trunk, to be a true one, they were given up to him. Saint Andrew fixed his residence at Novogorod, where he died, considered as a Saint. According to the Russians, his relics, the mill-stone, and the trunk, are yet to be seen there; where since that time, they continue to work miracles: so that people come in from all sides in pilgrimage to this place.

I saw an Archimandrite at Paris, who was convinced of the truth of all these facts. He would rather have submitted to lose his beard, than give up the most trifling circumstance of this narrative. I was the more surprized at it as he was a
man

man of good sense; and that he was not the abbot of that monastery, where the relics of this pretended saint are said to be deposited. These relics, and others of the like nature in many convents, bring great profits to the monks, to the scandal of religion.

I asked the archbishop of Tobolsky an account of the Russian Saints; and he mentioned very few; saying, that the bad custom of sending money to Rome for making Saints was unknown to them: and that Saints were acknowledged in Russia, when the synod had pronounced them such, and after the Empress had ratified their decision. Every time I saw this prelate, he chose to converse with me about religion, and particularly about the Pope. He thought it very extraordinary that his Holiness should receive the sacrament seated in an arm-chair. I first denied the fact; but when he told me, that a certain Russian had been a witness of it at the consecration of the last Pope, to avoid entering into disputes, which are ever disagreeable, I assured him the Pope was a cripple.

The archbishop had as much dislike to astronomy as to the Pope: he was always in a passion at the idea of the motion of the earth. He quoted passages, which he said were from St. Paul; though I could never find any passage in that apostle's writings contradicting the motion of the earth round the sun: I then advanced some astronomical truths; but, on these subjects, the prelate was always a heretic.

Although the priests of Russia are unfit, from their ignorance, to make proselytes, yet they have the folly of attempting to convert every body. Being one day at dinner with one of these prelates, after having drunk freely, he had a mind to convert my servant, who was a Lutheran, and served me in the double capacity of interpreter and cook, though but indifferently in either. As soon as the prelate had finished his discourse, the servant answered him with great anger, that a Lutheran was

full

full as good as a fchifmatic. The prelate immediately fnatched up a plate, and would have thrown it at the heretic's head, if I had not interpofed; telling him at the fame time, I had never read in fcripture, that it was cuftomary among the apoftles to break people's heads, in order to infure their falvation. I then fent my fervant away to dinner, and a few glaffes of *crematum* foon made us good friends again.

The churches are very ill built at Tobolfky, as they are throughout the Ruffian empire; there are no fuch beautiful monuments to be found among them, as among different churches in the reft of Europe. The churches here are, on the contrary, very fmall, generally rather dark, and badly ornamented. There are indeed many paintings in them, but thefe have neither drawing nor coloring; they are all placed, one above another, againft the wall of the naos, or body of the church. Four rows of thefe paintings conftitute all the ornaments of the cathedral at Tobolfky. The choir is in the middle, as it is in moft of our churches; but with this difference, that all the ceremonies, performed within the choir, are not expofed to public view. It is a facred place, where none but the priefts enter; the door is generally fhut, and only opened for a few minutes, either to give the bleffing, or perform fome other folemn and ftriking act, or in the great ceremonies exhibited on the outfide of the choir.

On thefe occafions the archbifhop is preceded by his clergy, whofe dreffes are very grand: their beard and hair loofely flowing, waving the idea of uncleanlinefs, gives them a very refpectable appearance. They form themfelves, in great order and with the moft profound filence, in a femicircle, on each fide of the door, and feem wholly taken up with the ceremony. At length the archbifhop makes his appearance in the middle of his clergy, with the mitre on his head, and the crofier in his hand. Sometimes he has neither of thefe, but carries a chandelier, with three branches, in his hand, adorned with wax tapers, or with relics; and gives the blessing with the relics or the chandeliers. This solemnity of the Greek church, is so awful to the people, that if there should be the least disturbance, as there is frequently in the Romish churches, all is hushed as soon as the doors are open; and the assembly waits with the deepest veneration for the sight they but seldom enjoy.

The ceremonial dresses are extremely grand, but inconvenient; the cope, instead of being open before, as it is in the Romish church, has but one single opening to let the head through, and the forepart of this garment is turned up over the arms.

The abbots have mitres similar to those of the bishops; but they differ much from the mitres of our prelates. The best idea that can be given of them is, to compare them to a bee-hive; they are covered with ornaments and jewels, which are commonly false.

The dresses of the Greek church, having been published by *M. Le Prince*, I thought it needless to give any fresh engravings of them; I therefore refer such of my readers, as may be desirous of knowing something more of these dresses, to that gentleman's representation of them, from whence a better notion may be gathered, than from any description I could give.

In the public ceremonies of the Greek church, the holy worship consists chiefly in action. These actions have a great effect on the people, but become ridiculous in the narrative.

I have seen the ceremony of the holy supper. St. Peter was represented by a fat well-looking monk, but who was perhaps little accustomed to these ceremonies, as he seemed aukward and foolish. The archbishop, on the contrary, had a free, easy countenance, and a sprightliness very expressive of his zeal.

Having

Having washed the feet of eleven monks, he then addressed himself to St. Peter: immediately a great dispute arose, which could not be heard, because the prelate had, at one of his sleeves, a square piece of stuff surrounded with bells, which made a great noise: but it might easily be perceived from the confusion and dejected look of the monk who represented Saint Peter, that he was not fond of disputes: he was at last completely disconcerted, by the bystanders bursting out a laughing; so that, in order to put a stop to this, they were obliged to wash his feet quickly. The archbishop gave a discourse on humility, and then went away.

In the Greek church, children of five or six months are brought to the communion table. I saw an instance of this at Tobolsky; a little child was waked out of his sleep for this act of devotion; he gave them to understand, by crying, that he had much rather have been excused; notwithstanding his tears, they made him partake of the sacrament; but, he could not be quieted till he was put to the breast.

Easter-day is set apart for visiting in Russia, as the new-year's day is in France. I affronted some people, very unwittingly, for want of knowing the customs of the country.

Being intent upon some astronomical calculations in the morning, I did not perceive a Russian come into my room. Unwilling, as I suppose, to disturb me, he had placed himself near me, unfortunately for us both; for starting up quickly to walk about the room, we struck each other so forcibly, that he fell backwards on the floor, and I upon a trunk. Although I was equally stunned with the accident, and surprized at seeing a stranger in my apartment, yet I went up to make him my excuses. I stretched out my hand, desiring him to be seated: he then offered me his hand, and gave me at the same time an egg. I was astonished at this, not having yet recovered the shock my head had received. Besides, I was quite at a loss what to answer him, for he talked to me all the while as if I had understood his language. I was continually bowing, and endeavouring to convince him by signs with my head, as with my hands and feet, how much I was obliged to him for all his civilities, till at length he went away seemingly much displeased. I was preparing to go to work again, when another Russian came in; who appeared evidently, from the unsteadiness of his gait, not to be fasting: he advanced to embrace me, but as he smelt powerfully of brandy, I endeavoured to keep myself out of the way of his mouth, but it was impossible to avoid it. This man also gave me an egg; and I then began to find out enough of this ceremony, to give him in return the egg I had just received; notwithstanding which he still seemed dissatisfied when he left me.

As to myself, I was so little pleased with these two visits, that I shut my door instantly, lest I should have a third: I fastened it with two nails, one at top, the other at bottom, as I had no bolt.

A few hours after I learnt that this was, as I said before, the usual visiting day. The men go to each other's houses in the morning, and introduce themselves into the house by saying, *Jesus Christ is risen*: the answer is, *Yes, he is risen*. The people then embrace, give each other eggs, and drink a great deal of brandy. As I had not complied with all these customs, I then found out why the Russian, who had visited me in the morning, had been displeased. I was the more sorry for it, as I could easily have satisfied them with a few glasses of brandy: besides, I was particularly attentive in complying with the customs of the country, without which precaution a man makes himself disagreeable to every body.

The afternoon is employed in visiting the women, who also go a visiting themselves: they are generally accompanied by the men; and they enjoy this pleasure of going out, very much,

much, as they are much confined at other times; the men indulge themselves in drinking the whole day. The room, where the visitors are received, is set out with all their finery. There is a kind of sideboard, raised in form of an altar, at the end of the apartment, where all the riches of the family, plates, dishes, knives and forks, bottles, glasses, candlesticks, &c. are set out upon several brackets, and placed in the nicest order. In the middle of the room is a table, covered with a carpet, which is garnished with Chinese sweetmeats, and a species of rasberries of this country, dried in the sun. On coming into the apartment, all the people place themselves, standing all along the benches which surround the table, the women first, and the men after them. Then the mistress of the house, with the utmost gravity, and without saying a word, kisses all the company round. When this ceremony is over, the men retire into another apartment, and the women are left by themselves in the first. There is also a table spread, with a carpet and sweetmeats, in the room where the men are.

The master of the house entertains his guests in this room, while his wife takes upon her the same office in the other. Some travellers have asserted, that the women of this country drink strong liquors to excess; but I have never found this. Coffee is served up to them, with a kind of bad beer, and some tea; and they seem to drink of these liquors, more from complaisance to the mistress of the house, than by choice. It is not so with the men, who are almost all drunk after three or four visits; for as soon as the company is seated, the master of the house brings in a kind of waiter, with glasses full of brandy, or other liquors of the like nature. He offers some to each guest, and it would be a great affront not to drink with him. After this a sort of mead is served up, some coffee, and between whiles some brandy. One must absolutely partake

take of all these liquors, and eat a few sweetmeats. The visit generally lasts half an hour, after which the men go back to the women's apartment; where, having been again saluted, the company goes altogether in a visit to the next neighbour. Thus the whole day is spent going about the town and drinking. After two visits were over, I was seized with such a violent pain in my head, that I was obliged to retire. I found myself still so much indisposed next day, that although I was very desirous of continuing my visits with those persons, who did me the honor to ask me, yet I should have given it up, had I not been assured, that I might be excused from drinking by staying among the women: but I perceived even at the first visit, that this was by no means agreeable to the men. A Russian, to whom I have often been obliged for his advice, confirmed me in this conjecture, so that I returned to the mens table, taking care to provide myself with a number of handkerchiefs, which were of great service to me. As soon as I had taken my glass of brandy, I emptied it into my handkerchief, on pretence of wiping my mouth; and, by this contrivance, visited the whole day without suffering any inconvenience. These visits generally last three days.

I observed, during the holy week, that it was very easy for the rich people in Russia, to acquit themselves of the duty of customary prayers. The priests go about into their houses, with the ornaments of the church, and every thing necessary for the divine service, adapted to the season; there they perform the service for a trifle, while the Russians are in bed, or in their other apartments.

Description of the city of Tobolſky, of its inhabitants, and of the manners and cuſtoms of the Ruſſians, &c.

SIBERIA was made known to the Ruſſians in 1563, by a private man in the neighbourhood of Archangel, whoſe name was Anika; and afterwards conquered by the chief of a band of ruffians, under the reign of John Baſilides. It was then governed by a Tartar prince of the family of the Uſbecs. This banditto, named Termack Timofeiwitz, at the head of ſeven or eight hundred Coſſacs, ravaged all the country about the rivers Occa, and Volga.

The Czar Baſilides ſent a body of troops againſt this chief of the Coſſacs; they obliged him to retire into the mountains that divide Ruſſia from Siberia, called Poias Zemnoy, or the Poias mountains. He croſſed this chain, going up the river Czauſowa, and fell back upon the territories of M. Strogonof, whoſe deſcendents have ſtill very conſiderable poſſeſſions in this diſtrict *.

This chief, at the head of a ſet of reſolute banditti, eaſily obtained of M. Strogonof all the aſſiſtances he required. He embarked with his company on the Tagil, and went down that river to the place where it empties itſelf in the Tura. Purſuing the ſame courſe on this river, he ſeized upon the city of Tumen, ſurprized Tobolſky, made priſoner the ſon of the Chan Zutchuin, a boy twelve years old, and ſent him to Moſco, with the offer of Siberia to the Czar of Ruſſia, by which he obtained his pardon.

Tobolſky, the capital of Siberia, was built on the ſide of the old city which was then called Sibir. It contains about fifteen

* It appears that he went up this river, as far as the confines of Bilimbacufkoi.

thouſand

thousand inhabitants, almost all Russians, or naturalized. Of the latter there are several Mahometan Tartars; the greater part of them live without the city, that they may perform with less interruption the ceremonies of their own religion.

The town is divided into two parts: the larger part is situated on the banks of the Irtyſz; and the other upon a small mountain, the summit of which is a platform extending to the east of Toboliky. The height of this mountain is about 25 toises above the river. The upper town is fortified, eastward and northward, by a rampart, bastions, and a ditch of six feet in breadth, bordered with palisadoes. All the fortifications are on the flat: the other parts of the city are from situation difficult of access; the southern part, on account of a deep gorge, the sides of which are very steep; the western part, because the Irtyſz flows at the foot of the mountain, which being composed of a very loose sand, cannot be scaled without great danger. Vast pieces are continually breaking from the mountain, fall into the river, and carry away every thing they meet. I have been an eye-witness of an accident of this kind. I was coming from a party of pleasure, where I had been in a boat with Mr. Pouſkin, his lady, and some other persons. We went up the mountain by a path leading to Mr. Pouſkin's house. We had scarce advanced a few steps, when we heard such a violent crash to the right-hand, that we were frightened. All the inconvenience we found, was being obliged to get up faster than we had intended.

The town has a governor, whose authority extends almost all over Siberia; and a court of chancery composed of fifteen counsellors, who regulate affairs as well civil as military. The governor is the president, and decides commonly with sovereign authority. This place being at the distance of near eight hundred leagues from the court, true accounts are seldom transmitted from hence to the throne; so that the governors

nors almoſt always abuſe their power, from the opportunity they have of doing it with eaſe.

In order to counterbalance this authority, Peter I. created a new office. The perſon inveſted with it, is called a Proctor: he is not dependent on the governor or the chancery: he ranks next to the governor, and part of the buſineſs adjudged by the chancery, or by the governor, cannot be finally determined without the ſanction of the proctor. This important poſt was at that time filled by count Apollo Pouſkin: a perſon as fit for the office as any one who could have been pitched upon. This miniſter poſſeſſes the moſt enlightened underſtanding, warmed with the love of truth and humanity.

As he is directed by the greateſt zeal and diſintereſted affection, it is in his power to procure his country the moſt eſſential advantages. He was kind enough to offer me a lodging at his houſe, and preſſed me ſo much, I could not refuſe him. Every inſtant I remained at Tobolſky, gave me freſh proofs of the obligations I had to him.

He had come to Tobolſky two months before me: where he lived with his lady in a retired manner, entirely taken up with the duties of his ſtation, and with the cultivation of literature, which he had ever been fond of. Being verſed in the French language, he had brought with him from Moſco, a ſelect library, conſiſting of the works of our beſt writers. He had an improved mind, joined to an uncommon politeneſs, and gentleneſs of manners. Free from national prejudice, he could not conſider his wife as a ſlave: ſhe was his beſt friend; and by the goodneſs of her heart, contributed to her huſband's happineſs.

M. de Soimanof, was governor of Siberia, he had ſerved in the navy in the reign of Peter I. and had acquired much aſtronomical knowledge, at St. Peterſburg, with M. Deliſle, of the Academy of Sciences. M. de Soimanof's abilities afterwards induced Peter I. to give him the command of a fleet on the Caspian sea. At the same time he was ordered to take the plan of this spot, and it is to him we owe the first accurate chart of that sea. After the death of Peter I. he was much persecuted by his enemies, who found means to have him banished. He was recalled; and, after various changes, the Czarina Elizabeth gave him the government of Siberia. As he had lived long at court, he was well acquainted with all its artifices. Although he was naturally a sincere man, the changes of his fortune had made him mistrustful and dissembling. His superior understanding made his enemies fear him: he was bold, enterprizing, capable of planning the greatest designs, and of carrying them into execution, had he been less advanced in years. It was an unlucky circumstance for me, that he could not speak French. It was evident to me, on many occasions, that I lost a great deal by not being able to hold a conversation with him, without my interpreter.

At Tolbosky, there is an archbishop, whose diocese extends over the greater part of Siberia. The prelate who then filled that see, was a native of Poland. He was not a man of great knowledge; but was perfectly well acquainted with the Latin tongue, and with the scriptures. His religious zeal was carried to the highest excess of fanaticism. He constantly persecuted the Mahometans and Pagans in the confines of Tobolsky, in order to convert them to the Greek religion: in other respects he was an exceeding well-bred, and very amiable man.

Besides these principal officers, there was also the Grand General at Tobolsky, whose rank in the army was very high. He was a weak man, and superstitious; believing, as well as the common people, that the overflowing of the Irtysz was caused by my arrival in the country; and that this stream would not sink into its channel again, till after I was gone.

All the counsellors of the chancery, and several merchants, live in a very reputable manner at Tobolsky. The garrison, consisting

consisting of two regiments of infantry, brings a great number of officers there, who are entirely engaged in pursuit of pleasure.

The clergy is composed of fifty monks, and twenty priests; three of this number, including the archbishop, are supposed to understand the Latin language.

These several states of the military, of juridical people, of the clergy, and of merchants, might form very agreeable societies any where else: especially as most persons employed under the government are sent there from St. Petersburg, and from Mosco.

At the distance of about an English mile, the city of Tobolsky presents a beautiful view; this is owing to its situation, and the number of small steeples it contains, most of which are covered with brass. But we lose this sight upon our entrance into the town; as the houses are all of wood, and ill-built: the governor's house, the chancery, the archbishop's palace, the town-hall, and a kind of citadel, are the only buildings built with bricks and stones.

It is scarce possible to walk along the streets in this city, on account of the quantity of dirt there is even in the upper town, except in some part of the summer. To obviate this inconvenience, there have been foot-ways made by planks in some streets, which is the general custom in Russia; but they are kept in such bad repair at Tobolsky, that you can hardly venture out except in carriages, which are indeed pretty common here, because wood, horses and their keep, are all at a very low price.

The men in Siberia are tall, stout, and well made, as they are almost all over Russia: they are excessively fond of women and drinking. As they are slaves to a despotic prince, they exert the same absolute authority over their slaves or inferiors, with still greater severity.

The women are in general handsome at Tobolsky: their skin is exceedingly fair, and their countenance agreeable; their eyes are black, languishing and down-cast; for they never dare look a man full in the face: they wear no caps, but use colored handkerchiefs, which they interweave so curiously among their hair, generally black and unpowdered, that this kind of head-dress gives them a very bewitching look. They all use paint, young girls as well as married women; and this custom prevails even among the servant maids, and some of the common people.

The women are commonly well-made till the age of eighteen or twenty; but their legs as well as their feet are always large. Nature in this respect seems to have had in view the bulk they usually acquire; which seems to want very firm supporters.

The baths, they use twice a week, contribute chiefly to spoil their shapes: they cause such a relaxation in all the parts of the body, that the beauty of the women is quite gone before they are thirty years of age.

Their dress at present is very much like that which is in use throughout Europe. The mens dress is exactly the same at Tobolsky, and all over Russia. Some merchants, the noblemen's stewards, and the common men are almost the only persons who have kept to the old dress, as well as to the custom of wearing the beard. I saw only a few gentlemen at Tobolsky, who had been disgraced, still conforming to these old customs, which they certainly had lately taken up again. The dress of the women at Tobolsky (I except the head-dress) differs from that used in Europe, only in our peculiar fashions, with which they are unacquainted; they generally wear a loose gown like a domino. On public days, their gowns are much like the robes formerly worn in France. This dress came from St. Petersburg to Tobolsky.

The men, as well as the women, are generally richly dressed: they get their stuffs and silks from Mosco, and sometimes from China; but at Tobolsky, as throughout Russia, both the sexes are very uncleanly, notwithstanding the baths they use twice a week. The women change their linen but seldom; and are unacquainted with that variety of undress, to which the Europeans are accustomed; and which is often more betwitching than the richest ornaments: so that there are few opportunities of being present at the toilet of the Russian women.

In the houses of people of the first rank at Tobolsky, as in most other parts of Russia, there is but one bed for the husband and wife, and sometimes one for the children: all other persons in the house lie promiscuously upon benches or upon matts, which they spread on the ground, in the different apartments*. There are no curtains to the beds; and instead of a bolster, the husband and wife have each of them seven or eight pillows, one less than the other, raised up in form of two pyramids. This bed is generally the principal piece of furniture. Sometimes there are at Tobolsky in bed-rooms, some wooden chairs, a large stove, and a small table.

In the whole city of Tobolsky, there was not a single house that had any carpeting in it; some beams placed one upon another, but made smoother than common, some benches and a few wooden chairs, made up all the furniture of their apartments.

At Tobolsky men are very jealous of their wives, as they are throughout the greater part of Russia: beyond the city of Mosco, however, they are seldom in company with them; spending most of the day in drinking, and generally coming

---

* In 1663, the people of quality used to lie upon boards or benches, on which a skin or other covering was spread: there was no furniture in the houses; and very few tables were covered with a cloth at meals. M. de Voltaire, histoire de la Russie, tom. i. pag. 20.

home drunk. The women seldom go out; they live wholly sequestered from society, given up to laziness and indolence, which are the causes of the depravity of their manners.

That kind of delicate love which proceeds from sensibility, and against which the severest virtue cannot always guard itself, is here totally unknown.

Here a lover never has the satisfaction of seeing the confusion and disorder of his mistress, endeavouring, but unable, to conceal her tenderness. Such situations are never met with in Siberia, nor in the greatest part of Russia, where the polished manners of the rest of Europe have not yet prevailed. In these barbarous regions, men tyrannize over their wives, whom they consider and treat as their slaves, requiring of them the most servile offices: in their matrimonial engagements they are obliged to bring them a handful of rods, in great ceremony, and to pull off their boots, as a token of the superiority of the husband, and the subjection of the wife. Availing themselves more than any where else of their superior power, they have established the most unjust laws, which neither the beauty nor delicacy of the sex have yet been able to abolish or soften. We are not therefore to be surprized, that that delicacy of sentiment which caracterizes the people of more civilized nations, is so rarely to be met with here. If such women are worth the attempt, boldness is often sufficient to insure success; but opportunities of this kind seldom occur, as women are scarce ever seen, but when their husbands are present; and if the least attention is shewn them on these occasions, it is very probable one may not see them a second time.

I saw some foreigners at Tobolsky, who had been there ever since the beginning of the last war; unacquainted with the customs of the country, they often experienced disagreeable consequences, from the idea that women were to be treated with the same politeness and attention here, as in the rest of Europe.

Europe. They afterwards became more cautious, being convinced of the neceffity of taking no notice of the ladies before their hufbands; and joining in with the convivial pleafures of the latter, foon found means of being admitted to greater familiarities with their wives in private. Thus the depravity of the fex in Ruffia is owing to the tyranny of the men.

The women are captivated merely by fenfual pleafures, often giving themfelves up to their flaves; among which they take care to chufe fuch as are moft healthy and robuft.

The manners of this people will never be improved, while the women are kept in a ftate of flavery, and do not partake of the pleafures of fociety. Although the men are remarkably fevere to their wives, yet are they very indulgent to their daughters. They think that married women fhould be entirely taken up with their hufbands, but that greater liberty may be allowed to the unmarried, thereby to give them opportunities of getting hufbands: they very foon avail themfelves of this freedom, without the confent of their parents, or the fanction of the church. At twelve or thirteen years, they are frequently no ftrangers to the other fex; but fuch is the inconfiftency of this people, that they expect their daughters fhould ftill be virtuous, while they allow them fuch liberty, as ought ever to be regulated by a good education; they alfo pretend to determine with an abfolute certainty, whether their daughters are ftill virgins; this is done by a jury of skilful women, who determine this matter by entering into the ftricteft examination, which, in other countries, would be confidered as very indecent.

On the day appointed for the marriage ceremony, after the parties have been joined by a prieft, as in our church, the lady's parents give an elegant fupper, at which the hufband's family is prefent, fome friends, and a magician, who comes with an intent to counteract the witchcraft which might be

R r practifed

practifed by other magicians, to prevent the confummation of the marriage. The new-married couple, attended by a godfather and a godmother, are conducted with the greatest ceremony into the nuptial chamber before fupper.

The magician walks firft, the godfather follows, conducting the bride: the bridegroom gives his hand to the godmother, and the bridefman his to the hufband's neareft female relation, who is one of the jury, which is generally compofed of three or four women. During this proceffion to the nuptial apartment, every thing is got ready for the feaft in the room where the company ftays; who wait only the return of the married couple to begin their mirth; being thoroughly perfuaded, that the decifion of the jury will be favorable to the bride.

The marriage chamber contains in general nothing but a bed, which is ufually very neat, and without curtains; the images given by the godfather and godmother to the married couple; a few chairs, and a table, with bottles of brandy, and glaffes, near which an old matron is placed.

The proceffion having reached the marriage chamber, the matron offers the bride a waiter, on which are glaffes filled with brandy and other liquors: the bride then prefents them to the magician firft, and afterwards to the whole company round; the magician prepares his magic art; the bride is then undreffed, and left with a fmall petticoat and an under-waiftcoat only; both of them made on purpofe for this day, which is confecrated to voluptuoufnefs. The bridegroom is alfo undreffed, and a nightgown thrown over him: the bride then kiffes all the company round, offers them again a glafs of brandy; and when every body has drank a fecond time, they retire into an antichamber, leaving the married couple alone with the matron, who affifts at the ceremony; in which fhe is the more interefted, as fhe receives a reward if the lady is acknowledged to be a virgin; whereas fhe is obliged, if the contrary happens,

to

to drink out of a broken glafs, in the midft of the company, which is confidered as a mark of ignominy.

After confummation, the jury of women is called in, who ftrip the bride quite naked, in order to decide whether fhe was a virgin. Among other proofs required upon this occafion, the infpection of the linen is what they moft depend upon, and when this anfwers to their wifhes, the fhift is placed in a box; they give the bride a clean one, drefs her, and then call in the magician, the godfather, and the bridefman. The matron, triumphant, gives the waiter again to the bride, who offers another glafs of brandy to all the people of the proceffion. The married couple are then led back to the company: the box containing the proof of the lady's virginity is carried firft; and upon the appearance of that, the mufic announces the triumph of the new-married couple. While the mufic is playing, the figns of the bride's virginity are fhewn to each of the guefts, and for feveral days after the box is carried round among all the neighbours. When all the company is perfectly fatisfied, the lady dances for a few minutes with her hufband, and every body fits quickly down to the table, where moft of the men commonly get drunk.

There were feveral marriages while I ftayed at Tobolfky; but I could never get any admiffion to any of the feafts; one lady in particular, otherwife a very amiable woman, was always againft it; faying, fhe was afraid I fhould think their ceremony ridiculous, and give an account of it to the public. In my way from Tobolfky back again to St. Peterfburg, I was invited to a wedding, and appointed bridefman, fo that I had then an opportunity of feeing the whole tranfaction.

In the beginning of the reign of Peter I. the Ruffians ufed to marry without having feen each other. The parents on the man's fide ufed to fend a kind of matron to the girl's parents: the matron then told them; *I know you have goods to difpofe of, and we have purchasers.* After some inquiries, and a few days spent in negociating the affair, the parents used to meet. If the lad was agreeable to the girl's parents, the day of the ceremony was fixed. The evening before marriage, the young man was brought to see his destined wife, who received him without speaking a word: one of her relations was engaged to converse with him. The next day, the lad used to send a present to the lady, consisting of sweetmeats, soap, and other things of the same kind. The box was never opened but in presence of her friends, who were immediately sent for: she then used to lock herself up with them, continually shedding tears while her friends were singing songs suitable to the occasion of her marriage.

There are no traces of these last customs remaining, except among the common people. European manners, which Peter I. endeavoured to introduce in his dominions, have abolished some of the ancient prejudices. From this period, marriages have been upon a different footing. Among the great, parents are influenced by fortune and high rank; and children, as it is the custom every where else, are seldom consulted.

European manners, however, have gained very little ground in Russia; because they are not conformable to the despotism of the government: they have nevertheless introduced luxury, and brought on a communication between Russians and foreigners; which has only contributed to make the Russians more unhappy, by giving them opportunity of comparing their state of slavery, with that of a free people.

As I have seen the Russians at the distance of eight hundred leagues from court, I have been enabled to acquire a competent knowledge of this people.

Upon the whole, there is very little society in Russia, especially beyond Mosco: neither is it possible there should be much, under a government where no man enjoys that civil liberty,

liberty, by which the safety of the citizen, in other countries, is secured. A mutual fear prevails among individuals; from hence arises mistrust, disguise, and deceit. Friendship, that sentiment which contributes to the happiness of our lives, has never been known in Russia; it supposes a sensibility which makes an absolute union of the two friends, and effusions of the heart, which divide their pleasures and pains reciprocally. As the men have but little respect for the women beyond Mosco, they are not attended to in company, although company is nothing without them. They are almost always confined to their houses; where they pass their tedious days among their slaves, without authority and without employment; they do not even enjoy the satisfaction of reading, for most of them know not how to read. The men are as ignorant as the women. They visit now and then with great ceremony: the governors and chief magistrates give grand dinners several times in a year. Relations also meet now and then, to keep the feast of their family saint; but they seldom admit any person at these feasts, who is not one of the family. At the great entertainments, both men and women are invited together, but they neither sit at the same table, nor in the same room. The mistress of the house does not appear in the mens apartments, till they are just sitting down to dinner; she brings in with her a large waiter covered with glasses full of brandy; which she presents, in a very submissive manner, to all the guests, who do not even look at her; the glasses are returned to her, and she withdraws immediately.

There are always a great number of people at these feasts; to which persons of all stations are invited. Officers, clergy, magistrates, and merchants, are all placed at the same table; but with this difference, that rank is more strictly attended to, than in any German court. Military men are placed according to their several ranks; and persons of other professions are disposed in the same manner: no regard is paid to birth.

All the dishes are served up at once. Their soup is made by cutting the meat into small pieces in the broth. They have some ragouts, which nobody who is not used to can eat of. The table is generally covered with several pyramids of roast meat; most of them composed of different kinds of game, the rest of butchers meat. Chinese sweetmeats are served up at the same time, and some made of the fruits of the country.

Their manner of sitting at table, and their customs, seem to be very similar to those which prevail in some districts of Germany; but they have adopted only the ridiculous parts of them, which they have even rendered still more ridiculous. A profound silence is observed during dinner; which is interrupted only at times by the healths that are drunk.

As soon as they sit down to table, each man pours into his glass some of the made-wine I have mentioned before; and then all rise to drink each others health. Each guest is drunk to by his christian and surname; and a drop of wine is swallowed to each person's health.

I have been at some of these dinners, where there were more than sixty people, all drinking to each other at the same time. Their attitudes, and the confusion of different sounds had a very singular effect. Peter not being able to make James hear him, was stretching himself over the table, and bawling out as loud as he could; at the same instant, he was interrupted by Francis, who was bowing to him, or by a knock of the head from Philip, who was turning about from right to left without perceiving the posture Peter was in. Philip's turn came next: as he was lifting his glass to his mouth, his neighbour gave him a jog of the elbow, and spilling part of his wine, interrupted him at the most interesting moment. Such scenes as these, varied in different ways, were repeated almost at every part of the table; and the pleasantry of them was enhanced, by observing the impatience of some of the people. As to myself, felf, I could never find an opportunity of drinking any one's health; but kept my head in conftant motion, to the right and left, and forwards. It is reckoned a qualification to catch the opportunity fo feafonably as to drink to every perfon's health, without defcending from one's dignity, or meeting with any accident.

The firft health being over, every body fits down, and is at liberty to eat for a few moments. Glafs tumblers of a cylindrical form, fix inches high, and four wide, are placed in different parts of the table. Every gueft within reach of one of thefe tumblers, takes it up and drinks out of it: it would be thought very unpolite, if he was to take a glafs, in order to avoid drinking out of the fame tumbler as his neighbour. This cuftom is not only difagreeable, but at the fame time very dangerous, on account of the fcurvy, which is extremely frequent in Ruffia.

When the company has eat for a few minutes, the Emperor's health goes round. This toaft is given in a different manner. A large glafs bottle, to which there is alfo a glafs top, is placed on the table before the perfon of the higheft rank. This perfon rifes from his feat, as well as his right-hand neighbour, to whom he gives the head of the bottle, and pouring fome wine into the cup, gives out the Emperor's health, bowing to the whole company. As foon as he has drunk, he gives the bottle to his neighbour, who paffes the top to the perfon fitting next to him. All the company drinks the Emperor's health in the fame manner, while a band of muficians is employed in finging fongs adapted to the ceremony.

The healths of the princes and princeffes of the royal family are then drunk in the fame order, and eating goes on for a little time longer.

The

The healths of all the guests are then carried round, with another glass bottle, which is not so beautiful as the first, and is covered with a crust of bread.

This toast goes round nearly in the same way as the former, except that when the lid of the bottle is given to one's neighbour, it is usual at the same time to tell him the christian and surname of the person whose health is going round; and this must be repeated making a bow to him: this custom is very troublesome to strangers, as the Russians have generally three or four christian names. This ceremony is carried on with the utmost gravity, and one must be very exact in the whole detail, which extends all round the table. However desirous I was of being exact, yet I was always puzzled when the toast came to me. I used to forget the number of saints named to me, most of which were never inrolled in our list. I was however very much mortified at this. Besides, I had usually for my neighbour a Russian, who was a very strict observer of rules; he had acquired by his exactness a right of presiding over the police of the table, and was very much out of temper, whenever any one was deficient in this point. This gentleman was so obliging as to set me right frequently; but on one occasion he was as much puzzled as myself, when two crusts of bread were presented to me from each side, one of which had fell several times, contrary to order, into the plates, and into the bottle. Not knowing whom I was to answer, nor what I was to do with these two crusts, I referred the whole affair to him, and sat down. He was informed, that, the company consisting of sixty guests, a second bottle had been called for, to hasten the ceremony; but he decided, that it was better to be detained two hours longer at table, than to neglect any of the usual forms.

At last, the company rose from table, and went into another room. I imagined at first, that the dinner was over, and
that

that we were now to drink coffee; but was much furprized at the fight of a table covered with Chinefe fweetmeats. Four fervants waited for the company, with bottles of mead, beer, and different liquors made with brandy. Others brought in waiters with glaffes. The company then fet in for drinking again; and from this time ceremony was at an end. The Ruffians, though accuftomed to this manner of living, feldom bear the quantity of liquors drank after dinner, which are not only very ftrong, but the drinking is alfo inceffantly continued till the evening. If the company chufes to take a walk, the bottles and glaffes are carried along with them; and this is looked upon as doing the honors completely.

Some travellers affert, that the women as well as the men give themfelves up to all the exceffes of drinking; but I have always feen the contrary. The women, after dinner, remain in the fame room, growing tired of one another; for it is impoffible it fhould be otherwife, where thirty women meet together without one man.

The inhabitants are much delighted with receiving vifits; vifiting is called *going in gaft*. As foon as the company comes in, the miftrefs of the houfe appears with her hufband, and kiffes them all on the mouth. She is often an old woman of feventy, who comes in hobbling along, with a fhaking head, and fome remains of a few rotten teeth; but whether fhe is young or old, ugly or handfome, the ceremony is ftill the fame; and it would be a crime, let what would happen, to fhew any figns of mirth upon thefe occafions. I knew a gentlemen in Siberia, who would fometimes come forward to meet the ladies at thefe vifits, and, inftead of appearing folemn as he ought to have done, would put on a fmiling countenance. One of his friends informed him, he behaved very rudely to the ladies, who did not however find fault; and very improperly to the men, who were much displeased with him.

When this first ceremony is over, the mistress of the house withdraws. She returns soon after, with a waiter and glasses full of liquors: every body rises, she offers them the liquors; the company bow to one another, drink, eat for some time, and then go away. The men sometimes converse between whiles, but the women never join in the conversation. If a stranger comes in, he invites the company to his house, who always comply with the invitation. They do not leave him, till they have drunk plentifully, and go from thence to drink with another neighbour. The whole afternoon is thus spent in visiting, and every man generally goes home drunk.

There is no other kind of social amusement in use throughout the whole nation from Mosco to Tobolsky; they dance sometimes, but that is very rare, except at weddings.

It is about fifty years since the women at Mosco and St. Petersburg have shaken off the yoke of slavery, to which they were subjected by their husbands. Before that time, they lived, and were treated in the same way as in other parts of Russia. If the manners have not been much bettered from this change, it is owing to their excessive depravity, before it took place. Throughout Russia in general, a man has much to answer for, if he is but agreeable.

Mosco appeared to me preferable, in many respects, to St. Petersburg. The city of Mosco not being more than two hundred short leagues distant from St. Petersburg, the governors are too near the sovereign, to be tyrannical; and the inhabitants far enough from the seat of government, not to be afraid of the freshold for flight indiscretions of society *.

Pleasure

---

* M. de Montesquieu observe, in the 12th chapter of his 12th book, wherein he treats of *suedita* words that, in the manifesto published by the late Czarina, against

Pleasure is sought after at Mosco, while the inhabitants can hardly venture to speak of it at St. Petersburg.

The common people in Russia, having no ideas of liberty, are much less unhappy than the nobles. Besides, they have but few wishes, and consequently, their wants are less: they are unacquainted with either industry or commerce, especially beyond Mosco. The Russian having no property of his own, is usually indifferent to every thing which might better his fortune. Even the nobles, who are constantly in fear of banishment, and of having their estates confiscated; are not so much employed in improving them, as they are in expedients to raise a speedy supply of ready money, to gratify their present inclinations.

The Russian country people live upon very indifferent kind of food; and therefore, readily giving way to laziness in their stores, they pass their lives in the debaucheries of women and brandy, which liquor however they are not always able to procure. If we were to judge of them merely from the languid life they lead, it might be imagined, that they have but few ideas; on the contrary, they are artful, cunning, and greater rogues than any other nation. They are also remarkably dextrous at thieving. They are not endowed with that courage which some philosophers have ascribed to the northern nations; the Russian peasants are, on the contrary, pusillanimous and cowardly to an incredible degree.

There are no principles of morality among them; they are more afraid of neglecting the lent-fasts, than of murdering a fellow-creature, especially if he is a foreigner; for they do not reckon foreigners among the number of their brethren.

---

against the Olgoroufki family in 1740, one of those princes is sentenced to death for having used some indecent expressions about the Czarina's person: another, for having misinterpreted her wise regulations for the good of the empire, and for having offended her sacred person by words not sufficiently respectful.

The Russian and the Polish slave seem to differ from each other in every respect: the Russian neglects agriculture; is generally immoral, crafty and subtle. On the contrary, the Polish slave takes a pleasure in cultivating the land: he is moral, and stupid. These contrarieties seem to me sufficiently accounted for from the different constitution of the two nations, exclusive of other causes, which may possibly have contributed to establish them.

The slave in Poland is in possession of lands which are his own property; it is natural, therefore, he should delight in improving them; since by that he is enabled to satisfy all his wants, and to enjoy the comforts of life, without having recourse to criminal actions. He is moreover subject to a set of free nobles, who may venture, in every instance, to be virtuous with impunity. If he is stupid, it is because he is enslaved. The Russian slave not having one inch of ground at his own disposal, agriculture is indifferent to him; he is willing to enjoy himself, and is fond of drinking brandy; but as he can seldom get it without theft, or trespassing against the laws, the fear of punishment makes him cautious and subtle.

Slavery has set aside all the rights of nature among the Russians; the human species is in Russia a commercial article, sometimes sold at a very low price; children are often forced from their mothers arms to be sold to persons given up to debauchery. The joy which other people conceive on the birth of their legitimate children is here unknown. This event, on the contrary, is a sorrowful one to a young woman, who knows that her child may be taken away from her, at the instant that he is playing on her knee; she suckles him, and takes a great deal of trouble in bringing him up; he grows, and the time draws near when she is in continual apprehension of losing him: she never can flatter herself that, in this beloved child, she shall find a support and a friend in her old

old age. If when somewhat farther advanced in life, the child perceives the tears starting from his mother in consequence of these dreadful reflections, he asks her the reason, presses her cheeks between his little hands, sooths her with kisses, and at length mixes his tears with hers.

The meanest animals enjoy the happiness caused by the birth of their young: Man, in Russia, is the only being who cannot partake of it. This depravity stifles all principles of humanity, and all kind of sentiment. Going, on my return from Tobolsky to St. Petersburg, into a house where I was to lodge, I found a father chained to a post in the middle of his family: by his cries, and the little regard his children paid to him, I imagined he was mad; but this was by no means the case. In Russia, people who are sent to raise recruits, go through all the villages; and pitch upon the men proper for the service, as butchers, in all other parts, go into the stables to mark the sheep. This man's son had been selected for the service; and had made his escape, without the father's knowledge; the father was made a prisoner in his own house; his children were his goalers, and he was in daily expectation of receiving his sentence. I was so much shocked with this account, and with the scene I beheld, that I was forced to seek another lodging immediately.

This practice has made the Russians cruel and inhuman: they are animals whom their masters think they must crush with a rod of iron, while they continue under the yoke *.

The Russian nobility, having cruel and wicked slaves constantly before their eyes, have acquired a severity which is not

---

* The common people in Russia are at present so corrupt, that they must be kept in a state of rigid servitude, while they continue enslaved: but any man who allows himself to reflect, will easily conceive, that, with proper care, they might be restored to liberty, without having any thing to fear from some inconveniences which may be thought to follow at first. While they are slaves, they will ever be vicious.

natural to them; as they crouch before their sovereign, to their superiors, and to all those from whom they have any thing to expect, they exercise the greatest rigor over all persons subject to their authority, or who have not the power to resist them.

The common people in Russia having nothing to contest with the sovereign, one might reasonably expect to find happiness among this class. In all other parts of the world, the country people get together on holidays: the fathers meet at a public house, oftentimes resting from their labours under the shade of a tree, and indulging in a cheerful glass; they discourse about increasing their stock, and sometimes their conversation turns upon politics, while a wretched fiddler, sitting on a cask, makes their children exquisitely happy.

Such pleasures are unknown in Russia: the common people dance now and then, chiefly on certain days of the Carnival; when they are entirely given up to debauchery and drunkenness: so that one can scarce venture to travel at such a time, for fear of being ill-treated by the mob. The peasants in Russia generally stay in their stoves on holidays, standing at the door without taking any exercise: laziness is the greatest pleasure they have, next to women and drinking. If a Russian peasant has got a little money, he goes to the public house by himself, spends it, and gets drunk in a few minutes: he is then no longer in fear of his fortune being taken from him.

The young country women sometimes amuse themselves, on fine days, by swinging upon a plank, balanced across a beam lying on the ground; they place themselves at the ends of the plank, and raise one another alternately five or six feet high with the greatest dexterity. The men never mix in these diversions, and indeed they are seldom with the women, out of their cottages.

Of the progress of the Arts and Sciences in Russia. Of the genius of the nation, and of education.

PETER I. ascended the throne of Russia in 1689; and immediately framed the design of enlightening his nation, sunk in ignorance for more than seven hundred years past. He undertook a journey into Europe, that he might become acquainted with the arts and sciences, and with every circumstance which could possibly tend to complete the designs he had formed. In the course of his journey, nothing escaped his notice; he visited the learned; he sought out the artist in his manufactory; made himself master of the art, and being thereby enabled to judge of the abilities of the artists, engaged them in his service, whenever he found them to excel.

All the sovereign powers interested themselves warmly in promoting the schemes of this great man; numbers of learned men and artists of all kinds, from the several parts of Europe, set out for Russia. Peter I. on his return into his own dominions, raised public buildings consecrated to the Arts and Sciences. Establishments, which in Europe were formed by degrees, arose in Russia all at once: the nobility laid aside their beards, as well as their ancient manner of dress: the women, before confined wholly to their houses, now made their appearance in public meetings, unknown in Russia till this period. The court became brilliant. Peter I. seemed to have formed a new nation, though he had made no alteration in the political constitution of the government: the nation remained in a state of slavery, which he still made more severe. He forced all the nobility, without distinction, to serve in the army. A number of young slaves were chosen out from among

among the people, and fixed in the academies and schools: of these some were destined to literature, others designed for the arts and sciences, without any regard to their particular talents or inclination. Peter himself visited the academies and the manufactories; and often took the plane and the chisel in his own hands; but snatched the pencil from the hands of a young artist, who was painting Armida in the arms of Rinaldo, and ordered him to be flogged *.

The successors of Peter I. pursued the same plan; the Academy of Sciences however gained a reputation; Bernouilli, Delisle, Herman, and Euler kept up the credit they had acquired in other countries; the Arts shone forth with some kind of splendor; but the Academy lost its repute, and the Arts sensibly decreased, as the great men first invited into Russia, either died, or left the country. The sovereigns still continued to supply their subjects with able masters, and to encourage and protect men of abilities; but, notwithstanding these advantages, not one Russian has appeared in the course of more than sixty years, whose name deserves to be recorded in the history of the Arts and Sciences.

Men of abilities invited into Russia from foreign parts, appear mostly to be discouraged, and not to persevere in their studies with the same earnestness as they did in their own country. In the year 1761, several foreigners of the first rank in the republic of letters, belonged to the Academy of St. Petersburg; among these may be mentioned M. Epiney, Leman, Braun, Tauber, Stelin, and Muler, formerly secretary to the Academy, and at present director of a school at Mosco, as I was informed at my return into France. The late Mr. Lomanosow, a Russian, was a man of genius; and would have made a conside-

* In the original, *faire donner les batogues*, a kind of punishment described hereafter.

rable figure in any other Academy. Mr. Rumoufki, as yet too young a man to have acquired any great degree of reputation, is poffeffed of great natural abilities, and a thirft after knowledge, very uncommon among the Ruffians.

Notwithftanding this number of learned men, it fhould feem as if genius in moft of them was weakened, as foon as they came into Ruffia, fo that the academies and fchools feem to derive their chief credit from the names only of the learned which are in Ruffia. The annals of the Sciences furnifh inconteftable proofs of this affertion, and any man who has not examined thefe, may be convinced of this truth, by confulting thoufands of travellers, who have refided at St. Peterfburg, and at Mofco.

This ftate of the Arts and Sciences in Ruffia implies a defect, the caufe of which muft be fought for, either in a want of genius peculiar to the nation, or in the nature of the government, and the climate. A philofopher*, whofe name will be held in veneration by the lateft pofterity, fpeaking of the difference of men with refpect to climate, reprefents the people of the North as having coarfer organs, and being animated with fluids of a groffer kind, better adapted to produce large robuft bodies than men of genius; but this philofopher would have us confider them, at the fame time, as a very brave, fimple, unreferved, unfufpecting people, without policy or craft, having few vices, and feveral virtues, a great deal of fincerity and honefty, and whofe difpofitions are not very amorous. When I travelled in Ruffia, I every where met with a people very different from what I expected to find, from the ideas of this celebrated philofopher. It muft be allowed however, that, in what he has faid on this fubject, he has confidered the people of the North independently of their

---

* Montefquieu, liv. xiv. chap. 2.

government; which has so far altered the nature of man in Russia, by subduing even those faculties which are least under the controul of the authority of the sovereign, that it is extremely difficult to ascertain the distinguishing caracter of the nation; and it is for this reason that I have hitherto confined myself to the relation of facts upon this point.

Other philosophers have been of opinion, that the differences observable in various nations with regard to genius, to abilities, and to the passions, arise merely from education, and the constitution of different governments. If this principle be admitted, the manners and genius of the Russians, must be accounted for from the despotism of their government. I made observations during my stay in this country, which may possibly throw some light upon this point; but, in order to make the conclusions more evident, it will be necessary to remind the reader of certain truths and opinions generally admitted *.

Man, as well as animals and plants, is composed of solids and fluids; fibres, vessels and glands compose the first solids, and the rest are derived from these. In man, the fluids are the chyle, the blood, and others which are secreted from this last fluid, or which proceed from its dissolution. These several substances constitute the human machine; but we still must have recourse to some first moving power which sets this machine in motion, and gives it life. All natural philosophers and anatomists place this first moving principle in elementary fire; some call it the universal spirit, the vitriolic acid, the phlogiston, the electric matter, &c. It is this primary fluid which gives life to the whole universe; but it is so subtile that it acts not upon our organs, but by the medium of the air,

---

* These truths and opinions are almost entirely taken from Mr. I: Cat's physiological works, tom. i. I here quote this learned man once for all.

and other secondary fluids which form our atmosphere, and bear some affinity to it.

The fluid of the universe therefore, or this universal spirit, is the immediate cause of the motion of fluids in our organized body; and these give rise to the elastic powers and vibrations of the vessels and of the nerves, and actuate the whole animal machine.

We inspire the fluid of the universe with the common air, and it is combined with our food, by the analogy it bears to these substances, or rather to the air they contain. The organs and fluids inservient to digestion separate the part of these aliments, and from thence make an extract of the chyle, in which the universal fluid receives a new modification. The chyle is then the primary fluid, from whence all others are derived, so that these last must necessarily partake of some of the properties of the former. The chyle then passing into the vessels through which the circulation is carried on, is changed into blood. This fluid, having attained its highest perfection in passing through the lungs, is driven by the heart through the aorta to all parts of the body, and is chiefly and immediately directed to the brain, where it is depurated through the finest strainers, and deprived of all its grosser particles, which remain in the blood; and from the union of this pure and highly depurated liquid, the animal fluid or nervous juice is formed; which is therefore the produce of all the aliments changed into chyle and blood, modified by this universal spirit, and combined with it. This fluid, which I shall hereafter call nervous juice, and which Mr. Le Cat names the animal fluid, is the chief organ of sensation and of the faculties of the soul: it exists in beasts as well as in men, and perhaps also in plants, with which our formation and growth seems to have a remarkable analogy.

The nervous juice makes a kind of lake in the brain; the ſpinal marrow is the principal channel which conveys it from thence, and the nerves are ſo many rivers or ſtreams which ſprinkle and vivify all the parts of the animal. The nerves being tubes, their texture is ſuch, that the ſides of the canals are compoſed of other much ſmaller tubes; which terminate by one extremity in the brain, and by the other on the ſkin, where they expand and form a net-work of nerves: the nervous juice having been depurated through the ſubſtance of the brain, is conveyed by the fibres of this organ, and poured immediately into the nerves: the groſſer part received into the cavity of the nerve, becomes the principle of motion, and the finer part of this nervous juice flows in the ſmall tubes of the ſides of the nerves; where, notwithſtanding the ganglions ſcattered throughout the nerves, it forms one continued ſtream, which becomes the organ of ſenſe. This nervous juice, as ſubtile as light, tranſmits inſtantaneouſly to the brain, all the impreſſions it receives. This account of the nerves, and of the nervous juice, eſtabliſhes the ſyſtem of our ſenſations, of our ideas, of the mind, of the genius, and of all the faculties of the rational ſoul.

By the method in which the nervous juice is formed, it appears to be the produce of our food combined with the univerſal fluid: it muſt therefore partake of ſome of the properties of our aliments, and, if I may be allowed the expreſſion, of the ſoil from whence it ſprings, as the fluid does which circulates through plants.

The univerſal ſpirit, although every where the ſame, acts upon our organs only through the medium of the air, and other ſecondary fluids of our atmoſphere. Its action and influence depend therefore on ſecondary cauſes; which is clearly evinced from the effects of cloudy and rainy weather. Some people can even foretel theſe changes of weather from the infirmities

firmities they are afflicted with; and those who enjoy the best state of health, are dull and heavy; the whole body is depressed, because the influence of the universal fluid being impeded, the action of the fluids which nourish our solids, and keep up the animal œconomy, is obstructed in a proportionate degree. Supposing then, that there was really a climate in which these natural causes were always the same, or in a proportion nearly equal, it is certain that men in such a climate would be affected in the same manner, and would seldom be endowed with the powers of genius.

Since then the atmosphere has such a powerful influence over the constitution of man, and consequently over his faculties, its effects must bear a mutual analogy to the different heights of the soil on which the man lives, independently of other local causes, which must also make some exceptions to this general law. This is a received opinion with respect to the vegetable system. In many instances, the height of the soil is determined by knowing the plants which grow upon it; and the height of the soil being given, we may tell what plants it produces. These facts are generally admitted, for better observations have been made on plants than upon men; possibly, because the change of place, and the mixture of one nation with another, having obliterated all marks of the original caracters of men, it has been more difficult to trace them, as Mr. Rousseau observes.

The atmosphere is composed of different fluids, vapours and exhalations, arising from the surface of the earth. If we suppose the atmosphere divided into layers, the first layer will contain the grosser particles; and in proportion as we rise, the air will become purer, be more elastic, and the universal fluid will become proportionally more active.

From these general opinions, we must acknowledge with Mr. de Montesquieu, the influence of the climate upon the inhabitants;

tants; perhaps this great man may have extended its effects too far.

It is equally evident from what has been said, that in any comparison we would make between climates and the caracters of men, it is necessary to attend to the height of the soil on which they dwell.

The kingdom of Russia, from St. Petersburg to Tobolsky, may be considered as one extensive plain, divided by a chain of mountains crossing from south to north at the 75th degree of longitude. In different parts of this plain, we meet with high places or platforms, as at Mosco, and Caccy, and hillocks or rising grounds in other parts, as on the road from St. Petersburg to Mosco; but the height of these is very inconsiderable. I have taken the level of this plain from St. Petersburg to Tobolsky, upon an extent of near seven hundred leagues; and I have crossed and taken the level of the chain in the same manner in two different places, about sixty leagues distant from each other. By these levellings I have obtained, very exactly, the heights of all the places in which I have made observations during my journey. These results, connected with the geography and other informations I have been able to acquire, have enabled me to determine the height of the Russian land, from St. Petersburg to Tobolsky, with more accuracy than was necessary for my present purpose.

I consider the country between St. Petersburg and Tobolsky, as one vast plain, of about seven hundred leagues from west to east, and five hundred leagues from south to north; bounded by the Baltic westward, by the Frozen Ocean to the north, by the Black Sea and the Caspian to the south, and by the river Irtyſz eastward. This immense plain is composed of divers others which form new plane surfaces. I have distinguished however but two of these: the lowest of them is situated near the sea, and extends sometimes as far as one hundred, or one hundred

hundred and fifty leagues, as from St. Peterſburg to Jachelbiza, over a diſtance of 90 leagues of 2000 toiſes each. I have determined the mean height of this plane at thirty-one toiſes above the level of the ſea, and that of the ſecond at fifty toiſes. The laſt reaches over the greater part of this plain, which I croſſed over, an extent of more than 400 leagues. Other intervening plains are ſometimes to be met with, as in the neighbourhood of Tobolſky. The height of the laſt plane ſurfaces is about fourſcore toiſes; but their extent is inconſiderable, and they draw near to the two former, lowering towards the north, and riſing to the ſouth.

The hillocks and platforms are found chiefly on the ſecond plane, which I have found to be one hundred and fifty toiſes. Theſe inequalities are not frequent: their height, with reſpect to the level of the ſea, is two hundred and twenty toiſes, and about ſeventy above the plane on which they ſtand; they often extend twenty leagues in diameter, and ſometimes more. The aſcent to the ſummit of them is eaſy and almoſt imperceptible. The mountainous country comprehends the chain of mountains which divides Ruſſia from Siberia. This is the only chain we meet with throughout this extenſive ſurface, of about ſeven hundred leagues in length, and five hundred in breadth. The ſituation of the chain is likewiſe upon this ſecond plane, which riſes one hundred and fifty toiſes above the level of the ſea. I have fixed the mean height of theſe mountains, from a great number of obſervations, at two hundred and ninety toiſes; and conſequently, they are not more than one hundred and forty toiſes above the plane they ſtand upon. There are however ſome few of them in the confines of Echaterinenburg and Solikamſky, which riſe as high as three hundred and nine, and four hundred and ſeventy-one toiſes.

From

From this account it appears, that this part of Ruſſia in general is compoſed of immenſe plains almoſt on a level. Such inequalities are not to be met with here, as in France; theſe have a remarkable effect on the varieties obſervable in the ſoil of the French provinces, and on the nature of the atmoſphere. Towards the ſouthern parts of this kingdom, theſe inequalities form mountainous countries, and, in the others, hills and hillocks, more or leſs raiſed: ſo that although France does not extend more than about two hundred and forty leagues from weſt to eaſt, and two hundred and twenty-five from ſouth to north, yet the produce varies in almoſt all its provinces, which are thirty-eight in number; and very ſtriking differences may alſo be obſerved in the inhabitants, independent of the general caracter of the nation. Such differences are univerſally noted between the inhabitants of Gaſcony, Normandy, Picardy, Bretany, Champaigne, and Berry: and have given riſe to the jokes that have been paſſed upon them.

Ruſſia is, on the contrary, almoſt on a level; and indeed the ſame vegetable productions are obſerved all the way from St. Peterſburg to Tobolſky; a ſmall quantity of corn, and ſome hemp, in an extent of near ſeven hundred leagues; and, from the gates of St. Peterſburg to thoſe of Tobolſky, going by Solikamſky, we meet with nothing but pines, firs, and ſome kinds of the lighter woods. This ſtriking uniformity prevails equally among the animals, and among the inhabitants; the rivers contain the ſame kinds of fiſh, except the ſterlet, which is more ſcarce as one comes nearer to St. Peterſburg. The ſame animals are found in the woods. The ſoil in the neighbourhood of Tobolſky being more ſwampy than in any other part, there are here a greater number of water fowl, and ſome of them indeed different from any that are found throughout the reſt of Ruſſia. Some fruit trees grow in the neighbourhood of Moſco; but theſe trifling exceptions

cannot

cannot be said to invalidate the general rule, which prevails in its full extent.

With regard to the men, whoever has been through one province knows all the Ruffians; they are of the fame ftature, they have fimilar paffions, fimilar difpofitions, and their manners are alike. There is not even the leaft variety in their amufements, in their exercifes, in their manner of cultivating the land, or in their drefs. This uniformity is apparent even in their houfes. The Wotiaks however, the Scheremichs, the Schuwafchi, and the Tartars, are exceptions to this general rule: thefe people, who have fixed themfelves in fmall diftricts of Ruffia towards the weftern borders of Siberia, have continued the drefs that was peculiar to them: fome have kept their religion, and fome their manners; but in every circumftance dependent on the climate, natural caufes have acted fo powerfully, as to bring thefe people to the fame ftandard, and make Ruffians of them all. The Wotiaks indeed are of low ftature, as we have before obferved in fpeaking of them.

I have taken notice of there being fome difference between the people who live in the higher countries and thofe who dwell in the plains; and have even mentioned fome inftances of this fort in the account of my journey, not knowing at that time that I fhould make ufe of them in the manner I am now going to do. In the higher parts of the country, I have found more vivacity and cheerfulnefs than in the lower grounds, efpecially at Makhneva. I have made the fame obfervations at Echaterinenburg, where the difference was ftill more obvious; and would be ftill more remarkable, on comparing the inhabitants of Mofco, with thofe of St. Peterfburg; although the government, as I have before obferved, contributes much to this difference in the two laft-mentioned cities. Thefe diftinctions however, between the inhabitants of the plains and thofe of the higher grounds, are not so apparent as they are in other parts of Europe.

The slope of the rivers in the immense plains of Russia is but small; the rain waters, and those which proceed from the melting of the snows, do not easily run off. These waters generally make the country very marshy: the earth, whose surface is almost entirely covered with wood, still contributes to make the atmosphere more moist; and the summer season does not last long enough, to admit of the soil being dried up by the sun. Hence the number of marshes met with in Russia, even in the middle of the continent, and at the distance of three or four hundred leagues from the sea.

The winter appears to be the only season in which the Russians can enjoy the benefits of a pure atmosphere; and then the cold is so intense, that all nature seems to be lifeless and totally inactive. All the inhabitants, shut up and confined within their stoves, breathe an air infected by exhalations and vapours proceeding from perspiration. They pass their time in these stoves wholly given up to indolence, sleeping almost all day in a suffocating heat, and taking hardly any exercise. This manner of living, and the climate, produces such a degree of dissolution in the blood of these people, that they are under a necessity of bathing twice a week all the year round, in order to get rid of the watery disposition prevalent in their constitutions, by raising an artificial perspiration.

We may readily conclude from what has been said, that the nervous juice in the Russians is inspissated and sluggish, more adapted to form strong constitutions than men of genius: their internal organs have lost their elasticity and vibratory powers; the flogging they constantly undergo in the baths, and the heat they experience there, blunts the sensibility of the external organs. The nerves being no longer capable of receiving impressions, cannot transmit them to the internal organs;

gans; and indeed M. de Montesquieu observes, that, to make a Russian feel, one must flay him *. The want of genius therefore among the Russians, appears to be an effect of the soil and of the climate.

This opinion might farther be confirmed by other arguments equally strong; but as this work is intended to relate facts only, I must not dwell any longer upon this digression, which may already have been tedious.

The spirit of invention is as uncommon among the Russians, as genius; but they have a peculiar turn for imitation. In Russia, locksmiths, masons, carpenters, &c. are formed as a a soldier is in other countries. Each regiment has, in its own corps, all the necessary artists; and is not obliged to have recourse to manufactures, as is the custom every else. They determine by the stature, what employment a man is most fit for. They give a soldier a lock for a pattern, with orders to make others like it, and he does it with the greatest dexterity; but the original must be perfect, otherwise he would copy it with all its defects, however easy it might be to correct them. The same may be observed with regard to artists and workmen of all kinds.

This particular talent of the Russians is so remarkable, that one may see it prevail in the nation, immediately on coming into Russia. One may easily perceive, that the Russians possess it in so eminent a degree, that they might have been formed into a very different people from what they are at present.

I have observed that the Russians were naturally cheerful; that they have the true spirit of society, and that they delight in it; these circumstances are evident in the Russians who travel into foreign countries. Why then is a Russian, at least in some respects, so different from what he might be? The nature of education and of the government will furnish the solution of this problem.

* Liv. xiv. chap. 2.

In a good government, the education of children fhould be directed to virtue, the love of our country, and the happinefs of fociety. Such an education is intimately connected with the political fyftem of a good government; but it fuppofes that the intereft of the fovereign fhould be the fame as that of the nation. The regularity and harmony of a good adminiftration confifts in the relations and exact combinations of thefe two interefts; this conftitutes the power of the fovereign, and the happinefs of the people. Hence arifes that love of our country, which induces every citizen to confider the good of the nation as his own; public gratitude infpires and keeps up the love of fame, brings forth great men, and infures them the veneration of pofterity.

The love of fame and of our country is unknown in Ruffia; defpotifm debafes the mind, damps the genius, and ftifles every kind of fentiment. In Ruffia no perfon dares venture to think; the foul is fo much debafed, that its faculties are deftroyed. Fear is almoft the only paffion by which the whole nation is actuated.

I have feen in their fchools, a young mathematician ftudying Euclid with a piece of wood faftened to his neck; and mafters commanding abilities, as an army is taught to exercife.

I was told by a famous foreign artift, who had the direction of one of thefe fchools, that he once found among his pupils one of a fuperior genius. Defirous of pufhing a young man forward, who might do him honor, he took great care in inftructing him; he was well pleafed to obferve the daily improvements of his pupil; but in a little time the young man ftopt fhort. The artift, having tried to encourage him by all kinds of mild proceedings, afked him at laft in a very friendly manner, why he had taken a diflike to his bufinefs. I am, anfwered the young man, flave to M * * *; when he finds that I am a proficient, he will oblige me to work in his houfe,

where

where I shall meet with such ill treatment, that I had much rather live in the same manner as my companions.

I have known several persons who were persuaded that the Russians were incapable of making any considerable improvements in any thing. I think this opinion is entirely groundless; such facts as I have been relating of this young slave, have given rise to this mistake. These facts, on the contrary, imply at least a great share of judgment.

The government has attempted to rectify some of these inconveniences, by ordering that all persons who should distinguish themselves at the schools, should no longer be slaves to their lords, but should belong to the state. In this case, the lords will either avoid sending their slaves to the schools, or will find some means of keeping them to themselves, so that they must still remain in a state of slavery.

I could mention a number of facts of the same kind as the former, of which I have been witness; but I shall pass them over, to avoid giving offence to some persons at present in Russia. The fatal effects of despotism are extended over all the arts, all the manufactures, and are conveyed into all the work-shops. The artists are chained down to their work. This I have seen frequently, especially at Mosco, and it is with such workmen that the Russians imagine they can imitate the manufactories of Lyons.

Peter I. was persuaded, and the whole nation continues in the same opinion to this day, that the Russians must be governed in this manner. There might be reason for this conduct in some respects, at the time that Peter I. came to the throne, but it is very strange that such a prejudice should still prevail in Russia.

The pride of the Russians is still a great hindrance to the progress of the Arts and Sciences in this nation. This is a national vice, and to be observed in all stations. As soon as a learner has made some little improvement, he thinks he knows as much as his master, and presently after, even more. The public in Russia is ignorant enough to suppose him equal, and among other disadvantages attending this false presumption, it adds to the disagreeable circumstances a foreigner is already exposed to, who is called into the country to instruct the Russians; so that foreign artists are often obliged to keep their pupils under, in order to preserve their own importance. Most of them, displeased with their situations, are less anxious about endeavouring to bring up good workmen, than they are about making a fortune, which they seldom carry off into their own country. I did not meet with one single foreigner in Russia, who did not look back with regret to the time he had spent among his fellow-citizens.

The nobles, devoted to the military service, send their children to the *Corps of Cadets*, a kind of college instituted for the education of the nobility, or bring them up in the midst of their families; they treat the governors intrusted with the education of their children with the greatest regard; but are often obliged to put their youth under the direction of masters very unequal to such a task, most of them being persons disappointed of the success they sought for in Russia. Such masters are seldom fit to form the young nobility; and the fathers, who are themselves ignorant, and debased by slavery, are still less able to contribute usefully to the education of their children, to mould their hearts, and inspire them with proper sentiments. The despotic sovereign does not fail to make them sensible of the danger of acquiring any kind of knowledge of which absolute power might be jealous.

It is easy to conclude from what has been said on this subject, that it is owing to the nature of the constitution and to want of proper education, that the Russians have made so little improvement in the Arts and Sciences; and that these people,

though

though deficient in genius, and deprived of the powers of imagination, would still be a very different nation in many respects, if they enjoyed the blessings of liberty. But the question is, whether they would make any considerable progress, even if they enjoyed this advantage. This I cannot take upon me to determine. It were perhaps to be wished, if we agree with M. Rousseau of Geneva, that this nation had never been polished. However this may be, it is certain, that the general turn and spirit of the nation seems likely to undergo a total change under the reign of the Empress Catherine. Convinced, as she is, that the learned man, in whom the genius for sublime geometry is combined, with a disposition for philosophy and literature, is capable of assisting her in her designs of establishing a good government, by enlightening the minds of her subjects, she has given this philosopher an asylum near her throne, and indulged him in the advantages of coming near a sovereign who honors and cultivates the Sciences. She entertains the learned Euller, whose mathematical labours have immortalized his name. This great man is employed a second time in instructing the Russians. What progress will they not make under the reign of this Empress? She has already taken all the necessary steps to insure the success of the observation of the Transit of Venus over the sun; many of her subjects are to observe it in different places of this extensive empire. Her views are, to form a new nation: Peter the Great first conceived the design, laid the plan, and made way for the event; the honor of completing the glorious undertaking seems to be reserved to the Empress Catherine.

Of the laws, of punishments, and of exile.

M. VOLTAIRE, one of the firft writers in Europe, tells us in his hiftory of Ruffia*, that in 1722 Peter I. finifhed the new code of laws begun in 1718, and improved under the Emprefs Elizabeth. Peter I. forbad all the judges, on pain of death, to deviate from this code, or to fubftitute their private opinions to the general law. This fevere decree was fixed up, and is ftill pofted in all the courts of judicature throughout the empire. He alfo forbad the judges, under the fame penalties, to receive any fees, and every man in office to accept of any prefents. Moens *de la Croix*, chamberlain to the Emprefs Catherine, and his fifter, Madame de Bale, lady of the bedchamber to the Emprefs, being convicted of having taken prefents, Moens was condemned to be beheaded, and his fifter, a favorite of the Emprefs, to receive eleven ftrokes of the knout. This lady's two fons, one chamberlain, and the other page, were difgraced, and fent to ferve as common foldiers in the army in Perfia †.

This feverity is greatly relaxed fince the death of Peter I. All the provinces I have paffed through, have their own courts of juftice, which are called chanceries: the tribunals relating to civil and criminal matters, depend upon the fenate, and upon the college of juftice. I have obferved that, in all courts of chancery at any diftance from the capital, juftice was almoft publicly fold, and the poor man, though innocent, was generally facrificed to the wealthy criminal.

* Tom. ii. chap. 13. des Loix, pag. 222.
† M. de Voltaire, pag. 277.

Since the accession of the Empress Elizabeth to the throne of Russia, the punishments are reduced to two kinds, the *padogi*, and the *knout*.

The padogi are considered in Russia merely as a correction of the police, exercised on the soldier by military discipline, by the nobility on their servants, and by persons in authority over all such as are under their command.

I saw this punishment inflicted at my return from Tobolsky to St. Petersburg. I looked out of a window, on hearing somebody cry out in the yard, where I saw two Russian slaves pulling a girl of fourteen or fifteen years of age by the arms; she was tall and well made. By her dress, she appeared to belong to some good family. Her head dressed without a cap, was reclined backwards; her eyes, fixed on one person, pleaded for mercy; which her beauty should seem to have insured her, independent of her tears. Nevertheless, the Russians led her into the middle of the yard, and in an instant stripped her to the waist; they then laid her prostrate on the ground, and placed themselves on their knees; one of them holding her head tight between his knees, and the other, the lower part of her body: rods were then brought, which they continued constantly applying on the back of this girl, till some one cried out, *Enough*. This unfortunate victim was then raised, so disfigured that she was scarcely to be known; her face and her whole body being covered with blood and dirt. This severe punishment led me to imagine, that the young girl had been guilty of some very flagrant offence: some days after I learned, that she was a lady's waiting-maid; and that her mistress's husband had ordered her to be punished in that manner, on account of some neglect. In any other part of the world, she might perhaps have been turned away, if her mistress had happened to be in an ill humour. The Russians think themselves obliged to treat their servants thus, in order to make them faithful. These unhappy slaves, finding so many petty tyrants in their masters, are obliged on this account to live in perpetual mistrust: so that even in the midst of their families, they are under a necessity of being constantly on their guard with every person who comes near them.

I never saw the punishment of the knout inflicted; but as I was going over St. Petersburg with a foreigner, who conducted me to see all the curiosities in the city, we stopped upon the spot where Mad. Lapouchin had suffered this punishment. The foreigner had been present on this occasion; and was still so much affected with the affair, that he gave me a particular account of it on the very spot. I shall relate the incident as he told it me, and as I found it in my journal.

Every body who has been at St. Petersburg, knows that Mad. Lapouchin was one of the finest women belonging to the court of the Empress Elizabeth: she was intimately connected with a foreign ambassador, then engaged in a conspiracy. Mad. Lapouchin, who was supposed to be an accomplice in this conspiracy, was condemned, by the Empress Elizabeth, to undergo the punishment of the knout. She appeared at the place of execution in a genteel undress, which contributed still to heighten her beauty. The sweetness of her countenance, and her vivacity, were such as might indicate indiscretion, but not even the shadow of guilt; although I have been assured by every person of whom I have made inquiry, that she was really guilty. Young, lovely, admired and sought for at the court, of which she was the life and spirit; instead of the number of admirers her beauty usually drew after her, she then saw herself surrounded only by executioners. She looked on them with astonishment, seeming to doubt whether such preparations were intended for her: one of the executioners then pulled off a kind of cloak which covered her bosom; her modesty taking the alarm made her start back a few steps; she turned pale, and burst into into tears: her clothes were soon

after

after ſtripped off, and in a few moments ſhe was quite naked to the waiſt, expoſed to the eager looks of a vaſt concourſe of people profoundly ſilent. One of the executioners then ſeized her by both hands, and turning half round, threw her on his back, bending forwards, ſo as to raiſe her a few inches from the ground: the other executioner then laid hold of her delicate limbs, with his rough hands hardened at the plough, and, without any remorſe, adjuſted her on the back of his companion, in the propereſt poſture for receiving the puniſhment. Sometimes he laid his large hand brutally upon her head, in order to make her keep it down; ſometimes like a butcher going to flay a lamb, he ſeemed to ſooth her, as ſoon as he had fixed her in the moſt favorable attitude.

This executioner then took a kind of whip called knout, made of a long ſtrap of leather prepared for this purpoſe: he then retreated a few ſteps, meaſuring the requiſite diſtance with a ſteady eye; and leaping backwards, gave a ſtroke with the end of the whip, ſo as to carry away a ſlip of ſkin from the neck to the bottom of the back: then ſtriking his feet againſt the ground he took his aim for applying a ſecond blow parallel to the former; ſo that in a few moments all the ſkin of her back was cut away in ſmall ſlips, moſt of which remained hanging to the ſhift. Her tongue was cut out immediately after, and ſhe was directly baniſhed into Siberia. This incident is known to all perſons who have been in Ruſſia. In 1762, ſhe was recalled from baniſhment by Peter III.

The ordinary puniſhment of the knout is not diſgraceful, becauſe every individual under this deſpotic government is expoſed to incidents of the ſame nature, which have often been the conſequence merely of court intrigues.

Ruſſians who have committed crimes with regard to ſociety, are condemned to the great knout. This puniſhment is generally uſed on the ſame occaſions, as racking on the wheel in France.

France. The great knout differs only in some particulars from the common knout: the criminal is raised into the air by means of a pully fixed to a gallows, and a cord fastened to the two wrists tied together; a piece of wood is placed between his two legs, also tied together; and another of a crucial form under his breast. Sometimes his hands are tied behind his back; and when he is pulled up in this position, his shoulders are dislocated.

The executioners can make this punishment more or less cruel: they are so dexterous, that when a criminal is condemned to die, they can make him expire at pleasure, either by one or several lashes.

Besides the punishment of the knout, that of breaking on the wheel was in use before the reign of the Empress Elizabeth. Sometimes criminals were impaled through the side: sometimes they were hanged by the ribs upon hooks; in which situation they lived for several days; as did women who were buried alive up to the shoulders, for the murder of their husbands. Beheading was a punishment equally inflicted on the common people as on the nobility.

It appears evidently from the example of the kingdom of Russia, that neither the death of criminals, nor the severity of their corporal punishments, do contribute to reform mankind.

The Empress Elizabeth has kept up the punishment of the knout only, as I have before observed; criminals are even seldom condemned to this; banishing of the nobility, confiscating their property, and putting the common people to public labour, have been substituted instead of it. I have known several persons, who blamed the conduct of the Empress Elizabeth in this respect, considering these punishments as too mild.

There may be some reason for this opinion with regard to crimes of a peculiar nature; but, it is evident that such persons were little acquainted with the nature of banishment as practised in Russia.

All criminals condemned to public labour are treated in the same manner; they are shut up in prisons surrounded by a large piece of ground, inclosed with stakes, fifty or sixty feet high; in bad weather they retire within side the prison, and when the season permits they walk about in the inclosure. They have all chains to their feet; and are kept for a very trifling expence, being generally allowed nothing but bread and water, or, according to the place they are in, some other food instead of bread. They are guarded by a certain number of soldiers, who lead them to the mines, or other public labours; where they are treated with the utmost severity. This punishment in many instances is not adequate to the crimes: it has not that effect on the minds of the Russians as one might expect, because they are slaves. It would certainly have a very different effect on a free and civilized nation; where a perpetual punishment of this kind would prove a more powerful restraint on the people than the fear of death. Some villains even look upon that moment as the end of all their sufferings, to which circumstance we may impute the resolution with which some of them have behaved on the scaffold; but I believe it might be very dangerous to expose such criminals, as they do in Russia, to the public view. The habit of seeing these unhappy people at length destroys sensibility; and this sentiment is of such importance to society, that every method ought to be taken to preserve it among people who are already possessed of it, or to excite it in the breasts of those who are yet strangers to it. I am persuaded that the disagreeable sight of such a number of wretches in chains as are met with in most of the towns in Russia, has contributed much to produce that ferocity and

savageness

favageness of caracter so remarkable among the inhabitants of this realm.

Persons condemned to banishment are not all treated in the same manner; some are shut up, and others allowed a little liberty. Count Lestoc, after having placed the crown on the head of the Empress Elizabeth, was banished with his lady. Lestoc was arrested first, and shut up in the fort of St. Petersburg. His wife was a native of Livonia, of one of the most noble families: she was maid of honor to the Empress before she married count Lestoc; and though living at court, had still preserved the noble pride, inspired by that liberty which the province of Livonia, conquered by Peter I., still enjoys. The countess of Lestoc being arrested, took off all the diamonds belonging to her dress, as well as her watch, and other trinkets, and throwing them at the feet of those who took her up, told them to lead her to the place they were ordered to conduct her to: she was shut up in the same castle with her husband, but in a separate apartment: all their effects were put under seal, in expectation of the sentence of the private court of chancery. These illustrious prisoners, given up to this odious tribunal, the judges of which were avowed enemies to count Lestoc, especially M. de Bestuchef, the first minister*, looked upon their ruin as inevitable, and therefore did not endeavor to offer much in their defence. Lestoc had received a sum of money from a foreign power in alliance with Russia, and it was to this power that the Empress Elizabeth was indebted for the crown. The receiving of this present was the great charge brought against count Lestoc; on being questioned, he owned

---

* I have read in some manuscript notes on Russia, that in 1741 the Empress Elizabeth had abolished the secret chancery on her accession to the throne, and had referred to the senate all the matters which used to be tried there; but it does not appear that this order was ever carried into execution. Count Lestoc and his peers have never been judged by the senate, nor by any real court of justice.

he had received it; but his judges having afked him the value of the fum; his anfwer was: *I do not recollect, but if you are defirous of knowing, the Emprefs Elizabeth can tell you;* and indeed, he had informed this princefs that this fum had been offered to him, on account of the favors fhe fhewed him; and the Emprefs had allowed him to accept of it.

The countefs of Leftoc, as fully convinced of the fentence that would be given, as fhe was of her own and her hufband's innocence, only begged one favor of the judges, that fhe might be beheaded; but that they would fpare her fkin, that is, that fhe might not receive the punifhment of the knout.

Notwithftanding all the contrivances of Beftuchef, the Emprefs Elizabeth would never confent that thefe prifoners fhould be condemned to the knout: all their eftate was confifcated; they were banifhed into Siberia, fhut up in different places, and not allowed to correfpond with each other.

The countefs of Leftoc had but one room to live in: her furniture confifted of a few chairs, a table, a ftove, and a bed without curtains, made of ftraw, with one coverlet; fhe got clean fheets but twice in the firft year. Four foldiers conftantly watched her, and lay in her chamber; from whence fhe was not allowed to ftir, even for the common neceffities of life: fhe had only a few fhifts to change now and then. Leftoc gave out at his return, that his wife had been furprifed, that the vermin, the neceffary confequence of the filth fhe was obliged to live in, had not alone been fufficient to deftroy her. She ufed to play at cards with the foldiers, in hopes of getting four or five pence to difpofe of as fhe pleafed, which however was not always allowed. Being one day out of humour with the officer who commanded, he fpat in her face, and afterwards made her captivity ftill harder.

Count Leftoc was ftill more unhappy, becaufe the vivacity of his difpofition made him very impatient of the leaft contradiction;

diction; and he was only indulged in the liberty of walking about his room, on condition that he avoided coming near the window.

The Empress Elizabeth, however, had allowed Lestoc, as well as his wife, twelve French livres *per* day, which was very favorable treatment in Ruffia; but thefe exiles were not permitted to touch the money allotted to them, left they fhould have employed it in bribing their guards: the officer of the guard therefore was treasurer, he was ordered to procure them all neceffaries, and he let them want for every thing.

A few years after, count Lestoc and his lady were fuffered to live together: they had then several apartments, and a fmall garden at their difpofal; the countefs of Lestoc worked in the garden, fetched water, brewed, baked, wafhed, &c.——Sometimes even the officer of the guard introduced company to them: one of his friends, who had conducted a party into Siberia, defired to fee the count. This officer having contracted a kind of intimacy with him, propofed a party of play. Lestoc won four hundred French livres: this fum was a fortune for the two exiles; they were foon after informed, that it belonged to the party this officer conducted. The countefs fell at her hufband's feet, intreating him to return the money to this imprudent foldier; Lestoc raifed her up, and fent the money to the neareft village to be diftributed among the poor.

After the banifhment of M. de Bestuchef, count Woronzof, the high chancellor, attempted feveral times to have Lestoc recalled, as he was thoroughly perfuaded of his innocence; but the Empress Elizabeth would never liften to his intreaties on this point: fhe was however particularly attentive in giving orders to have wine fent to him from time to time, knowing he was very fond of it.

Lestoc and his lady were at length recalled by Peter III. after fourteen years exile: Lestoc came to St. Petersburg in the dress of the lower sort of people, which is commonly made of sheeps skin *. All the noblemen of the court, and all foreigners flocked eagerly to see him, endeavouring to make him forget the time he had past in exile. The friendly proffers he received were sincere, because every body knew he was innocent; the Empress Elizabeth never had a subject more firmly attached to her; and he had constantly maintained his allegiance during his exile: he declared that M. de Bestuchef had been the cause of it, and that the Empress had only given way to the importunities of this minister.

Count Lestoc, though seventy-four years old, still preserved all that firmness, which had been so necessary to him when he placed the princess Elizabeth on the throne. He used to give a circumstantial account of this event, and of his banishment, in public company; although he knew very well that the story was highly disagreeable to the Russians, and that he thereby exposed himself daily to be banished again; nor were the admonitions of his friends of any weight with him in this matter. Peter III. having done him the honor of admitting him to his table, Lestoc spoke to him in the following terms: " Sir, my " enemies will not fail to do me all the mischief they can, but " I hope your majesty will permit an old man, who has but " few days to live, to prate on, and die in peace." He claimed all the effects that had been taken away from him when he was arrested; they had been already distributed among several private persons, according to custom. He declared he would take possession of them wherever he found them. He also demanded, that an account should be given him of his jewels, and of the money the officers of the guard had received during his

---

* In the original, *habit de mousic*.

exile. Count Leſtoc himſelf acquainted me with every thing I have mentioned concerning his baniſhment, and furniſhed me alſo with the particulars of the revolution by which the Empreſs Elizabeth was fixed on the throne.

Count Munic, equally great as a courtier and as a general, acted in a different manner. He never complained. Both Ruſſians and foreigners had the greateſt reſpect for him.

General Munic was of the talleſt ſize ; though advanced in years, and extremely thin, he had preſerved in the midſt of his misfortunes, a moſt agreeable countenance. He engaged all hearts by his politeneſs, and the gentleneſs of his diſpoſition.

Munic, had a daughter at the time of his baniſhment; who, as ſhe was too young to partake of her father's diſgrace, remained at St. Peterſburg. In this lady, a moſt beautiful form and all the charms of youth were at ſixteen years of age, united to the virtues, the gentleneſs, and the underſtanding of her father. The ſenſibility of M. de Witenhof could not reſiſt ſuch powerful attractions. He had the ribband of the order of St. Alexander Neuſki, and was not without views of ambition. He was not ignorant of the danger of marrying the daughter of the diſgraced general Munic; but he was in love, and obtained leave to be happy; nor has one day paſſed, in which he has not applauded his own reſolution.

Mad. de Witenhof was ſeparated from her father twenty years: ſhe knew him only by report, which publiſhed his misfortunes and his virtues. She lived at Riga, where her huſband was ſecond in command. On receiving the news of her father's recall, ſhe flew with M. de Witenhof to St. Peterſburg. The Emperor had juſt aſcended the throne, and joy prevailed throughout the capital ; but the tenderneſs of Mad. de Witenhof made her regret the duty of appearing at court even for a moment : ſhe ſet out next day with her huſband for Siberia. Munic, confined for twenty years paſt, had never received any

news

news of his daughter. He was returning from Siberia, unacquainted with his own deftiny, or any of the events which had taken place during fo long an interval. He was at this time more than fourfcore years old; his lady was with him. Mad. de Witenhof found her father in a mean habit made of fheep's fkin. Munic difcovered his daughter by her tranfports, and for the firft time fhed tears. His lady, oppreffed by the misfortunes of exile, attempted in vain to participate of the general joy: her organs, worn out by adverfity, were no longer fufceptible of pleafure. I have had the honor of feeing this refpectable family feveral times. The unhappy mother, though encouraged by the juft regard which was paid to her hufband at St. Peterfburg, by his own prudence, and by the refpect of the whole nation, was neverthelefs in perpetual terror. Whenever the door was opened, her countenance betrayed marks of uneafinefs.

All exiled perfons are not confined, as I have before obferved. While I was at a manufactory in Siberia, where I came to get fome things I wanted, made under my own infpection, a man, whom I took at firft for a Ruffian peafant, came into the fame place. His countenance was pale, his beard long and difgufting, his drefs was ragged, and his whole appearance expreffed the greateft mifery. Obferving that he fixed his eyes on me, and that there was a kind of uneafinefs diffufed over his fingular countenance, I could not avoid being furprized. I went up to him, in order to make fome inquiries; but how great was my aftonifhment, when under fuch an appearance I found a man of extraordinary learning. He converfed with me in Latin upon the fciences, upon government, and upon the interefts of the European powers, &c. I foon found that that he was one of the unfortunate exiles who live in this country. I was going on with my converfation, when I obferved a Ruffian foldier come in, who turned pale on feeing me with this man. As I was acquainted with the country, I winked upon the exile, who understood me, left off speaking, without turning about, and soon after went away. I took care not to follow him, however desirous I was of doing it. I searched for him in vain some days after, walking about in all places where I had hopes of meeting with him: I never saw him after, and imagine he must have been confined at least for some time.

Banishment in Siberia is a kind of state of reprobation; it makes a man so miserable, that although he lives among his fellow-creatures, every body flies from him; no person dares to have any kind of connection with him; but this is not so much on account of the crime he is supposed to have been guilty of, as for fear of the government.

The least unhappy of the exiles are such as are allowed to go into service among the Russians; they live at least with human beings. I have known some of these very well satisfied with their condition; living with merchants who had some regard for these unfortunate people. One of these exiles brought me one day a small phial full of a liquor which he assured me was a sovereign remedy against all diseases. It may readily be imagined that I gave him whatever he asked for it.

I have read in the works of some preceding travellers, that the exiles in Siberia were employed in hunting the animals which supply the Russians with their beautiful furrs. I have never been a witness of this practice, but indeed it was impossible for me to see every thing. Besides, the Russians are in general so mistrustful, that when they are asked any questions, even concerning matters independent of government, they always answer, *God knows, and the Empress*.

Of the population, trade, navy, revenues, and land forces of Russia.

THE power of a state arises from its population; altho' in many countries this circumstance is the least object of the attention of government. Depravity of manners, luxury, and the wretchedness of the people, are the chief impediments to population; since it is well known, that unlawful connections contribute but little to the propagation of the species. Luxury, by increasing our wants, makes us apprehensive of an increase of family, and misery often gets the better even of the desire of procreation.

In northern countries, the climate furnishes a fresh obstacle to population: the regions of the Laplanders, of the Samoiedes, and all the northern parts of Russia, have been always depopulated, and will ever be so, because of the unfruitfulness of the soil, and the bad quality of the food these people are obliged to live upon: this food contains hardly any nutritious juice, and all nature in these climates seems to be in a state of perpetual sluggishness, in which scarce any active principles are to be discovered. On the contrary, the deserts of the southern part of Siberia, and of all Russia, have been much peopled on account of their being situated in a more temperate climate. The emigrations of the Huns, and the Scythians, are proofs of this fact.

Almost all philosophers are of opinion, that the constitution has less powerful influence in the northern, than in the southern climates: the people of the north are less addicted to venery. Love is among them a chaste and lawful passion, while it is always criminal among the people of the south.

The obfervations I have made in Ruffia are entirely contradictory to this opinion; they make the Ruffians an exception to this general rule: and it fhould feem that this apparent contradiction may be accounted for from moral caufes. The women being left to themfelves, and fuffered to live in idlenefs, the effects even of their moft trifling paffions muft be powerful. Among the common people, men, women and children lie together promifcuoufly, without any fenfe of fhame. Hence their paffions being excited by the objects they fee, the two fexes give themfelves up early to debauchery. Although the baths weaken them at the time they make ufe of them, yet the flagellation they receive there promotes the circulation of the fluids, gives elafticity to the organs *, and animates the paffions. Thefe particular caufes muft necefsarily produce great alterations in the effects refulting from the climate.

That part of Ruffia which I paffed over, is the moft populous: it bears a mean degree between the frozen regions of the north, and the temperate diftricts of the fouth. Thefe laft countries are defert, on account of the numbers of people who have removed from thence; befides that they have been laid wafte by the conquefts of Gengifkan and his fucceffors. The route I took, is confequently the fitteft to give us an exact knowledge of the population of Ruffia.

I went into no one houfe during the courfe of my journey, without inquiring at what age the parents had been married, what number of children they had had, how they had been brought up, and what difeafes they had been afflicted with: in fhort, I neglected not the moft trifling circumftance from which any information might be gathered.

---

* Flagellation quickens the motion of the fluids, and increafes the elaftic power of the organs, although it deftroys the fenfibility of the nervous network before mentioned. The animal machine would foon be deftroyed with them, if they did not ufe bathing fo frequently.

Notwithftanding

Notwithstanding the varieties I found in the number of facts I collected, I may venture to affirm, that the young people are generally married about eighteen years of age; oftentimes much later, and in some instances at fifteen or sixteen. Women bear children till fifty, but that is uncommon: I found they were more fruitful than I thought them to be, because most of them are affected with the fluor albus, and that every where else this disease is a hindrance to population. These people having but few wants, are not apprehensive of the inconveniences of a numerous family: and indeed I have met with women who had had eighteen children; but such fruitfulness as this may be considered as a phœnomenon. These women however had but two or three alive out of this number. Several particular causes concur daily in depopulating these extensive dominions.

The small-pox carries off near one half of the children: this disease seems to have been communicated to this country from Europe. Several persons have assured me of this remarkable fact, that the wandering Tartars to the south of Siberia are scarcely acquainted with this cruel disease. They are so exceedingly shocked at it, that whenever any person is seized with it, he is left alone in a tent with provisions, and the rest of the band encamps in some other place. The Tartars who penetrate into Siberia are almost immediately attacked with this disease; many of them die, and such as have reached their thirty-fifth year scarce ever escape. The more remarkable these facts appeared to me, the more pains I took to have them authenticated. I cannot, however, bring any other authority for them, than the testimony of several intelligent persons whom I consulted on this point, and who could have no motive for imposing upon me.

Venereal disorders are diffused throughout all Russia, and in northern Tartary more than any where else. The men are much addicted to sodomy in Russia. Venereal disorders prevail

among

among all the people from St. Petersburg to Tolbosky. I found that they had penetrated as far as to the eastern regions of Siberia. This circumstance is attested by Mr. Gmelin in his journey into Siberia. This traveller asserts, "That the "Neapolitan disease may be said to be common to all the "inhabitants of the district of Argunskoi, men, women, "old, young, and even children. The effects of it cannot "be seen without horror, and without a compassionate re- "flection upon the fatal consequences the disease may be "attended with. The only medicine they take for it, is a "decoction of the bark of the white poplar, or of the larch- "tree with allum. The effect of this medicine being to turn "the virus upon the internal parts, must hasten the death of "many patients, who may perhaps be less wretched than those "who survive. The people are consumed by degrees. Such "as are not already destroyed by this cruel disease, are ren- "dered unfit for labor, and reduced to be starved to death in "a wholesome and fruitful country *."

The same traveller found few houses in the city of Tomsk, where there was not at least one person affected with this distemper. He knew whole families which were seized with it †. It has run through all this district with the greater rapidity, on account of the debauchery which prevails in both sexes, and because there is no effectual remedy in use against it. Most of the children come into the world with this disease. We know that the foetus is nourished by a fluid passing through the substance of the mother's womb; and this fluid being impregnated with the virus, the infection must be communicated to the child, even although he may have been untainted at his first formation. This virus produces many other distempers, unknown in the polished countries throughout the rest of

* Gmelin, tom. i. pag. 256.   † Gmelin, tom. i. pag. 157.

Europe, becauſe there the parents who are ſeized with it, have ſuch eaſy opportunities of relief. The little care the Ruſſians take of their children when ill, increaſes the mortality ſtill farther.

The ſmall-pox, venereal diſeaſes, and the ſcurvy, make ſo much havock in Ruſſia, that unleſs the government takes ſome meaſures to prevent their effects, they will put an end to the human ſpecies in this country.

Children who are really healthy, acquire remarkable ſtrength by the nature of their education. They are not only dipt in cold water, when baptized, even in the winter, but are likewiſe expoſed to the ſevereſt cold on coming out of their baths. The ſtrength acquired in infancy does not laſt long; their conſtitution is ſoon impaired by exceſſes in drinking brandy, and in women. I met with few old men in the courſe of my journey; ſome few I ſaw of ſixty and ſeventy years, and one of eighty, who was an old ſoldier. A ſmall cottage ſituated by the ſide of the road had been given him as a reward for his paſt ſervices. Sometimes the poſtilions ſtop at this hovel to reſt their horſes. As the man lived quite alone and forlorn in the midſt of theſe foreſts, he could not get either at women or brandy.

There are neither phyſicians nor ſurgeons among theſe people; nor is there in general any other remedy beſides their baths, except for an epidemical diſeaſe, which ſometimes prevails in theſe countries, and which I have never heard of in Europe. This diſtemper begins by tumors of the bigneſs of a ſmall apple; it becomes incurable in three days; but is eaſily cured if attended to at firſt. The cure conſiſts in chewing tobacco with ſal ammoniac, ſo as to make a poultice of it, which is applied to the tumor, after it has been punctured to the quick in ſeveral places. It were to be wiſhed that a more circumſtantial account might be given of this diſeaſe and its cure; but as I have not been able to gain any farther information concerning this point, I thought proper to confine myself to what I found in my journal.

The working of the mines is also one of the chief reasons of the depopulation of Ruſſia; more than one hundred thouſand men are employed in this buſineſs *, and it is univerſally known, that the working of mines is one of the cauſes of the deſtruction of the human ſpecies. This labor is not proper for any, except very populous ſtates; and is therefore leſs fit for Ruſſia than any other nation. Beſides, if we except the produce of the iron and copper mines, that of the gold, ſilver and lead mines is ſo trifling, that it ſcarcely pays for the charges of working them. It is true, theſe mines increaſe the coin, which is very ſcarce in Ruſſia; but gold and ſilver are imaginary riches: population, the cultivation of lands, and induſtry, conſtitute the eſſential riches of the ſtate, and of the ſovereign. The power of Spain is grown weaker ſince the expulſion of the Moors, merely becauſe the inhabitants of that kingdom have abondoned agriculture, in order to go and work the golden mines of Peru. The colonies which Spain has ſent into America have almoſt deprived ſome of the Spaniſh provinces of their inhabitants.

The empire of Ruſſia is continually depopulated, ſince the conqueſt of Siberia, by the numbers of inhabitants which are ſent into the deſerts of this vaſt province. Siberia may be more fatal to Ruſſia, than Peru has ever been to Spain. The Ruſſians loſe a great number of ſubjects without any compenſation for the loſs; while the Spaniards receive at leaſt the treaſures of Peru in return.

A friend of mine who has been a long time in Ruſſia, where his thoughts have been much taken up about the ſtate of this

---

* Voltaire, tom. i. pag. 52. & 54.

empire,

empire, has imagined that, in 1760, the number of its inhabitants might be computed at sixteen or seventeen millions. Mr. Voltaire reckons the number in 1747, at twenty millions, and at twenty-four, including the Ukraine, Siberia, and the rest of the conquered provinces *. But this famous writer in the same page makes this population much less considerable, by supposing that the Russian empire is nearly as populous as France. Every body knows that that kingdom does not contain more than twenty millions; and indeed Mr. Voltaire in his first calculation explains himself thus: " In 1747, Russia " contained six millions six hundred and forty thousand males, " who paid the capitation. In this calculation, children and " old men are included †; but women and girls are not; nor " boys born in the interval between the beginning of one " register, and the making up of another. Treble the num- " ber of taxable persons, including women, and girls; and " the result will be near twenty millions." This calculation is exclusive of the inhabitants of such provinces as do not pay the capitation; which Mr. Voltaire reckons about four millions; and is made only by trebling the six millions six hundred and forty thousand males.

In this computation the number of boys born in the interval between one register and another is included, without attending to the number of persons who die; a number, which in Russia is much greater than that of the persons who are born, since it has been already shewn that this country is daily depopulated. It appears therefore, that in order to determine the exact number of inhabitants in 1747, it will be sufficient

---

* Mr. Voltaire gives the state of population in Russia, tom. i. pag. 51, and the following: he has taken it from the calculation made in 1747.

† From this calculation it appears, that all males pay the capitation. There have been fresh regulations since made, by which all persons under ten years of age, are exempted from this tax.

to double the number of taxable perfons: the refult will then be, in even numbers, thirteen millions, and feventeen millions, including the inhabitants of the provinces who do not pay the poll-tax. In this calculation indeed, it is taken for granted, that the number of women and girls is equal to that of men and boys; although many people think the number of women and girls is generally greateft *. It is alfo fuppofed, that in the interval between one regifter and another, the number of births is equal to the number of deaths; whereas, it is evident from all which has been faid, that the number of deaths is much more confiderable. The number therefore of the inhabitants throughout the empire of Ruffia in 1747, may be taken at feventeen millions. The famous writer I have quoted, feems to have made all thefe obfervations. Suppofing the empire of Ruffia to contain nearly as many inhabitants as the kingdom of France, it may readily be concluded from thefe feveral calculations, that the number of inhabitants in Ruffia in 1760, was lefs than feventeen millions, including all the males, women, girls, and all perfons not fubject to the poll-tax in the various provinces. Whatever fuppofition we may admit of, the number of inhabitants could never amount to nineteen millions in 1760, without exaggerating the population.

Peter I. tried all poffible means to increafe the trade of his empire: he made commercial treaties with China, Perfia, and feveral European powers. Tobolfky, the capital of Siberia, was the center of the Chinefe trade; this was carried on by means of the caravans which fet out from Mofco, and were three years going and coming. The difhonefty of the Ruffian and Chinefe merchants made this trade very languid from the firft; and the difputes which have arifen at divers times between the two powers, have entirely put a ftop to it. The

* Some people think the number of men and boys moft confiderable.

laft

last differences have happened in consequence of the revolution which took place in 1757, in the nation of the Calmuck Zongors, after the death of Gaidan Tcheren in 1746. He was Kam of the Tartars inhabiting that part of the north of Siberia situated between Siberia and China, near the origin of the Irtysz. This whole nation has been exterminated by the Chinese. All such as have escaped, have taken refuge on the borders of the Volga, and put themselves under the protection of Russia.

The Russians have always endeavoured to extend their dominions towards the south: in 1761, they tried to make themselves masters of part of the territories, which the Calmuck Zongors had deserted. The Russians were fitting out a small armament for this purpose while I was at Tobolsky, and I learned in France, that the Chinese had obliged them to lay aside their design. The chief intention of the Russians was to seize upon the mountains, where they expected to find some mines of gold.

The Russian trade carried on with Persia, has been equally unsuccessful. The English had established a company, in order to carry on this trade by means of the Caspian sea: but the Russians took umbrage at it; and required that the sailors should be Russians, and that the ships should be built by the natives of the country. This trade was quite destroyed by the disturbances which happened in Persia. A few Armenians and Tartars of Bucharia, still continue however to bring into Russia some lapis lazuli, raw silk, and some wrought silks; and carry back with them furrs and leather. But this traffic is very much confined, as well as the Turkish trade, which is entirely in the hands of the Cossacks of the Ukraine. They sail down the river Don in boats as far as the city of Azoph, where they exchange furrs and the caviar, for coffee and Turkish stuffs.

Most of the canals projected for the facility of commerce, remain unfinished: the rest have not proved so useful as was expected: the only canals which deserve to be mentioned, are, that of Ladoga, and that of Wysnei-Woloczok. One may travel by means of these from St. Petersburg to the Caspain sea; but with this inconvenience, that the vessels are two years going and coming, because they sail against the current; these canals therefore are seldom used for this purpose.

The canal of Wysnei-Woloczok joins the Volga, with the river Mota, which empties itself into the lake Ilmen, from whence the river Wolchow rises, which communicates with St. Petersburg by the canal of Ladoga. This last canal is of the greatest consequence to the city of St. Petersburg, in bringing up the provisions necessary for the subsistence of the inhabitants. The bottom of the lake Ladoga, or Oz-ladoskoe, being composed of a very loose sand, there are such banks formed of it by storms, that the lake is not navigable.

It appears from all we have said, that the land-trade in Russia is very inconsiderable. The vast extent of land and the deserts which must be crossed, make this trade even almost impracticable. All these facts are known to intelligent men, who have been at St. Petersburg, and at Mosco. M. Voltaire gives us the same idea of this trade [*], and I have been confirmed in it, by penetrating into the inland parts of the Empire. Former travellers have been mistaken upon this point, because in their time it was a new object, with which the whole nation was much taken up, and from which great advantages were then expected.

On the contrary, the sea-trade which Russia carries on with Europe is extremely beneficial to the nation, because the exportation is always more considerable than the importation.

* Tom. ii. pag. 211.

In 1749, the exportation of the different articles sent out from the ports of Ruffia, was valued at three millions of roubles: and the importation at two million nine hundred thoufand roubles: The number of fhips which came up to St. Peterfburg, the chief port of Ruffia, was two hundred and fixty, in the year 1744; two hundred in 1745; two hundred and fifty-two in 1750; and two hundred and ninety in 1751; fo that we may reckon the number of veffels coming in to St. Peterfburg annually, two hundred and fifty.

The Ruffians * trade with the Swedes, the Danes, the inhabitants of Lubeck and Hamburg; with the Englifh, the Dutch, and the French. More than half this trade is carried on by the Englifh. Among the other nations, the Dutch fend the greateft number of fhips into Ruffia. There are few French veffels to be feen in the Ruffian ports. The French carry on this trade, only through the channel of other nations, by which means both parties lofe the advantages of a direct commerce.

* *Mercantile articles exported from Ruffia.*

Sables	Rhubarb
Foxes, black and white, &c.	Pitch
Ermins	Linfeed oil
Caft lambs	Ifinglafs
Tygers	Caviar
Black and white bears	Salt fifh
Wolves	Rofin
Common martens	Flax
Wild cats	Hemp
White hares	Thread
Beavers	Wool
Lynxes	Matting
Leather	Canvafs for fails
Greafe	Mafts
Honey	Iron
Pot-afh and woad-afh	Copper.

The

The Russians are not expert traders: the merchants are too dependent upon the sovereign, and upon persons in office. They have neither capital nor credit enough to deal largely. The principal merchants of Russia are no better than agents to foreign merchants. Besides, the sovereigns in Russia carry on several branches of trade on their own accounts. They have reserved the monopolies to themselves, which they distribute among the nobles. The mention of these facts is sufficient to point out the inconveniences of such an administration, and to shew that the Russians might carry on a more profitable trade.

The revenues of Russia are considerably increased since Peter I. Although these revenues vary according to the circumstances of the times, we may still form a pretty exact idea of them from the following account*, which I have taken from the state of the finances communicated to me by one of my friends.

Each taxable person pays into the royal treasury seventy copecs for the poll-tax, and all the peasants belonging to the Empress pay forty copecs more. In 1747, Mr. de Voltaire computed the number of males paying the poll-tax, at six millions six hundred and forty thousand †. Supposing an equal number of inhabitants at present in Russia, the produce

---

* *Goods exported from France into Russia.*

The French send into Russia, gold, silver, and silk stuffs, flax, cotton, and varieties of woollen drapery and stuffs, for men and women, stockings, boots, shoes, hats, feathers, bags and buttons; all sorts of hard ware and toys, gloves, watches, pins, spectacles, combs, belts, handkerchiefs, and many things of the same kind: wine, brandy, vinegar, oil; all sorts of spices; china, cheese, herrings, anchovies, sugar, cards, paper, glasses, looking-glasses, pipes for smoking, wax tapers, tobacco, &c.

† Voltaire, tom. i. pag. 55.

of the poll-tax may eafily be calculated. From the ftate of the finances which I have had in my own poffeffion, I have taken a copy of the reft of the revenues of Ruffia mentioned in the note *, and I find that the whole revenue of the empire, in even numbers, amounts to thirteen million four hundred thoufand roubles, or about fourteen hundred thoufand roubles more than in the year 1725.

Before the time of Peter I. the Ruffians had nothing but barges, or fuch kind of fmall fhipping, which they ufed on the rivers Volga and Don. At prefent the Ruffians have docks at Archangel, at Cronftat, at St. Peterfburg, at Revel, and many fhip-

* Revenues of the Ruffian empire.	Roubles.
Poll-tax, 6,640,000 males, at 70 copecs	4,648,000
The demeans of the fovereign, for 360,000 peafants at 40 copecs over and above the poll-tax	144,000
Annual produce of the public houfes, from the fale of beer and brandy	2,000,000
Sea and land tolls, and the excife of St. Peterfburg, Archangel, Wiburg, Narva, Revel, and Riga	3,150,000
Iron and copper *	240,000
Pot-afh and woad-afh	70,000
Rhubarb	30,000
Tar, and oil of fifh	180,000
The falterns	1,400,000
Stampt paper and the ftamp	200,000
The baths pay a tax which produces	14,000
The trade of canvafs for fhips †	110,000
The revenue of the coin	250,000
The revenue of the port	330,000
The trade of tobacco	76,000
The duties on the corn trade	160,000
Conquefts in Sweden	100,000
Conquefts in Perfia	300,000
Total	13,402,000

* This is the produce of the mines of the fovereign's demeans.
† This traffic has been granted exclufively to one private man, who pays this revenue out of it to the crown.

shipwrights of the nation are kept in employment. It appears from the state of the naval forces in 1756, compared to that which

This state of the Russian revenue may be liable to some objections, because it must necessarily receive different alterations, according to the changes of times and circumstances; but if the revenue is lessened in some particulars, it is increased in others; and according to the present state of the kingdom, the general result will always be nearly the same. I thought it best to give the account of the Russian revenue, as I found it in the abstract which was given me, without making any alteration, except with regard to the number of males paying the poll-tax, for they were confounded with the women. It appears therefore, that in 1767, the revenue of Russia in money might be settled at thirteen million four hundred thousand roubles in even numbers. M. de Voltaire found by a state of the finances of the empire in 1725, that, including the tributes paid by the Tartars, all the taxes and duties in money, the sum total of the revenues amounted to thirteen millions of roubles, exclusive of the taxes in kind *.

Since the year 1725 however, the customs have been considerably increased by the care that has been taken to prevent smuggling. I have reckoned the number of peasants belonging to the crown, and which pay forty copecs more than the ordinary poll-tax, at 360,000, whereas Mr. Voltaire makes them much more considerable in 1725. I have not included in this state, the revenue arising from the furrs which are brought from Siberia, any more than that of the drugs; but to make up for this, I have reckoned the number of males paying the capitation, at six millions six hundred and forty thousand, as Mr. Voltaire calculated them in 1725, when it has been shewn, under the article of population, that this number must at present be very considerably less. It is likewise evident, that for this reason it was proposed to make a new regulation, in order to increase the poll-tax forty copecs per head; but this regulation has never been carried into execution; and indeed, the Russians are not always able to pay the common taxes, as they are now rated. The arrears from 1724 to 1747 amounted to two million five hundred and four thousand roubles, which the Empress Elizabeth gave up to her subjects.

I have included in the above account, the revenue arising from the sale of the pot-ash and the woad-ash; but I have been assured in Russia, that this traffic existed no more, or at least that it was considerably lessened, on account of its being hurtful to the empire, by destroying the forests which stood the nearest at hand for felling; a fact, of which every one must be convinced.

The number of peasants belonging to the crown, lessens, not only because of the depopulation, but also because it is a custom among the sovereigns of Russia, to reward their subjects by giving them a certain number of peasants. This fact is universally known. The furrs of Siberie do not produce so large a revenue in money as it

* M. de Voltaire, tom. i. pag. 59.

which was given by Mr. Strahlenberg in 1720*, that the navy of Ruſſia has been conſiderably leſſened ſince that time.
Some

* The author wrote in 1730. Tom. ii. pag. 115. and 123.

has been thought. Theſe furrs are conveyed from the diſtance of fourteen hundred or even two thouſand leagues, into the magazines of Moſco and St. Peterſburg; in this courſe they paſs through ſuch a variety of hands, that the fineſt of them are ſcarce ever brought to theſe magazines. Beſides, the countries from whence theſe ſkins come, being daily more and more frequented by merchants who are ſettled in Siberia to carry on this trade, and by the number of military perſons who are ſent there; it is plain, that theſe people will rather ſell their fine furrs, than give them up to thoſe who are commiſſioned to raiſe this kind of tax. The private people in Ruſſia get the beſt part of their furrs by the help of the merchants, or by ſome of their friends in the army; and I know that many of the furrs belonging to the crown, grow rotten in the magazines in Siberia and at Moſco, for want of ſale.

In the account of the revenues of Ruſſia I have taken no notice of the profits ariſing from the ſale of drugs, becauſe I did not find it in my notes. The crown has reſerved to itſelf the profit of all the eſtabliſhments for apothecaries formed throughout theſe dominions, as well as the diſtribution of the medicines; the crown appoints all the perſons employed in this buſineſs; ſupplies all the drugs, and in ſhort furniſhes all the expences, and alſo receives all the profit. Although the expences of the crown are very conſiderable on this account, it is certain that when all charges are paid, the crown gains at leaſt the ſtoppages made on the troops for their medicines, and I have been aſſured that the profits were ſtill greater; but the apothecaries, having all fixed ſalaries, are not ſufficiently intereſted, to endeavor to increaſe pharmaceutical knowledge, becauſe they are never employed on their own accounts. It is alſo evident, from the preceding ſtate of the revenue, that the ſovereign has monopolized ſeveral branches of trade, whereas it is the buſineſs of the monarch only to protect commerce and make it flouriſh. Theſe abuſes are directly contrary to a good adminiſtration, and they ſubſiſt only becauſe it is impoſſible to alter every thing at once.

I have reckoned in this eſtimate, the revenue of the conqueſts on Sweden at one hundred thouſand roubles only whereas thoſe provinces brought a conſiderable revenue to Sweden; but they are now no longer ſubject to the poll-tax, and this moderate revenue is the produce of the imperial demeans of Ruſſia: theſe revenues are much diminiſhed by the grants that have been given of theſe lands to ſeveral individuals.

The circumſtantial account I have given of the revenue of Ruſſia, gives us an idea of the real riches of this kingdom, and its reſources, by ſhewing the nature of their taxes. The obſervations I have made upon this revenue, ſeem to prove that they may be ſettled at thirteen million four hundred thouſand roubles in money, I have known ſeveral perſons very well acquainted with Ruſſia, ſome of which

Some ships, however, are still built every year in the several ports of Russia; but the number of these must be proportionally diminished, for reasons which will be seen hereafter. The ships of war are stationed at Revel and Cronstat, and the small vessels at St. Petersburg; but these are not good harbors. The harbor of Cronstat is exposed to three great inconveniences, according to M. de Strahlenberg *. " The sea is not wide enough
" before the port, nor very safe, on account of the number
" of rocks and hidden sand-banks surrounding the harbor, so
" that ships cannot come out of it but when the wind is in
" certain quarters. Secondly, the ice remains too long there,
" and the sea is not forced from it till near the end of May.
" Thirdly, the ships rot very fast in these ports, because they
" lie always in fresh water: (I have been assured, that they
" did not last longer than ten years.) The port of Revel is
" too much exposed to storms, so that ships do not ride in
" safety there, as three of the largest vessels perished in one
" day even in the very port."

In the time of Peter I. many ships were built of deal; at present the principal parts of them are made of oak, and

* Strahlenberg, tom. ii. p. 127. These facts are confirmed by all persons who have been at St. Petersburg.

valued the revenue of the state at fifteen million of roubles, and others at thirteen or less; but the latter took into their account the deficiencies.

The coin is very scarce in Russia, not only for want of the first materials, but also because the number of roubles decreases annually. As this circumstance seemed to deserve the attention, the government endeavoured to discover the cause of it. It was found that the peasants and trading people who went into the towns, carried back with them in specie the profits arising from the sale of their provisions and goods, that they buried their fortune under ground, in order to conceal it from those on whom they were dependent, and that most of them dying without revealing the secret, this money was thus lost to the state. The endeavors which have been made to obviate this inconvenience have proved fruitless; for it will subsist as long as the people remain enslaved.

most

moſt of the veſſels are entirely built of this wood, which is found about the confines of Cazan *. This town is more than four hundred leagues diſtant from St. Peterſburg, taking the courſe of the rivers upon which the wood is conveyed. In this voyage it is neceſſary to aſcend the Volga for an extent of two hundred and ſixty leagues, which makes the conveyance of the materials for ſhip-building, extremely difficult. For this reaſon ſome deal is ſtill made uſe of; and it is well known that this wood is fit only for maſts, and that it is extremely bad for every other part of the ſhip. It ought to be leſs uſed in Ruſſia than any where elſe, becauſe there is freſh water in the chief ports of this empire, ſo that the veſſels rot very faſt.

From the account which has been given me of the maritime force of Ruſſia †, I find that in 1756, they conſiſted of twenty-two

---

* I have been aſſured that there was ſome oak brought alſo from Archangel, but in ſmall quantities.

† State of the ſhips of war which compoſed the naval powers in Ruſſia in 1756.

Ships of the line in the harbor of Cronſtat.	Year in which they were built.	Number of guns they carry.
Elizabeth, for repair		110
Zachariah Elizabeth	1747	99
Saint John Chryſoſtom	1751	99
Saint Nicholas	1754	80
Name unknown	1755	80
Leſnoy, in bad condition	1743	66
Sergius, in bad condition	1747	66
Raphael Archangel, in bad condition	1745	66
Uriel, in bad condition	1749	66
Gabriel, in bad condition	1749	66
Ingermania	1752	66
Name unknown	1754	66
Name unknown	1754	66
Pantlemont, in bad condition	1740	54
Name unknown	1756	66
Name unknown	1756	66

two ships of the line, six frigates, two bomb-ketches, two packet-boats, two fire-ships, and ninety-nine galleys.

According

At the port of Revel.	Year in which they were built.	Number of guns they carry.
Saint Alexander Newfschi, in bad condition	1749	66
Moschwa	1750	66
Saint John Chrysostom, the second, in bad condition	1749	66
The Northern Eagle, very bad	1735	66
Schlusselburg	1751	54
Verakil	1752	54
Total of first rate ships	22	
Frigates in the port of Cronstat.		
Jegudice	1746	32
Sealfil	1746	32
Name unknown	1754	32
Name unknown	1754	32
At the port of Revel.		
Michael Archangel	1748	32
Kreysel	1751	32
Bomb-ketches.		
The Thunder	1752	10
Jupiter	1752	10
Packet-boats.		
The Elephant	1752	36
Name unknown	1754	36
Fire-ships.		
Mitau	1747	
Holland	1747	

Galleys.

According to M. Strahlenberg, there were on the Baltic in 1730, thirty-six ships of the line, twelve frigates, nine small frigates, and two hundred and forty galleys.

When the ships companies and the galleys are complete, the number of officers, soldiers and sailors, amounts to twenty thousand two hundred and thirty-nine, and the persons employed in the admiralty, with the workmen in the several ports, to nine thousand eight hundred and seventy-nine; but the number of soldiers and sailors is by no means complete.

The officers are but little acquainted with the theory of navigation, and still less with the practice; because they seldom go to sea. The ships surrounded with ice, and lying in fresh water, perish in the ports. A great number of ships have been condemned, before one sail has been hoisted upon them, and many officers have gone through their several ranks, without having ever been once on board a ship. Besides, the Russians are too much afraid of the sea, ever to become good seamen; they have none who deserve to be called sailors; and the empire of Russia will never have any, till she carries on trade by her own self.

The land forces of Russia are divided into troops of the field, and troops of government. These two bodies are entirely different, the last forms a kind of militia, which is distributed on the borders of Tartary, and in the several provinces of this vast empire; the great extent of which requires a large body.

Galleys.

Galleys of 22 rows	32
Galleys of 20 rows	22
Galleys of 16 rows	45

Each galley carries six small iron guns, and on the forepart, two four and twenty pounders.

There are two oars in each row, and five soldiers to each oar. The galley is commanded by one officer, who has a pilot, and twelve sailors under him.

of troops, to keep the people in order, and protect Ruffia from the incurfions of the Tartars. Thefe troops are kept for thefe purpofes only; they are never brought into the field, and are not fit to act againft regular troops, being ill fubfifted, and ftill worfe difciplined. They are difpofed in a garrifon in the provinces fituated in Europe, or in the neighbourhood, and towards the borders of Tartary, that they may be readily brought together, in order to affift the different parts of the ftate, or to attack the powers at war with Ruffia.

I find by the account of the troops of this empire, that the eftablifhed army amounts to three hundred and thirty-one thoufand five hundred men. It muft vary a little now and then, as it appears from the feveral ftates of the army I have feen. In 1750, the regiments of infantry confifted of two thoufand two hundred and ninety-eight men; and the regiments of cavalry, and of the provinces, were lefs numerous than thofe of which I have given an account. The regiment of body-guards is no longer exifting, having been broken by Peter III. Upon the whole, thefe trifling alterations have no effect upon the general refult, which is always nearly the fame. Therefore I compute the eftablifhed army in Ruffia in even numbers at 330,000 men *.

In

---

* *Military ftate of the troops in Ruffia, fuppofing the regiments complete.*

Houfhold of the Emprefs.

Body-guards, or Leibz company	300
Life-guards, cuiraffiers	846
Horfe-guards	1223
Foot-guards { Regiments of Preobragenfki	3245
———— of Semenowfki	2436
———— of Ifmaelowfki	2436
The grand duke's regiment	846
Six regiments of infantry of eight hundred and forty-fix men	5076
Total	16408

In this number are included all the mechanics employed in the regiments, farriers, lockſmiths, carpenters, &c. the batmen, the ſervants of the artillery, and the ſervants of all the officers in the army; which ſervants are called Denſchik. There is a great number

This body of troops being entirely deſigned for the ſovereign's guard, never takes the field. Theſe ſeveral regiments are always in garriſon near the monarch's reſidence, to be entirely at his diſpoſal on all occaſions.

Ruſſian field infantry.

The Ruſſian infantry conſiſts of forty-ſix regiments*. Each regiment contains three battalions, and each battalion twelve companies of fuſiliers, and two of grenadiers. The number of grenadiers and fuſiliers is 2128; and the whole regiment including officers, &c. conſiſts of 2637 men †. But all the regiments are not ſo numerous: reckoning them at 2637 men, the forty-ſix regiments when complete will amount to 121,302.

Each regiment has four three-pounders along with it; and four ſmall mortars charged with grenades.

The Ruſſian cavalry conſiſts in a few regiments of horſe grenadiers, ſome cuiraſſiers, dragoons and huſſars.

Ruſſian field cavalry.

Four regiments of horſe-grenadiers, of 2489 men	9956
Four regiments of cuiraſſiers, of 1350 men	5400
Twenty-ſix regiments of dragoons, of 1350 men	35100
Six regiments of huſſars, one with another	12860
Total	63316

Fortification and artillery.

Fortification	750
Miners	210
Artillery and bombardiers	10000
Total	10960

* According to the different returns I have ſeen, the infantry has ſometimes conſiſted of 52 regiments; but it appears to me that ſome of thoſe regiments have been incorporated with others, belonging to the ſovereign's guard, which was formerly leſs numerous.
† The liſt of theſe will be given in the account of the expences of each regiment.

number of thefe: they are made foldiers after they have ferved a certain time. All the foldiers employed to guard the prifoners and criminals are likewife included; but I have not reckoned the irregular troops: thefe are composed of Coffacks, Zaporovians, Calmucks, Walacks; which are of ufe only in war time. They have no pay, but live upon their own plunder.

Ruffian infantry of government, which never takes the field; a kind of militia.

Twenty regiments of 1344 men, in the countries conquered from Sweden	26880
Thirty-two regiments diftributed in the feveral parts of Ruffia, Siberia, &c. They all, except four, confift of 1328 men, three of the four are of 664 men, and one of 1992	41168
Twenty regiments of 1077 men, diftributed in the Ukraine	21540
One regiment on the lines of the Ukraine	1248
Total	90836

Dragoons.

Four regiments of 1056 men	4224
Three regiments of 1220 men	3660
One fquadron at Mofco, of	546
Total of the cavalry of militia	8430

Recapitulation.

Houfhold of the Emprefs	16408
Field infantry	121302
Field cavalry	63316
Fortification, miners, artillery, bombardiers	10960
Infantry which never takes the field	90836
Cavalry of militia	8430
Total	311252
We have feen before, that the navy, reckoned complete, including officers and failors, amounts to	20239
Total of land and fea forces	331491

Thefe

These troops are not formidable of themselves, being generally ill mounted, and having no kind of discipline; but they are very terrible on account of the robberies they commit: they plunder and ravage all the countries through which they pass, and practise the most shocking cruelties. They are of but little use to the Russians in defending their camps, and are often very fatal to their army, by the consumption of provisions and forage. They have always a number of horses with them to carry off the booty. In the states I have seen of the army of Russia, this body of troops amounts to thirty or forty thousand men, sometimes more; if these are added to the military establishment, the number of troops in Russia will amount to about three hundred and sixty thousand men.

It appeared to me at first incredible, that there should be such a number of troops in a kingdom so much depopulated, and whose revenues are so moderate. I have had the military returns in my own possession, with the names, and account of the regiments. From these it is evident, that the army amounts to 330,000 in even numbers, exclusive of the irregulars. Mr. de Voltaire finds it nearly the same in 1725 *. But how the Russians can contrive to maintain such a considerable body of troops; whether it is necessary to the sovereign of this empire; or whether he should not rather lessen the military establishment, considering how much the empire is depopulated; and if the sovereign is obliged to maintain such a body of troops in time of peace, whether this can be admitted as a real proof of his power; are objects, the examination of which appeared to me so interesting to mankind, to Europe, and perhaps to Russia itself, that I took a great deal of pains to gain some insight into them.

* Mr. Voltaire reckons the number of sea and land forces, at 339,500 in the year 1725. tom. i. pag. 59.

In order to proceed with regularity, it is neceſſary to conſider the empire of Ruſſia in the ſeveral relations it bears to Europe, and to its Aſiatic neighbours; and we muſt alſo pay ſome attention to the extent of this realm. The political ſtate of Ruſſia with reſpect to Europe is well known. Several authors have written upon the connection this empire has with the neighbouring Tartars; but whether the political ſtate of theſe ſeveral powers has undergone any alteration or not, it is abſolutely neceſſary to ſpeak of it here. Beſides, that by this means, the authenticity of the facts related by preceding travellers will receive farther confirmation.

As we get farther diſtant from St. Peterſburg coming near to Kamtſchatka, the people are under leſs ſubjection, not only on account of the difficulty of ſending troops and proviſions towards the eaſtern part of this empire, but alſo becauſe the troops which are ſent, being not within reach of the ſovereign, the army, the governors, and all perſons in office, abuſe the authority they are inveſted with. Theſe people are always ripe for a revolt; an inconvenience inſeparable from all dominions of a vaſt extent. There are even in Siberia ſome people whom the Ruſſians have never been able to ſubdue ſince the conqueſt of that province. Among theſe are the Tchouktchi. The Joukagirs their neighbours, and the Koriachs are kept in tolerable ſubjection. All theſe people inhabit the extremity of the north eaſt of Siberia. Altho' they can be of little advantage to Ruſſia, yet that power is conſtantly at war with ſome of them in order to bring them into ſubjection. The Tchoutkchi are the moſt ſtubborn and cruel enemies the Ruſſians have. They have always preſerved their liberty, tho' the Ruſſians have the ſuperior advantages of fire-arms, and diſciplined troops to act againſt them. As the Ruſſians however were continually ſending freſh troops, they would have deſtroyed or ſubdued them in proceſs of time, if their neighbors the Joukagirs, had not
warned

warned them that such an event would certainly take place, if they still continued to use nothing but arrows against the fire-arms of the Russians. They advised them therefore to fall upon the Russian artillery as soon as they should meet with it, and to make themselves masters of it; assuring them they might easily compass this point, as the artillery was never very numerous. The affair turned out as the Joukagirs had foretold. Some years before I came to Tobolsky, a body of Russians marched against the Tchouktchi: the Russian general sent a small detachment forwards with some artillery: these troops were attacked and slain when they little expected it; a few soldiers only escaping to carry the news to the Russian general; who advanced immediately against these people, was beaten, and obliged to sue for peace. It was agreed by both parties, that the chiefs and some of the troops should meet together unarmed in a hamlet near the two armies. The Tchouktchi adhered strictly to the terms of convention; the Russians came to the appointed place to all appearance without arms; but they had concealed under their clothes a kind of cutlass, which the Russian peasants always carry about with them. The Russians agreed to every proposal the Tchouktchi made, and inticed them to drink such a quantity of brandy, that they were soon drunk; so that the greater part of them were killed while they were asleep. The Russians immediately marched and attacked the army of the Tchouktchi, which escaped into the mountains, their prince and the principal chiefs having been slain in the massacre the Russians had made of the troops of this nation. I was informed of this affair by a young prince, nephew of the chief of the Tchouktchi; and the truth of it was confirmed by the Russians who were my interpreters. The Russians had brought him prisoner to Tobolsky, where he had lived unfortunate, although not confined: he was maintained by the governor. This unhappy

prince

prince, anxious for the recovery of his liberty, had defired me to take him away along with me, as my fervant, and fent me a petition for that purpofe, which he had caufed to be writ in Latin, that I might underftand it. The Ruffians were ftill engaged in carrying on a war againft thefe unfortunate people in the year 1761, inftead of leaving them at peace among their frozen mountains.

Moft of the other people, as the Kamtfchadales, the Jakouti, the Tungoufes, although fubdued, are ftill always upon their guard againft the Ruffians: the Ruffians having fent fome engineers to turn the courfe of the river Amour, and examine whether a navigation might not be eftablifhed upon it; the people who dwell on the borders of this river, obliged them to lay afide their defign.

Many of the Tartar hords inhabit the countries fituated to the fouth of Ruffia: they oblige the Ruffians to keep a confiderable body of troops conftantly upon thefe borders, from the lake Baikal, as far as the confines of Poland. The Ruffians have even conftructed in moft of thefe places, lines of circumvallation, and forts at fmall diftances from each other. Thefe precautions are neceffary to defend the empire from the incurfions of the Tartars, and to maintain fuch as have been already conquered by the Ruffians, in proper fubjection. Moft of thefe Tartars wander from place to place, and live on plunder. They have ever been troublefome to the Ruffians in this part of the empire. Notwithftanding the lines and forts, they penetrate readily into Ruffia, when they advance in large bodies: they then plunder the villages, while the troops neareft at hand are collecting together, and go off with the fpoil as foon as thefe troops appear; fo that the deferts of the fouthern part of Ruffia, and chiefly of Siberia, are the moft powerful obftacles the Ruffians can oppofe to thefe people: thefe regions being uninhabited, there are no villages for the Tartars to plunder;

moft

most of them not daring to advance into the inward parts of the country, because of the number of troops the Russians always keep upon these borders; while the Russians endeavor always to live in peace with the rest of the Tartars.

The Russians however, have great advantages over the Tartars, who for the most part have nothing but arrows to act with against the fire-arms of the Russians. There are some nations among these wanderers who are not even acquainted with the use of fire-arms; but all the Tartars are warlike and brave. An event, which I have learnt since my return to Paris from the chevalier de St. Pierre, proves that some of them are totally unacquainted with fire-arms; and at the same time shews what kind of men the Russians have in their neighbourhood. A strong detachment of these Tartars advanced some years ago, to the frontiers of Siberia; the commandant of one of the Russian forts having espied them, and not knowing what was the intention of this body of Tartars, sent to let them know he would fire upon them, if they did not retire. The Tartars having assembled, held a council together, and sent afterwards to desire the commandant would fire upon them, which was done immediately. Several of them having been killed by one cannonade, they went a little farther off, held another council, and sent to desire the commandant would fire again: they retreated a little farther, and did not quit the ground till after the third cannonade. This fact shews, that if these people were instructed in the art of war, they would become formidable to the Russians.

The revolution which has taken place among the Calmuck Zongors [*], will give us still a farther idea of these people. This nation was become so powerful under the reign of Kal-

---

[*] According to some authors, Calmuczs Zungors, Kalmuks, or Calmucs Dsongars.

dan-Tcherin their Kam, that the Chinese and the Russians were both afraid of this prince. He died in 1746; and a civil war arose immediately after between his successors, which caused the ruin of this nation. The Chinese weakened it at first, by espousing alternately the cause of each of the pretenders to the crown; and after a ten years war in 1757, they crushed the new Kam, and destroyed his subjects; the unfortunate remains of which, to the number of twenty thousand families, made their retreat on the Wolga, and put themselves under the protection of Russia.

Several other branches of the Calmucks still inhabit this part of Asia. They have preserved the courage and bravery they had in the time of Gengis-kan, and his successors. It was with these same people, that these princes made so many conquests, and gave laws to all Asia. The Mongals situated between China and Siberia are descendents from these same Tartars, and are equally brave. Most of them are dependents of the Chinese empire, and are well trained to war. The Chinese are at war with these warlike people; and indeed their last Kam having retreated into Siberia, where he died, the emperor of China demanded him with so much warmth, that the Russians, after making many difficulties, were obliged to have the dead prince conveyed upon the frontiers of China: the Chinese took this method to be assured of the death of this Kam, whom they still feared.

The Russians inhabiting towards the south of Siberia, though subdued, are however most disposed to revolt. I have been able to ascertain this from my own observation, having pursued this route on my return from Tobolsky to St. Petersburg.

It is evident from this account of the interior parts of Russia, that the sovereign is always obliged to maintain a large body of troops to keep the subjects in awe, and to defend the country

country from the inroads of the Tartars: it is this body which is called the army of government, and which amounts to about one hundred thousand men: these troops are put to no other use; they never are engaged in war any where else, not only because it would be too dangerous to leave these provinces and the confines without defence, but also because these troops being scattered abroad throughout this empire, of near two thousand leagues in length, and about five hundred in breadth, it is not possible to put them all in motion, and collect them. On some occasions, they would come to the appointed place when the war was finished, for the roads are impassable in summer-time; bridges are not always to be met with, even on the road from St. Petersburg to Tobolsky, which is much frequented; so that, indeed, there is no travelling except in winter, in a sledge, and although my attendants were no more than three when I travelled through this country, yet I could not always find in the villages a sufficient number of horses to go on with. It is on account of these local difficulties, and the extent of this empire, that the Russians are not able to make any other use of the troops of government. They are neither trained up to war nor disciplined, and are therefore not held in much estimation by the people of the country. They are very ill subsisted, their pay not being more than about half of what the field troops receive. The soldiers have not quite one half-penny English *per* day; but they receive every month, as well as the field troops, two bushels of flower, and one bushel of oatmeal *per* man. This body of troops, consisting of near one hundred thousand men, does not stand the kingdom of Russia in more than one million one hundred and sixty thousand roubles; because the people are obliged to furthem with provisions for subsistence in kind. This tax, exclusive of the poll-tax and other customs, enables Russia to keep up a large body of troops, as the people furnish the same provisions to the field troops, from the commiffary's clerk, to the Denfchik or officer's fervant. The field troops are also stationed in garrifon in the most fertile provinces. By this management, the establishment of the fea and land forces, though confifting of three hundred and thirty thousand men, does not coft more than about fix million four hundred thousand roubles *.

According to the abstracts I have feen, the expences of the court in money, do not exceed two millions of roubles, including the fubfiftence of the corps of cadets, the academies and ministers in foreign courts; fo that these several expences,

and

---

* In order to determine the expence of the troops, I have extracted from the returns of the pay of the army, that of one regiment. It will be feen by the following detail, that the documents I have made ufe of, are fufficiently precife to juftify the inferences I have drawn from them.

Account of the annual charges of a complete regiment of thirty battalions, confifting of twelve companies of fufiliers, and two of grenadiers. The allowances for forage, which are always paid in money, are included in this account.

Ranks.	Numbers.	Appointments of each officer and foldier including the floppages for medicines.		Annual expence.		Rations of forage per month.	Rations of forage for fix months in the year.	In money at 90 copecs per ration.		Number of officers fervants.	Appointments and forage in money for the whole year.	
		Roub.	Cop.	Roub.	Cop.			Roub.	Cop.		Roub.	Cop.
Principal ftaff												
Colonel	1	585	0	585	0	17	102	91	80	6	676	80
Lieutenant colonel	1	351	0	351	0	11	66	59	40	4	410	40
Major	1	286	20	286	20	11	66	59	40	4	345	40
Second major	2	175	50	351	0	16	96	85	50	4	437	40
Each of thefe officers has a company.												

Ranks.

and those of the army do not amount to more than about 8,400,000 roubles; and as I have computed the revenue of Russia,

Ranks.	Numbers.	Appointments of each officer and soldier, including the stoppages for medicines.	Annual expence.	Rations of forage per month.	Rations of forage for six months in the year.	In money at 90 copecs per ration.	Number of officers servants.	Appointments and forage in money for the whole year.
		R. C.	R. C.			R. C.		R. C.
Lesser staff								
Quarter-master	1	117 0	117 0	4	24	21 60	1	138 60
Adjutants	2	117 0	234 0	8	48	43 20	2	277 20
Baggage-master	1	58 50	58 50	2	12	10 80	1	69 30
Pay-master	1	81 90	81 90	3	18	16 20	1	98 10
Commissary	1	81 90	81 90	4	24	21 60	1	103 50
Chaplain	1	64 35	64 35	3	18	16 20	0	80 55
Surgeon	1	175 50	175 50	3	18	16 20	0	191 70
Chief clerk	1	49 0	49 0	2	12	10 80	0	59 80
Surgeon's mates	2	117 0	234 0	0	0	0 0	0	234 0
Drum-major	1	6 57	6 57	0	0	0 0	0	6 57
Provost	1	7 57	7 57	0	0	0 0	0	7 57
Commissary's clerk	1	24 49	24 49	1	6	5 40	0	29 89
Clerk of the provisions	1	24 49	24 49	1	6	5 40	0	29 89
Chapel-master	1	42 1	42 1	0	0	0 0	0	42 1
Musicians and singers	6	6 57	39 42	0	0	0 0	0	39 42
Under provost	2	6 57	13 14	0	0	0 0	0	13 14
Captains	12	175 50	2106 0	5	360	324 0	0	2430 0
Lieutenants	16	117 0	1872 0	4	384	345 60	16	2217 60
Sub-lieutenants	30	81 90	2457 0	3	540	486 0	30	2943 0
Ensigns	12	81 90	982 80	3	216	194 40	12	1177 20
Serjeants	32	9 81	313 92	0	0	0 0	0	313 92
Masters at arms	16	9 48	151 68	0	0	0 0	0	151 68
Standard bearers	6	9 10	54 63	0	0	0 0	0	54 63
Camp-color men	14	9 10	127 47	0	0	0 0	0	127 47
Corporals	64	7 57	484 80	0	0	0 0	0	484 80
Clerk of each company	14	7 57	106 5	0	0	0 0	0	106 5
Barbers	14	6 57	91 98	0	0	0 0	0	91 98
Drums	40	4 7	162 80	0	0	0 0	0	162 80
Fifes	4	6 57	26 28	0	0	0 0	0	26 28
Grenadiers and fusiliers	2128	6 57	13580 96	0	0	0 0	0	13580 96
Foreign smith	1	59 10	59 10	0	0	0 0	0	59 10
Smiths	2	6 57	13 14	0	0	0 0	0	13 14
Foreign farrier	1	59 10	59 10	0	0	0 0	0	59 10
Farriers	5	6 57	32 85	0	0	0 0	0	32 85
Carpenters	14	6 57	91 98	0	0	0 0	0	91 98
Bat-men	71	7 2	458 42	0	0	0 0	0	498 42
Officers servants or Denschik	106	6 30	667 80	0	0	0 0	0	667 80
Servants of artillery	6	7 2	42 12	0	0	0 0	0	42 12
Total	2637	3069 18	27209 92	101	2016	1814 40	106	19024 32

In this account the stoppages for medicines and for hospitals is not included; the sovereign is at no expence for medicines.

Russia, at thirteen millions four hundred thousand roubles, there remain about five millions of roubles, for the other expences,

From the above abstract it appears, that the soldier has not more than about one pound, seven shillings, and four pence English *per annum*, or not quite one penny *per* day; but there are besides two bushels of flower, and one bushel of oatmeal given to him every month, as well as to each non-commissioned officer, from the commissary's clerk to the Denschik; but the sovereign has nothing to do with this expence: these provisions are furnished in kind by the subject, chiefly by such as are exempt from the poll-tax; and it is for this reason, that the troops are distributed throughout the most fruitful provinces, and throughout those which do not pay the poll-tax. The sovereign pays moreover for the soldier's coat, and for all that is necessary to complete him from head to foot. This expence amounts to about 12 roubles. The sum is drawn from the yearly stoppages on the soldier's pay, which should amount to 10 roubles 98 copecs *per annum*, whereas he receives only six roubles 57 copecs; but the whole expence for each soldier amounts to 10 roubles 98 copecs, or four roubles 41 copecs more than I have reckoned in the foregoing abstract; so that we must add about 10,293 roubles to the charges of a regiment, and then the whole expences of a regiment will amount to 39,317 roubles.

From this account it is very easy to form a pretty exact idea of the expences of the Russian forces, by means of the abstract I have given. I have calculated them in the following manner:

Forty-six regiments of infantry, making a body of 121,302 men, at 39,317 roubles *per* regiment, amount to 1,887,216 roubles.

The expence of a regiment of cavalry exceeds that of a regiment of infantry by 2630 roubles, or about one twelfth part. This proportion may be thought too little, but it must be considered, that forage is supplied by the subject, as well as provisions in kind, and that the horses being bought in the country, cost but little. The expence therefore of a regiment of cavalry, amounts to 41,947 roubles; and the forty regiments making a body of 63,316 men, amount to 1,677,880 roubles.

The guard of the Empress consists of a body of 16,380 men; almost as many as are in six regiments of infantry or cavalry. Every body knows that guards are more expensive than other troops. I shall however reckon their pay the same as that of the cavalry, or at 41,947 roubles; and the guards of the Empress then making a body of troops equal to six regiments, must take up 251,682 roubles, *per annum*. The charge of these troops is here rated as low as possible, their subsistence is not only much higher, but also the pay of most of these regiments is double to that of the others. But as I intend to consider, whether the Russian empire is able to maintain such a large body of troops as it keeps up, it is better to rate the expences somewhat below than above the mark. If we were to de-

expences, which are confiderable *. From thefe obfervations it fhould not feem probable, that Ruffia, with fuch a mo-

viate ever fo little from this principle, the military eftablifhment would exhauft the greateft part of the revenue of Ruffia.

The body of fortification, miners, artillery, and bombardiers, confifts of 10,960 men, which is equal to four regiments of infantry; and fuppofing the expences of thefe troops the fame as the guard of the Emprefs, they will amount to 167,788 roubles. In the abftracts I have had, it was computed at 300,000 roubles. I fhall reckon it the fame; and from thefe feveral calculations, the following refults are obtained.

Expence of the field troops.

	Men.	Roubles.
Houfhold of the Emprefs	16,380	251,682
Infantry	121,302	1,887,216
Cavalry	63,316	1,677,880
Fortification, artillery, &c.	10,960	300,000
Total	211,958	4,116,778

The pay of the troops of government is very different from that of the field troops. The coft of one of thefe regiments is not greater than about one half of the expence of a field regiment of the fame number of men. In the account I had, I found the expence of the army of government, or militia, compofed of

Expences of all the fea and land forces.

	Men.	Roubles.
Field army	99,266	1,161,155
	211,958	4,116,778
Total of the land army, and its coft	311,224	5,277,933
The fleet, the canal of Cronftat, the officers and the failors making a body of	20,239	1,200,000
Total of land and fea forces, and their cofts in money	331,463	6,477,933

* It has not been in my power to give a particular detail of thefe other expences, not having feen any account of them; but an explanation of the purpofes to which they are applied, will be fufficient to give us an idea of them, and will throw an additional light upon every thing that has been faid.

1ft, In the account of the expences of the troops I have omitted the appointments of the general officers. A field marfhal has 8140 roubles, and the other officers in proportion. Nor have I included the rewards beftowed upon the military people, either in penfions, or by granting them a certain number of the pea-

moderate revenue, can defray all other neceſſary expences, and at the ſame time keep up a body of troops of three hundred

ſants belonging to the crown, which is very often done; and it muſt be obſerved, that this laſt method of beſtowing rewards is the moſt coſtly to the ſtate; becauſe theſe peaſants are for ever loſt to the revenues of the crown, whereas penſions laſt only for life.

2dly, The arms and ammunition for all theſe troops: this muſt be a conſiderable article, though much leſs coſtly in this country than any where elſe; becauſe theſe people being ſlaves, all handicrafts are at a very low price.

3dly, The repairs of the public buildings, of the court, and many other extraordinary expences of the court and the ſovereign.

4thly, The miniſters living near the ſovereign, the high chancellor, the vice-chancellor, the high-ſteward of the imperial houſhold, the high-treaſurer, and the maſter of the horſe.

5thly, The council of war, compoſed of four field-marſhals, two generals of artillery, and twelve lieutenant generals; this council attends to the ſupplies of the army, and the promotion of officers, as far as the rank of lieutenant-colonel. Under this council is placed the board of ordnance, the commiſſariat, the military cheſt, the clothing board, the victualling office, the comptroller's office, and the war office eſtabliſhed at Moſco.

6thly, The admiralty, which has the cognizance of all affairs reſpecting the navy: it has the inſpection of all foreſts, and woods, ſituated on the large rivers. Under the admiralty there is firſt the commiſſary-general of the navy, whoſe buſineſs it is to pay every thing relating to this branch, as proviſions, and the ſubſiſtence. 2dly, The office eſtabliſhed for the care of the magazines, and all things neceſſary for the fitting out of ſhips. 3dly, The office for the building of ſhips, and all materials relating thereto. 4thly, The artillery and navy office.

7thly, The eſtabliſhment for foreign affairs, the buſineſs of which is to expedite all ſecret diſpatches, to pay the miniſters at foreign courts, and the penſions and gratuities given to theſe miniſters, to officers and other perſons. This eſtabliſhment regulates likewiſe all the extra-buſineſs of the ſtate. There is an office belonging to it at Moſco, which receives and diſtributes the monies allotted to theſe purpoſes.

8thly, Two colleges of juſtice; the one at St. Peterſburg, the other at Moſco. The adminiſtration of juſtice belongs to them. Peter I. ordered, that they ſhould take no fees, and aſſigned to the judges and clerks, ſalaries out of the public money *. On the contrary, there are no ſalaries given to the ſenate.

9thly, The treaſury appointed to receive the public revenues, except thoſe which ariſe from the poll-tax and the ſalterns. There is at preſent an office at St. Peterſburg for the adminiſtration of the revenues from the conquered provinces: all the other departments are at Moſco. I do not include in the treaſury the

* Voltaire, tom. ii. p. 228.

hundred and thirty thousand men: although I am convinced that this is a true state of the case, yet I will suppose the contrary, that this power is capable of maintaining such a body of troops, and at the same time of answering all the expences which necessarily attend the administration of so extensive an empire: it is however a certain and known fact, that Russia is enabled to keep its government and field troops in time of peace merely because there is little coin necessary to answer the expences, and that the people furnish provision for their subsistence in kind, and forage for the cavalry; provided that the greatest part of the troops is sent

number of persons employed in collecting the revenue, the tolls, the customs, the salterns, &c. All these persons are of no expence to the state, because they are paid by those farmers who are called *Otkoutckiki*.

10thly, The secretary of state's office, which directs the distribution of public money, and issues out orders to the treasury; the pay-offices established at St. Petersburg pay nothing without orders from thence.

11thly, The auditor's office appointed for receiving and examining the accounts of all the other offices.

12thly, The board of trade, which has the direction of the mines, the manufactures, the maritime customs, the tolls in the ports, and settles all the differences between the merchants.

13thly, The salt-office directs the revenue of the salterns, and receives the money which is paid into the imperial chest on that account; it appears that these two last offices (12 and 13) are not paid out of the royal treasury.

14thly, The several chanceries distributed throughout this vast empire, and all the governors and other military persons employed, who receive their appointments from the chanceries of their respective provinces, as well as a great number of other officers belonging to the court.

We may readily conceive, from this catalogue of the number of persons necessary for the business of all these offices, that the revenue of Russia would not be nearly sufficient to supply all these expences, if it was entirely taken from the revenues of the state. This point may easily be cleared up hereafter; I could have done it during my stay in Russia, if I had then had the account in as good order as I have given it here; but it was necessary first to collect all the materials, which took up a great deal of time. It is certain, however, that the expences of the army, as well as the appointments of some of the offices, are taken out of the royal treasury. Five millions of roubles therefore, are a very moderate revenue to supply the expences of the military alone; although in those branches relative to the making of the arms, the ammunition and the navy, there are many resources arising from the state of slavery Russia is in, which enable her to employ a number of hands, for these several purposes, at a very low price.

into

into the most fertile provinces; but all these advantages are lost in time of war, because it is impossible to export the provisions and forage beyond the limits of this extensive empire; and Russia being unable on account of its moderate revenue, to bear any extraordinary expences, it is most evident, that this power can not maintain upon its revenue, an army out of its own dominions. This is a truth known to all persons who are the least acquainted with the state of Russia; it was necessary, however, to examine the principles on which it is founded.

Supposing the sea and land forces of Russia to amount to three hundred and thirty thousand men, the field troops make up about two hundred and ten thousand, sixteen thousand of which compose the guard of the sovereign, and the rest of the army consists of one hundred and ninety-four thousand men. Many of these troops are employed to guard the criminals, and to conduct them to the mines. The detachments from regiments in Russia are considerable as well as the non-effectives. In the returns I have seen, the non-effectives amount to 700 in each regiment, consisting of 2637 men: this great deficiency in the Russian regiments is owing to the following causes. Part of the non-effective account belongs to the war-office. The provinces from whence the recruits are raised, are very far distant, and they are not easily brought together, because the roads are almost impassable: the Russians have the greatest aversion to the service, for which reason many of them desert, and many die of fatigue before they join the regiment; from which, these recruits are often seven or eight hundred leagues distant, and sometimes more. In the inner parts of the kingdom, I have seen how much the Russians dislike the army. I followed one of these parties for some time on my return from Tobolsky to St. Petersburg; after having quitted it on going into any town, where I stopped for seven or eight days, I often rejoined it the day after my setting out from thence, and I learned from the Russian officer who commanded the party, that the desertion was so considerable, that he did not expect to conduct one half of them to St. Petersburg, although he took up some regular troops on his way to prevent desertion. The countenance of each soldier was clouded with despair; and the recruits appeared like a set of wretches condemned to the gallies. Desertion is doubly injurious to Russia: for the loss of troops is not the only consequence of it; the deserters not being able to appear, lest they should be taken up, collect themselves into bands of robbers who infest the country: it is not from hearsay alone that I assert this fact, as I was obliged to take an escort with me at my return from Tobolsky, in order to travel across these provinces with any degree of safety.

Supposing the non-effectives at seven hundred *per* regiment, they will turn out to be seventy-five thousand at least in the field troops, which I have reckoned at two hundred and ten thousand men; from which the guard of the Empress consisting of sixteen thousand men, who are always near her, are to be deducted. The field troops are then reduced to about one hundred and twenty thousand men; from which we must still deduct a number of persons, included in the military state of each regiment in Russia, though they are never in action. Among these are the quarter-masters, the clerks, the barbers, the smiths, the farriers, the carpenters, the bat-men, both of officers and artillery, and several other people in office. These persons amount to more than three hundred *per* regiment, and more than thirty thousand among the field troops. If we afterwards consider the great number of soldiers detached from the regiments, it is easy to conclude, that although the standing forces of Russia amount to three hundred and thirty thousand men, including army and navy, yet this power cannot bring

bring into the field more than about seventy or fourscore thousand regular troops at once; and I have been acquainted with several officers, who were persuaded that there could never be more than sixty thousand effective fighting men in the Russian army. In the last war, the forces of Russia, both by sea and land, appeared to the highest advantage: all the troops that could be gathered together were brought from the inner parts of the empire, in order to send a large army into Germany. But upon examining the several campaigns of the Russians from the year 1757 to 1761, we find that their armies in general consisted of no more than one hundred thousand men, including the irregulars before mentioned, the workmen, the servants, and all other persons employed, who are reckoned in by the Russians among the troops. These last amounted to upwards of fifteen thousand men; and the number of irregulars was still greater; so that the regular troops could not amount to more than about sixty thousand men, and were often fewer. The army appears more considerable from my calculations, because I have supposed it to consist of three hundred and thirty thousand men; whereas, according to the state of it published by the Russians on the 16th of March 1760, a time when they ought necessarily to have had the greatest number of troops on foot, it amounted to no more than two hundred and eighty-four thousand men; and it is even probable, that the irregulars were included in that account.

A Russian army, however complete it may be at the beginning of a campaign, loses a number of men by sickness. This circumstance may appear extraordinary, because the Russian soldiers are generally stronger and more healthy than those of other nations: as they even lie upon straw or upon boards, without suffering any inconvenience. Besides, they do not desert when they are in the field, either from the difficulty of getting away, or from religious motives, or from their stupi-

dity,

dity, which may perhaps induce them even to be fond of slavery, or from their not knowing where to go, as they are unacquainted with any language but their own, or from their imagining that happiness is no where to be found but in the midst of the snows of Ruffia. It is true indeed, that in 1761, one hundred soldiers deserted from the single regiment of Azo in the course of a few days; but such incidents are so rare, that we may fairly conclude, there is no desertion among Ruffian troops when they have once joined the army. But the number of Ruffians killed in the last war, added to those who died of sickness, was so considerable, that I have known several of their officers, who were persuaded, that the Ruffian army was almost renewed every year. The mortality, prevailing in consequence of diseases to which the soldiers are exposed, seems to be owing chiefly to the following reasons. In treating of the manners and the climate it has been observed, that the constitution of the Ruffians requires that they should use vapour baths twice a week. The general officers, and some others in the army, are able to procure themselves the advantage of these baths; but it is impossible an army should have the same: neither would it be proper they should, if it could even be contrived, for the whole army would then be disabled from fighting two days in the week. The soldiers therefore not being able, while on service, to use these baths so necessary for their health, it is evident, they must be afflicted with many diseases, and a great number of them must perish; because their hospitals are so ill attended, that they hardly deserve that appellation. As there is a deficiency of physicians and surgeons at St. Peterfburg and at Mofco, this deficiency must still be greater in the army.

The officers in general are little acquainted with the art of war: this science, as extensive as it is complicated, requires a variety of other knowledge on which it depends. There are scarce any persons in Russia able to instruct others in these preliminary sciences.

The Russians have scarce any idea of Tacticks; they know not even the name of Xenophon, Herodotus, Polybius, &c. and are less acquainted with the great generals of the present age, from the nature of their atchievements, than from the report of their victories. It is, however, this art of ranging an army in the field, and teaching it a proper exercise, which often determines the fate of battles and of empires. All the Tactick of the Russians consists in forming their army in a crescent, in square, *en potence*, and sometimes in form of a triangle, and they seldom take the advantages of ground, because for the most part they are unacquainted with them. Although most of their field troops are perfectly well disciplined, they know not how to put their army in a proper order of march. They place the baggage, which is in great quantity, between the first and second line, sometimes promiscuously. Part of the army is employed in conducting the carriages, to which most of the soldiers fasten their arms; and the march of a Russian army is so disorderly, that it rather resembles the emigration of a people from one nation to another. The Russians are little acquainted with the custom of sending detachments forwards, or with the use of spies; their irregulars, which are designed to protect them during a march, to clear the suspicious places and to serve as scouts, are less attentive to these several circumstances, than to ravage and plunder the places through which they pass*; and indeed Marshal Appraxin was surprized on his march in 1767. General Fermer encamped near Kustrim in 1756, had not a sufficient notice of the king of Prussia's arrival, to prevent him crossing the Oder. Soltikoff marching into Silesia in 1759 was

---

* I have been assured, however, that towards the end of the last war, General Totleben, a foreigner in Russia, had disciplined some of the irregulars.

also

also furprized, and the moſt advanced regiments of his army were attacked on the place marked out for their encampment; the general being at that time a hunting. It is perhaps for this reafon, that the Ruſſians, though near Silefia, fell back every year into winter-quarters upon the Viſtula; at the diſtance of more than eighty leagues from the king of Pruſſia's army.

The officers have not the leaſt knowledge either of the forming of magazines, or of the diſtribution of proviſions. Flower and oatmeal is given to the foldiers, and one carriage for twelve men; and it is left to them to fettle their ovens and make their own bread. It often happens that, through fatigue or neglect, the foldiers are very ill fed. To thefe feveral circumſtances is owing the flowneſs of the military operations of their armies; which are formed into enormous bodies not eaſily put in motion.

Thefe facts have been confirmed to me by all the officers I have fpoke with, and by all foreigners who have been in the Ruſſian army. They are fo many inconteſtible proofs that the body of officers are little acquainted with the art of war.

The Ruſſian foldier, being forced into the fervice, is not actuated by any principle of honor or courage; but brandy, the dread of puniſhment, and the love of life, fometimes infpire him with a kind of bravery.

The artillery of the Ruſſians is very well ferved, and is always very numerous. The cavalry is chiefly compofed of dragoons and huffars, as they have but fix regiments of cuiraſſiers. This cavalry is too light to fuſtain the charge of common horfe; which by its weight alone will always be fufficient to bear down the Ruſſian cavalry. Their horfes, which are taken from their own country, are ſtrong and hardy; they are extremely fleet, but fo fmall that they fink under the weight of their riders. After a few months campaign, a great part of the

the cavalry is difmounted. I have been affured however, that the Ruffians fometimes got their horfes from Holftein; and indeed they might eafily procure them from thence, as well as the other powers of Europe; but the fcantinefs of the revenue will not admit of this additional expence. Every body allows that the Ruffian cavalry is the worft in Europe; but the fame cannot be faid of the infantry. One hundred years ago, it was faid that the infantry fought well, provided they had ditches or pallifades before them, that they might wait for the enemy under cover; but that they fled in a very cowardly way if they faw no place of defence. It is remarkable, that all thefe facts are to this day ftrictly true, although thefe troops are better difciplined. If the Ruffians fee an eafy retreat open to them, they think of nothing but running away; but if they are fhut up, and obliged to defend their lives, they become formidable troops. A Ruffian never fights for honor, but for life.

Thefe feveral opinions feem to be confirmed by the campaigns of the laft war. The king of Pruffia engaged near Silefia, againft the powerful armies of Germany, at the diftance of more than one hundred leagues from the eaftern borders of his own dominions, was never near enough to carry on a regular campaign againft the Ruffians. This monarch being able to act againft them only with fmall bodies of troops in that part of his kingdom, ufed to fuffer them to advance till they became troublefome to him, he then marched towards them with an intent to deftroy them, giving orders that none of them fhould be made prifoners; but this great king and his generals have almoft always fought the Ruffians where they had no open retreat; they were either thrown back upon their baggage in marches, or driven againft a river. Thefe are exactly the pofitions in which the Ruffians, who fight only for life, become formidable; they will not go forward one ftep

to

to attack the enemy; but if they cannot escape, they must be killed before the field of battle can be gained.

If we consider attentively the Russian campaigns which have made so much noise during the last war, we shall be astonished to find, that these people have never conquered any provinces, except such as the king of Prussia had evacuated, on account of their being too far distant from the body of his army; and that he could spare but few troops to act against them in those parts of his dominions.

The city of Kustrim being an advantageous post, the king of Prussia with a small body of troops, attacked general Fermer, who was besieging it: the Russians claimed the honor of the victory; the king of Prussia indeed retired with considerable loss; but general Fermer, having been joined next day by Romanzow's corps, raised the siege of Kustrim, and retreated into Prussia.

Soltikoff, after having gained two victories, one over general Wedél, who had no more than a small-corps to oppose to the whole Russian army; the other, over the king of Prussia, who attacked the Russian army combined with Laudon's forces near Francfort, did not obtain any other kind of advantage. This Russian general fell back also into Prussia without attempting to lay siege to any place, or to follow the king. Butturlin, who succeeded him, would never attack this monarch; although he was joined by Laudon, one of the best generals belonging to the Empress Queen; he rather chose to keep always at a distance, fearing to be attacked himself; he also retreated and took refuge in the dutchy of Prussia: At length Romanzow took Colberg in December 1761, after a siege of about four months.

All these facts imply, that the Russians have scarce made themselves masters of any other provinces except those evacuated by the Prussians in the beginning of the war; and that not only the officers have but little knowledge, but alfo that the troops are not very fit to form an attack, though, as I before obferved, they make a refolute ftand in their own defence when they have no retreat open.

Every body knows that the military eftablifhment contributes much to the depopulation of a ftate, and that in all governments the number of military perfons fhould be proportioned to the number of inhabitants; without which balance a nation would deftroy itfelf. If the army in France amounts to three hundred thoufand effective men in time of war, this number is confiderably reduced in peace; befides that there are more than twenty-feven thoufand foreigners in pay among thefe troops. Notwithftanding this prudent regulation, it is certain, that population does not increafe in France, if even it does not diminifh.

Ruffia, though lefs populous than France, is obliged on account of the extent of its dominions, to keep up in time of peace an army of near three hundred thoufand, or at leaft two hundred and fifty thoufand men, if the troops which are to take the field amount to about fifty thoufand. Such a confiderable body of troops muft be very injurious to the peopling of this ftate, in which other caufes of depopulation feem to foretel the total deftruction of the nation.

From all that has been faid, the following fummary may be collected.

The military eftablifhment of Ruffia, including the naval forces, the army of government, and the field troops, amounts to three hundred and thirty thoufand men.

Although the revenue of Ruffia does not exceed fixty-five or feventy million of French livres, yet the empire is able to maintain this confiderable body of troops; becaufe the pay of the foldiers in money is very trifling, and that the troops are

garrifoned

garrisoned in the most fertile provinces, which supply the provisions necessary for their subsistence in kind.

Russia, with so numerous an army, cannot bring into the the field more than sixty or seventy thousand effective regulars, and even by this the dominions are depopulated. This power not being able to bear any extraordinary expence, on account of its moderate revenues, is not able of itself to maintain such an army out of the empire, because the provisions which the people in the several provinces furnish, cannot then be conveyed to them.

The navy of Russia is weak, not only because there are but few ships, but also because the sea officers have as little knowledge as those of the land; besides, the Russians have no sailors, and never will have any while they do not carry on trade themselves.

The Russian artillery is very well served.

Their cavalry is the worst in Europe.

The infantry are the best troops they have; most of them are well disciplined: they are not fit for an attack, but defend themselves pretty well, even when not covered; when they are, they are very formidable, especially when there is no retreat open for them.

The corps of engineers have but little knowledge, and are incapable of conducting a siege. The Russians only know how to bombard a city.

I have thought the knowledge of these facts might be useful in Europe, because they remove the prejudices which have been entertained in regard to Russia; and this, if there is no other advantage attending it, is correcting a prevailing error. The inhabitants of Lubeck and Hamburg trembled at the name of the Russians. Poland and Germany, through which I have passed, considered Russia as one of the most formidable powers of Europe. The Russians entertained the same idea of their own empire, especially Peter III. and at the time I am now writing, France and a great part of Paris consider it in the same light. While I was at St. Petersburg, just setting out for Siberia, I received a letter from Paris, desiring me to take an accurate survey of this country, from whence whole nations were in a short time expected to emigrate, and, like the Scythians and the Huns, to over run our little Europe. Instead of such people, I found marshes and deserts.

In order to determine the power of Russia, the calculation must not be made in proportion to the extent of its dominions, as most writers have done; but rather in an inverse ratio of this same extent: in this view it will appear weak. In the present state of population and wealth in Russia, an army cannot be sent beyond the confines of the empire, without being ruined even by the victories it may gain; a Russian army in such a situation must be almost entirely destroyed, though the auxiliary subsidies supply the troops with subsistence: the officer's pay being very trifling, he is obliged to spend part of his own fortune out of the empire, and it is generally known, that Russia is always extremely attentive to prevent the exportation of coin, because it has already felt the ill effects of this practice: indeed, all the Russians allow that the last war has been extremely fatal to the state.

The sovereign of Russia would find the advantage of giving up the project of extending the empire; he should rather endeavor to collect and bring all his subjects together. This advantage would be considerable if all the northern part of Siberia was left to the bears, and the inhabitants were transported from this frozen region into the deserts of the southern parts of this province; which, from the temperature of the climate, and the fertility of the soil, are very proper to become the habitations of men. The only inconvenience attending this, would be, that the Tartars, being their neighbours, might learn the art of war from the Ruffians, as thefe have acquired it from the Swedes. However this may be, Ruffia, by bringing thofe people together, would no longer be obliged to maintain in time of peace, a large body of troops, which increafes the depopulation, and adds to the expences, without advancing the power of the ftate. By this alteration, its power would become much more confiderable, becaufe all its troops might then be employed in the defence of the empire; and if Ruffia fhould endeavor, as things are at prefent, to fet thefe people free, there will be the greateft difficulty in making this liberty compatible with its own ambitious views. The fovereign, while he remains abfolute mafter of the lives and fortunes of his fubjects, may maintain a confiderable army, by allowing a moderate fubfiftence to the foldiers, and to all perfons employed in the fervice of the army; but he will lofe this advantage, whenever thefe people become free.

From thefe feveral obfervations, it has appeared to me, that many perfons have entertained too high an idea of Ruffia, while others have been led into a contrary extreme. This power will always be formidable to the northern ftates in its neighbourhood.

F I N I S.

ERRATA.

Page 11. Line 20. *for*, fervility; *read*, fervitude.
16. ——— Last line but one, *for* painting, *read* sculpture.
17. ——— 6. *for*, well filled with trees; *read*, well planted; and insert the following words; kept in good order, and well stocked with deer, &c.
18. ——— Last line but one, *for*, six; *read*, two.
19. ——— Last line, *for*, cachra; *read*, cacha.
23. ——— 30. *dele*, but as.
23. ——— 31. *for*, we were determined; *read*, yet we were determined.
28. ——— 22. *for*, Tschoudowai; *read*, Tschoudoiwa.
34. ——— 20. *for*, more than one hundred feet; *read*, about fifty toises.
34. ——— 22. *for*, thirteen or fourteen feet; *read*, six or seven toises.
36. ——— 12. *for*, three hundred and eighteen feet; *read*, one hundred and fifty toises.
36. ——— 13. and 14. *for*, one hundred and thirty seven feet; *read*, sixty toises.
36. ——— 18. and 19. *for*, eight hundred and fifty feet; *read*, about four hundred toises.
40. ——— 11. *for*, are; *read*, were.
42. ——— 7. *for*, one foot high, and six inches wide; *read*, one foot wide, and six inches high.
60. ——— Last line but one, *for*, fourscore thousand; *read*, fourscore and three thousand.
61. ——— 25. *for*, than fifty; *read*, than from fifty.
63. ——— 12. *for*, Paiadinska; *read*, Paiudinska.
77. ——— 17. *for*, three hundred thousand and eighteen wersts; *read*, three thousand one hundred and eighteen wersts.
78. ——— 20. *for*, eclipse; *read*, planet.
78. ——— 29. *for*, construed; *read*, constructed.
109. ——— 26. *for*, these; *read*, those.
112. ——— 30. *for*, here are extensive; *read*, here extensive.
116. ——— 16. *for*, would; *read*, will.
117. ——— 19. *for*, Schuwachi; *read*, Schuwaschi.
120. ——— 40. Of the figures; column 3. *for*, 20 d. 9 m. 9 s. *read*, 20 d. 9 m. 0 s.
121. ——— 4. Below the table, *for*, 1,570,060 toises; *read*, 57,060 toises.
127. ——— 7. Above the table; *for*, 552 toises, 7 inches, &c. *read*, 552 toises 3 feet 7 inches, &c.
168. ——— 6. *for*, as that; *read*, as in that, &c.
177. ——— 17. *for*, but, it still; *read*, but it is still.
182. ——— 2. *for*, 41 ¾, *read*, 41 ¾.
190. ——— 21. *for*, amber; *read*, umber.
195. ——— 25. *for*, consists; *read*, consist.
199. ——— 18. *for*, crystallizations of a crystal matter; *read*, crystallizations of the nature of quartz.
207. ——— 11. *for*, was; *read*, is.
212. ——— 17. *for*, fossils; *read*, fossil.
220. ——— 5. of the note, *for*, flope; *read*, slope.
231. ——— 1. *for*, you; *read*, one.
247. ——— 1. of the notes, *for*, tom. ii; *read*, tom. i.
249. ——— 13. *for*, the 11th; *read*, the 14th.
277. ——— 7. *for*, fulse; *read*, false.
308. ——— 26. *for*, opportunity; *read*, opportunities.
315. ——— 16. *for*, stores; *read*, stoves.
320. ——— 26. *for*, Epiney; *read*, Epinus.
331. ——— 14. *for*, every else; *read*, every where else.
343. ——— 28. *for*, pence; *read*, halfpence.
358. ——— 10. *for*, Mota; *read*, Msta.
361. ——— 13. of the note, *for*, the revenue of the port; *read*, the revenue of the post.
364. ——— 7. of the notes, *for*, deserve the attention; *read*, deserve attention.
382. ——— Last line of the notes, *for*, p. 228; *read*, p. 223.

www.ingramcontent.com/pod-product-compliance
Lightning Source LLC
Chambersburg PA
CBHW030553300426
44111CB00009B/968